Jin Yong's Martial Arts Fiction and the Kungfu Industrial Complex

Jin Yong's Martial Arts Fiction and the Kungfu Industrial Complex

Paul B. Foster

LEXINGTON BOOKS
Lanham • Boulder • New York • London

Published by Lexington Books
An imprint of The Rowman & Littlefield Publishing Group, Inc.
4501 Forbes Boulevard, Suite 200, Lanham, Maryland 20706
www.rowman.com

86-90 Paul Street, London EC2A 4NE

Copyright © 2023 by The Rowman & Littlefield Publishing Group, Inc.

All rights reserved. No part of this book may be reproduced in any form or by any electronic or mechanical means, including information storage and retrieval systems, without written permission from the publisher, except by a reviewer who may quote passages in a review.

British Library Cataloguing in Publication Information Available

Library of Congress Cataloging-in-Publication Data

Names: Foster, Paul B., 1960- author.
Title: Jin Yong's martial arts fiction and the kungfu industrial complex / Paul B. Foster.
Description: Lanham : Lexington Books, 2023. | Includes bibliographical references and index.
Identifiers: LCCN 2022054170 (print) | LCCN 2022054171 (ebook) | ISBN 9781666921472 (cloth) | ISBN 9781666921489 (ebook)
Subjects: LCSH: Jin, Yong, 1924-2018--Criticism and interpretation. | Martial arts fiction, Chinese--History and criticism. | Kung fu--China.
Classification: LCC PL2848.Y8 Z5326 2023 (print) | LCC PL2848.Y8 (ebook) | DDC 895.13/52--dc23/eng/20221125
LC record available at https://lccn.loc.gov/2022054170
LC ebook record available at https://lccn.loc.gov/2022054171

∞™ The paper used in this publication meets the minimum requirements of American National Standard for Information Sciences—Permanence of Paper for Printed Library Materials, ANSI/NISO Z39.48-1992.

Contents

List of Figures	vii
List of Tables	ix
Preface	xi
Introduction: *Wuxia* Fiction, Film and Construction of the Kungfu Industrial Complex	1
1 Kungfu Cultural Literacy: Situating Jin Yong's Martial Arts Fiction	15
2 Jin Yong's Rhetorical Kungfu: Cultural Capital of Humor	45
3 Canonization, Cultural Capital, National Character	67
4 Kungfu Star Power: The Entertainment *Jianghu*	107
5 The *Kung Fu Hustle* Hustle	183
Glossary	211
Bibliography	221
Index	237
About the Author	243

List of Figures

I.1. Multidimensional Matrix of the Kungfu Industrial Complex, adapted from Hockx, *The Literary Field of Twentieth-Century China*, 8 — 8

1.1. Film supervisor Johnny To (center) has Andy Lau (left) and Tony Leung (right) prepare for their leading roles in *Cauldron* (1984) by reading Jin Yong's novel. Below: Leung reviews early film adaption — 20

1.2. Introduction credit screenshot and protagonists Guo Jing (Felix Wong) and Huang Rong (Barbara Yung), *Heroes* (1983), Episode 10 — 28

1.3. Introduction screenshots and protagonist Guo Jing (Hu Ge), *Heroes* (2008), Episode 1 — 30

1.4. Linghu Chong battles Asia the Invincible, *Wanderer* (2001), Episode 34 — 37

2.1. Wei Xiaobao demonstrating "cursing kungfu" after being scolded for using despicable (*beibi*) techniques to save Mao Shiba's life, *Cauldron* (1984), Episode 1 — 52

2.2. Wei Xiaobao secretly observes his "wife" being served by his prostitute mother, *Cauldron* (1984), Episode 34 — 60

3.1. "Method of Spiritual Victory," Ah Q in *The True Story of Ah Q* (1981) and Wei Xiaobao in television adaptation of *Cauldron* (1984), Episode 1 — 79

4.1. Tony Leung as Wei Xiaobao and Andy Lau as Emperor Kang Xi in television adaptation of *Cauldron* (1984), Episode 10 — 123

4.2. Brigitte Lin as Asia the Invincible, *Swordsman II* (1992) — 141

4.3.	Bruce Lee as Huo Yuanjia's disciple Chen Zhen, *Fist of Fury* (1972)	150
4.4.	Jackie Chan using Drunken Fist kungfu and scolded by his father, *Drunken Master II* (1994)	154
4.5.	Jackie Chan, *City Hunter* (1993), movie theater scene in which he learns from Bruce Lee how to fight tall opponents, direct homage to Lee's iconic fight in *Game of Death* (1978)	161
4.6.	Visual References to Bruce Lee's iconic costume in *The Game of Death* (1978), *Kill Bill* (2003), *Shaolin Soccer* (2001)	163
4.7.	Gordon Liu as Kangxi in the Shaw Brothers film adaptation of *Caldron* (1983) and as the dual role of Johnny Mo and Pai Mei in the *Kill Bill* films	168
5.1.	The *qinggong* (light-body kungfu) of Zhang Ziyi and Chow Yun-fat in *Crouching Tiger* (2000)	186
5.2.	Characters Liu Zhengfeng and Qu Yuan perform title song, "Xiao ao jianghu," *Wanderer* (2001), Episode 5	190
5.3.	Hong Qi and Ouyang Feng discussing the *jianghu* in *Ashes of Time* (1994)	198
5.4.	The old beggar peddling Jin Yong martial tomes at conclusion of *Kung Fu Hustle* (2004)	201
5.5.	*Companions* martial lovers, Yang Guo and Xiaolongnü, come out of retirement to battle the Beast in *Kung Fu Hustle* (2004)	203

List of Tables

1.1. Jin Yong's 12 Major Novels with His English Title Translations and Abbreviations (in italics) in Order of Initial Publication   23

1.2. Film Adaptations and Derivatives of *The Eagle-Shooting Heroes* by Year, Title, Dir, Studio and Stars, Compiled from Hong Kong Movie Database and Duoban Dianying   27

1.3. Television Adaptations of *The Eagle-Shooting Heroes* and Its Derivatives by Year, Director/Producer and Main Stars, Compiled from Duoban Dianying and Baidu   29

1.4. Selected List of Stars and Their Jin Yong Roles   39

Preface

This study of Jin Yong's martial arts fiction and the afterlives of his characters, plots, and kungfu techniques originates in my own reading of his novels for both entertainment and cultural edification. I've benefited throughout this process from many discussions on Jin Yong and the martial arts fiction craze in Taiwan with Su Taiyi and other friends. Fellow students back in graduate school days intrigued me with views on the relative realism of kungfu techniques in Jin Yong and Gu Long's novels. These forays led to research into the greater questions of the role of popular literature in society. Inspiration to pursue this research vis-à-vis the discourse of *jianghu* in discussions with fellow AAS conference panel participants Kirk Denton, Chen Xiaomei, Nick Kaldis, and our audience. Further thanks go to discussants and participants at numerous other conferences who provided valuable feedback on presentations targeting specific aspects of this research. I'm particularly grateful to Professor Petrus Liu for incisive feedback integrated into my book, as well as the detailed critique of my manuscript by anonymous reviewers whose challenges to my ideas helped guide the shape of the final drafts. I would also like to thank the School of Modern Languages for a research development grant to travel to Huashan, Taishan, Shaolin, Luoyang, and other places in Jin Yong's novels, as well as Professor Lin Haizheng for cultural guidance and adventures together throughout China. Inspiration comes in many forms, and I must credit my *qinggong* wire walking partners, Andy Peterson, and Eric Mintz for guidance along the way. Finally, no words can fully express the extent of my gratitude for the patience and support for this passion from my wife Julie and my sons Alex and Isaac.

PF
Atlanta, Georgia

INTRODUCTION

Wuxia *Fiction, Film and Construction of the Kungfu Industrial Complex*

Jin Yong, the grandmaster of *Xin pai wuxia xiaoshuo* (New school martial arts fiction) of the mid-to-late twentieth century, is recognized throughout East and Southeast Asia for the extensive wealth of his factual, fictional, and fantastical Chinese cultural constructions.[1] His twelve major novels were originally serialized over two or three years and typically run from 1600 to 2000 pages as individual works. These stories have engaged droves of readers, as well as viewers of the multiple film and television series adaptations, over hundreds of hours in what John Minford terms a "celebration of Chinese culture, of Chineseness, a fictional experience which is in some respects more "Chinese" than any of the available Chinese realities. . . . A Chinese banquet."[2] The influence of Jin Yong's works, both direct and indirect, in the construction of Chinese cultural knowledge worldwide is broad and far-reaching, promulgated by film and television production companies and a vast array of actors in Hong Kong, Taiwan, and mainland China from the latter half of the twentieth century into the twenty-first century.

Immediately at the turn of the twenty-first century Ang Lee's *wuxia* martial arts film *Crouching Tiger, Hidden Dragon* (hereafter, *Crouching Tiger* [2000]) broke down the door to the U.S. market and ushered in a host of great Chinese fantastical *wuxia* martial arts movies featuring swordsmanship, hand-to-hand combat, gymnastics, mystical energy forces, and battles in flight over rooftops, lakes, and atop bamboo groves. Whether because of high production values, fresh and exotic narrative elements, or fantastical *wuxia* techniques and plots common to Jin Yong's martial arts fiction, this adaptation of Wang Dulu's short, serialized novel from the 1940s used just a couple of hours to accomplish a feat that Bruce Lee and Jackie Chan's more "realistic" *wushu* martial arts-based kungfu film genre took three decades to do—the transnationalization of *wuxia* martial arts film and technical elements.

The turn of century timing was right. The fantastical elements of *wuxia* film found new markets globally as audiences became increasingly receptive to kungfu cultural products in the twenty-first century. The concurrent late twentieth-century opening of Chinese business, politics, culture, and language in the post-Cultural Revolution *kaifang* period starting in the 1980s paralleled the growth of *wuxia* film. Jin Yong's martial arts literature was immensely popular in the Chinese diaspora and during these decades came to wield massive cultural influence on the mainland, so much so that it became a window to both Chinese popular culture and its traditional high culture antecedents. Close examination of Jin Yong's novels and their television and film adaptations enables the deciphering of the cultural codes and other underlying elements necessary to fully appreciate the popularity of his stories and understand how Jin Yong's characters manage to sustain their cultural power in film, television, and other digital platforms over the decades.

This book examines the creation and manipulation of cultural capital associated with Jin Yong's martial arts stories and myths. His stories impart important Chinese cultural knowledge, and the connection of these stories and myths to authors, auteurs, performers, and critics operate in overlapping unison to construct and perpetuate the understanding of key elements of traditional and popular Chinese culture. Popular and high culture are bridged by the language of action informing narratives of power in martial arts fiction and film. Pierre Bourdieu's concept of "cultural capital," elaborated in detail below, is made both intelligible and relevant through examination of popular martial arts literature. Jin Yong's *wuxia* fiction operates in cultural discourse that exemplifies the inextricable relationships between "high" and "low" culture come to the fore with a prioritization of neither.

The concept of *wu* (martial) informs both actual *wushu* (martial arts) and the moral and ethically imbued concept of *wuxia* (martial chivalry) that authors like Jin Yong depict in their works. Critic Siu Leung Li notes the kungfu in *wuxia* film "means the cultural imagination of kung fu, not real-life martial arts."[3] The masterpieces of New School Martial Arts Fiction, written from the 1950s to the 1970s, played a seminal role in the construction of *wuxia* kungfu culture for more than half a century but the *wuxia* lineage reaches to antecedents far back in dynastic history. Some *wuxia* techniques are a form of fantasy or magical realism, such as the *qingshen gongfu* (light body kungfu) that enables practitioners to fly from rooftop to rooftop, or the invisible shock waves of *neigong* (internal kungfu power) that draw on a fighter's *qi* (internal energy force), which is then channeled through the palms in a burst of force. Beyond physical technique, social and ethical formulations that inform the martial society portrayed in Jin Yong's works operate according to cultural codes of training and interpersonal and social dynamics formed over centuries of martial narratives. Audiences rely on cultural capital, the linguistic and cultural knowledge founded in Chinese philosophy, religion, history, and cultural values constructed over the millennia, to thoroughly interpret and consume all manner of story elements, from the mundane to the fantastical. The novelist weaves all these elements together on the written page and connects with the readers' imagination. The filmmaker adapting these stories relied on highly trained/skilled actors and the invention of clever production techniques to represent fantastical elements. Audiences, for their part, required an abundance of the suspension of disbelief to enjoy the representations that authors like Jin Yong creatively conjured in their written works, at least until advent of digital imaging technology provided the powerful tools to accurately represent the surface-level fantasy in *wuxia* film and television. Film mediates the plots, subplots, and narrative and linguistic techniques through which the author connects to the reader. Those elements must be adapted by screenwriters, directors, producers, technical experts, and actors who are tasked with interpreting and reinterpreting martial and cultural concepts with technology and language. Audiences who had devoured Jin Yong's novels were drawn to film and television adaptions and participated in an expanding discursive feedback loop that impacted supply and demand for the works, eventually constructing a multidimensional integrated system I call the "kungfu industrial complex."

The kungfu industrial complex is a vast multidimensional cultural matrix of martial arts fiction, television, and film in a dynamic process of creating and sustaining related knowledge and mechanisms for its reification, reproduction, and commodification. Knowledge is connected by a myriad of threads from Chinese history, philosophy, literature, and language, which come together in the popular imagination as readers consume martial arts literature and the film and television adaptations thereof. The audience accumulates cultural capital through years of education and/or cultural experience and develops "kungfu cultural literacy" through consumption of martial arts novels, film, and television. This cultural capital functions in a cycle that facilitates both interpretation and appreciation of the works and associated phenomena.

The kungfu industrial complex matrix is multidimensional starting with the writer, reader, and critic. Using an abundance of imagination and creativity, the author constructs the stories, characters, and a vast array of associated tropes which play on the cultural capital of the readers to create meaning. The audience, both popular and academic, participate in discourse dissecting the characters and stories and contributing to their interpretation and validation (or not). The production industry, including directors, scriptwriters, actors, and technical personnel, designs and implements adaptations for screen congruent with the stories' specific cultural tropes and metaphors. Beyond print and film production mechanisms, the "industry" extends to all manner of cultural products such as music, comics, cartoons, computer games, associated with the original works and its spinoffs. Film, television, and physical products construct, reinforce, and (sometimes) challenge the world view and ideology of swordsman and martial arts practitioners who populate the fictional narratives.

In addition to the creative and physical mechanisms that facilitate the production of works and adaptations, the relatively more amorphous dimensions of time and place are crucial to the kungfu industrial complex. Time and place have an important role in the context of plot and narrative as well as the metanarrative discourse—the popular and academic feedback—to Jin Yong's fiction. This discourse encompasses a continuously developing body of temporally relevant knowledge that transcends the martial arts narratives through reception and interpretation. Interpretation varies by audience, be they situated by place in Hong Kong, Taiwan, mainland China, or the diaspora abroad. Reception also varies temporally, and thus China's opening to the outside world in the 1980s allowed the import of *wuxia* novels, films, and television series from elsewhere (Hong Kong, Taiwan, Singapore, and such). The popularity of "imported" media adaptations created space for new adaptations featuring "domestic" mainland actors and production crews.

Adaptation of martial arts fiction to screen also initiated the transcendence of ethnicity and place through the process of transnationalization as martial arts cultural tropes (if not the complete works themselves) were disseminated and adapted for the global marketplace. On the global level, film became a vehicle to transnationalize both actual martial arts and the more esoteric and fantastical aspects of *wuxia* martial arts fiction. A host of film, television, and singing stars are the physical faces that portray the fictional characters on screen. They demonstrate insofar as possible the real *wushu* and fantastical *wuxia* martial arts techniques found in the original texts. Actors, directors, and production crew interpret and reinterpret Jin Yong's (and other writer's) martial arts tropes with the effect of constructing and sustaining an "afterlife" for the fictional heroes and plots. The synergy of this artistic and commercial process simultaneously expands the dimensions of the kungfu industrial process in all its dimensions—all the while pursuing audiences and making vast fortunes.

At the very base of the kungfu industrial complex lies a long legacy of martial arts literature from the Ming and Qing dynasties (and earlier) that informs twentieth-century works of fiction and film. There are also real historical Chinese kungfu techniques, such as Taiji, which were developed centuries ago and practiced throughout the ages. Prior to widespread literacy, anecdotes of physical and philosophical training were skillfully woven by storytellers who entertained teahouse audiences.

Such storyteller's wrote prompt books that eventually became novels which more formally codified and transmitted historical characters, kungfu sects, and techniques. Fictionally embellished legends, such as the story of Wu Song killing a tiger bare-handed, may have first been fodder for popular entertainment starting with those teahouse storytellers and further developing with the rise of print capitalism of the late nineteenth and twentieth centuries as growing literacy and commercial development spurred magazines and newspapers to serve individual readers. The serialization of martial arts fiction helped sell magazines and newspapers as a first step. The development of film and television technology in the twentieth century then became a readily available platform for expansive transmission of martial arts narratives and characters. The commercial success of martial arts fiction in print and film continued and increased throughout the modern era. Commercial interests met popular demand for entertainment, capitalizing on the success of individual novels as they moved from original literary serial to individual hardbound novel, and then on to film and television series. Success of these works led to derivative works spinning-off of the characters into new plots, transforming cultural capital into economic success.

The kungfu industrial complex attained global reach as the production techniques, stars, directors, fighting styles, and underlying ideology of the works were gradually recognized and integrated into Hollywood films during the 1990s and 2000s. A prime example is the opening chase scene of *The Matrix* (1999) in which Trinity runs horizontally on vertical walls and across rooftops. It is no coincidence that such signature "light body kungfu" action appears in *The Matrix* and its sequels because these films employed the renowned action director Yuen Woo-ping from *Crouching Tiger*. The term kungfu means both "martial art/skill" and the "idea of martial arts." After running through an initial combat training program, the protagonist Neo of *The Matrix*, enthusiastically calls for more, and upon finishing states with awe and reverence, "I know kungfu." Films like *Crouching Tiger*, Zhang Yimou's *Hero* (2002), and to a lesser but important extent, *The Matrix*, portray other aspects of Chinese cultural philosophy beyond kungfu action. But it was the economic success of these films that legitimized the cultural capital associated with kungfu and related Chinese values. Success in the international film marketplace started with martial arts—*Crouching Tiger* earned $128 million in the United States alone,[4] *Hero* earned $177 million at the box office worldwide,[5] and *The Matrix* earned $463.5 million[6]—and reinforces and reconfirms the Chinese national sense of cultural self-worth.

Hero and *Crouching Tiger* function on a subtle ideological plane to affirm Chinese values such as the centralization of state power and the loyalty of individual and clan to the state. In this way, they suggest a cultural cohesion not dependent upon a nineteenth-century threat of Western imperialism. Chinese consciousness at the onset of the twenty-first century appears to be moving away from the obviously nationalist movies, which previously implied a China struggling with a twentieth-century sense of inferiority, toward an exploration of Chinese values and capabilities on their own terms. Martial arts films like *Crouching Tiger* played an important transitional role here, and movies like Wu Jing's *Wolf Warrior* (2015) seem to indicate a reversal of the "victim of imperialism" narrative toward an assertion of cultural superiority.

The global assimilation of symbolically powerful elements of the kungfu industrial complex is a measure of Chinese cultural success over the last half century. By successfully exporting its stars, directors, styles, and kungfu (along with such attendant notions as chivalry and valor), Chinese culture has a platform for expressing its values, exporting its cultural capital, and asserting cultural value. Western audiences have access to a more positive and proactive (thus complicated) China, and thus find liberation from the paradigm of prejudice constructed during the semi-colonization of China over the nineteenth and early twentieth centuries, or the Maoist failures and successes of the 1950s and 1960s.

WUXIA AND *GONGFU* (KUNGFU)

Hong Kong martial arts films are traditionally divided into two sub-genres, *wuxia* swordplay films and *gongfu* (kungfu) fist films, a demarcation particularly evidenced between competing studios and stars in the 1970s. Bruce Lee and Jackie Chan might privilege the "realism" of *wushu* in their kungfu film representations, but as critic Richard Meyers notes, well-produced *wuxia* movies actually surpass Bruce Lee's kungfu films with complicated plots and dazzling sets that "require the same level of acrobatic stunts."[7]

Chinese viewing audiences often came to the movies with an intricate knowledge of the *wuxia* plots because they had either read the original novels or seen one or more of the television dramatizations of the works. This accumulation of cultural capital starts with familiarity of the works of Ming and Qing martial arts fiction (and even earlier). A prior knowledge facilitates the audience's evaluation and appreciation of the novels and films. It is also requisite for authors, screenwriters, and actors to represent and adapt characters, plots, interactions, and kungfu techniques in various media. A prior knowledge also facilitates the discourse on the works in their various manifestations as audiences engage in culturally discursive comparison of the text to the various television series and film renditions.

Audiences may not literally believe in feats of flying and other magical-like exhibitions of the kungfu artist's *qi*, but they are primed to suspend disbelief and equipped to both critically assess and enjoy the directors' and actors' interpretations of well-known and much-loved material. Film adaptations are situated in a rich textual history and deep cultural discourse. In addition to Jin Yong's twelve quintessential martial arts epics and two shorter novels, works by authors of the New School Martial Arts Fiction includes seventy-three novels by Gu Long (1937–1985), thirty-three by Liang Yusheng (1926–2009), as well as works by less prominent authors. While credit for the *global* appeal of Chinese kungfu starts with Bruce Lee's iconic films in the 1970s, his films are situated within an elaborate world and world view of kungfu value based in martial arts plots and fantastical swordplay period dramas. Chinese *wuxia* swordplay films have at the base a cast of character and plot archetypes from Jin Yong, Gu Long, and Liang Yusheng's martial arts fiction.

Jin Yong's martial arts fiction played a formative role in kungfu cultural literacy as popular reading and viewing audiences developed early and repeated exposure to text, television series and film. Periodic repetition resulted in a deeply ingrained knowledge and virtually effortless recognition of characters, stories, and a broad swath of other cultural issues. An underlying premise of the analysis of culture is that culture is always in flux, changing and reflecting itself against interpretations of its past and visions of its future. Jin Yong's role in the construction of kungfu cultural literacy and the kungfu industrial complex created controversy associated with mainland China's opening to the West and its enthusiastic embrace of Hong Kong and Taiwan popular culture in the 1980s and 1990s. While Chinese literature has been a source of cultural pride for millennia, it wasn't until the twentieth century that vernacular fiction, the *xiaoshuo* (novel/fiction), was elevated to a prominent place in the literary canon. The vernacular fiction initially valorized by cultural authorities, however, was not *wuxia* fiction, but rather a realistic fiction informed by the Western literature advocated during the May Fourth era of the late 1910s and 1920s. It wasn't until the late twentieth century that the embrace of New School Martial Arts Fiction works by the Chinese population and (some) critics created waves in the Chinese literary world.

WUXIA FICTION AND CULTURAL CAPITAL

Martial arts film is an attractive theme that provides a segue into the much more complicated linguistic and cultural medium of *wuxia* literature, the base of this study. The conceptualization of kungfu industrial complex as briefly described above will be further elaborated throughout each of the chapters of this book. The kungfu industrial complex indicates a

8 Introduction

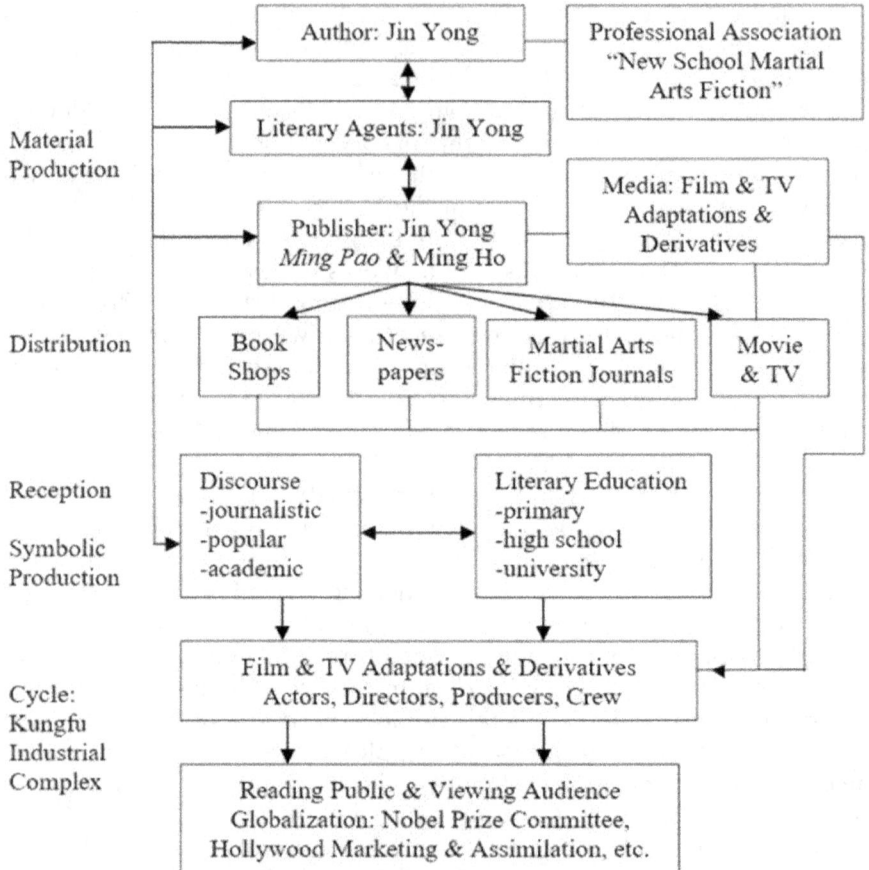

Figure I.1. Multidimensional Matrix of the Kungfu Industrial Complex, adapted from Hockx, *The Literary Field of Twentieth-Century China*, 8

multidimensional matrix of agents operating within cultural, social, and economic spheres that creates a type of intangible currency of interpretation, cultural capital, as well as associated social and economic capital. Pierre Bourdieu's theoretical conceptualization helpfully contextualizes the construction and workings of these types of capital, viewed as operating in a setting or "field," such as the literary field of modern China of the twentieth century, or the news world in Jin Yong's Hong Kong from the 1950s to 1970s. Bourdieu sketches out cultural capital as follows:

> Cultural capital can exist in three forms: in the *embodied* state, i.e., in the form of long-lasting dispositions of the mind and body; in the *objectified* state, in the form of cultural goods (pictures, books, dictionaries, instruments, machines, etc.), which are the trace or realization of theories or critiques of

these theories, problematics, etc.; and in the *institutionalized* state, a form of objectification which must be set apart because, as will be seen in the case of educational qualifications, it confers entirely original properties on the cultural capital which it is presumed to guarantee.[8]

The embodied state generally refers to the acquired cultural knowledge that people, audiences, actors, and associated production personnel possess. The objectified state refers to cultural products themselves. The institutional state refers to the institutions that confer value on the products through educational, academic, and critical discourse. Cultural capital operates complexly within overlapping fields in which these states interact. The structural schematic on the previous page (Figure I.1) is expanded to include the technological adaptations of television and film to demonstrate Bourdieu's idea of the literary field and assist in the visualization of the kungfu industrial complex as a complicated multidimensional matrix.[9]

This is a two-dimensional representation of a dynamic multidimensional phenomenon that cycles with time and space. The kungfu industrial complex is thus shorthand for the complex interaction of multiple fields (Bourdieu) described by the schematic above in which cultural capital, social capital, and economic capital manifest themselves instrumentally to produce and reproduce cultural, social, and economic value. Cultural capital has embodied, objectified, and institutionalized states manifest in the "agent" (person) author/reader/audience, the "object" (stories and characters), and the critical apparatus that reifies the value of the works. In addition to simple manipulation of this cultural capital as learned/accumulated knowledge to engage in interpretation, agents may also employ it in social and economic transactions, which involves interaction in one or more of the other fields diagrammed above.

Jin Yong is a complex agent in cultural capital in the sense that he occupies multiple places in this schematic: author, literary agent, publisher, and even screenwriter for film adaptations of his early novels. The situation is suitably complex because he comes to this nexus as with cultural capital and further produces cultural capital. My conceptualization of the kungfu industrial complex situates Jin Yong's original texts in extending circles of literary production and discourse which operate in the accumulation and manipulation of cultural capital in the form of linguistic, historical, philosophical, and moral elements of his imagined martial arts world. The chapters of this study address kungfu cultural literacy (the background knowledge crucial to interpret multiple levels of meaning in the narrative), rhetorical kungfu (textual power dynamics between characters), discourse kungfu (canonization discourse in the objectified and institutionalized forms of cultural capital), and star power (accumulation and manipulation of cultural, social, and economic capital). My analysis depicts the settings and agents in a variety of fields, for example, sussing out the impact of association with Jin Yong on the careers of the actors. These multiple dimensions of overlapping "fields," the textual dynamics, academic discourse, and entertainment forces, are constructed over the quintessentially important dimension of time—popularization depends on familiarization—which thereupon lead to further constructions of kungfu cultural capital, layer upon layer, in the sense that Bourdieu notes, "Cultural capital breeds cultural capital: because the aestheticizing disposition emphasizes formal similarities between works of art, it also assumes sufficient familiarity to make establishing similarities viable."[10]

This book investigates how Jin Yong's work are a study in culture motifs, stories, values, norms, philosophy, religion, and the language thereof. Analysis of the works and the extratextual production and discourse reflected against Bourdieu's concept of cultural capital is highly productive because such conceptualization brings together each dimension of the discourses in all their complexity. Consideration of Bourdieu's theory vis-à-vis martial arts fiction and film is also a test of the theory. If the storytelling is compelling it can both edify—manifest in the embodied state of cultural capital in the reader/audience who accumulates and "employs" it in post-textual discourse regarding the narratives—and construct a body of knowledge (cultural capital) that operates in fields of discourse associated with the story. What is the nature of cultural capital in such reinforcing cyclicity?

Literary discourse is one arena in which cultural capital is articulated in the institutionalized state. Such capital is accumulated and employed in credentialed discourse by students and academics who discuss, debate, and publish papers and books analyzing the author and works, validating their importance in our lives form every possible angle, furthering the construction of knowledge and constructing additional cultural capital. This institutionalized state cultural capital is not necessarily represented by a "degree" in Jin Yong studies (yet), but is related to the credentials of the critics, professors, and students who take classes and research the subject.

Jin Yong's stories initiated the construction of social and economic capital that at first was situated in the newspapers that serialized his stories, and then in bookstores as volumes of the works were individually published, and nearly simultaneously in television and film adaptations. Social and economic capital accrues to actors who portray the characters in film and television. For example, a successful portrayal of a particular role could enhance an actor's cultural capital (association with the famous role) and social capital (connections made with directors, actors, producers, and film companies), and thus position the actor to pursue other Jin Yong roles, or other roles within and without the martial arts genre, all of which (hopefully) would result in further generation of economic capital. Success begets success, which can be nicely measured in the number and quality of future roles, as well as economic compensation at the box office.

Compelling stories well told at the right time and populated by interesting characters and actors skilled enough to portray them results in the construction and enhancement of "star power," wherein an actor simultaneously symbolizes the role and embodies the cultural capital inherent in the role. Star power is comprehensive, a measure of all the various forms of cultural capital in its embodied, objectified, and institutional states, operating in social, economic, and symbolic discourses. The shared cultural capital of all the participants in cultural production, from technical production to audience consumption of the cultural work, contribute to the valorization of the work's "success."

Despite the ideological precepts promoted in the May Fourth era in the early twentieth century, which eschewed subject matter such as martials arts fiction for lacking social value, consumption of martial arts fiction continued throughout the period. Although Chinese literary discourse of the twentieth century continued to valorize the May Fourth authors and their works for their role in modernizing China and the Chinese people, the market for martial arts fiction continued throughout the 1920s, 1930s, and 1940s. The production of martial arts fiction accelerated in the middle of the twentieth century with the serialization of New School Martial Arts Fiction works in Hong Kong newspapers, just as the Chinese revolution was closing the door to the genre as the People's Republic of China was established in 1949. Hong Kong thereupon became the epicenter for martial arts fiction, and the works of author Jin Yong's (and other New School Martial Arts Fiction writers) were serialized in newspapers and adapted for film. The popular success of Jin Yong, Gu Long, and Liang Yusheng's novels was great, and concurrent advances in film and television technology facilitated multiple film and television adaptations. Derivatives and spinoffs of the characters and stories showed up in comics, digital games, and other media. While not ideologically touting a social mission, like the lauded works in the May Fourth era, Jin Yong's works "have been a continuous source of material for other products of mass culture,"[11] and transcend simple entertainment in their contribution to the unconscious social function of constructing the nation.

Jin Yong's novels map out the Chinese nation geographically, and the characters and their behavior became archetypical products that inform the national consciousness. For example, Jin Yong's final epic novel, *Lu ding ji* (*The Deer and the Cauldron*; serialized 1969–1972; hereafter *Cauldron*) provides a historically based fictional account of Qing imperial consolidation, intrigue, and international conflict, told with considerable irony and humor. *Cauldron* also encompasses elements of post-1949 PRC-Taiwan relations in pseudo-political allegory, as the protagonist Wei Xiaobao colludes with Ming loyalists traced to Taiwan. Wei Xiaobao also becomes an "international expert" as he travels to Russia to form an alliance to thwart Qing conspirator Wu Sangui's attempt to overthrow Kang Xi, and winds up foiling a coup against the Russian throne.

The construction of national identity in Jin Yong's works involves a critique of ethnicity, typically through the lens of ethnic conflict and inter-dynastic politics. Jin Yong's novels frequently turn on conflicts between ethnic groups struggling to dominate China. The cultural superiority of the Han—who make up a little more than ninety percent of the mainland's population—is ultimately reaffirmed through struggles over sacred kungfu texts, even if martial superiority on a dynastic scale is temporarily elusive. Novels like Jin Yong's *She diao yingxiong zhuan* (*The Eagle-Shooting Heroes*; serialized 1957–1959; hereafter *Heroes*) and *Tian long ba bu* (*The Demi-Gods and Semi-Devils*; serialized 1963–1966; hereafter *Semi-Devils*) demonstrate both the breadth of China's ethnicities and issues involving the discourse Han ethnic primacy.

In addition to helping fashion national and ethnic identity, the martial arts action in Jin Yong's fiction also provides a complex vision of Chinese social values that reinforce and sometimes challenge the audience's view of China, ancient and modern. Cultural values such as Confucian respect for hierarchy, central authority, education, and virtue are entwined with swordsmanship that resembles calligraphy (and vice versa), poetry recited while defeating foes, music as both high art and weapon, and loyalty to one's martial master and state. At the same time, the novels and film/television adaptations counterpose the qualities of individual rectitude with national aspirations.

This book is structured in five chapters. Chapter 1, "Kungfu Cultural Literacy: Situating Jin Yong's Martial Arts Fiction," describes a form of cultural capital necessary for audiences to makes sense of martial arts fiction and film. The elements of kungfu cultural literacy form the foundation of the kungfu industrial complex and are linked across interstices of language, story, history, and philosophy to make up an interpretive "code" of the matrix. Kungfu cultural phenomena are intelligible to the extent of cultural capital of the audience.

Chapter 2, "Jin Yong's Rhetorical Kungfu: Cultural Capital of Humor," is an exposition of one dimension of Jin Yong's literary art. Jin Yong's narrative/storytelling technique employs humor founded in popular linguistic forms of irony and satire, including cursing, sarcasm, flattery, and hierarchical wordplay. These are primary metaphorical vehicles that *bring together* a variety of kungfu cultural tropes which inform kungfu cultural literacy. This exposition of one dimension of Jin Yong's rhetoric demonstrates how language and the cultural capital interact in the construction of the kungfu industrial complex.

Chapter 3, "Canonization, Cultural Capital, National Character," analyzes the valorization of Jin Yong's work within the "field" of academic discourse by situating his novels in the canonization debate. This institutional dimension of cultural capital is essential to construction, maintenance, and further development of the kungfu industrial complex. Canonization is the normalization of the "value," or measure of cultural capital, that Jin Yong's fiction brings to the reader/audience/society at large. Canonization validates the author and works by sanctioning their cultural status. Discourse centering on the author's potential as a Nobel Prize candidate ups the ante by situating him as a national representative in global (transnational) cultural discourse.

Chapter 4, "Kungfu Star Power: The Entertainment *Jianghu*," is an interpretation of the human capital dimension of the kungfu industrial complex. Jin Yong's narrative/storytelling techniques (coding) connect elements of kungfu cultural literacy with his characters to create and propel his stories, entertain audiences, and increase readership. Similarly, the actors (as well as directors, producers, stunties, etc.) who reprise those characters in Jin Yong related television and film adaptations and spinoffs promote the stories and grow the audience while simultaneously acquiring technical training and further cultural capital as they build their own star power in a virtuous cycle. They thus contribute to the construction of the kungfu industrial complex matrix in dimensions of *time*, *place*, and *interpretation*. Jin Yong's works are reperformed repeatedly over decades and interpreted (and reinterpreted) by numerous top stars of each decade in Hong Kong, Taiwan, and mainland China. These stars become the contemporary faces of the iconic Jin Yong characters and complement (or sometimes displace) the actors who previously played those iconic roles. What were initially "two-dimensional" texts published serially to sell newspapers to the Chinese diaspora throughout Asia, eventually inspired the creation of film, television, and other media products and simultaneously constructed cultural capital in reputations of actors and production personnel associated with Jin Yong roles.

Finally, chapter 5, "The *Kung Fu Hustle* Hustle," brings all elements of the kungfu industrial complex together in an applied interpretation of Stephen Chow's film *Kung Fu Hustle* (2004). *Kung Fu Hustle* demonstrates a full-functioning kungfu industrial complex that manipulates the language, characters, sub-plots, plots, and values of Jin Yong's (and others') martial arts fiction. The "hustle" of *Kung Fu Hustle* is displayed through mature and comfortable "self-validation through self-satire" of those characters and stories. Complete recognition of self-satire and humor relies upon intricate understanding of the interpretive kungfu cultural code and the accumulation of related cultural capital.

NOTES

1. This chapter draws elements from my essay "The Geopolitics of Kung Fu Film," *Foreign Policy in Focus*, February 8, 2007, http://www.fpif.org/fpiftxt/3980.

2. "Kungfu in Translation, Translation in Kungfu," in *The Question of Reception: Martial Arts Fiction in English Translation* (Hong Kong: Lingnan College, 1997): 30.

3. Siu Leung Li, "The Myth Continues: Cinematic Kung Fu in Modernity," in *Hong Kong Connections: Transnational Imagination in Action Cinema*, eds. Meaghan Morris et al. (Hong Kong: Hong Kong University Press, 2005): 51.

4. Box Office Mojo by IMDbPro, accessed January 25, 2020https://www.boxofficemojo.com/title/tt0190332/?ref_=bo_se_r_1.

5. Box Office Mojo by IMDbPro, accessed January 25, 2020, https://www.boxofficemojo.com/title/tt0299977/?ref_=bo_se_r_1.

6. Box Office Mojo by IMDbPro, accessed January 25, 2020, https://www.boxofficemojo.com/release/rl2271446529/.

7. Richard Meyers, *Great Martial Arts Movies from Bruce Lee to Jackie Chan and More* (New York: Citadel Press, 1985, 2001): 68.

8. Bourdieu, Pierre, "The Forms of Capital," trans. Richard Nice, *Handbook of Theory and Research for the Sociology of Education*, ed. John G. Richardson (New York: Glenwood Press): 243.

9. The schematic is adapted from "Figure 2: Institutions of the literary field in West-European countries (Van Rees and Vermunt, 1996: 320)," in Michel Hockx, ed., *The Literary Field of Twentieth-Century China* (Honolulu, University of Hawaii Press, 1999): 8.

10. "Pierre Bourdieu," in *"The Johns Hopkins Guide to Literary Theory and Criticism,"* eds. Michael Groden, Martin Kreiswirth, and Imre Szeman, http://litguide.press.jhu.edu.proxy.library.georgetown.edu/index.html.

11. Dai Jinhua, "Order/Anti-Order: Representation of Identity in Hong Kong Action Movies," in *Hong Kong Connections: Transnational Imagination in Action Cinema*, eds. Meaghan Morris et al. (Hong Kong: Hong Kong University Press, 2005): 90.

ONE

Kungfu Cultural Literacy
Situating Jin Yong's Martial Arts Fiction

Jin Yong received the *Zhongguo gongfu zhizun dajiang* (The supreme award for Chinese kungfu) from the hand of Jackie Chan at a Global Festival held by Shenzhen Satellite TV, the Shaolin Temple, and Hong Kong TVB in Shenzhen on October 12, 2007.[1] The photograph of these two cultural icons demonstrates that both literary and physical kungfu are powerful elements in the discourse of Chinese kungfu in the entertainment industry. Jackie Chan spoke respectfully as he praised and contextualized Jin Yong's contribution and influence:

> Speaking of influence [in the martial arts world], I have to mention a person, because he used his pen to spread Chinese culture, Chinese martial values, and Chinese vistas to the whole world. Not only just Chinese people, he has caused a craze among tens of millions, over 100 million foreigners. I believe that everybody knows without me having to say who it is. Today I am truly extremely honored and delighted, he is the pride of Chinese people worldwide. Grandmaster Jin Yong.[2]

Hong Kong was ground zero for kungfu entertainment in the form of fiction, film, and television in the latter half of the twentieth century and Jin Yong and Jackie Chan represent the pinnacles of cultural production. The backstory to this industry is crucial to understanding the globalization of kungfu and its appeal in the late-twentieth and early twenty-first centuries.

Jin Yong was not merely the romanticized solitary author sitting alone in his study cranking out installments of his fiction day after day, but also a businessman and newsman. In addition, he was friend and colleague to fellow New School Martial Arts Fiction leading writers Liang Yusheng and Gu Long. Moreover, Jin Yong was friends with a range of other martial arts fiction writers, directors, and actors, and associated with them in Taiwan and Hong Kong:

> In the 1960s and 1970s I went to Taiwan and Taiwan martial arts fiction writers came to Hong Kong. We gathered to drink, play mahjong [or cards]

and chat. I was the main host, so they all called me *"bangzhu"* (gang leader). This gang probably was the *hunao bang* (mischievous gang), and its members were mainly Gu Long, Wo Longsheng, Zhuge Qingyun, Ni Kuang, and Xiang Zhuang. Besides them, there was also [director] Zhang Che, [actor] Wang Yu, and so on.[3]

He frames his recollection in terms of martial arts fiction metaphor, he is the "gang leader," and humor as the "mischievous gang." Jin Yong indicates close interaction with important players in martial arts cultural production at the very time he was writing and adapting his novels for screen: *wuxia* martial arts fiction writers Gu Long, Wo Longsheng, and Ni Kuang, as well as director Chang Cheh (Zhang Che) and top Shaw Brothers Studio film star Jimmy Wang Yu, who came to prominence in the *wuxia* martial arts classic *Du bi dao* (The one-armed swordsman, 1967).

The kungfu industrial complex is a vast matrix informed by linguistic terminology as well as a myriad of connections between classic Chinese martial arts novels which lay out the world view and ideology of the swordsman and martial arts practitioners. This includes portrayal of legendary heroes like Huang Feihong (Wong Fei-hung) in modern Hong Kong martial arts movie from 1960s; transnationalization through the vehicle of Bruce Lee in his 1970s kungfu films and visual references in later movies;[4] the careers of a multitude of subsequent film, television, and singing stars; the cross-fertilization of actors and the characters they portray; the real and exaggerated martial arts techniques that dazzled audiences long before digital imaging made possible closer representation of the mystical and fantastical elements of the original texts; and the heroic efforts of the directors, crews, and producers who brought the cultural products to life and sustain the afterlife of the myriad of heroes and heroines.

Kungfu cultural literacy has a long lineage tracing back to characters and stories from traditional fiction of the Ming (and earlier) and narrative elements drawn from history and philosophy. As a prelude, note that kungfu cultural literacy is the measure of the accumulation of cultural capital that encompasses a deeply ingrained impression of (1) the texts: the novels themselves, the plots and subplots, archetypical characters, fighting schools and styles, sacred or secret martial arts texts, individual fighting techniques; (2) cultural (and kungfu) values rooted in philosophy, military strategy, history, medicine, geography, and associated metanarrative; and (3) kungfu commercialization: productions in film, television, media, comics, cartoons, computer games, internet memes, and the associated technology and personnel requisite to produce and disseminate associated commodities (writers, directors, cast, crew, theaters, etc.).

KUNGFU CULTURAL LITERACY AND CULTURAL CAPITAL

Crouching Tiger is a prominent example of the ballet of swordsmanship, hand-to-hand combat, gymnastics, mystical energy forces, and fantastical special effects in *wuxia* films in which characters fly over rooftops, cling to walls, and channel their *qi* into lightning bolts delivered through the palm of the hand or fingertips. Audiences are primed for these elements of Chinese kungfu culture by *wuxia* film and the martial arts novels that preceded film. The surface level action in *Crouching Tiger* is for the most part intelligible to all viewers. Reading the novel on which it is based would make a deeper level of understanding possible (corrected for the inevitable convenience of adaptation). Deeper levels of understanding are dependent upon "kungfu cultural literacy," which relies on a multitude of both obvious and unobvious cultural knowledge including but also beyond the kungfu related values and ideological structures of martial arts fiction and film.

From a literary critical point of view, Bourdieu's notion of cultural capital helps lend interpretive clarity to the idea of kungfu cultural literacy. Note that while I use "literacy," Bourdieu uses the term "competence" which enables the use of cultural capital. Education, socialization, and other experience create "a form of knowledge, understanding or internalized code which equips the social agent with a competence for deciphering artistic works."[5]

Films like *Crouching Tiger* are cultural products that are an inseparable combination of cultural, social, and economic capital. Economic capital might be roughly approximated by box office revenue and production costs, although multiplier effects certainly exist. Cultural and social capital are less statistically measurable but equally important. In order to successfully attain deeper levels of understanding and resonance of a novel or its adaptation to a film (or television series), the audience requires linguistic cultural capital at relatively deeper levels including knowledge of the rules and values of the martial arts world including its mysticism and symbology. Moreover, the actors, scriptwriters, directors, and crew require linguistic cultural literacy to inform their interpretations and representations of the action from the novel into the film. Cultural capital doesn't end with the embodied state where audiences and actors seemingly nodding in silent agreement of understanding. Films also contribute to the social and economic capital of the actors and production crew, which can in turn be leveraged for future economic capital as they hone their production craft.

In the current example, *Crouching Tiger* suggests that higher levels of cultural capital might enhance a viewer's appreciation of the fantastical elements of the kungfu beyond surface level. Viewers/readers with this cultural capital "trade" it in discussion on blogs while academics do an elevated version of this through film and literature reviews. An audience might suspend disbelief while trying to comprehend or construct an interpretation that makes sense. This may require some conscious investigation of Chinese culture, history, or geography, not to mention language, which in turn might accrue to the reader/audience further kungfu cultural literacy and facilitate deeper appreciation of the story's nuance. The acquisition process is a continuous feedback loop with repeated reproduction of cultural capital—individual and communal interpretations that inform readers, audiences, actors, production crew, in all the various dimensions necessary to make and interpret an adaptation. Successful manipulation of cultural capital leads to further social capital and economic capital through awards, additional roles, bragging rights, etc.

The kungfu industrial complex is constructed by and encompasses the process of production of cultural capital, playing on a relationship between texts, films/television adaptations, actors, directors, distributors, and consumers as individual cultural capital is acquired and translated into symbolic and economic (and sometimes political) capital. Literary texts are adapted into film text; literary characters are embodied by actors; the characters wander a vast *jianghu* (martial world) that describes a nation typically (but not always) separate from officialdom; they employ martial techniques that are founded in fictional lore; they represent historical kungfu sects sometimes in actual locations such as *Crouching Tiger*'s Daoist Wudang Mountain; the economic and cultural success of the film begets sequels; the actors' star power (a product of the interaction between cultural, social, and economic capital) is enhanced by institutional recognition; directors accumulate cultural capital which is sometimes engaged, such as when the action director becomes director of the sequel (the case in *Crouching Tiger*'s 2016 sequel); the storyline and myths repeats with variations; a star (e.g., Michelle Yeoh) returns for the sequel and other stars, such as Donnie Yen, are incorporated into the film, enhancing or exploiting their cultural capital (star power) to assure or increase box office. The plot and subplots appeal to the audience's linguistic and cultural knowledge/sensibilities within the culturally literate group, and likewise challenge that of the nonculturally literate group, which may initially lack kungfu sufficient linguistic and cultural literacy but may gradually accumulate it through repeated exposure and/or education. The actor's enhanced star power might be viewed as a career breakthrough in personal, ethnic, and global terms, as *Crouching Tiger*'s Zhang Ziyi notes: "Because of movies like *Crouching Tiger, Hidden Dragon*, and *Hero* and *Memoirs of a Geisha*, a lot of people in the United States have become interested not only in me but in Chinese and Asian actors in general. Because of these movies, maybe there will be more opportunities for Asian actors."[6]

Although complex and intangible, cultural capital is acquired, possessed, and manipulated by both readers/audiences and those people involved in production alike. It can be learned gradually from one text to the next, from one film to the next. Actors may benefit from cultural capital to inform the roles they play, then accumulate symbolic capital from those roles by association with a specific role and/or production. Then their symbolic capital can be leveraged into economic capital through further opportunities in film and television. When the authors, actors, directors, et al., participate in bringing the stories and characters "to life" they are constructing the kungfu industrial complex.

The kungfu industrial complex in turn thus trades on multiple elements of Chinese culture that audiences learn over time as they acquire kungfu cultural literacy—from classic popular novels to actual kungfu schools, from philosophical Confucianism, Daoism to Buddhism, from traditional China to modern China, from the spatial geography of dynastic China to the "imagined community" or nation of modern China, and more.

There is a linguistic distinction between "kungfu" and "martial arts"—both terms overlapping and shared between the Chinese words *gongfu* (kungfu), *wushu* (martial arts/technique)—and *wuxia* ("knight-errant," "martial chivalry," or "martial arts" as adjective), as well as *wugong* (kungfu ability/skill/technique). "Kungfu" is a fundamental component of the latter three terms in Chinese, connected through the character is *wu* (martial or military). The twentieth century saw a rise in the term *wuxia xiaoshuo* (martial arts fiction/novel).[7] Premodern Chinese used a range of terminology such as *xia*, *youxia* (traveling or wandering *xia*), and *xiayi* (*xia* righteousness/righteous loyalty).[8] The character *wu* (martial or military), which is used in the three terms above, also forms the general abstract concept *wuyi* (literally, "martial arts"). However, the term "martial arts fiction" in Chinese is formulated as *wuxia xiaoshuo*, because this term encompasses the idea and moral virtues of "chivalry," akin to the English term "knight-errant" when put it into action in Chinese through the linguistic formulation, *xing xia zhang yi* (to do martial chivalry and uphold virtue/righteousness). The greatest martial artists in the *wuxia* world either studied a martial text or wrote one, which elevates them to an ideal "cultured" hero expressed in the linguistic formation *wen wu quan cai* (talented in both literary and martial arts). *Wuxia* kungfu cultural capital thus valorizes the literary and culture alongside the martial.

Much of the fiction classified as *wuxia xiaoshuo*, especially Jin Yong's fiction, encompasses both fist and sword, as well as *qi* (internal energy/force) and a host of other weaponry. The issue is English translation, an interpretive "art." That said, to address kungfu cultural literacy the terms *wuxia* and kungfu will be differentiated when necessary to discuss genre attributes. This differentiation is useful when discussing Hong Kong

Figure 1.1. Film supervisor Johnny To (center) has Andy Lau (left) and Tony Leung (right) prepare for their leading roles in *Cauldron* (1984) by reading Jin Yong's novel. Below: Leung reviews early film adaption

martial arts film, which can initially be divided into subgenres of *wuxia* "swordplay" films acted in ancient costume (*guzhuang*) and featuring fantastical feats (often by virtue of wire work), and kungfu film which stress more realistic fighting displays (*wushu*) of fist and feet and generally eschew fantastical feats. *Wuxia* films integrate sword wielding heroes and heroines, but also feature use of fist combat. In contrast, Bruce Lee and Jackie Chan generally used their fists and weapons without edges and did not usually act in ancient costume per se. What brings these two together is how *wuxia* and kungfu are structured by the same cultural ideological system, the martial school structure with its hierarchy and all its linguistic and culturally informed values.

Reading and viewing audiences develop an attuned sense of kungfu cultural literacy through long and repeated exposure to text, television, and film, which results in a virtually effortless recognition of characters from classical fiction and martial arts fiction of the twentieth century. Top students in the 1980s and early 1990s Taiwan were pressured by parents to forgo reading martial arts fiction during high school in favor of their studies so as to survive the brutal preparation for college entrance exams. This resulted in the phenomenon of the first semester at university sometimes being referred to as the "Jin Yong Semester,"[9] whereupon students satisfied pent up frustration at denial of these works by binge reading through his collected works day and night. The concept of kungfu cultural literacy refers to a deeply ingrained knowledge of Chinese history and culture necessary to both consciously and unconsciously understand the martial arts novel beyond the surface linguistic level, but rather at progressively deeper levels of the cognitive, emotional, and subconscious/psychological.

Jin Yong is one extremely productive node in the multidimensional matrix of kungfu cultural literacy. This study of the kungfu industrial complex relates the corpus of elements of Jin Yong's martial arts fiction and the entertainment industry, television, film, and music connections at every level. In this context kungfu cultural literacy is a measure of the audience's varying depth of conscious and unconscious understanding and engagement with Jin Yong's characters, plots, sacred texts, invented kungfu, subversion of cultural norms, television series, films, and other extensions of Jin Yong identifiers.

Extended Jin Yong identifiers are a measure of cultural capital and the breadth of impact of Jin Yong's works in the kungfu industrial complex. For example, Jack Ma, founder of the Chinese tech giant Alibaba, uses a nickname Feng Qingyang drawn from a renowned swordsman in Jin Yong's *Xiao ao jianghu* (The Smiling, Proud Wanderer; hereafter *Wanderer*): "At Alibaba, those who have been influenced by Jin Yong are not limited just to 'Feng Qingyang' Jack Ma. Following Jack Ma, who is deeply steeped in Jin Yong's cultural influence, all the workers at Alibaba have taken 'nicknames,' so Alibaba has 'Guo Jing,' 'Miao Renfeng,' 'Xiaoyaozi.'"[10] The example of Jack Ma, currently China's richest person, having a Jin Yong nickname is intelligible on the surface insofar as one recognizes the connection to Jin Yong. Digging deeper, the reader needs a sufficient level of kungfu cultural literacy to identify the personality and martial features of the fictional character from whom his nickname is derived. Feng Qingyang was the greatest swordsman of the Huashan Sword Sect but also a reclusive hermit (the reason for which requires high level kungfu cultural literacy). He taught one of Jin Yong's most recognizable characters, Linghu Chong, but stipulated that Linghu Chong keep his tutelage secret. One also needs to know that Feng's sword style was called *Dugu jiu jian* (The nine swords of Dugu). Another critical piece of knowledge that Feng is a direct martial descendant of Dugu Qiubai, whose name literally means "Dugu Seeking Defeat." The connotation is unintelligible unless one knows the back story: that Dugu Qiubai was the greatest swordsman ever and was so dedicated to the way of the sword he yearned for a worthy opponent who might defeat him. Here are four or five levels of kungfu cultural literacy necessary to guess the possible reason that Jack Ma might have taken Feng Qingyang as his nickname. This might help explain that after Jin Yong died in late 2018, Jack Ma reportedly said: "On the last day of October, Jack Ma blogged in commemoration of Jin Yong, 'Without the gentleman [Jin Yong], I don't know if we'll still have Alibaba or not.'"[11] While it is impossible to know for sure what Jack Ma meant by this, the character Feng Qingyang was quite cryptic, teaching Linghu Chong a lesson analyzed throughout the 1600-plus pages of the novel: "The most fearsome [kungfu] moves in the world lies not in martial ability, but in conspiracy, treachery and traps."[12] This is a prominent example of both the depth of influence that Jin Yong and his works have on his readers, the progressively deeper levels of kungfu cultural literacy necessary for interpretation, and the extent of afterlife of his works in the kungfu industrial complex.

JIN YONG'S WORKS

Jin Yong's works were originally serialized daily over many years in newspapers or martial arts fiction magazines. John Christopher Hamm's *Paper Swordsman* (Hawaii, 2005) details the variety of versions from serialization to individual partial editions, both homemade and rip-offs capitalizing on Jin Yong's name and the works' popularity.[13] Eventually Jin Yong started his own publishing company to produce his revised works, Ming Ho Publication Corporation Limited.[14] To date there have been three editions and numerous printings of *The Collected Works of Jin*

Yong in Hong Kong, Taiwan, and mainland China. According to Jin Yong, he wrote for fifteen years, from 1955 to 1970, dates of convenience since he actually finished the serialization of his last novel in 1972, and then spent ten years from 1970 to 1980 revising all his works for publication.[15] The serialized original works are typically referred to as the *jiu ban* (old edition), the collected works finally completed in 1981 and published by Ming Ho (Minghe) are referred to as *xin ban* (new edition), and the second revision finished in 2006 is called the *xin xiu ban* (new revised edition).[16] The new edition of his collected works contains thirty-six volumes.[17] The first official, not pirated, introduction of a work of Jin Yong's fiction into mainland China was in 1980, when *Heroes* was published serially in Guangzhou's *Wulin* (Martial forest) magazine just as China opened to the outside world.[18] An official simplified-character edition of *The Collected Works of Jin Yong* was published in mainland China in 1994.[19]

Table 1.1. Jin Yong's 12 Major Novels with His English Title Translations and Abbreviations (in italics) in Order of Initial Publication

Shu jian en chou lu	書劍恩仇錄	[*Book and Sword,* Gratitude and Revenge]
Bi xue jian	碧血劍	[The Sword Stained with *Royal Blood*]
She diao yingxiong zhuan	射雕英雄傳	[The Eagle-Shooting *Heroes*]
Shen diao xia lü	神鵰俠侶	[The Giant Eagle and Its *Companion*]
Xueshan feihu	雪山飛狐	[*Flying Fox* on Snowy Mountain]
Feihu waizhuan	飛狐外傳	[*The Young Flying Fox*]
Yi tian tu long ji	倚天屠龍記	[The Heaven Sword and the *Dragon Sabre*]
Lian cheng jue	連城訣	[*A Deadly Secret*]
Tian long ba bu	天龍八部	[The Demi-Gods and *Semi-Devils*]
Xia ke xing	俠客行	[*Ode to Gallantry*]
Xiao ao jianghu	笑傲江湖	[The Smiling, Proud *Wanderer*]
Lu ding ji	鹿鼎記	[The Duke of Mount Deer (The Deer and the *Cauldron*)]

Titles references for Jin Yong's works are indicated in italics above.[20] Most of Jin Yong's stories are quite long, ranging from two to five volumes at approximately four hundred pages per volume. The geography of the stories encompasses large swaths of China, from Mongolia and Manchuria in the north to Yunnan and Sichuan in the south and west. For example, the locations in *Heroes* extend from the Gobi Desert in Inner Mongolia in the north to Xiangyang in Hubei province; *Semi-Devils* covers nearly all of China from Mongolia to Manchuria in the north to the southern reaches of China's Yunnan Province, where the former state of Dali (937–1253) existed, and to the western state of Xixia (1032–1227) which occupied part of today's Inner Mongolia and Gansu Province. Jin Yong's texts often include maps of the geographical areas traversed in the plot and other culturally related errata such as paintings or inscriptions.[21] One map in volume 4 of *Heroes* compares four great world empires, featuring Genghis Khan's Mongol Empire occupying the greatest territory.

Specific scenes in Jin Yong's works are grandiose, with huge armies doing battle, such as the grand scale description of the Mongol battles in *Heroes* and the battle where Xiao Feng (a.k.a. Qiao Feng)[22] saves the Qidan emperor from a coup while on a hunting trip in *Semi-Devils*. A banquet may be attended by several hundred or several thousand martial heroes. For example, the retirement party for Liu Zhengfeng, an elder of the Hengshan Sect in *Wanderer*, depicts five hundred guests in attendance.[23] Later in *Wanderer* a meeting on Songshan depicts a couple thousand participants in attendance to ostensibly consolidate the five separate mountain sword sects into a single "Five Mountains Sword Sect."[24] A great gathering of heroes (*yingxiong dahui*) in *Dragon Sabre* counts the fighters of all sects who've come to meet at the Shaolin Temple and arrives at four thousand six hundred.[25] Woven into the structure of Jin Yong's works are elements of history and legend, good versus evil, the cycle of revenge and retribution, obligation and loyalty to one's martial master and brethren, character development and individual martial improvement, a search for the martial book of secrets, the struggle to be "Number One" in the martial world, and the defense of the Empire against threats from within and without. The plot of *Book and Sword*, for example, turns on attempts of an ethnic Han secret society to overthrow the Manchu Qing Dynasty woven with an item of popular folklore from Jin Yong's hometown that regarded the Qianlong emperor as a Han Chinese. These elements are intertwined with Chinese aesthetics, medical, philosophical, and religious practice and inquiry taken from Daoism, Buddhism, Confucianism, and other orthodox and unorthodox strands of popular culture. There is a whole array of interpersonal relationships with the tensions and conflicts they spark: master and pupil, sworn brothers, lovers, husband and wife, parent and child, and brothers and sisters of martial sects. The love relationship is one common organizing principle in a number of Jin's works, Yang Guo's relationship with Xiaolongnü in *Companion* being the foremost example. Their relationship is complicated by the fact that they are also master and pupil, which violates a Confucian code of ethics held dear by the "upright" sects of the *jianghu* martial world and becomes a critical subplot driving the narrative.

Another overarching organizing principle is the battle between good and evil, which may be undermined by the conflation of good and evil and challenged or critiqued by main characters like Linghu Chong in *Wanderer*. Linghu Chong is forced to choose between good and evil, orthodoxy and heterodoxy, as he navigates the *jianghu* and struggles with the hypocritical dogmatism of his upright Huashan Sect martial master, Yue Buqun. Linghu Chong discovers a world that is complex, with good amid evil, evil amid good, righteous behavior by those in heterodox sects, and nonrighteousness behavior by those in orthodox sects.

A typical Jin Yong's plot device is the search (or battle) for a book of martial secrets which might ensure the practitioner a chance to become "number one" in the *jianghu*. In *Wanderer* this text is the *Bixie jianpu* (Sword manual to ward off evil).[26] The search for the sword manual leads to the destruction of its putative author's clan and catalyzes turmoil in the *jianghu*, involving competition between numerous orthodox sects and individuals who are mobilized to search for it. Revenge, a third common thread that weaves Jin Yong's stories together, becomes the *raison d'être* for the character Lin Pingzhi, whose grandfather had ostensibly authored the sword manual. Lin sacrifices love, reputation, and progeny to avenge the death of his family and the loss of their fortune.

THE CONSTRUCTION OF CULTURAL CAPITAL: AN OVERVIEW OF JIN YONG'S WORKS AND IMPACT

Locating Jin Yong and his works in both historical and literary historical context is important in order to set up the discussion of cultural capital in the kungfu industrial complex. Kungfu concepts owe a debt to fiction as they traverse the media divide to television and film. The debt of *wushu* (martial arts) to *wuxia* (martial chivalry) is situated within the values and value structure of popular culture where these linkages become comprehensible. The locus classicus of kungfu fiction can be traced back at least as far as the Ming Dynasty novel, *Water Margin*, and then followed through the Qing Dynasty to works of fiction from China's Republican Period (1911–1949). The latter half of the twentieth century sees a geometric acceleration of New School Martial Arts Fiction, which were originally serialized in Hong Kong and Taiwan newspapers and magazines from the 1950s through the 1970s and then adapted for television and film. Jin Yong is the undisputed master of this New School.

Jin Yong's background informs the cultural capital of his readers, much like participation in social media plays a part in the construction of cultural and social capital of netizens of the twenty-first century. He was born Zha Liangyong in 1924 to a prosperous family in Haining County, Zhejiang province, to the south of Shanghai, China. He went to Hong Kong in 1948 to work at the newspaper *Dagong bao*, where he wrote on international issues involving China. In 1952 he started work at *Xin wanbao* (which belonged to *Dagong bao*) as the editor of a supplement and wrote movie critiques, as well as some movie scripts. At *Xin wanbao* he met other martial arts writers, particularly Liang Yusheng, with whom he became good friends, and turned his hand to writing martial arts fiction in installments for newspapers. In 1955 he started the serial publication of his first novel, *Book and Sword*, in *Xin wanbao*. Besides writing fiction, Jin Yong was also a journalist, and editor. He serialized *Royal Blood* in 1956 and started *Heroes* in 1957, both published in *Xianggang shangbao* (Hong Kong Commercial Daily). After publishing his first three novels serially in someone else's newspaper,[27] in 1959 he started his own newspaper, *Ming Pao*, wherein he serially published *Companion* and many of his later novels. Jin Yong's martial arts fiction was crucial to the initial financial success of his newspaper as readers returned daily to follow the characters and narratives he created.

Synergy between Jin Yong's newspaper and the other magazines and journals he established facilitated the marketing of his martial arts works through advertisements, letters to the editor, and even a Jin Yong discussion forum. Hamm details in *Paper Swordsman* the background of Jin Yong's rise through parallel journalism and fiction writing. This included starting his own publishing company to put out his revised works, which were polished for a more literary read.[28] Jin Yong himself later wrote that his own fiction writing emphasized Chineseness in form and language, and stressed that his *wuxia* fiction was entertainment for the masses, thus specifically rejecting the role of literature as "serving society" which leading writers of the twentieth century advocated during the idealized literary reform period of the May Fourth era of the 1910s and 1920s.

Jin Yong's martial arts novels are the most poignant example of New School of Martial Arts Fiction that arose in the British colony of Hong Kong after the establishment of the PRC in 1949. Jin Yong attracted readers to his newspapers with his martial arts fiction, became exceedingly rich, (at one point listed as the sixty-fourth richest person in Hong Kong with $1.2 billion in the 1990s) and is arguably the best selling/most read Chinese novelist of all-time, writing a total of thirty million or so Chinese characters in approximately 15,000 pages of text. It is quite possible that Jin Yong's readership is greater than that of any other writer in world history, however, statistics on readership are difficult to come by, especially considering the long history of pirating his works in mainland China and Taiwan in the 1960s, 1970s, and early 1980s. But to get an idea of scale, a 1996 interview article estimates 100 million copies of Jin Yong works were sold, including pirated versions, but not including translations.[29] Another report states that more than 500,000 sets of Jin Yong's collected works were sold by Beijing's Sanlian Bookstore in the Mainland between 1994 and 1996 alone.[30]

In order to grasp the impact that Jin Yong's works had in popular media of film and television, it is instructive to examine the variety of adaptations of *Heroes*, which was serialized between 1957 and 1959 in *Hong Kong Commercial Daily* (*Xianggang shangbao*). His other major works follow similar process and scale. The following tables indicate the speediness and extent to which *Heroes* was adapted, first as a film in 1958 when it was still being serialized in the newspaper and nearly sixty years later as a spin-off by directors Zhu Lingfeng and Diao Yu called *The Eagle Shooting Heroes Eighteen Palms Subduing the Dragon* prepares to drop.[31] In addition, derivative works based on plots and subplots appear in both television series and film, and provide prequels and/or in-depth background narratives to Jin Yong's original works. The plethora of adaptations and readaptations contributes to and increases the complexity of cultural capital vis-à-vis Jin Yong, his novels, and his characters. Initial successes by actors in earlier productions might become iconic, and the next adaptation of the same work might challenge that iconic interpretation, sometimes successfully and sometimes not. The third, fourth, or perhaps fifth adaptation (or later) may eventually transcend the earlier iconic version because of new talent, technology, or some combination of these. Moreover, successive generations of viewers may have successive valuations of what constitutes the iconic version. Students might debate with teachers or perhaps even argue with grandma or auntie about the relative evaluation of each rendition. Cultural capital is malleable and operates in a feedback cycle, especially considering the time dimension as the extensive list of adaptations and derivatives as film and television series below indicates. The tables below indicate the frequency of adaptation of *Heroes* by the year as a measure of the cultural currency of just one of Jin Yong's novels.

Table 1.2. Film Adaptations and Derivatives of *The Eagle-Shooting Heroes* by Year, Title, Dir, Studio and Stars, Compiled from Hong Kong Movie Database and Duoban Dianying

1958. *She diao yingxiong zhuan* (Story of the Vulture Conqueror). Dir. Hu Peng. Emei Film Co. Starring Walter Tso Tat-Wah and Yung Siu-Yi.
1959. *She diao yingxiong zhuan* (Story of the Vulture Conqueror). Dir. Hu Peng. Emei Film Co. Starring Walter Tso Tat-Wah and Yung Siu-Yi.
1977. *She diao yingxiong zhuan* (Brave Archer). Shaw Brothers Studio. Dir. Chang Cheh. Starring Alexander Fu Sheng and Kelly Niu Tien.
1978. *She diao yingxiong zhuan 2* (Brave Archer 2). Shaw Brothers Studio. Dir. Chang Cheh. Starring Alexander Fu Sheng and Kelly Niu Tien.
1981. *She diao yingxiong zhuan 3* (Brave Archer 3). Shaw Brothers Studio. Dir. Chang Cheh. Starring Alexander Fu Sheng and Kelly Niu Tien.
1993. *She diao yingxiong zhuan zhi dong cheng xi jiu* (The Eagle-Shooting Heroes: Eastern and Western Accomplishments). Dir. Jeffrey Lau. Starring Leslie Cheung, Brigitte Lin, Maggie Cheung, Tony Leung Chiu-wai.
1994. *Ashes of Time*. Dir. Wong Kar-Wai. Starring Brigitte Lin, Maggie Cheung, Leslie Cheung, Tony Leung Chiu-wai.
2019. *Xiao xi gu: She diao yingxiong zhuan* (Star of Tomorrow: Legend of the Eagle Shooting Hero). Dir. Mo Zhiying and Zhou Yuyu. Starring Shi Xiaosong, Tao Yuxi, and Xiaoyang Boyan.
2021. *She diao yingxiong zhuan zhi xiang long shiba zhang* (Legend of the Condor Heroes: The Dragon Tamer). Dir. Zhu Lingfeng and Diao Yu.
2021. *She diao yingxiong zhuan zhi jiu yin baigu zhua* (The Legend of Condor Heroes: The Cadaverous Claws). Dir. Daniel Fu Dung.

Figure 1.2. Introduction credit screenshot and protagonists Guo Jing (Felix Wong) and Huang Rong (Barbara Yung), *Heroes* (1983), Episode 10

Table 1.3. Television Adaptations of *The Eagle-Shooting Heroes* and Its Derivatives by Year, Director/Producer and Main Stars, Compiled from Duoban Dianying and Baidu

1976. *She diao yingxiong zhuan* (The Eagle-Shooting Heroes). Commercial Television. Dir. Xiao Sheng. Starring Bai Biao and Michelle Yim.
1983. *She diao yingxiong zhuan* (The Eagle-Shooting Heroes). TVB. 59 episodes. Dir. Wang Tianlin. Starring Felix Wong and Barbara Yung.
1988. *She diao yingxiong zhuan* (The Eagle-Shooting Heroes). China Television Company, Ltd. (Taiwan). 36 episodes. Dir. Li Chaoyong. Starring Huang Wenhao and Idy Chan.
1992. *Zhong shentong Wang Chongyang* (Rage and Passion). TVB. 20 episodes. Dir. Yu Mingsheng. Starring Ekin Cheng and Fiona Leung.
1993. *She diao yingxiong zhuan zhi jiu yang zhen jing* (The Mystery of The Condor Hero). TVB. 20 episodes. Dir. Li Rengang. Starring Julian Cheung Chilam, David Chiang Da-wei, and Fiona Leung.
1994. *She diao yingxiong zhuan* (The Eagle-Shooting Heroes). TVB Jade. 35 episodes. Dir. Li Tiansheng. Starring Julian Cheung Chilam and Athena Chu.
1994. *She diao yingxiong zhuan zhi nan di bei gai* (The Condor Heroes Return). 20 episodes. TVB. Dir. Su Wancong. Starring Ekin Zheng and Marco Ngai.
2003. *She diao yingxiong zhuan* (The Eagle-Shooting Heroes). Ciwen Movies and Television. 42 episodes. Yu Min. Starring Li Yapeng and Zhou Xun.
2008. *She diao yingxiong zhuan* (The Eagle-Shooting Heroes). Chinese Entertainment Tianjin Ltd. 50 episodes. Dir. Li Guoli. Starring Hu Ge and Lin Yichen.
2017. *She diao yingxiong zhuan* (The Eagle-Shooting Heroes). Zhejiang Huace Film & TV Co. Ltd. 52 episodes. Dir. Jiang Jiajun. Starring Yang Xuwen and Chen Yitong.

This lengthy list applies to only one of Jin Yong's twelve major novels. There are long lists for adaptations of many of his other novels as well. *Heroes* is the first of three loosely connected works that are referred to together as "The Condor Trilogy" (*She diao san bu qu*): *Heroes*, *Companion*, and *Dragon Sabre*. The plot of the approximately 1,600-page novel is continued and expanded in *Companion*, which also runs about 1,600 pages. Characters from these two novels set up *Dragon Sabre*, which again clocks in at 1,600 pages. In addition to the list of television series and films above, an English translation of the trilogy was published in 2018.[32]

With such lengthy novels, film adaptations are typically done in numerous parts and episodes. Television series typically adapt the entire work (or a derivative subplot such as those listed above). Listing the adaptations of Jin Yong's other works in film, television series, derivatives (graphic novel, cartoon, manga, game, etc.), and English translation provides a qualitative sense of their cultural penetration. *Book and Sword* has two two-part film, two film, and seven television adaptations. *Royal Blood* has one two-part film, two film, and five television series adaptations. *Companion* has three two-part film, one film, and nine television series adaptations. *Flying Fox* has one two-part film and five television

Figure 1.3. Introduction screenshots and protagonist Guo Jing (Hu Ge), *Heroes* (2008), Episode 1

series adaptations. *Young Flying Fox* has three film and one television series adaptation. *Dragon Sabre* has three two-part film and nine television series adaptations. *Semi-Devils*[33] has three film and six television series adaptations. *Gallantry* has one film and four television series adaptations. *Wanderer* has two film and eight television series adaptations. *Cauldron* has two film and seven television series adaptations. The year these adaptations appeared gives an indication of the sustained presence of Jin Yong in cultural discourse over eight different decades starting in 1958, with one adaptation (and sometimes more) in forty-nine different years.

In sum, nearly every year a Jin Yong film or television series came out, and some years multiple adaptations appear. Movie and television versions of Jin Yong's works began to appear soon after publication of his novels (he himself also worked in script writing and directing). He started his own company to publish his revised works. Almost all his works exist in multiple versions over the years, along with computer games, internet games, websites, comic books, and translations. The production of television series of the most popular novels continues with new versions coming out every few years. The nearly constant reading, production, viewing, and reception over so many years is a clear, albeit abstract, measure of the cultural capital of Jin Yong's novels—great cultural capital propels great cycling and recycling of the works. The economic and social capital that the directors, cast, and crew generated is immense. This data indicates that Jin Yong became a virtual cultural industry unto himself, somewhat analogous to the Disney empire. An example of his reach in Asia is that contemporaneous to *Wanderer*'s serialization in Hong Kong and Singapore during the late 1960s, *Wanderer* also appeared in twenty-one newspapers in Saigon in three different languages: Chinese, Vietnamese, and French.

LINGUISTIC CULTURAL CAPITAL: HIERARCHY OF INDIVIDUAL, FAMILY, GROUP, STATE

Cultural capital does not exist in a vacuum but is rather based in long tradition and modulated through a discourse of cultural value, which itself is manifested in tension between high and low culture. Archetypical scenes from Chinese fiction throughout the dynasties are referenced in Jin Yong's novels. These scenes include terminology and minor plot elements that connect Jin Yong's martial arts fiction with a rich intertextual literary and cultural discourse. In the preface to the 1994 Joint Publishing simplified character edition of his collected works, Jin Yong references the roots of martial arts fiction:

Martial arts fiction continues the long tradition of Chinese classical fiction. The earliest Chinese martial arts novels should be exciting literary works in the Tang tales of the marvelous such as *The Curly-Bearded Hero, Hong xian, Nie Yinniang,* and *The Kunlun Slave.* After that is *Water Margin, The Three Heroes and Five Gallants, The Story of Hero Boys and Hero Girls,* etc. Modern relatively serious martial arts fiction even more emphasizes righteousness, moral integrity, sacrificing oneself for others, upholding the weak against the strong, national spirit, and traditional Chinese ethical views.[34]

Martial arts fiction is wrapped around the idea and mythology surrounding the "hero" (*yingxiong haohan*), who is typically situated within a martial sect and set of friendships modeled on the hierarchical family structure. Jin Yong's novels explore not only martial relationships but also romantic relationships of these heroes and other characters. A fundamental aspect of the hero's social milieu is the concept of the "sworn brotherhood" in which people without blood lineage may become martial relatives (brothers, sisters, uncles, aunts, grandfathers, grandmothers, etc.) and form a martial sect in which characters adhere to orthodox relationship hierarchies based on age and generation along the lines of traditional Confucian filial hierarchy.

Deviation from the structure of Confucian hierarchy among some of Jin Yong's characters, such as the peer-to-peer brotherhood established between of the elderly Zhou Botong and young Guo Jing on Peach Blossom Island in *Heroes*, helps drive Jin Yong's narrative through subversive irony and humor. Jin Yong's novels exemplify the transmission of the "richness of traditional literary content" and "literary scholarship in popular literature" to the reader and the simultaneous subversion of those same traditions. For example, Jin Yong creates characters that uphold the martial world's values and subvert them. The historical existence of the *xia* (knight-errant) can be traced back at least as early as the Warring States Period (ca. 475–221 BC) recorded in Sima Qian's Han dynasty classic the *Shi ji* (Records of the grand historian), written about 94 BC. This text contains a section called *Youxia liezhuan* (Biographies of knights-errant) that connects the value of the promise (one's word) and degree of righteousness of the knight-errant: "To save people from distress and relieve people from want: is this not benevolence? Not to belie another's trust and not to break ones promises; such conduct a righteous man would approve. That is why I wrote the 'Biographies of Knights-errant.'"[35] The idea of the knight-errant is thus firmly situated in Chinese history with a lineage going back more than two thousand years. Reference to the knight-errant is found in a variety of works of premodern Chinese literature, from poetry to drama to fiction. In terms of kungfu cultural literacy, it is significant to note that Jin Yong's works contain a plethora of intertextual references to celebrated Chinese history, philosophy, calligraphy, and art, as well as literature. One highly visible example originates from a poem by the Tang dynasty poet, Li Bai, entitled "Xia ke xing" (Song of the knight-errant) from which Jin Yong drew the title for one of his novels, *Xia ke xing* (*Ode to Gallantry*; serialized 1966–1967). Another layer of intertextuality is that Li Bai's poem itself draws lines regarding the knight-errant, *shi bu sha yi ren, qian li bu liu xing* (He would kill a man every ten paces and go on for a thousand miles without stop), which derives originally from the Daoist philosophy classic, the *Zhuang Zi* (389–286 BC).

In addition to references to poetry and philosophy, fundamental works of kungfu cultural literacy include three Ming Dynasty works counted among the *Si da ming zhu* (The four great classical Chinese novels), which contain the roots of the archetypical language of the sworn brotherhood. First note that the three kungfu related Ming novels are *Three Kingdoms*, *Water Margin*, and *Journey to the West*. The usage of the language of martial brotherhood, are much earlier than these three works, and as Petrus Liu notes: "Jin Yong imitated the language of vernacular fiction in general (not just *Three Kingdoms*) to create an aura of premodern China and speech patterns. But it's not that fiction (Luo or Jin Yong) actually gave rise to such expressions; rather, fiction simply represented Chinese society and its characteristics as they were."[36] That said, the prototypical demonstration of the sworn brotherhood appears in chapter 1 of Luo Guanzhong's *Three Kingdoms*, which begins with the famous "Peach Garden Oath," literally referred to as "*Taohua haojie san jie yi*" (Three heroes swear brotherhood in the peach garden). It is here that the three protagonists, Liu Bei, Guan Yu, and Zhang Fei swear an oath of brotherly filiality which is mirrored on numerous occasions throughout Jin Yong's works:

> They declared: Although we three, Liu Bei, Guan Yu, and Zhang Fei, are of different birth, we now become brothers, and will work with common purpose to get through this crisis and help those in distress. We repay our country above and bring peace to the people below. Though we weren't born on the same year, same month, and same day, we pledge to die on the same year, same month, and same day (*bu qiu tongnian tongyue tongri sheng, dan yuan tongnian tongyue tongri si*). Heaven and Earth witness our intent and if we betray our righteous loyalty and forget our obligation, may Heaven and humanity mutually punish us.[37]

There are two parts of the oath that frequently appear in parts of Jin Yong's works, first the title of the chapter: "*Taohua haojie san jie yi*" (Three heroes swear brotherhood in the peach garden), and derivative language based on *jie yi*. The second part is the pledge: "Though we weren't born on the same year, same month, and same day, we pledge to die on the same year, same month, and same day." Traditional family hierarchy is typically recognized as the archetype for social structure from the level of individual to the family, to the village, towns, cities, counties, provinces and finally the empire. Liu Bei, Guan Yu, and Zhang Fei first establish a hierarchy among individuals (themselves) recognizing Liu Bei as the elder, and the other two as second and third brothers, respectively. This creates a family-like nucleus that will help direct their decisions in battle and loyalty in martial alliances and thus guide them on the path of upright social relations while they attempt to conquer all of China.

Jin Yong replicates and manipulates this Ming era loyalty oath centuries later. The title phrase of *"jie yi"* ([bond of] righteous loyalty—swear brotherhood) is cited throughout Jin Yong's works in a variety of formulations. The pledge to die on the same day is repeated nearly verbatim virtually in every one of his works both initially upon swearing brotherhood and then later as a reminder of the characters' sworn loyalty. There is occasionally a twist, as in chapter 14 of *Book and Sword* where the protagonist and leader of the Red Flower Society directly references the Peach Garden Oath participants by name, but asserts that the quality of their brotherhood/sisterhood in fact surpasses that of the original because they will *succeed* in realizing their sworn ambition to die together the same day, whereas the original members of the Peach Garden Oath did not.[38]

At the very start in chapter 1 of *Heroes* Jin Yong uses the trope of sworn brotherhood when Yang Tiexin recalls swearing brotherhood with protagonist Guo Jing's father in the same terms of the Peach Garden Oath.[39] Although Yang Tiexin attempted to fulfill his brotherhood oath with Guo Jing's father, he made the conscious choice to abandon it in order to stay alive and save Guo Jing's mother from death, a clearly higher virtue that also had the effect of continuing the story.

Other works also reenact this brotherhood trope for narrative continuity as well as to reinforce *wuxia* values. In chapter 41 of *Semi-Devils* nearly the exact wording of the Peach Garden Oath is used in when Duan Yu reminds Xiao Feng of their brotherhood oath to fight to the finish despite his "lack" of martial skills which would ironically further imperil them.[40] In chapter 8 of *Cauldron* Wei Xiaobao is inducted into the anti-Manchu Heaven and Earth Society, which has the Peach Garden Oath as part of its *raison d'être*, along with "recovering the Ming and exterminating the barbarians."[41] Jin Yong manipulates this specific element of cultural capital by identifying the metaphorical origin in the Peach Blossom Garden of *Three Kingdoms* and explicitly relating it to Wei Xiaobao's understanding of the "hero" founded on the Yangzhou storytellers he listens to in teahouses at every chance.[42]

Wei Xiaobao is a kind of "antiheroic" hero, a protagonist who aspires to heroic stature, but given his lack of kungfu skills, his young age, small physical stature, and lowly social status as the son of a prostitute, he must instead use his wits and extraordinarily fine-tuned social sensors to navigate the *jianghu* martial world. The reader's grounding in kungfu cultural literacy (i.e., cultural capital) would clarify the irony of the antihero taking the position of hero. Wei Xiaobao manipulates this oath instrumentally for personal and social gain. In chapter 5 of *Cauldron*, he "becomes brothers" (*jie wei xiongdi*) with the Qing official Suo'e'tu, who teaches him how to skim great riches while searching the residence of deposed official Ao Bai. In chapter 28 he "swears brotherhood" (*jiebai cheng le jinlan xiongdi*) with Yang Yizhi, one of the Ming traitor Wu Sangui's officers, to get his help tricking the beautiful Ah Ke into marrying him. In chapter 38 Wei Xiaobao uses the process of becoming sworn brothers instrumentally to trick two opponents into sparing his life. Wei Xiaobao's varied uses of the sworn brotherhood trope demonstrates his instrumental understanding of it as a tool that can be manipulated in lieu of kungfu skills for personal benefit—a subversion of the original cultural value.

An important variation of the brotherhood oath is located in the spirit of the often used Jin Yong expression for swearing oaths of brotherhood: *you fu gong xiang, you nan tong dang* (share fortune and shoulder hardships together), which is an idiomatic expression from the Qing era.[43] For example, in chapter 18 of *Wanderer*, Linghu Chong and Xiang Wentian kowtow to each and become sworn brothers using the oath: *lishi ta ri you fu gongxiang, you nan tongdang* (swear to share fortune and shoulder hardship together). This sworn oath is found throughout Jin Yong's works and it is used both seriously in martial defense and for subverting convention with humor in order to propel the narrative. Examine chapter 16 of Jin Yong's *Heroes*, when Guo Jing becomes sworn brother with Zhou Botong, who is two generations his elder: "Zhou Botong kneeled down next to him and declared loudly: 'Old rascal Zhou Botong today becomes sworn brother with Guo Jing, and from now on we share our fortunes and our hardships. If I break this oath, may all my kungfu be lost, and may I not even be able to defeat a kitten or puppy.'"[44] Becoming brothers despite such age difference both demonstrates the appropriateness of Zhou Botong's nickname, *lao wantong* (old rascal), as well as puts Guo Jing in position to learn high level kungfu from him for the purpose of narrative progression (surprising others who underestimate him based on previous knowledge). Such humorous subversion of the typical martial values is one of Jin Yong's narrative strategies to create tension that helps propel his plot and sub-plots.

THE CULTURAL PENETRATION OF JIN YONG'S WORKS

Jin Yong is the de facto leader of Chinese literature appointed by the marketplace through the dollars of his readers, the reach of his works, and the frequency with which adaptations of his works enter the entertainment world. As previously mentioned, woven into the structure of Jin Yong's works are elements of history and legend, good versus evil, the cycle of revenge and retribution, obligation and loyalty to one's martial master and brethren, character development and individual martial development, a search for the martial book of secrets (a "holy grail" or sacred text), the struggle for domination to be number one in the martial world, and defense of the Empire against threats from within and without. There is a whole array of inter-personal relationships with the tensions and conflicts they spark—master and pupil, sworn brothers, lovers, husband and wife, parent and child, martial brothers and sisters. Jin Yong's works depict a broad expanse of Chinese aesthetics, medicine, philosophy, and religion.

The extent of the cultural penetration of Jin Yong's works is immense. Starting with a 1978 Shaw Brothers film, there are three movies from the early 1990s stemming from *Wanderer* alone, as well as seven television series spanning four decades, the most recent debuting in 2013 and again in 2018. Contemporary stars and superstars such as Chow Yun-fat (Zhou Runfa), Liang Jiaren, Jet Li (Li Lianjie), Brigitte Lin (Lin Qingxia), Richie Jen (Ren Xianqi), Ma Jingtao, and Li Yapeng appear in these movies and television series, as well as a host of other movies directly or indirectly related to Jin Yong's works, to which I'll return below.

The unsung heroes of all these kungfu cultural products are the film studios, directors, scriptwriters, and producers that form the industrial nexus to bring Jin Yong's works (as well as those of others) into life in visual media. For example, over a period of five years from 1977–1982 the director Chang Cheh filmed at least six of Jin Yong's works. There are also the directors Tsui Hark (Xu Ke) and Ching Siu-Tung (Cheng Xiaodong), who individually or as a team are responsible for some of the most exciting kungfu films of the last twenty years, including *Seven Swords* (2005) and the *Huang Feihong* movie series (1992–1997) that starred Jet Li.

In works such as *Wanderer*, the plot maps out internal struggles for leadership and hegemony in the martial world played against the larger canvas of a battle between good and evil. This is one example of how Jin Yong's works operate in the construction of the image of the Chinese nation or empire. *Wanderer* depicts a *jianghu* martial world mapped from north to south by the Yellow River and the Yangzi River and punctuated by five sacred mountain peaks home to the orthodox schools of swordsmanship. Hengshan in the far north of Hubei Province, Huashan in Shaanxi Province, Songshan in the central China, (physically near to Wudangshan and the Shaolin Temple), Taishan in the east, and Hengshan in Hunan Province in the south. The western region is demarcated by Qingchengshan in Sichuan Province, and the eastern provinces

Figure 1.4. Linghu Chong battles Asia the Invincible, *Wanderer* (2001), Episode 34

marked by cities of Fuzhou and Hangzhou. Distances traveled by the heroes are great since action takes place in most of these locations.

A high production value and relatively faithful television adaption of *Wanderer* that came out in 2001 starring Li Yapeng as Linghu Chong and Mao Weitao as Dongfang Bubai (Asia the Invincible). Linghu Chong uses *Dugu jiu jian* (The nine swords of Dugu) style to confront Asia the Invincible, who is indisputably the best martial artist in the world.

Linghu Chong's acrobatics in this scene where he enters the cocoon spun by Asia the Invincible are incredible (Figure 1.4). Equally fantastic is Asia the Invincible's kungfu, so much so that he uses only an embroidery needle to fight his enemies. Despite his unparalleled swordsmanship, Linghu Chong is repelled and must execute a magnificent series of backflips to avoid the deadly needle. After he wipes a drop of blood off his forehead (in a somewhat Bruce Lee like fashion), Asia the Invincible compliments his swordsmanship. By rights he should clearly be dead, but his excellent sword technique has saved him and duly impressed his opponent. Here is a common Jin Yong trope that fighters may be out to literally *kill* the opponent, but they still show respect for the excellence of each other's kungfu through dialogue or interior monologue.

After *Wanderer*, Li Yapeng also starred in the forty-two-episode series of *Heroes* produced in 2003. His star power grew fast, as a December 2004 gossip report which mentions him indicates:

> Although a new star, he's rapidly shooting up the charts of favorite faces in China's youth scene. His fame stems from his performances in various TV love stories and was secured by his central role in the *gongfu* show *The Story of the Eagle-Shooting Heroes*, taken from the tales of kungfu novelist Jin Yong. Li isn't above using his pretty face to secure his fortune, and lately he's appeared on advertisements for products as varied as hair shampoo and PDAs. And why not? The golden days of a golden boy are but short.[45]

How short are the "days of a golden boy" in truth? It depends. The career trajectory of many now famous actors, some of whom are even recognizable to a Western audience, is the subject of chapter 4 of this book. They are all familiar fodder for gossip in the media and among Hong Kong, Taiwan, and mainland Chinese audiences. Their works include hundreds of films and television series, many based on Jin Yong's novels. It is not definitively clear if these stars became famous *because* of their roles in Jin Yong films and television adaptions, or if they landed the roles because of previous fame, but it is safe to say that these many "Cantopop" stars solidified their credentials during the production of television series and movies, and then transcended Jin Yong works by moving into other period dramas as well as modern gangster film and kungfu comedies and serious dramatic movies. Examples of this include Andy Lau in *A World Without Thieves* (2004) and *House of Flying Daggers*

(2004), and Tony Leung Chiu-Wai in *Ashes of Time* (1994) and *Hero* (2002). Here note that *Ashes of Time*, the English name for *Dong Xie Xi Du* (literally, "Eastern Heretic and Western Venom"), loosely draws upon Jin Yong's characters Ouyang Feng (style name Xi Du) and Huang Yaoshi (style name Dong Xie) from *Heroes*. Analysis and interpretation of this pivotal film is the subject of later chapters in this book.

Throughout this book I place building blocks to support the argument that Jin Yong's fiction is a fundamental glue that binds the pop culture matrix of television series, films, and stars, thereby enabling "star power" and composing a virtuous circle between the actors, their roles, and their visibility (and thus marketability) in popular culture. The adaptations are the interstices of Jin Yong's texts and characters and the stars of Chinese/Hong Kong/Taiwan film and television from the latter half of the twentieth century and into the early twenty-first century. The list of stars from the 1970s to 2000s gives a first indication of the powerful connection between stars and Jin Yong roles (table 1.4).

Table 1.4. Selected List of Stars and Their Jin Yong Roles

Actors	Jin Yong Characters Played
Adam Cheng	Chen Jialuo/Qian Long/Fu Kangan, Zhang Wuji
Alexander Fu Sheng	Guo Jing, Yang Guo
Andy Lau	Yang Guo, Kang Xi
Athena Chu	Huang Rong, Ah Ke, Chen Yuanyuan
Barbara Yung Mei-ling (Weng Meiling)	Huang Rong
Brigitte Lin	Dongfang Bubai, Long'er, San Gongzhu, Li Canghai/Li Qiushui, Murong Yan
Bryan Leung Kar-yan	Xiao Feng (a.k.a., Qiao Feng)
Chow Yun-fat	Linghu Chong
Danny Lee	Duan Yu, Ouyang Ke, Jin She Langjun
Ekin Cheng	Chen Jinnan, Zhan Zhixing/Nandi Duan Zhixing
Esther Kuan	Huo Qingtong
Felix Wong Yat-wah (Huang Rihua)	Guo Jing, Yuan Chengzhi. Hu Yidao, Xiao Feng
Gong Li	Tianshan Tonglao
Gu Tianle	Yang Guo
Hu Ge	Guo Jing
Hu Jun	Xiao Feng
Huang Xiaoming	Yang Guo, Wei Xiaobao
Idy Chan	Xiao Zhao, Wang Yuyan, Xiaolongnü, Huang Rong
Jacky Cheung	Hong Qigong
Jet Li	Linghu Chong, Zhang Wuji
Julian Cheung Chi-lam	Guo Jing
Leon Lai	Hu Fei

(Continued)

Table 1.4. Selected List of Stars and Their Jin Yong Roles (Continued)

Actors	Jin Yong Characters Played
Leslie Cheung	Yang Guo, Ouyang Feng, Huang Yaoshi
Li Yapeng	Linghu Chong, Guo Jing
Liang Jiaren	Lu Zhangke, Xiao Feng, Guo Jing, Linghu Chong, Hong Qigong, Hu Dedi
Liu Yifei	Xiaolongnü
Michael Miu Kiu Wai	Yang Kang, Huang Yaoshi
Ma Jingtao	Linghu Chong, Zhang Wuji
Pan Yingzi	Xiaolongnü
Ray Lui	Hu Fei/Hu Yidao, Wen Tailai, Yideng
Richie Jen	Linghu Chong, Yang Guo
Rosamund Kwan Chi-Lam	Ren Yingying
Sharla Cheung	Empress Dowager, Ren Yingying, Zhao Min, Yin Susu, Purple Yuen, Jiu Gongzhu, Ah Zi
Shu Qi	Xiao Jinyu
Stephen Chow	Wei Xiaobao
Tony Leung Chiu-Wai	Wei Xiaobao, Zhang Wuji, Shi Zhongyu/Shi Potian, Ouyang Feng
Tony Leung Fa-Kai	Duan Huangye, Huang Yaoshi
Vincent Zhao	Chen Jialuo
Wu Mengda	Jiang Sigen, Peng Zhanglao, Lu Zhuangzhu, Han Tiemo, Huang Zhonggong, Tieguan Daoren, Zhou Zhongying, Hai Dafu, Gui Xinshu
Yuan Biao	Yuan Chengzhi
Zheng Peipei	Empress Dowager, Producer—Dragon Sabre, Yang Guo, Wei Xiaobao
Zhong Hanliang	Kang Xi, Xiao Feng

It should be apparent from the sample of adaptations and the quality and quantity of stars playing roles listed above that Jin Yong and his characters reach deep into the Chinese cultural consciousness in a large variety of media, from literary text to film and television.

Important to the appreciation of kungfu fiction and film is "suspension of disbelief," a vital concept in literary theory that describes how the reader's reception of a work of literature is initially facilitated. The reader reconstructs a narrative in his/her mind based on accepting the prism of reality portrayed by the author, be it realistic or fantastical, without allowing a disbelief of seemingly impossible unrealistic actions to distract his/her reading. This also occurs in film reception, particularly in action films and fantasies where exaggeration and imagination are key to stunts. In the world of kungfu fiction and films the reader must readily accept the possibility of fantastic events like training one's *qinggong* light body kungfu to allow one to fly. Moreover, readers must accept that martial artists can master their *qi* in order to send laser-like blasts and defend with force field like strength. The reader brings cultural capital to interpretation of the *wuxia* narratives, but unlike the top martial artists who are idealized cultured heroes "talented in both literary and martial arts," the reader can only increase their kungfu cultural capital through the act of reading/viewing, not their martial ability.

Fantastic and fantasy elements give rise to important questions. What is real literature? What is reality? What is realism? What is real? This is relative. A recent blog gets at this issue in its title: "Qinggong zhende cunzai ma? Gudairen hui, xiandairen que buhui? Kanwan zhongyu mingbaile!" (Does light-body kungfu really exist? The ancients could do it, why can't modern people? After finishing reading I finally understand!).[46] The blogger cites a Tang Dynasty history that records the acrobatic feat of an official which generates the appellation of *roufeixian* (literally, "flesh flying immortal")—resembling *qinggong* (light body kungfu) in name and action.[47] Furthermore, a 2015 video of a Shaolin monk doing a hundred- and twenty-five-meter run on top of straw mats floating on water simulates the ancient art of *qinggong* as an example of the training needed to approach such skill.[48] A glance at modern trials bicycle star Fabio Wibmer's *qinggong*-like feats confirms such training possibilities.[49] These are two examples of how an important element of Jin Yong's fantastical kungfu have both historical precedent and contemporary cultural relevance.

This chapter has situated Jin Yong and his works and contextualized the basis of "kungfu cultural literacy" through which Jin Yong's audience accumulates the cultural capital to comprehend the fantastical martial arts represented in his *wuxia* fiction and respective film adaptations. The basic elements of kungfu cultural literacy are the foundation for the kungfu industrial complex and act as links connecting the interstices of language, story, history, and philosophy, which in turn manifest the interpretive "code" of the matrix. Kungfu cultural phenomena are intelligible to the audience's degree of internalization of cultural capital—how well the code is internalized—as well as to the degree that the directors, actors, and crew draw upon cultural capital as they reify the author's plots, subplots, and characters in production. In the next chapter I examine some specific elements of Jin Yong's rhetoric, a variety of kungfu cultural tropes, which inform kungfu cultural literacy as an example of the linguistic and literary depth necessary to access the code (i.e., accumulate the cultural capital) to interpret the works and their importance in the kungfu industrial complex.

NOTES

1. "Zhongguo gongfu quanqiu shengdian" [Chinese kungfu global festival], October 12, 2007, http://baike.baidu.com/view/1197603.htm.

2. My translation—unless otherwise specified, all translations in this book are made by the author. "Zhongguo gongfu quanqiu shengdian (6)" [Chinese kungfu global festival (part 6)], October 12, 2007, 10:20–11:00, http://www.tudou.com/programs/view/XG_GS__1ODY/.

3. Jin Yong, "Xiaoshuo chuangzuo de jidian sikao—Jin Yong zai bimu shi shang de jianghua" [A few points to contemplate on the creation of fiction—Jin Yong's remarks at the closing ceremony], in *Jin Yong xiaoshuo yu ershi shiji Zhongguo wenxue: guoji xueshu yantaohui lunwen ji* [Jin Yong's fiction and twentieth-century Chinese literature: collection of essays from an international academic conference], ed. Liu Zaifu et al. (Hong Kong: Minghe she, 2000): 27.

4. Lee plays Chen Zhen, a student of the actual historical hero Huo Yuanjia, in his movie, *Jing wu men* (*Fist of Fury*, 1972).

5. Pierre Bourdieu, *Distinction: A Social Critique of the Judgement of Taste* (London: Routledge, 1984): 22.

6. Quoted in "Interview magazine: Ziyi—July 2006," in "archive.is: webpage capture," accessed June 29, 2017, http://archive.is/appb.

7. Hamm tracks down the currency of the term *wuxia xiaoshuo*, finding it "as far back as the Warring States period, the bisyllabic compound *wuxia* gained currency only in the early years of the twentieth century. It was borrowed from Japanese usage." *The Unworthy Scholar from Pingjiang: Republican-Era Martial Arts Fiction* (New York: Columbia University Press, 2019): 79.

8. I follow Stephen Teo's usage of the translation as "chivalry or "knight-errantry" "there is no cultural consensus about *xia*" with the proviso that it is Chinese culturally informed chivalry/knight-errantry, not King Arthur's Knights of the Round Table. Stephen Teo, *Chinese Martial Arts Cinema: The Wuxia Tradition*, 2nd ed. (Edinburgh: Edinburgh University Press, 2016): 3.

9. Based on personal conversations with students at Taiwan National University in 1992–1993. This first semester was referred to as "Jin Yong *xueqi*." Another Taiwanese friend informs that those were probably the most obedient of students who waited until university to read Jin Yong, because as freshmen and sophomores in high school she and some of her friends were reading Jin Yong day and night during winter and summer break. That said, as juniors and seniors in high school they were too busy preparing for the college entrance exam to have time to read Jin Yong.

10. "Alibaba upper management all take nicknames from Jin Yong's novels, Jack Ma is called 'Feng Qingyang,' what are others called?" accessed January 20, 2020, https://new.qq.com/rain/a/20181105A14EKN.

11. Ibid.

12. Jin Yong, *Xiao ao jianghu* [*The Smiling, Proud Wanderer*], vol. 28 of *Jin Yong zuopin ji* [*The Collected Works of Jin Yong*], 2nd ed. (Taibei: Yuanliu chubanshe, 1992): 396.

13. Hamm, *Paper Swordsman*, 181–184.

14. Ibid., 183.

15. Jin Yong, "Houji" [Afterword], *Lu ding ji* [The duke of the Mount Deer], vol. 36 of *Jin Yong zuopin ji* [The collected works of Jin Yong], 2nd ed. (Taibei: Yuanliu chuban gongsi, 1992): 2120–2121.

16. Researcher Chen Mo has a slightly different nomenclature, generally referring to these three versions as *jiu ban* old edition), *liuxing ban* (popular edition), and *xin xiu ban* (new revised edition). Chen also recognizes that there were small revisions that were made when the serialized stories were combined in volumes at first, which would technically constitute four, rather than three, versions, noting that it is difficult to find those original serialized versions (231). See "Jin Yong banben" [Jin Yong editions], *Chen Mo ping Jin Yong xilie* [Chen Mo critiques Jin Yong series], vol. 13 (Beijing: Haitun chubanshe, 2014): 231. Even more complicated is that throughout his book Chen's footnotes cite the "popular edition" as the "Beijing Sanlian Bookstore Edition," and the "New Revised Edition" as "Taibei Yuanliu New Revised Edition," and a reprinting of the original serialized works as the "Taibei Zhongli Bookstore Edition" (231, fn. 1 & 2).

17. Although most sources cite 1980, Leng Xia's chronology shows Taiwan's Yuanjing Publishing House first formally published it in 1979. Leng Xia, *Jin Yong zhuan* [Biography of Jin Yong] (Taibei: Yuanjing chuban shiye gongsi, 1995): 544.

18. Leng Xia, *Jin Yong zhuan*, 544.

19. Ibid., 547.

20. The English translations are taken from the copyright plates in the Chinese language Yuanliu Publishing edition of Jin Yong's collected works. Abbreviations follow John Christopher Hamm, *Paper Swordsman*, 311–313.

21. *Tian long ba bu* [*The Demi-Gods and Semi-Devils*], vols. 1–2, 5; *Xiao ao jianghu* [*The Smiling, Proud Wanderer*], vol. 3; and *Lu ding ji* [*The Deer and the Cauldron*], vols. 4–5.

22. Note that *Semi-Devil*'s plays on the ethnicity of Xiao Feng, who before he discovers his Qidan heritage has the surname Qiao. The remainder of this book refers to his surname as Xiao.

23. Jin Yong, *Xiao ao jianghu* [*The Smiling, Proud Wanderer*], vol. 1, 2nd ed., *Jin Yong zuopin ji* [The collected works of Jin Yong] (Taibei: Yuanliu, 1992): 232.

24. Ibid., 1303.

25. Jin Yong, *Yi tian tulong ji* [*The Heaven Sword and the Dragon Sabre*], vol. 4, 2nd ed., *Jin Yong zuopin ji* [The collected works of Jin Yong] (Taibei: Yuanliu, 1992): 1496.

26. Note that this is pronounced "*pixie*" in the forty-episode television adaptation produced in 2001 starring Li Yapeng but pronounced "*bixie*" in the Mandarin dubbing of Zhou Runfa's thirty-episode 1984 television adaptation.

27. Hamm, *Paper Swordsman*, 311–312.

28. Ibid., 184.

29. Simon Elegant, "The Storyteller: What makes Louis Cha's martial arts novels so wildly popular in Asia?" *Far East Economic Review* (September 5, 1996): 38.

30. Yu Huiming, "*Wuxia xiaoshuo ershi nian huimou*" [A look back at twenty years of martial arts fiction], January 21, 2002, http://www.people.com.cn/GB/paper39/5269/551667.html.

31. Douban dianying, "Shediao yingxiong zhuan zhi xiang long shiba zhang (2021)", accessed March 26, 2022, https://movie.douban.com/subject/35043784/.

32. Translated by Anna Holmwood, the first in the twelve-volume trilogy is titled *A Hero Born: Legends of the Condor Heroes*. See Xing Yi, "Legends of the Condor Heroes: a tale of loyalty and betrayal," *The Telegraph*, December 4, 2017, accessed June 25, 2019, https://www.telegraph.co.uk/china-watch/culture/legends-of-condor-heroes/.

33. Note that the 1987 Yuanliu collected works edition calls this *The Semi-Gods and the Semi-Devils*, not using "Demi-Gods" and adding article "the" to Semi-Devils.

34. "Jin Yong Zuopin ji (Sanlian ban) xu" [Preface to the Joint Publishing edition of *The Collected Works of Jin Yong*], accessed June 3, 2016, http://cnnovels.com/wx/jingyong/014.htm.

35. James J. Y. Liu, *The Chinese Knight-Errant* (London: Routledge and Kegan Paul, 1967): 14.

36. Petrus Liu, private communication, December 2016.

37. Luo Guanzhong, *Sanguo yanyi* [Romance of the three kingdoms] (1970, 2 vols., Hong Kong: Zhonghua shuju, 1987): 4.

38. Jin Yong, *Book and Sword*, 594.

39. Jin Yong, *Heroes*, 39.

40. Jin Yong, *Semi-Devils*, 1739.

41. Jin Yong, *Cauldron*, 309.

42. Ibid.

43. The origin of this idiomatic expression is in chapter 5 of Li Baojia, *Guanchang xianxing ji* [Record of the current state of officialdom], accessed May 25, 2016, http://chengyu.game2.tw/archives/25427#.V0Y4_-RH7fc.

44. Jin Yong, *Heroes*, 660.

45. "Gossip: Most Wanted Men," accessed May 26, 2008, http://www.cityweekend.com.cn/en/beijing/features/2002_11/Gossip_MostWantedMen.

46. Chengshi Langzi, "Qinggong zhende cunzai ma? Gudairen hui, xiandairen que buhui? Kanwan zhongyu mingbaile!" (Does light-body kungfu really exist? The ancients could do it, why can't modern people? After finishing reading, I finally understand!), January 20, 2021, https://www.163.com/dy/article/G0PMFO4M0543NQXQ.html.

47. Years ago, a fellow graduate student explained with utmost sincerity that the ancient arts practiced in sacred kungfu texts such as those discussed by Jin Yong, were lost over the ages, so nobody can do those feats now, but it is still "real," that is to say those were things that the trained martial artist could do at one time before the secrets were lost.

48. "Shaolin monk runs atop water for 125 meters, sets new record," August 29, 2015, posted September 2, 2015, https://www.youtube.com/watch?v=YrncG8NvZJI.

49. "Wibmer's Law–Fabio Wibmer," accessed July 18, 2021, https://www.youtube.com/watch?v=ZDbNe3mS0aw.

Two

Jin Yong's Rhetorical Kungfu
Cultural Capital of Humor

Humor is often a low-brow form of art and Jin Yong's use of it doesn't depart from this standard, so how could it be considered within the "cultural capital" that Bourdieu theorizes?[1] Bourdieu analyzes the cultural formation of "taste" which informs literary value. The idea of "rhetorical kungfu" addressed in this chapter draws on Bourdieu's sense that comedy, extended to humor, is a form of symbolic violence, "the process whereby power relations are perceived not for what they objectively are but in a form which renders them legitimate in the eyes of the beholder."[2] There is an inherent irony here as "eye" of the beholder (reader/audience) varies individually with habitus, the embodied form of cultural capital. Writer, reader, and characters operate in overlapping ironies of interpretation based on the extent to which they "get" the joke. Audience recognition of linguistic codes is directly related to the reader's cultural capital and indirectly related to its manipulation by the writer throughout the narrative. Bourdieu differentiates between highbrow, middlebrow, and lowbrow tastes in comedy, and identifies the highbrow function to "legitimate" what comedy embodies cultural capital. Jin Yong's characters, however, typically use lowbrow humor, but competent readers recognize the irony of (mis)understanding between the characters who manipulate humor to fight their adversaries or defend themselves. In a sense, the interpretation of lowbrow humor becomes a highbrow reading activity. The examples discussed in this chapter improve Bourdieu's cultural capital formulation by demonstrating how the instrumental use of symbolic violence through lowbrow humor operates across class levels.

This chapter explores an important aspect of Jin Yong's literary art, his employment of humor through irony and satire founded in the popular linguistic forms of cursing, sarcasm, flattery, and hierarchical wordplay. These primary metaphorical vehicles *demonstrate* how a variety of kungfu cultural tropes work together to construct kungfu cultural literacy and transmit a cultural capital "code" which that connects narratively across the interstices in the multidimensional matrix of the kungfu industrial complex represented (two-dimensionally) in the Introduction (Figure I.1). In addition to kungfu cultural literacy, literary reception/canonization, and symbolic reproduction via adaptation and the associated cultural capital of star power, the authorial style/technique addressed in this chapter also provides a glimpse into some of the key characters in Jin Yong's novels, fundamentally reifying an "original text" dimension of kungfu cultural literacy.

Readers in the Ming dynasty and May Fourth era were necessarily well educated because of the educational investment it took to become literate—perhaps the most fundamental measure of cultural capital in the pre–social media world. The development of the Chinese novel arguably emanated from early storytellers who performed in teahouses of dynastic China, thus making stories accessible to nonliterate audiences who had the opportunity to become familiar with the protagonists and antagonists of stories like *Water Margin* and *Journey to the West*. Wei Xiaobao, the illiterate protagonist of Jin Yong's final novel, *Cauldron*, is a fictional example of such an audience member. He learned much of his martial rhetoric in such teahouse settings. In the modern era of nearly universal literacy (abetted by film and television adaptations), kungfu cultural capital acquired through reading Jin Yong's novels and/or viewing their adaptations to screen is broad-based by the last decades of the twentieth century. Jin Yong's propensity to interpolate "high" literary art such as Tang and Song poetry, quotes of Daoist and Confucian philosophy, as well as social and historical context into his novels means his audience assimilates both high and lowbrow cultural capital through reading.

The discourse of literary value situates individual works in pre- and post-textual (and supra-textual) continuum; thus, the literary work is a tension of forces and lineages, also termed discourses. Viewing Jin Yong's works from the perspective of cultural capital has the result of highlighting partialities in the perspectives of critics, readers, and authors. The author is not ground zero for cultural capital, but simultaneously a transmitter, interpreter, and constructor in a time instance. As such, Jin Yong's humor both embodies and also engages in subversion of some linguistic, cultural, and social tropes that rely on reader recognition of the norms on which he plays in the text. It is instructive to see an example of the *lineage* through one element of Jin Yong's rhetorical kungfu. To wit, examine the following three archetypical literary characters demonstrate the temporal continuity of lowbrow ironic humor:

> Sun Wukong: Virtuous son, you're the one being unreasonable. How is it that the son likes to beat his father? (*Xianlang, ni que meili, nali erzi hao da ye de?*).[3] (Wu Cheng'en, ca. sixteenth century)

Ah Q: What is the world coming to nowadays, with sons beating their fathers! (*Xianzai de shijie tai bu chenghua, erzi da laozi*).[4] (Lu Xun, 1921–1922)

Wei Xiaobao: Hey, hey, cuckold son-of-a-bitch, what the hell are you dragging me/your father for? (*Wei, wei, wugui erzi wangbadan, nimen tuo laozi ganshenme?*).[5] (Jin Yong, 1969–1972)

These characters each valorize a quintessential element of rhetorical kungfu: first person raising of one's own status above that of one's interlocutor. Arrogant first-person reference using the term *laozi* (father) translate as "I" and is the fundamental example of what I term "hierarchical kungfu" (*beifen gongfu*), one of four primary elements of Jin Yong's rhetorical kungfu. Hierarchical kungfu functions within an ideological prism that views social relations in terms of family (and extended family) relations. The term *laozi* (your father/old man), and its parallels such as *laoye* (father/grandfather/respected old man) are the simplest form of a wide range of hierarchical kungfu rhetoric that employ family relationships as a weapon. Referring to oneself as *laozi* ("I") is an intergenerational insult, put-down, dissing, or expression of arrogance by raising oneself a generation (or more) over the opponent (operatively meaning something like the ironic question "Who's your daddy now?").

An indistinct line can be drawn over four centuries from Ming Dynasty Sun Wukong to Republican era Ah Q to the 1970s Wei Xiaobao. All three of these characters experienced violence at the hand of stronger adversaries. Sun Wukong fought a pantheon of supernatural beings as he traveled to the "West" (referring to India in Ming era context here) in the capacity of bodyguard to the monk Xuan Zang and here complains of the unreasonableness (*ni que meili*) of the son beating his father (*nali erzi hao da ye de?*). Ah Q fought village bullies and elders and psychologically coped with his suffering by employing the phrase "the father is beaten by his son" to console himself, "what's the world coming to?" Similarly, Ah Q also metaphorically defended Chinese national psychology in compensation for the shame of being defeated in the Sino-Japanese war of 1895, as well as being later colonized and oppressed by numerous foreign nations throughout the first half of the twentieth century.[6] Wei Xiaobao is bullied by adult martial artists and manipulates hierarchical kungfu similar to Ah Q and Sun Wukong, with added rhetorical flourish by directly cursing his enemy as *wugui erzi wangbadan* (cuckhold son-of-a-bitch) while terming himself *laozi* (I, me, your father). Each of these archetypical characters employs a highly acute rhetorical and comic flexibility that derives its force from a tension between appellations of generational differentiation (*beifen*) to psychologically attack their enemy. Wei Xiaobao's further curse, "cuckold son-of-a-bitch," demonstrates a use of rhetorical kungfu that directly highlights the aspect of sexual innuendo associated with *laozi* and its various derivatives. Each of these characters operates in a unique discursive space but maintain commonality. Wei Xiaobao is no more than thirteen years old at the start of *Cauldron* and he employs hierarchical kungfu to directly compensate for his lack of kungfu skill and his low position in the social hierarchy. He wields that position with considerable irony as he employs *laozi* because his mother is in fact a prostitute and he doesn't know his father. Ah Q uses the term *laozi* to place himself a generation above the village elder, pulling "psychological rank," thus imagining himself superior and thereby subverting Confucian status and age hierarchies to achieve a "spiritual victory" (*jingshen shengli*) while he suffers a real beating. At its base, the mechanism of hierarchical kungfu operates on the conscious or unconscious insinuation of "sexual innuendo" to insult one's opponent. The joke works because by using *laozi* the speaker infers that he is sleeping with the addressee's mother (in other words, "I am your father"). There are a number of variations that similarly use other family relationship terms to insult/attack one's interlocutor, such as the insinuation that the speaker is sleeping with the opponent's sister. This terminology is set within a larger context of family relationships that inform verbal interactions between martial artists and the family like structure of martial sects.

Academic discourse on Jin Yong and his contribution to Chinese literature and culture often identifies his fiction as a "vehicle for cultural transmission."[7] Chen Mo's extensive collection of writings on Jin Yong address a wide variety of aspects of his characters, plots, and various adaptations. My examination of Jin Yong's rhetorical kungfu is an additional interpretive explanation of how and why his works have maintained tremendous pop cultural appeal over many decades. In brief, Jin Yong's breadth of linguistic, literary, and cultural references (high culture) operate in tandem with humor (low culture) to enable the lasting pop culture resonance of his works. Additionally, the periodic adaptation and readaptation of Jin Yong's novels across a variety of media forms a self-fulfilling virtuous cycle that has a commercial and cultural multiplier effect enhancing the construction of cultural capital, which by extension becomes a paradigmatic process in the construction of the kungfu industrial complex. Jin Yong's original texts remain (nearly) the same, but periodic television adaptations introduce new audiences (as well as old) to his characters and stories through the vehicle of attractive new stars and improved technology. The rhetorical kungfu of the original is generally well preserved across the adaptations. Such reperformances revitalize the discourse about his martial arts fiction through reintroduction of the characters and stories even if some of the adaptations might be critical failures.

Jin Yong's humor related rhetorical kungfu can be divided into four tropes: "cursing kungfu" (*maren gongfu*), "sarcasm kungfu" (*fengci gongfu*), "flattery kungfu" (*ma pi gong*), and "hierarchical kungfu (*beifen gongfu*). These are major groupings, and he also employs other rhetorical devices that typically turn on subversion of some Chinese cultural norm. Li Tuo asserts "Jin Yong's writings continue and develop a mighty and ancient tradition of writing" and suggests his language developed into a "distinctive vernacular" and could be called "Jin-style vernacular."[8] Petrus Liu importantly notes the rhetoric of Jin Yong's choice of naming in both *Cauldron* and *Semi-Devils*, using the original Chinese characters to indicate the wordplay in his analysis:

> Both *Cauldron* and *Semi-Devils* are actually deliberately intertextual references to the fourth great classic novel, *Dream of the Red Chamber*. Wei Xiaobao 韋小寶 (偽小寶) is actually Jin Yong's humorous play on 賈寶玉 (假寶玉), the protagonist of Dreams whose clan is in a tangled relationship with another, the 甄 (真). The struggle between the 賈 and 甄 family, between 真真假假—or as one would put it, what is reality and what is a dream?—constitutes the main allegorical and thematic nexus of the Chinese classic. In naming his protagonist 韋小寶 and making him a bastardized version of the most famous literary character in Chinese (say a Chinese Hamlet) and a bastardized parody of his own fiction (in the sense that Xiaobao knows no kungfu and is more of an antihero than anything else), Jing Yong's uses the rhetoric of "humor" and relies on readers cultural literacy.[9]

Rhetorical specificity at the micro-level which relies on the reader's cultural literacy, noted by Liu above, is matched on the macro-level. Critic Chen Pingyuan regards Jin Yong's success as intricately related to the "wealth of historical and general knowledge" within his novels. Chen also cites Yan Jiayan, who praises Jin Yong's novels for "their richness of traditional literary content, and literary scholarship in popular literature," suggesting they "should be called cultural novels (*wenhua xiaoshuo*)."[10] The assessments of these critics directly connect to Bourdieu's concept of cultural capital, which sees the popular form of language consciously drawing from deep cultural roots. Jin Yong's rhetoric draws deeply on Chinese culture and the language of its literary masterworks.

CURSING KUNGFU

Cursing kungfu is found throughout Jin Yong's works, but perhaps best exemplified by the protagonist Wei Xiaobao in *Cauldron*. Wei Xiaobao is the thirteen-year-old street-smart spawn of a brothel in Yangzhou, a thriving city near the intersection of the Yangtze River and the Grand

Canal. The novel is among Jin Yong's longest works, measuring approximately 2000 pages, and is set in the early Qing dynasty (1644–1911). The initial chapters depict young Wei Xiaobao traveling from Yangzhou to Beijing, where he is captured by a high-ranking eunuch and taken into the Forbidden City. He unwittingly earns the friendship of the young Emperor Kang Xi by engaging him in kungfu training matches without knowledge his opponent's status. His willingness to physically hit the young emperor engenders Kang Xi's trust because nobody else in the palace would dare "fight" him for real. In addition to this most improper behavior toward the emperor, Jin Yong's narrative supplies numerous other examples to imply that Wei Xiaobao's street upbringing is quintessential preparation for learning to survive palace intrigues and navigating the official world. Wei Xiaobao manipulates connections with a marvelously attuned social sensibility, a "social kungfu" as it were, as a series of events leads to his intersection with the *jianghu* martial world in humorous and historically (but fictionalized) accurate ways.

Wei Xiaobao helps Kang Xi dispose of a regent with imperial ambitions, as well as other opposing officials as Kang Xi comes of age and consolidates his rule. As he assists the Manchu emperor, Wei Xiaobao ironically stumbles into membership and leadership of the anti-Manchu Heaven and Earth Society (*Tian di hui*). Wei Xiaobao rises in Qing officialdom while simultaneously assisting the Heaven and Earth Society in their plot to kill another high Qing official, the Ming traitor Wu Sangui. Here Wei Xiaobao ironically services the interests of both the Heaven and Earth Society and Emperor Kang Xi. Wei Xiaobao collects seven wives along this narrative trajectory. One wife is a Qing princess, two others are Ming loyalists, and one is the former wife of the leader of the Mystical Dragon Cult (*Shen long jiao*), a powerful anti-Manchu martial sect—a pseudo-allegorical reference to the Gang of Four and Chairman Mao's Great Proletarian Cultural Revolution, which was in high tide at the time Jin Yong wrote this novel (serialized from 1969–1972).

Wei Xiaobao's physical kungfu is abysmal. He usually accomplishes his feats through cleverness, trickery, and coincidence, not "orthodox" martial arts. Jin Yong's plot design and multiple ironies are adroit and compelling. Portrayal of the use of power by Wei Xiaobao, Kang Xi, and other officials, makes this novel seem like a primer for navigating contemporary elite social circles that require skills of flattery, manipulation of connections, sensitivity to intrigue, and the like. Equipped with a few technologically advanced weapons to make up for his lousy kungfu skills—an impenetrable Kevlar-like vest and a super-sharp dagger that can cut through ordinary steel—Wei Xiaobao manages to escape dangerous situations and survive near death experiences. When he does actually learn a few kungfu moves, it turns out to be a type of "fleeing" kungfu that enables him to escape in tight circumstances. Such kungfu is highly suited to his personality and poor kungfu and plays on the last of the popular *Thirty-Six Strategems*, "escape is best strategy" (*zou wei shang ji*).[11] Wei Xiaobao's real kungfu, however, is metaphorical. It lies not in martial arts but rather in his acute understanding of human relations and social psychology, which he employs through of a variety of linguistic rhetoric. His "cursing kungfu" demonstrates humor, irony and satire, tools necessary to successfully navigate the official world, the martial arts *jianghu*, and the streets of Yangzhou. Jin Yong validates the power of Wei Xiaobao's cursing kungfu in scenes that depict even Emperor Kang Xi learning his vulgar expressions (a high departure from decorum), and humorously signals Kang Xi's pardon for Wei Xiaobao's overtly disloyal acts.

In line with his brothel upbringing, Wei Xiaobao loves to curse and is marvelously inventive and vulgar at it. Near the beginning of this long story, salt merchant subordinates and official troops try to capture the minor hero Mao Shiba at a Yangzhou brothel. Wei Xiaobao helps Mao escape. Ethical and linguistic dynamics of the martial world come to the fore as Wei Xiaobao attempts to coerce/convince Mao to take him along to Beijing. Mao resists taking him because he is angry that Wei Xiaobao used unethical methods to help defeat their enemy:

> Mao Shiba said sternly, his expression becoming even more ferocious: "Why did you throw ashes in Shi Song's eyes?" Wei Xiaobao was very frightened, took a step back and said trembling: "I . . . I saw that he was going to kill you." Mao Shiba asked: "Where did the ashes come from?" Wei Xiaobao said: "I . . . I bought them." Mao Shiba said: "Why the heck did you buy ashes?" Wei Xiaobao said: "You said you were going to fight with somebody and I saw you were already wounded, so . . . so I bought ashes to help you." Mao Shiba was furious and cursed: "Little bastard, your grandma's (*xiao zazhong, ni nainaide*), where did you learn that technique?"[12]

First note the kungfu cultural literacy point that Wei Xiaobao saved Mao's life, but because he did so in an unethical manner Mao was furious at the breach, insinuating that he would have rather died than lose honor by being perceived as not fighting fair. Continuing, the narrator says:

> Wei Xiaobao's mother was a prostitute, and he didn't know who his biological father was. He most hated people cursing him as a little bastard and he couldn't help flaring up in anger and cursing: "Your grandma's old bastard, screw the Mao family's seventeen or eighteen generations, cuckold son-of-a-bitch (*ni nainaide lao zazhong, wo cao ni Mao jia shiqiba dai lao zusong, wugui wangbadan*), what do you care where I learned it from? You stinking bastard, nearly dead old shellfish (*ni zhe chou wangba, sibutou de lao jiayu*)."[13]

Figure 2.1. Wei Xiaobao demonstrating "cursing kungfu" after being scolded for using despicable (*beibi*) techniques to save Mao Shiba's life, *Cauldron* (1984), Episode 1

Having been angered at suffering his most detested curse, Wei Xiaobao counterattacks with curses in multiple. While the sexual related curses are superficially decodable, the curse directed particularly at eighteen generations of Mao's ancestors is effective on the ideological level since Wei Xiaobo is leveraging against the norm of Confucian propriety that holds family lineage in highest esteem. The narrative continues:

> Mao Shiba spurred his horse over and reached out with his long arms grabbing him by the back of the neck and lifting him in the air, shouting: "Little devil, you still going to curse?" Wei Xiaobao kicked both legs wildly and yelled: "You thieving bastard, stinking turtle, corpse on the road, pig cut by a thousand slashes (*ni zhe zei wangba, chou wugui lucao shi, gei ren zhanshang Yiqian dao de zhuluo*. . . ." He was born in a brothel and had learned countless curses in all dialects from north to south. Now his anger flashed up and his mouth was full of obscenities.[14]

Mao Shiba is stymied, unable to find leverage over the kid who relentlessly curses him and keeps upping the ante "in all dialects from north to south." These excerpts demonstrate important dichotomies that are used for leverage in cursing kungfu: old verses young, strong verses weak, kungfu skilled verses unskilled. Although seemingly outmatched at each level, Wei Xiaobao still wins out with his exceedingly colorful cursing, culminating with the declaration, "If I'm afraid of a dog bugger like you then I'm not a real hero (*yingxiong haohan*)!"[15] This final assertion is tantamount to near total comic subversion of *jianghu* martial values which glorify the "real hero" as the pinnacle of ideological virtue in the martial world, quite the opposite of protagonist Wei Xiaobao at this point in the story. The curses in the adaptation are minor in comparison to those in the original text. Mao relents and allows Wei Xiaobao to accompany him to Beijing for the ostensible purpose of watching Mao fight a top Manchu hero, the regent Ao Bai. Here at the beginning of the long story Wei Xiaobao has already demonstrated some of the cursing and low-down fighting tricks, as well as other types of linguistic kungfu (hierarchical kungfu, and insults), that he uses throughout the novel, in both the *jianghu* martial world and the world of officialdom.

FLATTERY KUNGFU

Flattery kungfu one weapon in Wei Xiaobao's arsenal in *Cauldron* but is exemplified especially well in excerpts from Jin Yong's *Semi-Devils* (serialized 1963–1966). *Semi-Devils* is a fascinating story of conflicts of personal character, ethnic nationalism, and international conflict set in a Song Dynasty that is under military pressure from the north by Qidan (Mongols), Tanguts (Xi Xia) and Jurchens (Jin Dynasty). Three young heroes become sworn brothers and mutually support each other at critical junctures in the narrative.

The eldest of the three heroes is Xiao Feng, leader of the Beggar Gang, the biggest kungfu sect in the *jianghu*. Xiao Feng's character is straightforward and upright and his kungfu is unrivaled. He is the victim of an ethnically based power struggle within the Beggar Gang, the immorality of which is cast into stark relief by his virtuous model conduct in both his martial arts actions and his concurrent tragic love story. The confluence of these two subplots provides significant momentum to Jin Yong's narrative. The second hero, Duan Yu, is the scion of the small southern dynasty of Dali, located in present day Yunnan. Duan Yu's father and uncle rule Dali as prince and emperor, respectively. They possess a marvelous One-Yang-Finger kungfu (*Yi yang zhi*), the secret of which is passed down generationally through their family. The young Duan Yu is highly intelligent and well educated, but not *jianghu* worldly-wise. Much to the chagrin of his father, he eschews learning kungfu while growing up, instead delving deeply into the cultural arts, philosophy, and such. Duan Yu leaves Dali to escape the pressure to study kungfu. His cultured and youthful demeanor betrays his ignorance of the nitty-gritty real world outside the palace and generates several conflicts involving a variety of martial warriors. In ironic contrast to his refusal to learn kungfu, Duan Yu has propitious encounters through which he inadvertently acquires powerful kungfu skill—a process that Jin Yong repeats in other works to the extent of becoming a kungfu cultural trope. He subsequently encounters Xiao Feng, who mistakes him for the antagonist Murong Fu, a leading hero with whom he is connected by an expression exalting their prominence in the martial arts world as *bei Qiao Feng nan Murong* (in the north there is Qiao Feng, in the South there is Murong). Qiao/Xiao Feng and Duan Yu test each other's drinking and light-body kungfu, and ultimately become sworn brothers after their true identities emerge.

The theme of good versus evil in *Semi-Devils* is played against the backdrop of conflict between Han, Qidan, Yan, Xi Xia, and Jurchen ethnicities. Ironic dichotomies, a staple of Jin Yong's narrative techniques, show moral Qidan folk such as Xiao Feng pitted against immoral Han folk; scheming Yan folk (Murong Fu) pitted against both Han and Qidan people. Minions follow the line of ethnicity with which they identify and act on the basis of whatever "greater good" corresponds to their ethnicity. The rules of the *jianghu* martial world, including the imperative of revenge that results in vicious cycles of revenge killings, provide a metanarrative against which these subplots unfold. Early in the story Duan Yu meets with attack by Nanhai E'shen, the third member of a loose confederation of the Four Great Evildoers (*Si da e'ren*). This excerpt both puts the upright/good kungfu sects into relief against evil and initiates a narrative strand that will eventually develop into a challenge to the rightful rule of the Dali state which, when the top Evildoer makes claim to Dali's throne, is revealed to have changed emperor's years previously under ethically questionable circumstances.

The unskilled Duan Yu employs rhetorical kungfu of flattery in an early scene in the novel. Duan Yu and Mu Wanqing are at the top of a mesa, under attack from foes. Nanhai E'shen arrives to capture them but takes a liking to Duan Yu, recognizing that he has the potential to be an ideal disciple (the shape of his head being similar to his own is his prime criteria). Nanhai E'shen also threatens to ravage the veiled Mu Wanqing because she has killed his only disciple and reaches to remove her veil. This creates a conundrum for Mu Wanqing because her master made her swear that she would marry the first man to see her unveiled face (a corrective to her master's own unrequited love story subplot). To avoid having to marry Nanhai E'shen, she raises her veil for Duan Yu instead. In addition to reinforcing the primary *jianghu* value of honoring one's word (stated variably, but quite commonly as *shuohua suanshu*) to her master, this is also a twist typical in Jin Yong's stories wherein he "tests" the honorability (or not) of the martial artist by presenting them an extreme conundrum. Nanhai E'shen is enraged and Duan Yu resorts to flattery to save both their lives:

> [Duan Yu] stood next to Mu Wanqing and said: "So your honor's nickname is Nanhai E'shen, and your martial ability is the number... number... yeah in the world. I've long heard your honor's great name like thunder in one's ears. In the last few days, I've come to know many real heroes, and in truth your martial ability (*wugong*) is the most awesome. I threw a pile of rocks down on you but to my surprising not one hit you. Your honor's martial ability is so magnificent it is really outstanding." To himself he thought, "Although I've praised him greatly, his martial ability is indeed awesome, so this flattery really isn't unconscionable."
>
> Hearing Duan Yu praise his martial ability as awesome, Nanhai E'shen was really full of himself. He chuckled drily twice and said: "Punk (*xiaozi*), your ability is ordinary, but your insight is pretty good. Get the eff out of here, I (*laozi*) will spare your life."[16]

Shameless flattery worked to save his own life, but Nanhai E'shen still wanted to ravage Mu Wanqing so Duan Yu invokes adds to flattery another element of the martial code to save her—prohibition against bullying the weak:

> [Duan Yu] hurriedly said: "Everywhere in the *jianghu* it is said that Nanhai E'shen is a truly great real hero. Not only wouldn't he bully an injured gal, he wouldn't even hit a wounded guy. Everyone also says that Nanhai E'shen wouldn't even fight against one single man, the more numerous his opponents, the happier he fights. This is what shows how awesome his honor's martial ability really is."[17]

In addition to appealing to the martial ethic that a true hero would not bully the weak, whether female or injured male, Duan Yu furthermore ups the ante (leveraging against the implied shame) by asserting that such a powerful hero fighting *only one* able-bodied male would not be fair. Furthermore, Duan Yu invents a list of martial artists who have praised his kungfu, so numerous he can't remember, to which Nanhai E'shen responds, "Punk, you're interesting. Next time you hear somebody say I'm really heroic you must remember their names well."[18] Later in this scene, Duan Yu continues his flattery by raising Nanhai E'shen's rank, which is actually number three of the Four Great Evildoers, to number two and then to number one. Nanhai E'shen replies: "Right, right! Punk, you are really smart, you know I am an evildoer who couldn't be eviler. Number One won't do, but number two is right."[19] Not only does Duan Yu save their lives through his flattery, but he also eventually even tricks Nanhai

E'shen into becoming *his* "disciple." Each step in this vignette plays on elements of the martial code, including the comic position of Nanhai E'shen becoming Duan Yu's disciple (again tricking him into staying true to his word). Duan Yu humorously demonstrates flattery here to great effect, with the aftereffect of also saving himself and Mu Wanqing from Nanhai E'shen's evil brethren because she is now his master's "wife" and ravaging her would violate his own martial lineage. Although knowingly going against his own conscience, Duan Yu rationalizes such shameless flattery through recognition of the extreme danger facing them. His flattery is all the more ironic because in doing so Duan Yu also violates the *jianghu* dictum that a "real man" or "true hero" would rather die than submit or betray his values (go against his conscience). Like Wei Xiaobao, who ironically proclaimed himself a "real hero" despite his sleazy actions, Duan Yu, at this point in the narrative, is also an "antihero" who saves himself and his associates by resorting to rhetorical kungfu.

SARCASM KUNGFU

Semi-Devils is also the locus of a seminal example of sarcasm kungfu that explicates the level of cultural capital help make Jin Yong's humor work. This kind of kungfu is practiced most adroitly by the secondary character Bao Butong, a subordinate of the conflicted antagonist Murong Fu. Bao is a straightforward fighter who takes issue in unique fashion with whatever anybody says, thus the appellation "different" (*bu tong*) is explicit in his given name. In the following example he satirizes disciples of the Constellation Sect, shameless flatterers who have been conditioned by the unpredictability of their master and sect brotherhood to believe that flattery, not physical kungfu, is the best way to advance one's status in their sect. This "truism" is confirmed through interactions with their master, Ding Chunqiu, and held throughout the sect hierarchy. As such, it stands in stark ideological contrast to *jianghu* norms that promote the upright hero as a fighter willing to act and die in defense of the martial values, being true to one's word.

Bao Butong's confrontation with the Constellation Sect disciples generates much humor because of the overlapping ironies in the interplay between the *jianghu* norm of truth telling, sarcasm directed at falsehoods (including flattery), and flipping the falsehoods into relative truth (not recognizing the sarcasm). Bao Butong's confrontation with the lackeys starts with him sarcastically praising the sect for their unmatched kungfu. The disciples excitedly ask what he sees as their "most awesome" kungfu. Bao replies:

"How could it be only one kind? There are at least three kinds." The sect brethren were even happier, and asked in unison: "Which three kinds?"

Bao Butong said: "The first is flattery kungfu (*ma pi gong*). If you don't master this kungfu, I'm afraid that in your sect you won't live more than half a day or a day at most. The second is trumpeting kungfu (*faluo gong*). If you don't loudly brag about the virtues of your honorable sect's martial ability, not only will your master look down on you, you'll also be ostracized by the others in the sect and won't have a foot to stand on. The third kind of kungfu, well, that is shamelessness kungfu (*hou yan gong*). If you don't murder your conscience, be shameless and brazen, how can you successfully practice flattery kungfu and trumpeting kungfu, these two great amazing kungfu [techniques]?"[20]

Bao Butong expects the Constellation Sect disciples to attack him in response to his ridicule but is surprised that they instead agree with his analysis. He increases his sarcasm by adding flattery and feigned humility, asking them to explain why they agree. One member is "elated" at his flattery and explains:

"Naturally, the most important secret is to praise our master to the heavens. If his honorableness were to fart . . ."

Bao Butong cut in and replied: "Of course it is also fragrant. Furthermore, one must loudly inhale and exhale to appreciate it in one's heart. . . ." That person said: "You are quite right, but there is a small defect. It isn't 'loudly inhale and exhale' but rather 'loudly inhale and softly exhale.'" Bao Butong said: "Right, right, your great immortalness's instruction is right. If you loudly exhale you can't avoid appearing to dislike master's fart . . . it isn't too fragrant."[21]

The Constellation Sect disciples are impressed by Bao's acumen and suggest that he is a perfect fit to join their sect, if only he hadn't already joined an "unorthodox sect" by mistake. Bao's sarcasm is explicit in Jin Yong's narrative, which also makes clear that he and his martial brothers are both "angry and amused" to observe such "shamelessness." The narrative here is hilarious to the reader as well and even richer in humor than the limited excerpts cited indicate. Jin Yong must have found great amusement writing this chapter (among others). The rhetoric of irony is thick and may be parsed into flattery and sarcasm. Bao's sarcastic flattery is received as compliment by the Constellation Sect members, who magnify the irony by reverse the meaning of "orthodox" and "unorthodox" kungfu. Sarcasm kungfu and flattery kungfu operate here in unison. Bao Butong fully expected a fight because of his extreme and (what he thought was blatant) sarcasm, but the Constellation Sect members flipped the script, recognizing it as straightforward praise. Ironically, Bao's flattery, though not flipped, was still interpreted positively, as deserved, and also recognized as one mainstay of the sect's kungfu. Bao unknowingly elicited a detailed explication of flattery kungfu by its foremost practitioners. The ever-sarcastic Bao Butong had even referred to himself as *xiaozi* (kid/ punk) while satirizing them, an ironic reversal of hierarchical kungfu, which typically elevates oneself above one's opponent with the use of a *laozi* (I, your father) equivalent. This brings us to a more detailed analysis of hierarchical kungfu in below.

HIERARCHICAL KUNGFU

Hierarchical kungfu is the most extensive and (potentially) vicious type of rhetorical kungfu it directly challenges *jianghu* martial world order. The irony of hierarchical kungfu tests the cultural capital of reader/audience through a humor that pivots on the subversion of the Confucian principles of filial piety and its associated value of hierarchical respect for elders, and recognition of one's place in the hierarchy. This is a key pillar in the structure of the martial sect and the *jianghu* martial world. The examples of Ah Q and Sun Wukong were noted at the beginning of this chapter. Sun Wukong is an insolent and mischievous but highly skilled martial expert who refers to himself throughout the Ming novel as "*Lao Sun*" (Old Sun). In contrast, Lu Xun's Ah Q is a pathetic antihero who attains deeper levels of comic irony because his clever use of hierarchical kungfu results in the inflation of his own ego and demonstrates what Lu Xun termed the "method of spiritual victory" (*jingshen shengli fa*), a process by which one may achieve ultimate psychological victory despite actual physical defeat. The power behind this linguistic play of words turns on the term *lao* (old, respected), which derives authority from the Confucian moral virtue of *xiao* (filial piety). Filial piety demands unwavering respect toward one's father, elders and, by extension, one's social superiors.

Jin Yong's character Wei Xiaobao wields the appellation *laozi* (I; your old man/father) with utter abandon, even if at times he must think it to himself rather than verbalize it out loud for fear of a beating. Jin Yong fills the pages of *Cauldron* with variation upon variation of such generationally related verbal warfare, often mimicking Ah Q and Sun Wukong's lament. For example, when captured by Mystical Dragon Cult member Tou Tuo (who doesn't know his identity), Wei Xiaobao pretends that "his uncle" is Wei Xiaobao and that Tou Tuo's fellow cult member Liu Yan is his uncle's master. Wei Xiaobao is an expert using his words and wits in such convoluted situations and he tricks Tou Tuo into releasing him. Part of his technique is to play on relationships, real or imagined, and use self-deprecating humor to convince his opponent of his seriousness. This strategy is effective because nobody would typically make fun of himself in such a life and death situation, so he is underestimated. Although his kungfu abilities are quite poor, he effectively uses his verbal abilities to attack psychologically. Attacking requires some degree of care, however. Cursing Mao Shiba, Wei Xiaobao's attack was head on because he estimated that Mao would not cause him real harm. But he also can also attack obtusely when the risk of harm is serious, a technique Jin Yong's narrator calls "going around the bend and curse somebody" (*rao wanzi ma ren*). Wei Xiaobao manipulates the expression, "the son beats his father," as he attempts to escape Tou Tuo who grabs him by the scruff of the neck, and adds a generation to the curse, implying that Tuo Tuo is his grandson, saying "the grandson is holding up his grandfather" (*sunzi ti yeye*).[22]

Although Wei Xiaobao's martial kungfu is limited, he recognizes direct, indirect, and analogous dimensions of cursing. Wei Xiaobao employs all the humorous elements rhetorical kungfu described in this chapter, sometimes simultaneously (they are interconnected and overlapping). His cursing nomenclature is rich and employed either verbally or in his interior monologue to set himself above his adversaries. For example, the eunuch Hai Dafu who captured and brought him into the Forbidden City is referred to as old turtle/cuckhold (*lao wugui*), the Empress Dowager is old whore (*lao biaozi*), and Liu Yan is big fat pig (*da fei zhu*) or sow (*muzhu*). The humor of his splendid and varied verbal kungfu often turns on information of which Wei Xiaobao's interlocutor is unaware (and this is perhaps key to his survival). When Wei Xiaobao says "you're just like my mother," which should translate as the utmost compliment, he actually means that Liu Yan is a whore, but she takes no offense because she doesn't know his mother is a Yangzhou prostitute.[23] Jin Yong takes this joke to its pinnacle when Wei Xiaobao visits the Yangzhou brothel where he himself grew up and finds one of own "wives" disguised as a man (itself a martial arts fiction trope) in the company of one his enemies. Both his "wife" Ah Ke and his enemy are being entertained by his prostitute mother as he looks on in secret. He recognizes her two clients, thinking "'My old lady is whoring my mom.' Only to see Ah Ke extend her hand and push [his mother] Wei Chunfang,"[24] whereupon Wei Xiaobao gets mad thinking, "Little whore, you're pushing your mother-in-law, you have no sense of propriety!"[25]

Even the bastard spawn of a prostitute like Wei Xiaobao knows that there should be "propriety" in the social hierarchy. It is not the fact of the brothel that is at issue, per se, but rather the irony that Wei Xiaobao is actually a bastard who doesn't know his father. Jin Yong's humorous rhetorical kungfu here hinges largely on the subversion of ethical-moral concepts important to Chinese culture. Upright and proper women don't work as prostitutes, nor do they have children out of wedlock. Wei Xiaobao

Figure 2.2. Wei Xiaobao secretly observes his "wife" being served by his prostitute mother, *Cauldron* (1984), Episode 34

may make such use of hierarchical kungfu just because he is at the lowest, most disrespected level of society. He plays on particular words like *lao* (old), which when added to an appellation means "respected." Wei Xiaobao cannot escape the narrative reality of his name "little treasure" (*xiaobao*), but he unexpectedly manages to transcend the "meanness" (*xiao*) of his brothel birth by becoming a high official, a martial sect leader, as well as friend and confidant to the young Emperor Kang Xi, all of which earn him the respect of members of officialdom and various sects in the martial *jianghu*.

Jin Yong's narrative logic proves that Wei Xiaobao both publicly and privately considers himself superior to his associates, including Emperor Kang Xi. His sense of superiority is expressed through a subversive subtext that manipulates the method of Ah Q-like spiritual victory playing on the use of *lao* and *xiao* for generational raising and lowering in verbal battle. This is a shared psychological-linguistic kungfu technique found in both Ah Q and Sun Wukong: all three characters us the arrogant first-person self-reference or demeaning second person address to either raise himself a generation above his enemy or lower his enemy a generation below himself in a tactical play of verbal warfare designed to demean or "dis" their opponent.

Wei Xiaobao highlights the play between generations young and old in complex and opposing worlds: the brothel and the palace; the dirty streets and the *jianghu* martial world; the orthodox court and the *jianghu* martial world; friend to Kang Xi and leader of the anti-Manchu Heaven and Earth Society. Wei Xiaobao is a complex example of the values of the worlds he straddles. Note that Jin Yong states that he was in fact consciously thinking of Lu Xun, Ah Q, and Ah Q's method of spiritual victory when writing *Cauldron*:

> When I wrote this book [*Cauldron*] I often thought of the Chinese people's method of spiritual victory emphasized in Lu Xun's "The True Story of Ah Q." The concept of spiritual victory is indeed widespread and has been around quite a long time in China. But it is not limited to China. Sometimes when I am abroad, I also discover that people from just about everywhere have their own method of spiritual victory. So, I try to explore from another angle the special characteristics of the Chinese people.[26]

Wei Xiaobao possesses enormous quantities of two crucial positive features that Ah Q virtually lacks, those of *yiqi* (righteous loyalty to one's friends) and *renqing* (human sentiment). Wei Xiaobao is thus a positive, well-rounded complement to Lu Xun's negative critique of the national character in the form of Ah Q (and other characters). *Yiqi* is the factor that makes him a martial hero, even though his martial abilities are minimal. It may be for this reason that Wei Xiaobao is Jin Yong's greatest practitioners of hierarchical kungfu—his martial ability is so pathetic that he makes up for it in dialogue and interior monologue through which he creatively raises himself generations above his interlocutors in his speech and thoughts to gain psychological superiority.

Only twelve or thirteen years old at the beginning of the novel, Wei Xiaobao is young by any standard and not respected in any of the worlds he inhabits—he lacks social and economic capital in all dimensions. The amount of kungfu cultural capital he does possess is acquired mainly from frequenting the teahouses where he hears the storytellers tell the tales of heroes of yore. Although his kungfu skills are poor, his knowledge of the ethical and moral structure of the *jianghu* are firm. In the *jianghu* he is viewed as young and untalented, thus underestimated by his opponents. As *Cauldron's* narrative demonstrates, he becomes Kang Xi's closest friend and confidant and accrues immense social and political capital (power) although in the Qing court he is perceived as crude and ignorant due to his illiteracy. Because he is Kang Xi's friend, the older officials flatter and bribe him to gain his favor. His kungfu cultural capital informs his understanding of the leadership hierarchy in both *jianghu* and official worlds and this in turn cycles back to increase his cultural capital through accumulation of experiences that act as a survival guide to navigate intrigue in both worlds. His status in both these worlds rises as a matter of coincidence after he assists Kang Xi by capturing and then, by a stroke of luck, killing the top Manchu general and de facto ruler, the regent Ao Bai. He cements Kang Xi's trust and friendship and simultaneously wins the leadership of one of the branches of the anti-Manchu Heaven and Earth Society (they have kidnapped in their attempt to kill Ao Bai, and he stumbles into leadership). He becomes rich and powerful by skimming the spoils of Ao Bai's fortune, quickly learning the technique from another high official and using his connection to Kang Xi to demand bribes from officials.

The narrative framing structure repeats in numerous subplots, such as when Wei Xiaobao is sent to become a monk at the Shaolin Temple where he rescues the Emperor's father; or when he travels to Russia as an advisor to a Russian Princess and foils a rebellion. Similarly, he works *yiqi* and *renqing* connections to avoid execution to become a leader in the Maoist styled Mystical Dragon Cult, and then navigates the rescue of many Heaven and Earth Society martial brethren in the face of Imperial troops, managing to save his life, and that of his seven wives as Kang Xi sends him into exile on a deserted island. In each of these sublots the *jianghu* martial world virtues, particularly *yiqi* and *renqing*, guide his decisions and actions, and create opportunities for him to survive and thrive. Wei Xiabao uses his *jianghu* cultural capital, along with a lot of coincidental luck, to navigate extreme situations where he not only saves his own life but also ingratiates himself to powerful benefactors. Jin Yong imbued

Wei Xiaobao with the four overlapping humorous elements of rhetorical kungfu (cursing, flattery, sarcasm, and hierarchy) to balance against the improbability of a street urchin making a successful path to wealth and power and love.

APPLIED CULTURAL CAPITAL

Cultural capital is typically an abstract theoretical concept that is not quantified in measurable detail. However, the interpretation of literary humor, though still abstract on the whole, can be viewed as an area in which cultural capital is "applied" and measured. The analysis of the types of rhetorical kungfu that constitute a common thread in Jin Yong's humorous narrative technique in this chapter takes cultural capital from the abstract into the concrete as three levels: first it is a measure of the individual reader or audience member or actor's level of linguistic cultural acuity – the audience needs access to specific linguistic tropes to facilitate engagement with the texts, films, and other media. In other words, interpretation of the rhetorical kungfu humor here is a relative degree based on the particular reader's level of cultural capital which relies on linguistic, social, political, philosophical, historical, and other culturally specific knowledge (such as Chinese medicine and traditional concepts of physiology). At this first level every reader or audience member has access to the narrative through the linguistic rhetoric designed by the author—humorous rhetoric works well to quantify it because humor starts as a relatively facile measure of understanding, did the reader get the joke or not. This superficial level of cultural capital is possessed by nearly everyone with linguistic competence to understand surface level metaphors. But audiences have varying levels of appreciation of the texts, partly in relation to their own cultural capital. The second level of cultural capital requires access to the metaphorical and relies upon the relation of language to simple metaphor to complicated metaphor and requires greater knowledge to understand "why" the linguistic joke works. For example, knowledge of cultural background elements such as understanding of the Confucian value of respecting one's elders and the ability to identify threats to that value. This level of cultural capital is also accessible to readers moderately conscious of contemporary pop cultural trends.

Understanding "why" the humor works is also a matter of degree because there are different levels of the why in the ways of understanding. Thus, the third level of cultural capital is symbolic, which is defined here in relation to interpretation of the interaction between simple and complex, or between complex and complex, cultural metaphors. In Chinese there is a historical split between vernacular and classical language that is not completely demarcated but may be addressed in general terms. Access to classical or ancient Chinese requires an investment of time and education much akin to a Western student required to study Latin and Greek to gain access to foundation texts from religious and philosophical traditions. However, in the West there is a relatively long tradition of vernacular translation of those texts upon which modern students can rely for accurate interpretation. In China elementary knowledge of classical Chinese is helpful because newspapers and documents often incorporate a relatively high degree of "bookish" language derived from classical Chinese. While grounding in history and philosophy in modern education in China can be done without a deep foundation in classical Chinese, many tropes in modern Chinese are drawn directly from classical, and access to those relies upon a relatively more thorough grounding in cultural, social, political, and historical knowledge. For example, Jin Yong's strategic rhetoric includes ideas from *Sunzi Art of War*, such as the saying "know yourself and know the enemy and you'll win every battle" (*zhi ji zhi bi, bai zhan bai sheng*),[27] which is a common modern variation of the classical original, "know the enemy and know yourself and you'll not suffer misfortune in a hundred battles" (*zhi bi zhi ji, bai zhan bu dai*).

At each of the three levels of cultural capital identified above in this "applied" reading the linguistic and simple metaphor act as an entryway into understanding (to "getting" the joke) the humor. Perhaps this explains in part why audiences of different education levels can all appreciate the humor in Jin Yong's works even if not immediately aware of the deeper levels and dimensions on which the humor works. The interested reader can do further investigation—educating oneself—by checking the historical, social, and political, etc. references that facilitate the metaphors and thereby increase their own cultural capital.

Cultural capital also seems to be a forum of discourse where everyone possesses some amount, and the amount increases and decreases in relation to how it is used. The passive reader or film/television viewer may never use it beyond the linguistic level of appreciation of the text or performance. On the other hand, that same reader may engage that cultural capital in discussion of Jin Yong's characters or stories, or the stars that populate the media adaptations thereof, which position the reader to gain some benefit, say invitation to tea or other social engagements. Part of the reading audience is involved in a slightly more formal discourse regarding Jin Yong and his works. That is the subject of the next chapter which elaborates the literary and academic discourse surrounding Jin Yong's entry into the canon of twentieth-century Chinese literature. The popular reception of Jin Yong preceded the academic reception and is most important in the construction of the kungfu industrial complex because this is the first instance that economic capital derives from cultural capital. The second instance of economic and cultural capital synergy involves the important step in the construction of the kungfu industrial complex where Jin Yong's "low culture" popular martial arts fiction was valorized through "high culture" academic discourse.

The preceding two chapters describe certain fundamental features that serve as a basis of the kungfu industrial complex along the dimensions of *authorial production* and *audience consumption*, both depicted qualitatively in terms of kungfu cultural literacy. Just as the kungfu industrial complex cannot exist without the author, the texts, and the audience, it also requires a forum of validation literary discourse to legitimize its status and provide momentum for its continuation. The next chapter turns to analysis of the discourse of canonization that provides such legitimization—literary and social/cultural critique—not directly subservient to economic mechanisms and interests.

NOTES

1. Parts of this chapter are adapted from my article, "Jin Yong and the Kungfu Industrial Complex," *Chinese Literature Today*, vol. 8, no. 2. (2019): 68–76.
2. Pierre Bourdieu and Jean Claude Passeron, *The Inheritors: French Students and Their Relation to Culture* (Chicago: University of Chicago Press, 1979): xiii.
3. Wu Cheng'en, *Xi you ji* [The journey to the west], 3 vols. (Beijing: Renmin wenxue chubanshe, 1996): 528.
4. Lu Xu, "A Q zhengzhuan" [The true story of Ah Q], in *Lu Xun quanji* [The complete works of Lu Xun], vol. 1 (Taipei: Gufeng, 1989): 492.
5. Jin Yong, *Cauldron*, 286.
6. William Lyell notes in his translation of "The True Story of Ah Q": "[C]ontemporary readers saw Ah Q as representing China in miniature: continually humiliated by the imperialist powers, China had gained 'psychological victories' by boasting about the superiority of her ancient civilization." *Lu Xun: Diary of a Madman and Other Stories* (Honolulu: University of Hawaii Press, 1990): 109, fn19.
7. Hamm, *Paper Swordsman*, 136.
8. Li Tuo, "The Language of Jin Yong's Writing: A New Direction in the Development of Modern Chinese," trans. John Christopher Hamm, eds. Ann Huss and Jianmei Liu, *The Jin Yong Phenomenon: Chinese Martial Arts Fiction and Modern Chinese Literary History* (Youngstown, NY: Cambria Press): 44.
9. *Stateless Subjects: Chinese Martial Arts Literature & Postcolonial History* (Ithaca: Cornell University Press, 2011): 139–140.
10. Chen Pingyuan, "Transcending 'High' and 'Low' Distinctions in Literature: The Success of Jin Yong and the Future of Martial Arts Novels," trans. Jianmei Liu and Ann Huss, eds. Ann Huss and Jianmei Liu, *The Jin Yong Phenomenon: Chinese Martial Arts Fiction and Modern Chinese Literary History* (Youngstown, NY: Cambria Press): 63.
11. Jin Yong, *Cauldron*, 979.

12. Ibid., 72.
13. Ibid.
14. Ibid.
15. Ibid., 73.
16. Jin Yong, *Semi-Devils*, 145.
17. Ibid., 146.
18. Ibid., 147.
19. Ibid.
20. Ibid., 1308–1309.
21. Ibid., 1309.
22. Jin Yong, *Cauldron*, 740.
23. Ibid., 567.
24. Ibid., 1608–1609.
25. Ibid.
26. Quoted in Zhang Dachun, "Jin Yong tan yi lu" [Jin Yong talks about art], in *Zhuzi baijia kan Jin Yong (di si ji)* [Philosophers and writers of all schools read Jin Yong (vol. 4)], ed. Shen Deng'en, vol. 17 of *Jin xue yanjiu congshu* [A collection of Jin-ology research] (Taibei: Yuanjing chubanshe, 1985): 37–38. Originally published in *Zhongguo shibao*, October 30, 1970.
27. Jin Yong, *Semi-Devils*, 541.

Three

Canonization, Cultural Capital, National Character

Literary critics have long engaged in heated discourse about the value of certain works and authors.[1] High literature and its proponents have a history of dominance of the discourse of literary value and unsurprisingly pop literature is devalued with terms such as pulp fiction. In order to be valued as literature a work must fall within the parameters of the typical measures of literariness including character and plot development, adroit manipulation of symbols and metaphors, stylized writing, and such. A solid background in classical education, the deeper the better, facilitates access to and excellence of literary works in their greatest complexity. For pop literature, on the other hand, such a deep grounding in the classics is not requisite to appreciate and enjoy the works because entertainment appeals on the surface level. As noted in the preceding chapters, Jin Yong's popular novels are imbued with multiple levels of meaning and the readers' varying levels of cultural capital allows access to proportional levels of interpretation. Attenuation to metaphor, symbol, and allegory varies by the individual reader's cultural capital. Literary critics traditionally act as gatekeepers to the canon. They interpret and critique literary works and contribute to the academic (as well as popular) discourse that determines their relative value. The measure of value may be challenged by numerous factors, but economic success of a popular author, which may correlate with popular acclaim, was not traditionally one of them, neither in premodern China, nor in the Republican era, and especially not during the early decades of the People's Republic. This changed after China opened to the outside world and embraced the import of popular culture from Hong Kong, Taiwan, and the West.

Since the early twentieth century the greatest symbolic signifier of literary value has been the Nobel Prize in Literature—the ultimate valuation of cultural capital and cultural authority that an author can achieve. The first mainland located Chinese recipient of the Nobel Prize in Literature in 2012 was the author Mo Yan.[2] Mo Yan was also nominated for the inaugural Newman Prize for Chinese Literature in 2009, which he received for his novel *Life and Death Are Wearing Me Out* (2006). Interest in seeing a successful Chinese recipient of the Nobel Prize in Literature had been alive in literary discourse for nearly a century, as Jon Kowallis notes: "In 1927 Lu was considered for the Nobel Prize in Literature, for the short story "The True Story of Ah Q," despite a poor English translation and annotations that were nearly double the size of the text."[3] Lu Xun himself recognized that he and his works were not worthy of the Nobel Prize, stating "there are a lot of better writers than me in the world and they can't get it."[4] The international prize was seemingly out of reach, as Julia Lovell sums up, because of limited cultural and linguistic literacy, not just because of Lu Xun's own sense of the inadequacy of modern Chinese literature, or his "rejection of tokenism," or challenges to his ability to continue writing due to politics that impinged upon the literary world at that time, or "an aversion to the political, national, collective uses to which he could be put as a Nobel winner by the ruling government."[5] Putting aside Lu Xun's culturally conditioned modesty about the ability of his works to meet the of standards for a Nobel Prize, the early discussion of Lu Xun as a contender clearly demonstrates that China and Chinese literature had been on the radar of the Nobel Committee long before Mo Yan was awarded the prize in 2012.

In 2009, nearly eighty years after Lu Xun comments on the Nobel Prize, Jin Yong was considered for the Newman Prize for Chinese Literature for *Cauldron* and speculation about the merits and possibilities of Jin Yong as a candidate for the even more prestigious Nobel Prize occupied the Chinese literary world.[6] A Nobel Prize in Literature for Jin Yong would have had the dual effect of further valorizing his status in Chinese literature and recognizing his place in the canon of world literature, a controversial topic during the 1990s. The debate surrounding his canonization plumbed the depths of the discourse of "high" versus "low" (elite versus popular) literature. For example, critic Chen Pingyuan asserts:

> Few people will disagree when you call Jin Yong a master of popular fiction, but as soon as it becomes necessary to incorporate his achievements into literary history, even complete outsiders are quick to express their righteous indignation. To put it simply, in the eyes of experts and of normal readers, popular fiction is no [sic] real "literature." This common bias against popular literature is rooted in the "myth of literature" that was constructed during the May Fourth period.[7]

Chen's frank remarks here emphasize the common understanding that popular literature just doesn't make the cut as literature by May Fourth standards. Contrast Jin Yong's own take on May Fourth literature: "Modern Chinese fiction that is considered New Literature is really quite divorced from the Chinese literary tradition. It can hardly be called Chinese fiction.

Ba Jin, Mao Dun, Lu Xun—they all wrote foreign fiction in Chinese."[8] Jin Yong doesn't see modern Chinese fiction carrying on the lineage of Chinese literature. How does his own martial arts fiction relate to Chinese high cultural literary tradition? There are numerous strands contributing to this well-known debate, including quite disparaging remarks about Jin Yong's works by contemporary writer Wang Shuo, as well as controversy surrounding replacing Lu Xun's work with Jin Yong's in some school textbooks. The upshot is that the prestige of writers and the Chinese literary world was deemed to be at stake, and this was directly related to the self-image of the Chinese people.

The concept of cultural capital and national identity theory both validate Jin Yong's popular literature as "real literature." Pierre Bourdieu's ideas of cultural capital dovetail with Benedict Anderson's analysis of national identity to provide insight into both Jin Yong's contribution to the national identity discourse, literary canonization, and the construction of the kungfu industrial complex. Canonization requires the assessment of relative cultural, social, and political capital of the writer within the field:

> Bourdieu insists that rather than taking either aesthetic or ideological statements on their own terms, we should look first at the composition and forms of capital structuring a given field and then at the competition between agents aiming to secure or maintain their capital reserves (and to secure the dominance of one form of capital over another).[9]

A rigorous debate among writers and literary authorities indicates that there are vested interests of each party (Bourdieu's "agents") behind the scenes in competition for both market share and authority in literary circles—the markers of economic capital, social capital, as well as cultural capital. Bourdieu's conceptualization of types of capital are both clarified and complicated by Benedict Anderson's ideas on the relationship of the literary establishment and national identity.

National identity helps to shape or structure the field in which competing writers or critics (agents of discourse) vie for dominance of the literary world. In *Imagined Communities* (1991), Anderson identifies the rise of the press and the literary establishment, what he refers to as "print capitalism," as the primary vehicle in the construction of the concepts of nation and nationalism. Accordingly, literature and the popular press nurtured an abstract sense of unity between people separated by spatial, temporal, and communicative barriers.[10] The constituent elements of print capitalism are phenomena that resulted from the industrial revolution and the broadening of the educated middle class, both of which are crucial to "imagining the nation." Literature and journalism symbiotically linked readers with other readers, readers with authors, and readers with the events of the state. Readers' views of themselves, society and the world in general were thereby shaped—resulting in the psychological and social construction known as the "nation." This is not a static state, but rather a constantly fluid condition that adjusts to developments in the literary world within a meta-discourse of national identity.

It is not just high cultural artifacts and ideology that participate in the construction of national identity and the nation. Pop culture discourse plays an equally if not more important role and presents the gatekeepers of high culture with a challenge. How and why does a pop culture phenomenon like martial arts fiction become accepted by the gatekeepers of high culture? May Fourth era writers introduced literature in the vernacular and wrote about subject matters in everyday life, arguably promoting the popularization of literature that previously valued classical language and forms. The foremost writer of the era was Lu Xun, who wrote essays and novels renowned for critique of a largely negative national character which he summed up in "The True Story of Ah Q" (serialized 1921–1922; hereafter *True Story*). Jin Yong recognizes Lu Xun's status and notes how commentators have linked them together, while also downplaying the connection:

> I like creating novels, but I am only a common writer and very willing to listen to everyone's critique. Criticism is fine, and instruction is also fine as both can make me better and help my later creations. Today Mr. Sun Lichuan said in his presentation that I had a few commonalities with Mr. Lu Xun. For example, we are both from Zhejiang, and I can't get out of that. He also said we both are concerned with the times, concerned about the prosperity of the nation, and both also lived and wrote in areas under foreign control. But he didn't point out our differences. The biggest difference is that Lu Xun is a great author, and I am just a common writer.[11]

Like Lu Xun's own comments on his own worthiness for the Nobel Prize noted above, Jin Yong is modest about his status, a trait that he has written into characterization of the best fighters in his novels. Jin Yong uses the trope that the more modest the fighter, the greater his/her kungfu, an element of kungfu cultural literacy that is largely outside the ken of typical Western heroic character who often celebrates his/her own greatness. While this dichotomy is not absolute, Jin Yong's assertion "I am just a common writer" could be recognized by Chinese and non-Chinese readers as something of a "humble brag." Given the great degree of contemporary cultural influence of both Lu Xun and Jin Yong, their mutual modesty belies their importance. The similarity of these two authors at the cultural level is clear. First, for Lu Xun, Leo Ou-Fan Lee notes what might be called a CCP "machine" of canonization that turned Lu Xun into a cultural industry:

In the People's Republic of China, a veritable Lu Xun "industry" has turned out an impressive quantity of artifacts: at least three editions of his complete works, and numerous collections of his individual writings (some are reproductions of his original drafts); thousands of books and tens of thousands of articles; museums and exhibitions, children's books and drawings; paintings, photographs, portraits, sketches, cartoons, slides, sculptures, films, music (including operas and ballets), plays, posters, bookmarks, coupons, and badges and pins of many sizes.[12]

This veritable industry of Lu Xun artifacts functions to reify the author's works and characters, thus commodifying the cultural capital of the author measured in product volume and facilitating readership interest/investment in attaining that associated "objectified cultural capital." Lu Xun's popularity is based in part on the resonance of his characters and stories with the readership, and in part on the prestige associated with his position in the literary and academic discourse of the era. In Lu Xun's era his resonance with readers was based in large part on his insight into the foibles of national character, a critical issue in the May Fourth construction of national identity. In the era after his death, Lu Xun's resonance was at least based on the prestige he had attained as a writer/thinker and the mythologization of such in service to the revolution.

Similar to the "veritable industry" of Lu Xun artifacts, there is a plethora of cultural products spun off from Jin Yong's works, particularly movies and television series, which have tangible and intangible effects on the construction of national identity and the nation. Jin Yong's works operate in a further dimension that Lu Xun's works did not reach—the kungfu industrial complex. The actors and the directors and production crews who designed and implemented the sets for the multitude of Jin Yong productions have experiences and careers that often transcend Jin Yong's works. While actor Yan Shunkai gained notoriety after he played Ah Q in the 1981 adaptation of Lu Xun's novella, the number of film adaptations of Lu Xun's works is limited. In terms of tangible effects, actors who played Jin Yong characters could find that success leading to other roles that directly influence their careers. Intangible effects are subtler, for example, the indirect associations of individual actors with character roles/types and the cultural/social values associated with such types.

In addition to the similarity of an "industry" of cultural artifacts related to Lu Xun and Jin Yong, I argue that these two authors are directly related through their critique of Chinese national character in *True Story* and *Cauldron*. The discourse of national identity is not static, but rather in flux from decade to decade, generation to generation, and construction of national identity is not an individual but rather a group dynamic that encompasses the historical discourse while it simultaneously incorporates new contemporary phenomena. Lu Xun wrote in Beijing during the 1910s and 1920s then later from the relative freedom of the foreign concessions of Shanghai in the late 1920s and 1930s. Jin Yong wrote a generation later in the British colony of Hong Kong during the mid-twentieth century. Lu Xun created several characters that informed his critique of national character, Ah Q being the most prominent. Jin Yong created numerous characters and stories that depict the national character and remain relevant into the twenty-first century. Lu Xun was admired as a hero of the revolution and revered as the "soul of the nation" (*minzu hun*). Jin Yong earned many awards and honors, including a doctorate in Oriental Studies from Cambridge University for his dissertation on Tang Dynastic history.[13] Lu Xun was made a symbol by the cultural authorities of his time. While Chinese cultural authorities did not mythologize Jin Yong as a symbol of his time, the Chinese literary field finally came to recognize the importance of Jin Yong's works and accomplishments in the 1990s. The most coveted literary award, the Nobel Prize for literature, would have been important to both China and Lu Xun in the early part of the twentieth century. Similarly, this award *would have* been the pinnacle achievement for both Jin Yong and the Chinese literary world at the end of the century.

The Nobel Prize is an institutional form of recognition of the recipient's cultural capital as well as a mechanism that more generally creates the opportunity to acquire social and economic capital in the literary and entertainment fields. In other words, the Nobel Prize valorizes not only the author's talent and works, but also the investment of the author's readership in accruing cultural capital, the knowledge of which may translate to social and economic capital at varying levels. The Nobel Prize also functions to both domestically and globally enhance the international legitimacy of the Chinese literary field, regardless of whether the author would be the first or the twelfth Chinese recipient. In a Chinese literary field arguably divided into Mainland, Hong Kong, and Taiwan regions, a Nobel Prize for Jin Yong could have had a long-term unifying effect across physical political boundaries. In the discourse of national identity, the writers, works, and characters both construct and transmit knowledge of what is the national character. A writer both demonstrates and produces cultural capital (as well as other forms of capital) through his/her works and the subsidiary cultural artifacts (objectified cultural capital) related to them. Readers themselves may identify with the characters who depict national character, or with the narrative situations confronting the characters (the logic of how the national character is expressed), or even with the author constructing the national character narrative. In this light, Lu Xun's Ah Q was received as the epitome of the (negative) national character, and Lu Xun's penetrating analysis of China and his countrymen through *True Story* and other works earned him posthumous deification with the (positive) appellation of "soul of the nation."

Given the deep cultural penetration of Jin Yong's works and characters in text, film, and television to the mass of audiences, as well as his concomitant role in construction of Chinese national identity vis-à-vis Anderson's framing process noted above, I argue that contrary to Jin Yong's stated modesty about his literary achievement, his works indeed have a serious social function transcending entertainment—a function that denied to the genre of his works, neither recognized by the elite literary intellectuals of twentieth-century Chinese literature, nor many contemporary critics—that of the construction of twentieth-century Chinese national identity. Jin Yong's works unconsciously contribute to constructing the idea of nation physically as they map out the Chinese nation geographically. His archetypical characters participate in constructing the national identity through their actions, attitudes, and behavior. In addition, the adaptation of his works in television and film facilitated the translation of cultural capital into economic capital, leading to both character identification and mega-profits, furthering the construction of national identity while constantly growing the audience base. The construction of national identity resonates with the construction of the kungfu industrial complex, both of which reify and reinforce the power of Jin Yong's status in a virtuous feedback cycle of literary authority and cultural capital construction.

This chapter will demonstrate that Lu Xun and Jin Yong operate as in complementary discursive construction of a healthy and balanced cultural consciousness expressed through widely different approaches to literature and society. Although writing in the British colony of Hong Kong, Jin Yong was not operating in a Chinese cultural vacuum. I argue that Lu Xun's caustic negative critique of national character, crystallized in *True Story* is both replicated in its negative elements in Jin Yong's epic martial arts fiction and also complemented by Jin Yong's positive, heroic expressions of national character. After a "century of humiliation" predating Jin Yong, Jin Yong's novels are an expansive rounding out of Chinese national character which add a positive complement to national identity and pride. While Jin Yong famously critiqued Lu Xun as a writer of "foreign fiction in Chinese" noted above, seeming to deny the place of his works in the canon, his assertion intersects with a May Fourth cultural discourse of "Chineseness" from which Lu Xun and his novels cannot be separated. By invoking these discourses Jin Yong ironically facilitates a space for continuity between Lu Xun and his works and the Chinese literary tradition. Jin Yong's "foreign fiction in Chinese" assertion may be refuted through analysis of his own works vis-à-vis Lu Xun's from the perspective of the discursive continuum of the construction of national character. In terms of the larger discursive project of the construction of the Chinese nation, national identity, and character ("imagining the nation") examination of these seemingly unrelated literary giants together provides an enhanced understanding of literature's role in the construction of the "nation" as well as a wholistic Chinese national character/identity.

LU XUN'S NEGATIVE CRITIQUE OF NATIONAL CHARACTER

Writing in the first four decades of the twentieth century, Lu Xun and his May Fourth colleagues attacked traditional culture and values in general. They disparaged the genre of martial arts fiction for lacking serious social value, classifying it as subset of works written by the so-called Mandarin Duck and Butterfly school (*yuanyang hudie pai*).[14] In contrast, valorization of vernacular literature of the May Fourth Movement era by the literary establishment zeroed in on the works of Lu Xun and his critique of national character for his contribution to the literary history of modern China. This phenomenon is summed up by the writer Feng Jicai:

> In doing an inventory of twentieth-century literature we all discover a wonder: Lu Xun's oeuvre of novels is the smallest, but his influence is the greatest. He doesn't have the type of fear we writers have—if we don't have a huge work, we won't be great writers. He made it to the pinnacle of contemporary Chinese fiction with a slim volume of short- and medium-length fiction. Moreover, he was never at the mercy of any fickle market, and he himself was never on television. How could this be?
>
> If we look at it from a cultural angle the root of this miracle is clear at a glance. It is because of his particular cultural angle—the critique of national character.[15]

Given that his artistic oeuvre is so modest in size—two collections of short stories, a collection of prose poetry, classical poetry, a collection of fictionalized stories from myth and legend, and a collection of reminiscences from his childhood, it is ironic that Lu Xun is considered China's greatest modern writer. However, in addition to his literary works, Lu Xun also wrote volumes of *zawen* (essays) that richly map out many of the contours of intellectual activity in the literary world of the 1910s, 1920s, and 1930s, including his view of national character. In fact, Leo Ou-fan Lee argues that Lu Xun's sixteen volumes of essays "constitute a genre of his artistic contribution to modern Chinese literature."[16] Lu Xun's short stories are collected in *Nahan* (A call to arms, 1924) and *Panghuang* (Wandering, 1926). His collection of twenty-three prose poems is called *Yecao* (Wild grass, 1927). *Gushi xinbian* (Old tales retold, 1926) is a collection of eight stories, myths, or legends, fictionalized by Lu Xun. *Zhao hua xi shi* (Dawn blossoms plucked at dusk, 1932) collects ten reminiscences of Lu Xun's childhood. Lu Xun's classical poetry consists of over sixty poems written for various occasions, such as inscriptions for other works.[17] Moreover, a huge research "industry" on Lu Xun began not long after his death. In the process of mythologizing Lu Xun's status and contributions to modern Chinese literature, cultural authorities, or agents (literary critics and historians), built up both his image as China's leading writer and their own credentials as interpreters of his works. This resulted in the construction and transmission of cultural capital at multiple levels within a growing field of Lu Xun studies.

Ah Q, the main character of his longest work, the novella *True Story*, was immediately interpreted metaphorically by Chinese readers and critics as "the crystallization of Chinese qualities,"[18] a "national type," and a "'composite photo' of Chinese qualities."[19] *True Story* was published serially in the literary supplement to the Beijing newspaper *Chenbao* (The morning gazette) from December 4, 1921, to February 12, 1922. Consisting of nine chapters and fewer than fifty pages, it is Lu Xun's longest individual work of fiction. Ah Q's character is the manifestation of a pantheon of negative traits, from ignorance to cowardice, from bullying the weak to cowering before the strong, culminating in the "method of spiritual victory" (*jingshen shengli fa*), a mechanism of self-delusion he uses to turn physical defeat into spiritual or psychological victory. Early commentators generally agree that Ah Q is a negative manifestation of the Chinese national character (*guominxing*). Lu Xun's characterization of Ah Q was so compelling that it generated phrases such as "Ah Q-ism" (*A Q zhuyi*) and "Ah Q thought" (*A Q sixiang*) which were used to describe such negative, stereotypical behavior of the Chinese people.

JIN YONG AND NATIONAL CHARACTER COMPLEMENTS

Many characters in Jin Yong's works exhibit elements that parallel Lu Xun's negative critique of national character. Linghu Chong in Jin Yong's novel *Wanderer* and Wei Xiaobao in *Cauldron* are two prime examples that validate Lu Xun's negative critique by replicating Ah Q characteristics. Moreover, *Wanderer*'s protagonist Linghu Chong periodically plays a Lu Xun-esque critical consciousness by humorously manipulating elements of Lu Xun's national character critique. However, as demonstrated in analysis below, *Wanderer* and *Cauldron* also supply a host of "positive" manifestations of national character that are either lacking in Lu Xun's writings or even attacked by Lu Xun as "national essence." Such positive elements of the national character are expressed through Wei Xiaobao's adherence to the heroic code of the martial *jianghu* and Linghu Chong's heroic actions and attitudes. These actions and attitudes are firmly grounded in traditional Confucian (and other) virtues notably absent in Lu Xun's critique of Ah Q.

The contribution of literature to the construction of national identity implies a broad readership among the population. Jin Yong's balanced depiction of national character is ultimately consumed by a huge readership that far surpasses the audience of *True Story* despite the fact that Lu Xun is still "ranked" as the number one author of Chinese literature in the twentieth century and *True Story* is his representative work. Lu Xun's negative critique of national character in *True Story* runs to nine chapters in weekly installments, about 50 pages as a single novella. Jin Yong's valorization of both positive and negative national character runs to 2000 pages in *Cauldron* and approximately 1600 pages in *Wanderer*. The broad consumption by these two works by Jin Yong's much broader readership is a step in the construction of national character that overwhelmingly counterbalances and complements Lu Xun's dark, negative national character critique.

Terms and motifs from the Ah Q lexicon can be found in literary critique of Jin Yong's martial arts novels, and thus explicitly connect Lu Xun to Jin Yong in the discursive dimension. For example, Jin Yong scholar Chen Mo refers to Wei Xiaobao, the main character of Jin Yong's *Cauldron*, as Kang Xi's "spiritual victory substitute" (*jingshen shengli de daiyong pin*).[20] Ye Hongsheng book on martial arts fiction includes a section titled "Liu Taibao yu A Q jingshen" (Liu Taibao and Ah Q Spirit).[21] In another section Ye refers to *A Q shi* (Ah Q style) and *A Q jingshen* (Ah Q spirit).[22] One of the main components underlying these neologisms is Ah Q's "method of spiritual victory." The reputation of Lu Xun and Ah Q endure in late twentieth-century intellectual discourse, which still refers to Lu Xun and his national character critique to discuss reform of the national character in rapidly changing contemporary China.[23]

Analyzing "Occidentalist" discourse in the May Fourth period, the contemporary critic Shu-mei Shih points out that "the essentialization and reification of the so-called Chinese national character" was done to repudiate the "Chinese-ness" that it represented, "which was necessary for the entrance of and into the Western universal."[24] While Lu Xun and much of May Fourth national character critique was intent on changing/repudiating the largely negative national character, half a century later Jin Yong, in contrast, created characters with a holistic combination of both negative and positive elements of national character. Thus, Jin Yong's works recoup some of the "Chinese-ness" that Shih notes was repudiated here. Jin Yong's balanced portrayal of national character, a measure of "Chinese-ness as demonstrated below, may in part explain the popular resonance of martial arts fiction. When popular resonance is factored into literary valuation, Jin Yong and his stories and characters rank favorably against Lu Xun's.

JIN YONG'S VIEW OF "CHINESE-NESS" AND CRITICISM OF LU XUN

Jin Yong's immense popularity in China and other parts of East and Southeast Asia qualifies him as possibly the best-selling Chinese author of all time (if not the all-time best-selling author in the world). An indication of the intensity of demand for his works in the early 1980s is found in comments made by an official at China's Bureau of Publications in 1984. Jin Yong laughingly reported to one interviewer that the official complained to him that the pirated copies of his fifteen novels were "responsible for the lack of paper to print textbooks on."[25]

In the record of Jin Yong's discussion of Lu Xun with Ikeda Daisaku published in 1998, he is very respectful of Lu Xun and appears to know his works well.[26] In contrast, recall that this did not seem to be the case in a 1981 interview with the telling title "Against the Authors of 'Foreign Books in Chinese Language,'" where Jin Yong asserted that Lu Xun's fiction is hardly "Chinese." Jin Yong's rationalizes this assertion by emphasizing that *form* is vital to the expression of "Chineseness" in writing:

> I believe the form is the key thing, since the spirit can reflect modern themes and ways of thinking. Still, in reality, "spirit" is not easily divided into modern or ancient. "Form" is different. Chinese art has its own unique forms, in music, painting, costume, drama, dance, poetry, and song. You can sense them at the first encounter; in fact, this is cultural.[27]

Jin Yong takes issue with the May Fourth literary establishment in terms of the cultural identity of Chinese literature, saying specifically, "Ever since the May Fourth movement, intellectuals seem to have felt that fiction only exists in foreign forms, and that Chinese forms are not fiction."[28] Jin Yong regards form as the primary cultural signifier, rather than spirit because spirit may bridge the divide between ancient and modern. In contrast, I propose national character as a critical discursive mediator between the "spirit" and "form" to which Jin Yong refers above. As Jin Yong says in the quotation above, "you can sense them [unique Chinese forms] at the first encounter." This is not unlike Feng Jicai's remark quoted above that Lu Xun's greatness rests in his "particular cultural angle—the critique of national character." Analyzing Jin Yong's works from the standpoint of national character gives equal weight to form and spirit in "Chineseness" because, by Jin Yong's own logic, "you can sense it at the first encounter." National character bridges the perceived divide between form and spirit and thus supersedes Jin Yong's prioritization of form.

Jin Yong also differentiates his writing from the May Fourth literary tradition by arguing that "influencing society" is a side-effect of literature, and not "the goal" of literature. Jin Yong says, "Martial-arts fiction, of course, doesn't do that [i.e., serve the revolution—influence society]."[29] His denial of a social role for literature, including his own, is echoed by contemporary intellectuals and writers, such as Feng Jicai, who perceives three different levels of martial arts fiction: the lowest level of works appeal through stimulation by mystical swords and strange events; the next level of works are dynastic dramas with flying and wall-walking and feminine sentiment; and the best, or highest level of works include historical and cultural elements.[30] Jin Yong's fiction encompasses all three levels, and fits into the highest category by virtue of extensively woven historical and cultural features. However, as might be expected of a member of the contemporary literary establishment which places a premium on "high" literature, Feng is not convinced of the longevity of this genre as serious literature, it may "momentarily hold the attention of the strait-laced professors" but can't "keep the attention of writers whose imagination is equally developed."[31] Although Jin Yong specifically rejects the idea of "serving the revolution," he doesn't have control over how his novels are interpreted by readers and critics, nor how the cultural capital related to his works informs the discourse of literary value or is manipulated or objectified. Precisely because portrayal of the national character is an important function in the construction of the nation and national identity, Jin Yong unintentionally achieves an important social function. Analysis of *Wanderer* and *Cauldron* serve to clarify this phenomenon.

NATIONAL CHARACTER COMPLEMENTS: LINGHU CHONG (*WANDERER*) AND WEI XIAOBAO (*CAULDRON*)

Founding a national character *rooted in traditional values* was not what the antitraditional, iconoclastic, anti-Confucian Lu Xun had in mind, but those traditional values are one reason readers identified deeply with Jin Yong's characters and works. There is an intuitive sense of identification with these positive, idealized attributes—a sense of recognition that draws and expands on the already known. Lu Xun never prescribed a positive national character, per se, but did express an intention to "change" the national character through self-examination: "[M]y method is to make the reader unable to tell who this character can be apart from himself, so that he cannot back away to become a bystander but is bound to suspect that this may be a portrait of himself if not of every man, and that may start him thinking. Not one of my critics has spotted this, however."[32] Having already rejected the old value structure upon which a new national character might have been imagined/constructed, Lu Xun does lend credence to the idea that readers may change themselves, but he seems only to have seen an abyss, a vacuum of national character after his negation of the old one. The new ideological formations being imported from the West couldn't instantaneously bring a different, non-Western, Chinese national character to life. Lu Xun saw the defects of the Chinese people all around him from such a dark place and that it was difficult to specifically elucidate how to transform the Chinese mentality and value structure beyond, but at least he understood that it required readers to confront the darkness and start the introspective process of change.

Jin Yong scholar Chen Mo argues that Wei Xiaobao, the protagonist in *Cauldron*, Jin Yong's last work, may surpass Ah Q as the ultimate negative representation of Chinese national character.[33] Jin Yong says he was consciously thinking of Lu Xun, Ah Q, and Ah Q's method of spiritual victory when writing *Cauldron*.[34]

This contradicts his previously noted denial that martial arts fiction might have a social function ("serving the revolution"), implicitly

Figure 3.1. "Method of Spiritual Victory," Ah Q in *The True Story of Ah Q* (1981) and Wei Xiaobao in television adaptation of *Cauldron* (1984), Episode 1

acknowledging a potential social role of national character critique. Wei Xiaobao is an "antihero" like Ah Q, but two crucial positive features complement Lu Xun's negative critique of the national character arguably as Jin Yong points out: "The important features of his disposition are the adaptability to his environment and loyalty to his friends."[35] This is a first glimpse of the complement to Ah Q's negative characteristics. Jin Yong's stress on loyalty to one's friends (*yiqi*) and human sentiment (*renqing*) are the common aspects of characterization found throughout his fiction: "'Loyalty' has an important effect on unity and engagement in the struggle for survival. 'Human sentiments' have an important effect on dispelling internal contradictions and mitigating internal conflicts."[36] However, Jin Yong himself inadvertently becomes a critic of national character by disputing the view that Wei Xiaobao is its representative:

> There are numerous good and bad points of the Chinese in the person of Wei Xiaobao. But Wei Xiaobao is certainly not a representative type of the Chinese people. National character is a broad concept, and Wei Xiaobao is an individual, a person with a personality. Liu Bei, Guan Yu, Zhuge Liang, Cao Cao, Ah Q, Lin Daiyu, and so on, all have some special features of the Chinese, but none can be said to be a representative type of the Chinese people (*Zhongguoren de dianxing*). The temperament of the Chinese people is too complex. Ten thousand novels couldn't complete its depiction. Sun Wukong, Zhu Bajie, Sha Seng [of the classic *Journey to the West*] are not people, but in their person are some special characteristics of the Chinese people because the person who wrote these "demons" is a Chinese person.[37]

Jin Yong wrote modesty as part and parcel of the martial arts master's social interaction, the rule being that the more modest the master, the better his kungfu. In the canonization discourse, Jin Yong is modest of his own "value" vis-à-vis Lu Xun, recall him saying that "The biggest difference is that Lu Xun is a great author, and I am just a common writer."[38] In this brilliant (kungfu) move Jin Yong lowers himself vis-à-vis Lu Xun, which actually may be an assertion of his superiority. Instead of ten thousand novels necessary to depict the Chinese character, Jin Yong has fifteen novels totaling approximately 150,000 pages which sketch out many of its crucial elements. Though Jin Yong argues against viewing Wei Xiaobao as a representative of Chinese national character, he validates the idea that the national character can be described through literary works. Furthermore, the multitude of adaptations as television series, movies, manga, computer games, radio broadcasts, blogs, and literary critiques, which magnify Jin Yong's national character depiction in contemporary pop culture via the kungfu industrial complex demonstrates in both "spirit" and "form" that Jin Yong provides a well-rounded picture of the national character beyond the individual character of Wei Xiaobao.

Chinese critics readily situated Wei Xiaobao in the discourse of Chinese national character. Chen Mo sees Wei Xiaobao as surpassing Ah Q as a representative of negative Chinese national character and advocates studying the Chinese national character by investigating Wei Xiaobao. He concludes that contemporary Chinese society's "general mood, environment and cultural traditions" will not improve if Wei Xiaobao's "contemptible and shameless" character survives.[39] Although Wei Xiaobao may be worse than Ah Q, Chen still marvels at the excellence of Wei Xiaobao's characterization. This can be seen in one of his book chapter titles, "Zhongguo wenhua de jingling yu guaitai—Wei Xiaobao" (Chinese culture's spirit and freak).[40] In terms of the literary field of cultural production, in addition to being author, Jin Yong occupies the space as critic and actively engages in the discourse with cultural critique of his own work, analyzing Wei Xiaobao as antihero:

> On the one hand he stresses the code of brotherhood/loyalty (*yiqi*)—on the point of loyalty I'm afraid it is related to the arduousness of the environment in which he lives. On the other hand, he eats, drinks, whores, and gambles, and also often plays some dirty tricks and intrigues, and so on and so forth. This can also be regarded as a particular type of Chinese person. He is an "anti-hero," but this [type] is also quite true and widespread.[41]

Esteem for, and conformity to, the martial code makes Wei Xiaobao a hero. At the same time, the array of vices Jin Yong notes here makes him an antihero. This complexification of contradictory attributes makes his characterization far broader than Ah Q's. He is a far more negative representation of the national character than Ah Q. At the same time, his extreme negative attributes are balanced by two hugely positive attributes, adaptability, and loyalty, which provide the reader excellent characteristics to emulate. Many positive heroes in Jin Yong's works lack Wei Xiaobao's negative attributes. The protagonist Xiao Feng in *Semi-Devils* is an ideal representative of the positive moral virtues of upright martial arts sects and demonstrates that assimilation of Chinese culture and Confucian moral principles supersedes his Qidan ethnic identity, despite ostracization of his peers who embrace crude identity politics of ethnic biological determinism. Ironically, the non-Han Xiao Feng can stand as Jin Yong's poster child for the positive influence of traditional Chinese culture to supersede ethnic biological determinism. Here is evidence that cultural capital is learned, embodied, and manifested through the thought, behavior, and actions of Jin Yong's heroes.

The positive side of Jin Yong's national character is grounded in traditional Confucian values and virtues such as *zhong* (loyalty), *xiao* (filial piety), *ren* (benevolence, humaneness), and *yiqi* (righteous loyalty, justice, chivalry, or honor).[42] It also includes an appreciation and celebration of the traditional Chinese aesthetics of music, calligraphy, poetry, and painting, as well as the arts of drinking tea and wine, as intensely represented page after page throughout Jin Yong's works. The greatest martial artists are ideal "cultured" heroes with balanced proportions "talented in both literary and martial arts" (*wen wu quan cai*). For example, *Wanderer*'s Linghu Chong is a martial warrior who becomes schooled in traditional aesthetic virtues by the martial artists he meets as the story progresses. At the start of the narrative he already had a love of wine, a fundamental characteristic of the hero in martial arts fiction, but he is visited by Zu Qianqiu, who teaches him the *art* of drinking wine (*pinjiu*) paired with the proper vessels to bring out the greatest flavor. Zu Qianqiu arrives with sixteen different types of wine and appropriate vessels, readily finding Linghu Chong a fast learner as they sit and imbibe. As typical in Jin Yong's stories, this doubles as a narrative ploy—Linghu Chong unknowingly consumes a medicine that may save his life. Elsewhere in the story, Linghu Chong is taught other finer cultural arts by martial opponents whose kungfu is expressed through their specific cultural art, such as music of the zither, calligraphy of the master Zhang Xu, or the landscape paintings of master Fan Kuan.

In the May 1980 "Afterword" to *Wanderer*, Jin Yong identifies the idea of the title of this novel as a general characteristic also found commonly in real life during any dynasty, the pursuit of a "free and carefree" life:

> The carefreeness of [the musical composition which is the title reference] *Xiao ao jianghu* is the object of the type of character Linghu Chong is pursuing. Because what I wanted to portray was a universal personality, a commonly seen phenomenon in life, so there is no historical setting to this book. This means such circumstances can occur in any dynasty.[43]

Presumably of Han ethnicity, Linghu Chong is a complex character in which to locate national character complements because he walks a line between the orthodox and the heterodox realms of the martial *jianghu*, untainted by complications of ethnicity that beset Xiao Feng in *Semi-Devils*. Through association with upright sects (*zheng pai*), as well as unorthodox sects (*xie pai*), Linghu Chong becomes a critical consciousness, recognizing the similarities of these opposing sects within the value structure of the *jianghu*, and thus occupies a privileged position from which to critique the dogmatism of each sect. *Wanderer*'s litany of Ah Q cross-references demonstrates the negative features of national character, as well as challenges to them, and stands as a complex example of national character complements ripe for national character analysis.

The plot of *Wanderer*, unlike many of Jin Yong's other stories, does not revolve around external threats to China's territorial and political integrity. It rather maps internal struggles for leadership and hegemony in the martial world played out against the larger canvas of battle between good (*zheng*) and evil (*xie*).⁴⁴ The geographical expanse of this work delineates the reaches of the nation. The reader is treated to a *jianghu* physically mapped from north to south by the traditional *zhongyuan* (central plains), encompassed by the Yellow and the Yangzi rivers, and punctuated by the five sacred mountain peaks home to the orthodox schools of swordsmanship: the northern Hengshan in Hubei, the more centrally located Huashan (Shaanxi) and Songshan (Henan), Taishan in the east (Shandong), and the southern Hengshan in Hunan. Additionally, a map in volume three of *Wanderer*, locates the western region by reference to Mount Qingcheng in Sichuan, and locates the eastern coast by reference to the cities of Fuzhou and Hangzhou. Because action takes place in most of these locations, the distances Linghu Chong and other characters travel are tremendous.

Read as a near political allegory,⁴⁵ *Wanderer* is a natural choice to positively complement Lu Xun's critique of the national character. There are many examples of Ah Q types of negative expression found in the action, ideas, and language of *Wanderer*'s characters: *numu er shi* "glaring fiercely" (tied to Ah Q's "angry look-ism" *numu zhuyi*) is portrayed as a tactic to use when feeling powerless and having no other immediate recourse to action; use of the rhetorical kungfu signifier *laozi* (old man/father/"I") as an arrogant form of self-reference (described in the previous chapter as *beifen gongfu*—hierarchical kungfu); stereotypical and comical exposition on how nuns are unlucky with reference to the curse of "may you have no progeny" (*jue zi jue sun*); the ubiquitous idea of muddledness (*hutu*); ironic use of Confucian "rectification of names" (*ming zheng yan shun*); the practice of the demeaning self-slap; Ah-Q thought expressed in Buddhist parable; hypocrisy of the Confucian "upright gentleman" (*zhengren junzi*); obsession with being "Number One" (Number One–ism); antievolutionary psychology comparing people with lower forms of life; theatricality; and even an example of Ah Q-style "one-downsmanship."

In many of these instances Jin Yong uses these Ah Q characteristics ironically or sarcastically just as Lu Xun used them. However, *Wanderer*'s protagonist Linghu Chong often expresses sarcasm, unlike Ah Q in *True Story* where it is the narrator of Lu Xun's novel who indirectly accounts for much of the irony. Contrary to Wei Xiaobao in *Cauldron*, there is no explicit evidence that Jin Yong was ever thinking of Lu Xun's Ah Q as a model when he wrote these Ah Q-like references into *Wanderer*. He was possibly playing on some deeply held conceptions in traditional Chinese society, such as a popular prejudice regarding illicit sexual relations between monks and nuns. As a national character complement, however, Linghu Chong's positive heroic character becomes an ironic contrast to Ah Q when he expresses or critiques Ah Q-style features. This brings the national character complement into even starker relief. The example of Ah Q-style one-downsmanship helps demonstrate this notion.

In chapter 13 of *Wanderer*, Linghu Chong is found suffering an internal injury and has lost his strength. His master erroneously suspects he has stolen a book of secrets, the *Bixie/Pixie jianpu* (Sword manual to ward off evil), because of a startling advance in his swordsmanship. In addition, Linghu Chong is depressed that his sweetheart, Yue Lingshan, has fallen in love with his martial brother, Lin Pingzhi. As a result, he is literally a mess: dirty, bloodstained, gambling, and drinking himself further into despair. At this point in the story Lin Pingzhi's rich maternal grandfather hosts the entire Huashan Sect in Luoyang. Lin Pingzhi's relatives misinterpret Linghu Chong's appearance and behavior as a slight against their honor and moreover suspect that he has stolen the Lin family's *Sword Manual to Ward Off Evil*. Lin Pingzhi's cousins confront Linghu Chong after saving him from a severe beating at the hands of some town idlers. They berate him saying: "You are the number-one disciple of the Huashan Sect and can't even handle a few Luoyang hooligans. Ha, ha. Others don't know it, but doesn't this mean you're flaunting a false reputation (*langde xuming*)?"[46] Linghu Chong responds in Ah Q-style one-downsmanship saying: "I don't even have a false reputation [to speak of] in the first place, so I can't talk about 'flaunting a false reputation.'"[47] He is clearly speaking ironically since he has secretly learned an awesome style of swordsmanship called *Dugu jiu jian* ("The nine swords of Dugu") which he used to save the entire Huashan Sect from humiliation and death by instantaneously blinding fifteen enemies in one magnificent maneuver. This is not the Lin family's "secret" style, but nobody knows the difference. Additionally, because he has promised not to reveal the name of his teacher, Feng Qingyang, or the name of the style everyone thinks he is lying. This creates deeper misunderstanding, a narrative technique that Jin Yong commonly employs to advance the plot in his stories.

Linghu Chong's character is open, forthright, and relatively humble, so he does not brag of his feats. His calculated humility in the face of insults from Lin Pingzhi's cousins is cuttingly sarcastic and results in further bullying (the cousins painfully dislocate both his elbows). Compare Linghu Chong's one-downsmanship tactic to Ah Q's. Ah Q one-downsmanship as a "means of psychological victory" when faced with similar derision and bullying: "'Ah Q, this is not a son beating his father, it is a man beating a beast. Let's hear you say it: A man beating a beast!' Then Ah Q, clutching at the root of his queue, his head on one side, would say, 'Beating an insect—how about that? I am an insect—now will you let me go?'"[48]

Linghu Chong resorts to Ah Q-like irony by lowering his own reputation into the negative zone—he "can't talk about 'flaunting a false reputation'" since he does not even have that—lowering himself even farther than Lin's cousins originally suggested. But because of his "heroic" disposition (a well-deserved righteousness earned by his honesty, forthrightness, strong sense of loyalty, and factual innocence of the presumed crime) his sarcasm is an insult to his tormentors, not to himself, and he consequently suffers further verbal and physical abuse. There are a number of expressions in Jin Yong's martial arts lexicon that are used to describe this type of unyielding fortitude, such as *ning si bu qu* (rather die than submit) and *junzi ke ru, bu ke qu* (a gentleman may be insulted but he will not yield), or even *shi ke sha bu ke ru* (you may kill the gentleman/scholar, but not insult him).[49] Ah Q, on the contrary, lowers himself to avoid being bullied further and gives his tormentors the feeling they have won. In the end, however, Ah Q's maneuver gains him a spiritual victory: "In less than ten seconds, however, Ah Q would walk away also satisfied that he had won, thinking that he was the 'Number One self-belittler,' and that after subtracting 'self-belittler' what remained was 'Number One.' Was not the highest successful candidate in the official examination also 'Number One'?"[50]

Linghu Chong's "spiritual victory" is that of the righteous hero who maintains the moral high ground—expressed by his sarcastic "one-downsmanship"—even though he suffers additional physical pain as a result of his sarcasm. Ah Q's "spiritual victory" requires that he convince himself of a specious status by claiming to be "Number One," unaware of sarcasm or irony. Linghu Chong recognizes his actual superiority even while lowering himself, whereas Ah Q feels himself actually superior because he is "Number One" when it comes to self-demeaning. While Ah Q's "Number One–ism" is not directly replicated by Linghu Chong in this context here, the psychology of his Number One–ism is mirrored quite closely in the novel and appears throughout Jin Yong's other works.

Linghu Chong has a sense of the compulsion to be "Number One," a dimension of rhetorical kungfu, but does not revel in it ("Number One–ism") like Ah Q, who needs it to assuage his psyche. For example, having been banished from his martial sect for a year "to face the wall" in a cave high on Huashan, Linghu Chong calls himself "Huashan Sect's number one troublemaker" (*Huashan pai diyi daodangui*).[51] Linghu Chong expresses remorse at being the number one troublemaker. In another episode, Linghu Chong's identification with Ah Q-style psychology of "Number One–ism" is replicated more closely. After being captured by an old woman (the nun Yilin's mother) and hung up from the rafters in a remote temple on Hengshan, the old woman sticks a sign on him that he cannot see to read. Linghu Chong imagines how he is going to pay her back: "I'll hang her up and put a sign on her. What should I say?

The Number One bitch in the world! No, if I call her Number One in the world who's to say she wouldn't in fact like that. I'll write 'The Number Eighteen bitch in the world' and make her bust her brain trying to figure out who those other seventeen bitches ahead of her are."[52] Linghu Chong does not rationalize "Number One–ism" with respect to himself here, but reads it into his tormentor, suggesting that she might enjoy being called "Number One" even if she was hung up from the rafters and insulted. This clever observation puts Linghu Chong (and thus Jin Yong) on a similar level of critical consciousness as author/narrator Lu Xun when he wrote this feature into Ah Q's character. In fact, the sign that the old woman hung on Linghu Chong says that he is the "Number One blind guy in the world, a sexless bitch"—referring to both his refusal to marry the young nun Yilin (who is really her daughter) and the fact that he is disguised as a woman. Linghu Chong's position reminds him that just the night before he had discovered the monks Bujie and Tian Boguang hanging in a tree with similar "Number One in the world" signs stuck on them. Reasoning with the old woman in order to save his life (or to put it politely, that of his progeny), Linghu Chong says he cannot marry Yilin because he is in love with Ren Yingying and if he changed hearts then "he would be stealing Bujie's 'Number One in the world' appellation."[53] Here he humorously and ironically mirrors Ah Q's Number One–ism. After he is free and captures the old woman, he hangs her in a tree with the message "the number one jealous person in the world."[54]

In addition to "one-downsmanship" and "Number One–ism," there is a third aspect of Ah Q's spiritual victory prevalent throughout *Wanderer* that takes the form of rhetorical kungfu: arrogant self-reference of hierarchical kungfu. Ah Q worked this rhetorical kungfu into his method of spiritual victory while suffering a beating by asserting, "It's as if I were beaten by my son" (*Wo zong suan bei erzi dale*),[55] or lamented, "What is the world coming to nowadays, with sons beating their fathers!" (*Xianzai de shijie tai bu cheng hua, erzi da laozi*).[56] This word play turns on the Confucian moral virtue of filial piety, which holds it unthinkable to even express disrespect toward one's father, not to mention actually hitting him.

Jin Yong takes pains to explain this hierarchical kungfu humorously in *Wanderer* through the young nun Yilin of the northern Hengshan Sect. Yilin has escaped from the notorious rapist Tian Boguang thanks to Linghu Chong's trickery (Tian's swordsmanship is far superior to his own at this point). She narrates the episode to the assembled leaders of the Five Mountains Sword Sect Alliance. In her long and detailed discourse, she naively explains that Linghu Chong used the appellation *laozi* when talking to Tian Boguang, and asks: "Master, don't you think it's funny? Big Brother Linghu is not Tian Boguang's dad, but he calls himself 'your old man.'"[57] Much embarrassed, her martial master explains to her in front of the other alliance leaders that this expression is vulgar speech of the alleys. Of course, Linghu Chong is using this hierarchical kungfu as a "provoking strategy" (*ji di zhi ji* or *ji jiang ji*) trying to make Tian Boguang angry under the premise that this might compromise his martial ability and give him a chance of saving Yilin's honor and life (morality holds that the unchaste unmarried woman is expected to commit suicide if her honor is violated).

Other more complex examples of hierarchical kungfu in *Wanderer* also echo Ah Q's mentality. The hunchback Mu Gaofeng uses it by referring to himself as Old master (*laoyezi*) when he tries to take Lin Pingzhi as a disciple with the goal of obtaining Lin's *Sword Manual to Ward Off Evil*. At the same time Master Yu Canghai of the Qingcheng Sect aims to kidnap Lin and force him to give up the book. While looking directly down his nose at Yu, Mu addresses Lin as "a good kid" (*hao haizi*) and "an obedient kid" (*guai haizi*). Besides the fact that Yu is extremely short in stature, Jin Yong clarifies that Mu is using rhetorical kungfu against Yu by adding the comment, "as if he [Mu] were saying it to him [Yu]."[58] In an interesting variation of this tactic, Mu Gaofeng also addresses Linghu Chong's master, Yue Buqun, saying: "How is it that you are almost sixty and suddenly you have returned to your youth? You look just like you are my child."[59] Yue, for his part, had just addressed Mu in the first-person moniker of "little brother" (*xiaodi*) as a courtesy lowering himself, but Mu takes advantage of his politeness to demean him a full generation to his "child."[60]

Use of a wide variety of humbling self-reference, the opposite of using the arrogant *laozi*, is stock and trade of martial arts family relationship-based personal monikers. When such self-reference is taken to the extreme the result is insults based on a Darwinian scale of evolutionary development. This is born out in *True Story* when tormentors insist that Ah Q call himself a "beast" (*chusheng*) and he "one-downs" them by calling himself an "insect" (*chongzhi*) instead. Linghu Chong uses similar one-downsmanship in *Wanderer* when sarcastically refer to himself as "not even as good as a beast" (*lian chusheng ye bu ru*) while ironically "apologizing" to an enemy who is threatening the Huashan Sect. Linghu Chong furthermore punctuates this insult by explicitly denying that he is referring to the enemy interlocutor while he obviously is.[61]

Variations of self-lowering or devolutionary psychology are found in other situations in the novel. One character lowers himself and his daughter to the level of a "dog" because he realizes that he has offended Linghu Chong and only just learned of Linghu Chong's close connection to his benefactor. To wit, Linghu Chong is kidnapped by Lao Touzi and about to be killed to harvest his blood, which contains a medicine he unknowingly drank. Zu Qianqiu rescues him and explains the entire situation. The mortified Lao Touzi apologizes profusely to Linghu Chong using both generational lowering with the first-person pejorative self-reference "little person/punk/kid" (*xiaozi*) and at the same time raising the much younger Linghu Chong a generation above himself by calling him "venerable old Linghu" (*Linghu yeye*). Moreover, Lao Touzi demeans his own beloved daughter's nearly extinguished life by calling hers a "dog's life" (*gou ming*).[62] Though resigned to death himself, Linghu Chong now realizes that he has unknowingly consumed a rare potion painstakingly prepared over many years that was to have saved the daughter's life, so he doesn't take offense at the attempt to kill him. Verbally, Linghu Chong maintains the lines of generational respect by referring to Lao Touzi, who is old enough to be his father, as "venerable senior" (*lao qianbei*). Moreover, he sees the justice of saving the daughter's life while sacrificing his own. Here the narrative suggests that this is because he believes he does not have long to live anyway, but that is secondary because the reader has already encountered episodes where Linghu Chong has been willing to sacrifice his life in the name of chivalry itself. Linghu Chong thereupon performs a crude blood transfusion by feeding the daughter his blood and subsequently saves her life though nearly dying himself.[63] The reader sees Linghu Chong in a "heroic" role exhibiting characteristics of chivalry (by trying to save the life of the daughter) and mental clarity (reasoning that he will be dead soon anyway) that is quite in contrast to Ah Q's muddled survivalism.

The list of Ah Q similarities in *Wanderer* is too long to address in its entirety. A final example of Linghu Chong as a positive national character complement is found in his epic battle with the rapist Tian Boguang. Here Jin Yong details Linghu Chong's natural sense of chivalry—a willingness to die in order to save his martial sister-in-arms, the young and beautiful Buddhist nun Yilin. Linghu Chong's chivalry is based on the code of loyalty (*yiqi*), which stipulates that beyond defending the weak he must assist Yilin because she belongs to the Hengshan Sect and is thus a fellow member of the Five Sacred Peaks Alliance. Linghu Chong is constantly a hair's breadth from death during this long episode because Tian's martial abilities far exceed his own. Out of his sense of *yiqi* Linghu Chong will not leave Yilin despite this mortal threat. Interestingly, in the long process of battle Linghu Chong actually develops a mutual sense of brotherly loyalty (*yiqi*) with Tian Boguang because Tian intentionally passes up many opportunities to kill him out of respect for Linghu Chong's unwavering loyalty toward Yilin—a reflection of true heroic nature that Tian, despite being an evil rapist, admires.

Linghu Chong realizes he will eventually lose the fight with Tian Boguang and urges Yilin to escape while he distracts Tian in battle. Yilin, however, does not pick up on his ploy and instead stays to join Linghu Chong in the losing battle out of her own sense of *yiqi*, thus risking both their lives. Linghu Chong calls her "muddled" (*hutu*), and resorts to the strategy of cursing her and her master in the hope that she will be so offended that she'll finally just leave (so perhaps he too can escape with his life). When this strategy fails, Linghu Chong begins an exposition on how nuns are "unlucky." His comments that "as soon as one sees a nun, one is bound to lose his stakes/bet" (*yi jian nigu, feng du bi shu*).⁶⁴ This motif is also repeated elsewhere in the novel. One of the harsher curses that Linghu Chong hurls at Yilin is that of "having no progeny" (*jue zi jue sun*).⁶⁵ In *True Story* this curse was directed at Ah Q by a young nun. However, in *Wanderer* Linghu Chong curses the nun using the phrase as an adjective (the expanded version of his actual curse is too vulgar to repeat here). Yilin is so concerned with Linghu Chong's safety that she still does not leave. Yilin's narration of this part of the story in front of the leaders of the Five Sacred Peaks Alliance includes a dialogue that validates the stereotype that nuns are indeed "bad luck." After describing the scene, Yilin asks her master: "Master, older brother Linghu's subsequent unfortunate death, was it because . . ., because he saw me and then his luck turned bad?"⁶⁶ The other leaders tacitly agree with Yilin's suggestion, as indicated by the knowing smiles on their faces in reaction to hearing this exchange between the two nuns.⁶⁷ The issue of illicit relations between monks and nuns is addressed later in more detail in the process of clarifying Yilin's paternity through the introduction of her father, the monk Bujie. Her father explains that he was a butcher and only became a monk after falling in love with her mother, a nun, because this was the only way he could stay close to her. Bujie says he did not realize that as a monk he would have even less access to her because of proscriptions against sex. Although Bujie is not the sharpest tool in the shed, his discovery of the proscriptions is used to reinforce the popular idea/stereotype of illicit sexual relations between monks and nuns.⁶⁸

Although Linghu Chong was highly disrespectful in his use of these stereotypes, he is conscious of using them instrumentally, manipulating them both intentionally and sarcastically in order to rescue Yilin. The irony both reveals and reinforces an entrenched belief about "unlucky nuns," but at the same time also highlights Linghu Chong's cleverness and chivalry. In the end, Linghu Chong succeeds in saving Yilin and his heroic character impresses those listening to Yilin's story, as well as his opponent, Tian Boguang. Throughout the novel Linghu Chong's character continually impresses the people he meets regardless of their martial affiliation. His openness to questioning the orthodox dogma about good versus evil puts him at odds with his uptight Confucian master time and time again, and eventually results in his expulsion from the Huashan Sect. Although personally devastated by his expulsion, Linghu Chong is conversely recognized for his upright character by other martial leaders. Ultimately, Linghu Chong is even appointed head master of the northern Hengshan Sect even though this sect is populated entirely by nuns. Without going into the backstory, validation of this extremely strange situation comes from the abbots of the Shaolin and Wudang sects (the two most respected kungfu sects in the martial world) when they formally paid full tribute in ceremony. Besides earning the accolades from virtually all the orthodox leadership except for his own master, Linghu Chong also receives congratulations from the "evil" unorthodox Sun Moon Cult. Throughout the *jianghu* he is a real hero—the true *yingxiong haohan*.

Here is the national character complement steeped in understanding of the Ah Q-style mentality, using the terminology instrumentally and at the same time critiquing the mentality as a "critical consciousness" wielding it sarcastically. His martial ability is superb, but it is not his martial ability that is the focus of his character, but rather a combination of his cleverness, forthrightness, and adherence to the fundamental principle of *yiqi*, chivalrous loyalty to friends, that forms his heroic character. Such is the power of *yiqi* in his personality that Linghu Chong would not even kill the rapist Tian Boguang because Tian had spared his life many times during their battle. Linghu Chong initially sees this as a debt to be repaid and not a friendship, but subsequent events, including Tian Boguang's swearing off evil and truly changing his ways, prove Linghu Chong right in the end as Tian really reforms his behavior. Linghu Chong's character is thus depicted through the process of discovering that there is "good amid the evil, and evil amid the good," and he survives and flourishes as an example of the independent hero between supposed worlds of good and evil.

As a complement to Lu Xun's national character critique, Linghu Chong is portrayed as a critical consciousness in struggle with all elements of his surroundings, including the traditional Confucian senses of propriety, convention, and conduct within the orthodox school of swordsmanship. From the vantage point of the discursive construction of the nation, or Anderson's conception of "imagining the nation," Jin Yong's novels and the many cinematic and television representations of his stories and characters seem to play an antiauthoritarian role, but they also reify popular conceptions of justice. The analysis above makes the case that Jin Yong's novels are indeed imbued with a serious social function. Consider the following commentary by Geremie R. Barmé, who posits a complementary dimension of the social function of martial arts fiction:

> The traditional popularity of the exploits of knight-errant heroes witnessed a revival on the Mainland from the early 1980s, and the growth of martial arts literature, films and television series has had a massive impact on Mainland culture and the Mainland imagination ever since. This phenomenon is intertwined with a complex of popular sentiments that includes: the mass response to the official negation of Cultural Revolution ideology, a spiritual confusion resulting from de-centeredness, the desperate desire for the cre-

ation of a fantasy realm and a vague yearning among people to see justice dispensed by some gallant figures.⁶⁹

As a contemporaneous pseudo-allegory of the Cultural Revolution written while Jin Yong was also writing critical commentary in his Hong Kong newspaper, it is not surprising that readers versed in the horrors of the Cultural Revolution would read Linghu Chong as a sympathetic character giving hope for the Chinese people. Framing Linghu Chong as a national character complement, we see justice dispensed by a gallant and relatively independent figure who was wrongly suspected by his master, physically abused while in a weakened state, and expelled from his home school of martial arts—familiar injustices to victims (and introspective perpetrators after the fact) of the Cultural Revolution. Despite this train of events, Linghu Chong went on to earn the respect of the martial world in large part due to his sense of chivalry/loyalty (*yiqi*), buttressed by his unyielding sense of filial respect for his (hypocritical) master and his open disillusionment with the dogma of contending factions of good and evil. Here is a hero whose positive character complements Ah Q's negative one, while at the same time operating within the discourse of Ah Q's negative manifestation of national character. Although written some forty-five years after *True Story*, *Wanderer* validates Lu Xun's characterization of Ah Q by depicting Linghu Chong and other characters reveling in a litany of Ah Q-style characteristics right alongside positive and heroic qualities drawn from traditional Chinese values. The cohesion of Jin Yong's negative national character manifestation in *Wanderer* and *Cauldron* with that of Lu Xun's Ah Q, in addition to the ironic (not recognized by Jin Yong himself) May Fourth-like nation-building function of Jin Yong's works, strongly challenge Jin Yong's own assertion that Lu Xun was writing foreign fiction in Chinese—both authors participate vigorously in the national character discourse.

Although Jin Yong stressed form and language and deemphasized spirit in his account of the necessary qualifications for "Chineseness" in literature, the widespread depiction of Ah Q spirit (mentality) in the words and actions of Jin Yong's characters resonates strongly with those found in Lu Xun's works, so strongly that it undermines Jin Yong's own emphasis on form. In a sense, this is Jin Yong's tribute to Lu Xun. Although he may not have intentionally written Ah Q qualities *per se* into his characters (with the major exception of Wei Xiaobao), the closeness to Lu Xun's vision fills Jin Yong's pages and silently validates Lu Xun's reading of national character. So, despite Jin Yong's implication that he himself wrote "Chinese" fiction and Lu Xun wrote "foreign" fiction in Chinese, both authors featured the national character writ large in their works. This reading of national character complements bridges the dichotomies of high/low, old/new, intellectual/popular, Chinese/foreign, and social purpose/entertainment literature. Jin Yong and Lu Xun come together in complementary fashion in the discourse of national character and Jin Yong's martial arts fiction is quintessentially "real literature" through its function as a cultural product and discursive instrument in the construction of Chinese identity.

REASSESSING THE CANON OF TWENTIETH-CENTURY CHINESE LITERATURE

The language of modern Chinese literature has been an important topic of discourse since the May Fourth literary reforms promoted the use of vernacular Chinese and discarding of the classical in the late 1910s and 1920s. After the opening of China in the 1980s, Chen Pingyuan cites articles from the 1930s written by Qu Qiubai and Zheng Zhenduo, who arrive at the same negative conclusion about works of martial arts fiction in the early twentieth century. Chen states: "Despite the popularity of Jin Yong and others' works which attracted scholarly notice in the 1980s, in the minds of orthodox literati (*wenhuaren*) martial arts fiction is still 'cultural garbage' that poisons the youth."[70] Jin Yong and other writers of martial arts fiction may have achieved commercial success of over the decades, but their works were still viewed as "cultural garbage" with deleterious social effects. Economic capital associated with martial arts fiction may be significant, but the orthodox view of the literary establishment strongly resisted recognizing the cultural capital of martial arts fiction.

Criticism of Jin Yong's classical Chinese infused language, minus the regionalist denigration of dialect influence, is nearly an echo of the May Fourth snobbery toward "Mandarin Duck and Butterfly" literature. Such criticism is summed up by Perry Link, who notes, "many [works] employed a mixture of styles—causing May Fourth detractors later to describe the standard mode as 'half-classical-but-not-vernacular.'"[71] Link furthermore cites May Fourth charges against the martial arts fiction genre as replete with "hackneyed themes and characters."[72] Complicating this picture are comments by contemporary literary critics, such as Liu Zaifu, who come to exactly the opposite conclusion in their analysis of Jin Yong's language. Liu asserts that Jin Yong's language is "an authentic vernacular" and is not removed from the social masses like the "new vernacular" of the May Fourth writers.[73] Liu Zaifu, moreover, maintains that "Through his writing, Jin Yong raised the expressive standard of the vernacular."[74] Despite Liu Zaifu's contention, it should be noted that Jin Yong's peculiar vernacular from the 1950s to 1970s is not always viewed as close to colloquial Chinese, but has been termed a *"Jin shi baihua"*

(Jin-style vernacular language) which stems from the old style (premodern) vernacular, and carries on a tradition found in earlier Republican era twentieth century martial arts fiction.[75]

Linguistic continuity places Jin Yong's works as a continuum stemming premodern fiction through Republican era martial arts fiction. National character complements places Jin Yong next to Lu Xun on the spectrum of constructing the national identity and insinuates a significant contribution to the construction of cultural capital. Authors who can stand next to Lu Xun and not be overshadowed are extremely rare. Moreover, incorporation of Jin Yong's works in certain school textbooks since the 1990s is evidence that he might be near to supplanting Lu Xun as a literary cultural icon. Lu Xun endeavored to construct a modernity *apart* from tradition.

Discourse surrounding Jin Yong's late entry into the canon of twentieth-century Chinese literature provides an opening for the reevaluation of the Chinese national character discourse that had been guided by Lu Xun's overwhelmingly negative analysis, as well as introduce Jin Yong's place in literary discourse. But beyond the national character discourse, there are a number complex relationships between the most important issues in modern Chinese literary discourse that were triggered by Jin Yong's initiation into the canon in the 1990s as the Number Four writer (Lu Xun was ranked Number One): the vernacular language movement, "high versus low" literature, mass literature, canonization, and the introduction of market forces in literature, as well as the general reevaluation of twentieth-century Chinese literary history. Chen Pingyuan, professor of literature at Beijing University, describes the controversy at the time: "When Beijing Normal University's Wang Yichuan and others published their *Anthology of Masters of Twentieth Century Chinese Literature*, they ranked Jin Yong as number four, after Lu Xun, Shen Congwen and Ba Jin, but before Lao She. Mao Dun was not ranked at all. This action attracted media attention and was hotly debated for a while."[76] Bourdieu's concept of cultural capital advocates examining how agents operate in the cultural field (authors and critics here), and thus the "ranking" of Lu Xun and Jin Yong on this illustrious list describes a certain moment in the state of the cultural field, related directly to the discourse of Jin Yong's canonization. Jin Yong's entry into the canon brought the issue of "high versus low" literature to the forefront. The basic problem, spelled out clearly by Chen Pingyuan as noted above, is that martial arts fiction is not considered "real literature" by anyone, experts or lay readers alike. In the May Fourth discourse of literary value, popular fiction is something to be dismissed as written for entertainment or written to teach a lesson.[77] Accordingly, a work is not literature unless it fulfills a serious social function, is capable of description, conveys new thoughts, and is not for profit.[78] Chen notes that literary historians have dealt with the high/low issue in three ways: by writing separate histories of popular (low) fiction; by trying to fit popular fiction into the orthodox history; or by noting that the opposition between high and low is one of the characteristics of twentieth-century Chinese literature.[79] But in the end, popular literature is not considered by anyone as "real" or "true" literature.[80]

Situating Jin Yong's martial arts fiction firmly in the discourse of constructing the Chinese nation and national character strongly challenges the idea that his fiction is not "real" literature. Recall that the psychological construction of nation, as described by Benedict Anderson, is accomplished reader by reader, viewer by viewer, through communal consumption of oral, written, and visual texts across temporal and spatial boundaries. Considering its deep cultural penetration in text, film, and television, Jin Yong's martial arts fiction clearly performs a serious social function beyond entertainment. Such a function for this genre was recognized neither by the May Fourth literary establishment nor by many contemporary critics but qualifies Jin Yong's works as "real" literature in the spirit of Liang Qichao as well as Lu Xun. Jin Yong's entry into the canon is one step toward changing the intellectual and popular bias against the entertainment fiction that many people read and love but do not consider to be "literature," as Professor Chen indicates.

Chen Mo asserts that Jin Yong's literary accomplishments are not second to any past recipients, and comparable to eminent authors such as Shakespeare.[81] However, Chen was not optimistic that Jin Yong would receive the Nobel Prize given issues such as translation difficulties, particularly concepts such as *wu* (martial), *xia* (chivalrous "knight"), *jianghu* (martial world), *yiqi* (righteous loyalty), and a host of other culturally specific concepts from the rich legacy of Chinese philosophy and history. These terms tie to East-West cultural differences that relate to an appreciation of values and aesthetics inherent in Jin Yong's oeuvre. Chen Mo points out that from a modern Western perspective the *jianghu* is weird and difficult to understand.[82] Chen Mo points out that Chinese themselves look down on popular literature and won't recommend such works.[83]

Chen Mo's pessimism regarding the odds that Jin Yong might have won the Nobel Prize may be tempered by the canonization discourse in which multifaceted critique of Jin Yong, both positive and negative, have raised the consciousness of both readers and critics regarding the "value" of popular works, their cultural capital. Admittedly, J. K. Rowlings is not being considered for a Nobel Prize in literature despite the huge impact of her Harry Potter series worldwide, so cultural capital related to literature is not based solely on popularity, at least not yet. The canonization discourse both influences and is influenced by cultural capital of the sparring critics, or "agents" in Bourdieu's parlance, "we should look first at the composition and forms of capital structuring a given field and then at the competition between agents aiming to secure or maintain their capital reserves."[84]

The celebrated fight over Jin Yong's place (or not) in canon of Chinese literature was important in terms of Jin Yong's literary valorization and the construction and maintenance of the kungfu industrial complex. Beyond construction of national identity, the canonization battle helps describe the field in which agents (authors and critics) struggled to assess Jin Yong's cultural capital. Canonization is both an assessment of a certain, albeit unspecified, level of cultural capital, as well as a bestowment of additional cultural and economic capital. The construction of the kungfu industrial complex requires the creation and maintenance of authorial cultural capital, which may be challenged by the literary establishment on ideological grounds but is enhanced by the economic capital of the author's literary and other related endeavors. The term "canonization" broadly covers both the reception of the author and/or works by both the specialists and the popular reader. The specialists are gatekeepers who hold sway in literary discourse, but popular appeal is (ironically) an equalizing or even dominating factor given that the economic success of the author cycles back to have a clear bearing on his/her social and cultural capital.

Jin Yong's canonization takes place in the complex cultural landscape of a modernizing China, in which his novels were promoting traditional culture in contrast to a century of cultural modernization that frequently pitted cultural authorities against tradition. This is evident in the May Fourth era of the early twentieth century and the PRC-era Maoist Cultural Revolution. The canonization discourse brings cultural authorities, both official and organic, into the kungfu industrial complex as authors, critics, and academics stake out positions in the valorization of Jin Yong's work. As Chen Mo notes: "Jin Yong and his novels are Chinese cultural products, and at the same time are transmitters, molders, expressers, ponderers, and assessors of Chinese traditional culture. . . . Not only are Jin Yong's novels related to traditional culture, they are also intimately related to modern culture and even Western culture."[85] The fight to bring martial arts fiction into the canon inevitably involves elite biases about what is true literature, or the bias of "high verses low" literature. Jin Yong's assertion quoted above "that Lu Xun is a great author, and I am just a common writer" may be read as a reflection of this bias, humility aside. The basic problem is that martial arts fiction was not considered "real" literature by most literary experts and even by the general readership, as Chen Pingyuan points out, because it is written for entertainment and wasn't perceived to fill a serious social function or convey new thoughts. The preceding analysis of national character complements is a strong argument for assigning significant value to the role of popular fiction.

JIN YONG'S ULTIMATE CANONIZATION

Recognition of Jin Yong's literary status in the People's Republic of China increased throughout the 1990s. Over the previous three decades his newspapers and martial arts fiction, as well as television and film adaptions, made him exceedingly wealthy. He is arguably the most widely read Chinese novelist of all time. Simon Elegant's 1996 interview of Jin Yong estimated that 100 million copies of Jin Yong works were sold, including pirated versions, but not including translations.[86] The reach of his works, which were serialized in newspapers, viewed as movies and television series, read as comics, and even played out as computer games, make Jin Yong the de facto leading writer appointed by the marketplace, virtually a cultural industry in himself.

The final steps of Jin Yong's entry into the canon of Chinese literature encompass the first two decades of the 2000s in the form of official validation through inclusion in Chinese middle school and high school texts. Viewed from the perspective of Bourdieu's ideas of cultural capital, the embodied form, the objectified form, and the institutionalized form, are all addressed by inclusion in textbooks. This is particularly poignant when such inclusion is matched by shortening or removal of previous literary texts from the canon (Lu Xun, etc.). In the wake of the debate spurred by Wang Shuo's criticism of Jin Yong in 1999, a 2001 media report indicating that revisions of middle school language class materials would include Jin Yong's work "caused of intense debate in all quarters."[87] The negative attention to Jin Yong in the educational context seemed to give the upper hand to critics:

> Objectors said that martial arts fiction is a popular literature with entertainment as its purpose, of low intellectual value, and if it was selected for textbooks it would be difficult to have positive educational influence on students. Many parents and teachers also worried that the depiction of violent killing and romantic language in martial arts fiction would have a bad influence on students. After this, the Department of Education announced: Jin Yong's work won't become mandatory material for students. People's Education Publishing also said at the time that it wouldn't use Jin Yong's novels.[88]

Despite this controversy, when the People's Education Publishing textbook appeared in November 2004, the table of contents showed chapter 1 as the complete text of Lu Xun's novella, *Diary of a Madman*. Chapters 5 and 6 were selections of martial arts fiction, drawn from Wang Dulu's *Crouching Tiger, Hidden Dragon* and Jin Yong's *Semi-Devils*, respectively. The reaction to this news was concern that such "leisure entertainment" literature would "lead students astray," but the publisher noted that the textbook also included foreign fiction and poetry as well. While researchers, teachers and students were reported to have varying degrees of dismay or support, detractors lamented the return of the "four great populars" (*si da su*):

> "The four great populars are back again!" On the sina.com website some bloggers repeated these six characters 30 times (some people call "Qiong Yao's television series, Jackie Chan's movies, the Four Heavenly Kings, and Jin Yong's novels" as the "Four great populars"), in order to express their objection to Jin Yong's novels being selected for high school reading material.[89]

In an interview in August 2007 Beijing University professor Kong Qingdong was asked about Wang Shuo's criticism that "Jin Yong portrayed a bunch of very unbrilliant Chinese images in his novels," thus challenging Kong's reference to Jin Yong "designer of national image." Kong responded:

> This is not contradictory. Jin Yong's novels depict many unbrilliant Chinese people. Aren't Chinese people not unbrilliant? Isn't Wei Xiaobao unbrilliant? Zhang Wuji is unbrilliant. Li Mochou is also unbrilliant. Saying that Jin Yong depicted many unbrilliant Chinese people is correct. Wang Shuo's novels also depict many unbrilliant Chinese people. But we can also say they are all reflections of Chinese people. Heroes of any nationality are always a small minority and brilliant people are a small minority. If you want to actually reflect reality, then the majority of people are unbrilliant. So, I say Jin Yong depicts all kinds of Chinese people types over a broad landscape. Therefore, I say he is the designer of the national image. If you're going to understand Chinese people, I feel that you must remember Wang Shuo, also read Lu Xun, and read Wang Meng, and you also have to read Jin Yong. Only then will you know how the Chinese people really are.[90]

Kong has an instrumental view of indoctrination into the national character that comes through the process of reading, stating directly, "reading their [marital arts] novels you naturally get an education in critique of the national character."[91] This is a reification of the social function of literature—accumulation of cultural capital in order to "understand the Chinese people" and "know how the Chinese people really are." Jin Yong's vast audience ingests, digests, and regurgitates the characters, emotions, scenes, plots and sub-plots of the books, movies, and TV dramas until his characters become a part of the common cultural vernacular, in the process of reification of the kungfu industrial complex. As a result, Jin Yong's martial arts fiction transcends entertainment to serve a serious social purpose—the mapping of nation and national character through a heroic, critical and comical literature that character by character, value by value, and plot by plot facilitates the step-by-step construction of late twentieth-century Chinese cultural identity. Kong Qingdong also put the issue in this way:

I think that a very good national character, a worthy people with the hope of development, should maintain a spirit of both the *wu* (martial) and the *xia* (chivalry), and should not be biased. Only having the martial without chivalry, it is easy to lose justice. Only having chivalry and not the martial is just talking strategy on paper [not reality], should be [like] Duke Xiang of Song. If there is both the martial and chivalry, then this nation will develop well.[92]

The example of this professor from China's most elite university highlights the view that national character plays an important role in the construction of cultural capital. Reading novels of all types, not just martial arts fiction, instills a critique of the (negative) national character which is found in a lineage from the May Fourth all the way up through both Wang Shuo and Jin Yong. Remedial measures available to inculcate a worthy national character are found in the martial and the chivalrous elements in the novels. The professor is operating within a canonization discourse here in 2007. That year Jin Yong's fiction was viewed as increasingly replacing Lu Xun's in secondary school textbooks:

> Recently, a hot topic on the Mainland web is entry of martial arts fiction into the classroom. Continuing the selection of *The Demi-Gods and Semi-Devils* for mandatory reading in Beijing Education Publishing's high school language textbooks, in September of this year Jin Yong's *The Flying Fox on Snowy Mountain* also replaced Lu Xun's "The True Story of Ah Q" appearing in the table of contents of extensive preparatory language reading texts at Beijing City High School. This momentarily caused a chorus of approval and objection. Whether worrying that Jin Yong was "invading" Lu Xun [territory] or cheering "belated "justice," both conflicting thought tides made people have to think deeply about what kind of literature China really needs.[93]

This claim that an individual work of Jin Yong's is directly replacing one of Lu Xun's here is accompanied by statistics that indicate 23.6 percent of netizens think it's a good thing, 16.38 percent think it's bad, and 49 percent are noncommittal,[94] which at the minimum indicates an amount of awareness of readers regarding these two authors and their works. Not all authors have the popular cultural capital and status of Lu Xun and Jin Yong, however, which complicates the situation since older famous authors such as Zhu Ziqing were also being gradually phased out, adding to the stir in literary and intellectual circles. Such phasing out has been accompanied by the introduction of other late twentieth-century and early twenty-first-century authors such as Yu Hua and Jia Pingwa, but Jin Yong is a clear flashpoint because of the genre martial arts fiction.[95]

Perhaps the final step in the long process of Jin Yong's canonization (if there is ever a "final" step given that it is a process in continual evolution) came with the April 2013 report that Jin Yong's *Heroes* has been selected for inclusion on a list of 900 books that *elementary* school libraries must have on their shelves, while also noting that many parents had typically forbidden such martial arts fiction for their kids.[96] Attitudinal changes about popular fiction were afoot, as demonstrated by the list, which also includes *Harry Potter*, *Sophie's World*, and Shakespeare with the primary goal "to raise the children's' interest in reading." This level of structural legitimization in elementary and high school libraries and curriculum is an indication of the increasing strength of cultural capital associated with popular works. Here Jin Yong's works are listed alongside great works of world literature and culture, both the phenomenal Shakespeare and the remarkable *Harry Potter*. Even though he didn't win a Nobel Prize, Jin Yong's status in the canon of Chinese literature was cemented and he thus won the battle for cultural authority and cultural capital.

I've argued that Jin Yong significantly enhanced the critique of national character, adding a rich literature of positive complementary national character attributes to the national identity, positively assessed vis-à-vis Chinese literary giant Lu Xun. The discourse of academic canonization is a crucial dimension of the kungfu industrial complex through the valorization of popular literature as "real literature" by the gatekeepers. The fundamental status of Jin Yong within the kungfu industrial complex comes first and foremost from his works, characters, and stories (which are told and retold over the decades). Association of Jin Yong with most highly acclaimed Lu Xun and his works, characters, and concerns enhances Jin Yong's "literariness" and challenges the literary and cultural critics who were inclined to devalue or ignore popular literature. The discourse of canonization, literary sparring vis-à-vis Lu Xun, probably even raised Jin Yong's profile both within literary establishment and among the readership who were alerted to the controversy. Beyond demonstrating how Jin Yong's oeuvre constitutes a complementary construction to the negative national character depicted in *True Story*, Jin Yong by example shows why/how such popular works can be valorized as literature: national character critique serves a positive social function, Jin Yong sanctioning Lu Xun's negative critique while also ultimately becoming the example of a balanced, positive national character.

SOCIAL FUNCTION OF LITERATURE AND CULTURAL CAPITAL

The idea of literature in the service of nation-building has a lineage dating back through the May Fourth at least as far as the late-Qing reformer Liang Qichao, a journalist and publicist who in his 1902 article, "On the relationship between fiction and the government of the people" called for the use of the novel, and thus vernacular Chinese, for promotion of national consciousness.[97] As demonstrated above, Jin Yong's martial arts fiction ironically transcends his own emphasis on form and language as the elements that make his literature "Chinese" (as opposed to "foreign fiction in Chinese" written by Lu Xun et al.) by bringing a "high May Fourth purpose" to this poorly regarded traditional genre. The idea of "serving the revolution" is a transient trope when expanding the temporal dimension of literary-social-historical-political critical analysis to cover centuries, rather than merely decades. The literary canonization debate plays an ironic role in solidifying the status of Jin Yong's martial arts fiction in Chinese literary tradition. Jin Yong's literary awards and consideration for nomination for the Nobel Prize, even if not realized in the end, accrue cultural capital to Jin Yong, as well as social and economic capital in terms of contracts for further television adaptations, honorary degrees and honorary positions at numerous Chinese universities, and even a meeting with China's leader, Deng Xiaoping.[98]

Jin Yong and his works contribute to the project of "imagining" the nation and the national character, which becomes an underlying element of his literary appeal, and thus an important element in his accumulation of cultural as well as political capital, a step in the construction of the kungfu industrial complex. Jin Yong's works don't directly "serve the revolution" per se, and often actually critique the revolution. Despite this contradiction, Jin Yong's semi-political allegory in *Wanderer* stands out as an example of critique of the Cultural Revolution, and thus serves the revolution insofar as it argues against the extreme excesses that challenge the moral authority of the contemporary leadership during that period. "Serving society" or "serving culture" are more precise ways of terming Jin Yong's relationship to the construction of Chinese cultural capital.

NOTES

1. This chapter contains material highly adapted from my essay previously published in *Twentieth-Century China*: "Jin Yong's Linghu Chong Faces off against Lu Xun's Ah Q: Complements to the Construction of National Character," *Twentieth-Century China*, vol. 30, no. 1 (November 2004): 82–117. Reprinted with permission of *Twentieth-Century China*.

2. This qualification is made because the Chinese were born and raised, but French naturalized citizen Gao Xingjian won the Nobel Prize for Literature in 2000. From this example it is clear that although China has long embraced the accolades accrued by ethnic Chinese as a national honor, there is a political ideological calculus to consider.

3. Jon Kowallis, *The Lyrical Lu Xun* (Honolulu: University of Hawai'i Press, 1996): 3.

4. Lu Xun, "Zhi Tai Jingnong" (To Tai Jingnong), in *Lu Xun quanji*, 1989, vol. 11: 573.

5. Julia Lovell, *The Politics of Cultural Capital: China's Quest for a Nobel Prize in Literature* (Honolulu: University of Hawaii Press, 2006): 83–84.

6. Haiyan Lee, "Mo Yan, Inaugural Newman Laureate, Honored in Oklahoma," *The China Beat*, March 10, 2009, http://thechinabeat.blogspot.com/2009/03/mo-yan-inaugural-newman-laureate.html.

7. Chen Pingyuan, "Literature High and Low: 'Popular Fiction' in Twentieth-Century China," in *The Literary Field of Twentieth Century China*, trans. and ed. Michel Hockx (Honolulu: University of Hawaii Press, 1999): 116.

8. Jin Yong, "Against the Authors of 'Foreign Books in Chinese Language': An Interview with China's Most Popular Writer of Adventure Novels," trans. Marty Backstrom, ed. Helmut Martin, *Modern Chinese Writers Self Portrayals* (Armonk, NY: M.E. Sharpe): 173.

9. "Pierre Bourdieu," in *"The Johns Hopkins Guide to Literary Theory and Criticism,"* eds. Michael Groden, Martin Kreiswirth, and Imre Szeman, http://litguide.press.jhu.edu.proxy.library.georgetown.edu/index.html.

10. See the discussion in Benedict Anderson, *Imagined Communities*, rev. ed. (London: Verso, 1991): 37–46.

11. Jin Yong, "Xiaoshuo chuangzuo," 28.

12. Leo Ou-Fan Lee, *Voices from the Iron House: A Study of Lu Xun* (Bloomington: Indiana University Press, 1987): 190.

13. "China's most celebrated martial arts fiction writer Louis Cha has died aged 94," St. John's College, University of Cambridge, January 11, 2018, accessed December 30, 2020, https://www.joh.cam.ac.uk/chinas-most-celebrated-martial-arts-fiction-writer-louis-cha-has-died-aged-94.

14. In his treatise on this "school" in early twentieth-century China, Perry Link notes that the name *Yuanyang hudie pai* (Mandarin duck and butterfly school) was applied disparagingly. Perry Link, *Mandarin Ducks and Butterflies*, 7–8.

15. Feng Jicai, *Shouxia liuqing: xiandai dushi wenhua de youhuan* [Show leniency: The suffering of modern city culture] (Shanghai: Xuelin chubanshe, 2000): 121.

16. Leo Ou-fan Lee, *Voices from the Iron House: A Study of Lu Xun* (Bloomington: Indiana University Press, 1987): 110.

17. Ibid., 41–46.

18. Mao Dun, "Da Guotang xiansheng" [Reply to Mr. Guotang], *Xiaoshuo yuebao*, vol. 13, no. 2 (February 10, 1922): 5.

19. Zhou Zuoren (Zhong Mi), "A Q zhengzhuan" ["(On) The true story of Ah Q"]. Reprinted in *Lun Xun yanjiu xueshu lunzhu ziliao huibian (1913–1980)* (1913–1980) [A corpus of data of academic theses and works on Lu Xun (1913–1980)], gen. ed. Zhang Mengyang, vol. 1 (Beijing: Zhongguo wenlian, 1985): 29.

20. Chen Mo, *Gudu zhi xia—Jin Yong xiaoshuo lun* [The solitary knight—a treatise on Jin Yong's novels], 3rd ed. (Shanghai: Sanlian shudian, 1999): 107

21. Ye Hongsheng, *Lun jian: wuxia xiaoshuo tan yi lu* [Discussing swords—a record of artistic discussion on martial arts fiction] (Shanghai: Xuelin chubanshe, 1997): 240–242.

22. Ibid., 239.

23. In addition to Feng Jicai's article quoted above, see Bao Jing, ed., *Lu Xun "guominxing sixiang" taolun ji* [Collection of discussions on Lu Xun's "national character ideas"] (Tianjin: Tianjin renmin chubanshe, 1982).

24. Shu-mei Shih, *The Lure of the Modern: Writing Modernism in Semicolonial China, 1917–1937* (Berkeley: University of California Press, 2001): 131.

25. Elegant, "The Storyteller," 38.

26. Jin Yong & Ikeda Daisaku (Chitian Dazuo), *Tanqiu yige canlan de shiji* [Seeking a splendid century] (Hong Kong: Minghe she, 1998).

27. Jin Yong, "Against the Authors," 173.

28. Ibid.

29. Ibid., 177.

30. Feng Jicai, *Shouxia liuqing*, 109.

31. Ibid., 110.

32. "Da Xi zhoukan bianzhe yan" (Reply to the editor of *Theater Weekly*). In *Lu Xun: Selected Works*, trans. Yang Xianyi and Gladys Yang, vol. 4, 2nd ed. (Beijing: Foreign Languages Press): 141.

33. Chen Mo, *Gudu zhi xia*, 256.

34. Zhang Dachun, "Jin Yong tan yi lu" [Jin Yong talks about art], in Du Nanfa et al., *Zhuzi baijia kan Jin Yong (4)* [Philosophers and writers of all schools read Jin Yong (4)]. *Jin xue yanjiu congshu* [A collection of Jin-ology research], vol. 17 (Taibei: Yuanjing chubanshe, 1985): 37–38.

35. Jin Yong, "Wei Xiaobao zhege xiao jiahuo!" [This little punk Wei Xiaobao!], in Liu Tiansi, *Wei Xiaobao shengong* [Wei Xiaobao's mystical power], *Jin xue yanjiu congshu* [A collection of Jin-ology research], vol. 12. (Taibei: Yuanjing chubanshe, 1985): 156. Originally published in *Mingbao yuekan* (October 1981).

36. Ibid., 165.

37. Ibid., 174–175.

38. Jin Yong, "Xiaoshuo chuangzuo," 28.

39. Chen Mo, *Langman zhi lü—Jin Yong xiaoshuo shenyou* [A romantic journey—a mental journey through Jin Yong's novels] (Shanghai: Sanlian shudian, 2000): 385.

40. Chen Mo, *Gudu zhi xia: Jin Yong xiaoshuo lun* [The solitary knight: a treatise on Jin Yong's novels], 3rd ed. (Shanghai: Sanlian shudian, 1999).

41. Jin Yong, "Wei Xiaobao," 38.

42. Lin Yiliang also makes this point in conversation with Jin Yong. See Lu Li, "Jin Yong fangwen ji" [Record of calling on Jin Yong], in Weng Lingwen et al., *Zhuzi baijia kan Jin Yong (3)* [Philosophers and writers of all schools read Jin Yong (3)], *Jin xue yanjiu congshu* [A collection of Jin-ology research], vol. 16 (Taibei: Yuanjing chubanshe, 1985): 48.

43. This is dated May 1980. Jin Yong, "Houji" [Afterword], *Wanderer*, 1684.

44. For a discussion of the basic plot structure of *Xiao ao jianghu*, see Chen Mo, *Langman zhi lü*, 318.

45. Ibid.

46. Jin Yong, *Wanderer*, 544.

47. Ibid.

48. Lu Xun, "A Q zhengzhuan," trans. Yang and Yang, 110–111.

49. Used by Jin Yong in chapter 42 of *Semi-Devils*, and elsewhere. The formulation extends from the *Book of Rites* in reference to the Confucian gentleman.

50. Lu Xun, "A Q zhengzhuan," trans. Yang and Yang, 110.

51. Jin Yong, *Wanderer*, 305.

52. Ibid., 1544.
53. Ibid., 1549.
54. Ibid., 1574.
55. Lu Xun, "A Q zhengzhuan," trans. Yang and Yang, 109.
56. Ibid., 112.
57. Jin Yong, *Wanderer*, 126.
58. Ibid., 162.
59. Ibid., 202.
60. Ibid.
61. Ibid., 436.
62. Ibid., 625.
63. Ibid., 628–629.
64. Ibid., 129.
65. Ibid., 128.
66. Ibid., 129.
67. Ibid.
68. Ibid., 486.
69. Geremie R. Barmé, "TRINKET," 42–43.
70. Chen Pingyuan, "Qiangu wenren xiake meng—wuxia xiaoshuo leixing yanjiu" [Knight errant dream of the literati through the ages—research on types in martial arts fiction], in *Chen Pingyuan xiaoshuo shi lun ji* [Collection of Chen Pingyuan's essays on the history of fiction], vol. 2 (Shijiazhuang: Hebei renmin chubanshe, 1997): 998.
71. Perry Link, *Mandarin Ducks and Butterflies*, 59.
72. Ibid., 63.
73. Liu Zaifu, "Huiyi daoyan: Jin Yong xiaoshuo zai ershi shiji Zhongguo wenxue shi de diwei" [Conference keynote speech: The status of Jin Yong's novels in twentieth-century Chinese literary history], in *Jin Yong xiaoshuo yu ershi shiji Zhongguo wenxue: guoji xueshu yantaohui lunwen ji* [Jin Yong's fiction and twentieth-century Chinese literature: collection of essays from an international academic conference], ed. Liu Zaifu et al. (Hong Kong: Minghe she, 2000): 20.
74. Ibid., 21.
75. Li Tuo, "The Language of Jin Yong's Writing," 44.
76. Chen Pingyuan, "Literature High and Low," 132–33, fn. 2.
77. Ibid., 120.
78. Ibid., 120–125.
79. Ibid., 116.
80. This predilection is mirrored in the English-language reference materials on twentieth-century Chinese literature as well. Apart from Perry Link's book *Mandarin Ducks and Butterflies*, which itself only touches on early twentieth-century martial arts fiction, most other works do not give this genre more than a few sentences. See, for example, C. T. Hsia's *A History of Modern Chinese Fiction 1917–1957* (New Haven: Yale University Press, 1961); Lao and Goldblatt, eds., *The Columbia Anthology of Modern Chinese Literature* (New York: Columbia University Press, 1995); McDougall and Louie, *The Literature of China in the Twentieth Century* (New York: Columbia University Press, 1997); as well as Michel Hockx, ed., *The Literary Field of Twentieth-Century China* (Honolulu: University of Hawaii Press,

1999); and Idema and Haft, *A Guide to Chinese Literature* (Ann Arbor: University of Michigan Press, 1997).

81. Chen Mo, *Jin Yong wenhua* [Jin Yong culture], in *Chen Mo ping Jin Yong xilie* [Chen Mo critiques Jin Yong series], vol. 7 (Beijing: Haitun chubanshe, 2014): i.

82. Ibid., iii.

83. Ibid., v.

84. Jon Beasley-Murray, "Pierre Bourdieu," in *The Johns Hopkins Guide to Literary Theory and Criticism*, 2nd ed., eds. Michael Groden, Martin Kreiswirth, and Imre Szeman (Baltimore: Johns Hopkins University Press, 2005), accessed July 26, 2017, http://litguide.press.jhu.edu.proxy.library.emory.edu/cgi-bin/view.cgi?eid=37.

85. Chen Mo, *Jin Yong wenhua*, xvii.

86. Simon Elegant, "The Storyteller," 38.

87. "Tian long ba bu ruxuan gaozhong yuwen duben" [*The Demi-Gods and Semi-Devils* selected for high school language reader], *Jiaoyu, Renmin wang* [edu.people.cn], March 2, 2005, accessed May 11, 2016, http://edu.people.com.cn/GB/44071/3212362.html.

88. Ibid.

89. Ibid.

90. "Kong Qingdong jiaoshou zuoke da yuwang tan wuxia wenzi fangtan shilu" [The accurate record of Professor Kong Qingdong's visit to cq.qq.com discussing martial arts fiction language], August 28, 2007, http://cq.qq.com/a/20070828/000510.htm.

91. Ibid.

92. Ibid.

93. Wang Jingwen, "Jin Yong qudai Lu Xun yuwen keben de beihou" [Behind the scenes of Jin Yong replacing Lu Xun in language texts], September 10, 2007, accessed June 13, 2022. https://www.epochtimes.com/b5/7/9/10/n1828703.htm.

94. Ibid.

95. "Jin Yong ruxuan Lu Xun chu: Beijing yuwen keben gaige zheng yi ru chao [In with Jin Yong and out with Lu Xun: the tide of discussion of Beijing language textbook reform], August 18, 2007, accessed May 16, 2016, http://www.chinareviewnews.com/doc/1004/3/2/1/100432100.html?coluid=0&kindid=0&docid=100432100.

96. Li Li, "*She diao yingxiong zhuan* ruxuan Beijing Zhaoyang qu xiaoxue tushuguan jiben shumu" [*The Eagle-Shooting Heroes* selected for the basic library reading list at Beijing Zhaoyang district elementary school], April 2, 2013, http://news.ifeng.com/society/2/detail_2013_04/02/23800442_0.shtml. See also this television news report: "*She diao yingxiong zhuan* ruxuan Beijing Zhaoyang qu xiaoxue jiben shumu, Huaren online" [*The Eagle-Shooting Heroes* is selected for Beijing Zhaoyang elementary school basic reading list, Huaren online], accessed May 11, 2016, https://www.youtube.com/watch?v=yIEN87BHE94.

97. Liang Qichao. "Lun xiaoshuo yu qunzhi zhi guanxi" [On the relationship between fiction and the government of the people], *Xin xiaoshuo* (1902), trans. Gek Nai Cheng, in *Modern Chinese Literary Thought: Writings on Literature, 1893–1945*, ed. Kirk A. Denton (Stanford: Stanford University Press,1996): 74–81.

98. In addition to earning his own master's and doctorate from Cambridge University, Jin Yong has at least four honorary doctorates, including one from Cambridge. In 2007 Jin Yong was set to receive "an honorary doctorate by National Chengchi University (NCCU) in recognition of his outstanding long-term contribution to Chinese-language writing and literature, as well as his assiduous attitude toward learning. . . . Jin Yong received an honorary doctorate from Cambridge University in 2005" "Kung fu novelist Jin Yong to receive honorary degree," *Taipei Times*, May 8, 2007, accessed December 30, 2020, http://www.taipeitimes.com/News/taiwan/archives/2007/05/08/2003359966. In addition, in 2011 Taiwan's National Tsing Hua University "conferred an honorary doctoral degree" on Jin Yong "for his influential contributions to Chinese-speaking society." "Novelist Jin Yong given honorary doctorate by Taiwanese university," *Taiwan News*, December 19, 2011, accessed December 30, 2020, https://www.taiwannews.com.tw/en/news/1791891.

Four

Kungfu Star Power
The Entertainment Jianghu

It wouldn't have been surprising if Jin Yong had won the Nobel Prize for literature based on the impact of his stories on Chinese society and culture and the challenge they present to a century of Chinese political and cultural discourse. Ironically, he was a "counterculture" author: counter the Chinese revolution in both his celebration of Chinese traditional identity and the critical allegory in his key works, particularly the near Cultural Revolution allegory found throughout much of *Wanderer*. Jin Yong was a storyteller. Kungfu cultural literacy, the cultural capital of kungfu humor, and Jin Yong's canonization after China's opening demonstrate various dimensions of his storytelling and situate him within the thousand years of tradition to which John Minford, English translator of *Cauldron*, refers:

> Perhaps the most helpful Chinese starting point for such readers [of martial arts fiction] would be the kungfu movies of Bruce Lee and Jackie Chan, products that have travelled to the West in a way that the Chinese written word, by and large, has not. But Bruce Lee and Jackie Chan are just the tip of the iceberg. Their films are only a fraction of the vast kungfu film industry, and that industry itself is only one of the most recent growths of a much older tradition of Chinese storytelling that goes back well over a thousand years. Since at least the tenth-century crowds have gathered in Chinese teahouses, marketplaces, and parks, to hear stories told of the great heroes of their past, often to the accompaniment of a drum and musical instrument.[1]

Jin Yong's stories are read and reread, played and replayed, adapted and readapted, discussed and debated in pop culture, as well as in institutes of higher learning nationwide and worldwide. Academic discourse, teaching classes on Jin Yong and martial arts fiction, and using Jin Yong's works for language and cultural instruction are institutional dimensions of cultural capital that complement the pop culture discourse of Jin Yong's work in the kungfu industrial complex.

Jin Yong's mid-twentieth-century martial arts fiction formed the basis for many "swordplay" television series and movies. The kungfu styles, characterizations, plot elements, and overall ethical/moral culture found in these novels are traceable at least as far back to Chinese fiction from the Ming Dynasty, particularly the novels *Three Kingdoms* and *Water Margin*. However, technological developments in film and television appear to have fortuitously coincided with the advent of New School Martial Arts Fiction and resulted in acceleration of the popular culture disseminated through such media after World War II. The stories, adaptations, songs, actors, and singers are set against a backdrop of the production and distribution systems for film in Asia in the era:

> Through the martial arts films, Mandarin cinema achieved what historian Stephen Teo has called "a kind of pan-Chinese internationalism" within the region. Swordplay films might be shot in Korea or Taiwan, while kung-fu movies might take place in Malaysia or Thailand (the locale of Lee's *Big Boss*). Martial artists and actors from Southeast Asia and Japan became stars in Hong Kong productions. By the early 1970s the Japanese had begun to cut back production and had fewer low-budget action pictures to export, so Hong Kong martial-arts movies faced little competition. To satisfy censorship regulations, kung-fu films circulated in three versions: the tamest cut went to Malaysia, Thailand, and Taiwan; a stronger one was made for Hong Kong; and the bloodiest version went to Europe and North America, where censorship was lenient.[2]

The films and television series classified as "kungfu" and *"wuxia"* in Chinese are separate genres which overlap in the kungfu industrial complex, especially in terms of the globalization of martial arts film where they are complementary and simultaneous manifestations of one another. Stephen Teo notes, "kung fu evolved out of *wuxia*."[3] *Wuxia* martial arts fiction, film, and television don't leave out or discount kungfu, but rather include kungfu martial skills alongside swordplay and the use of other weaponry, albeit often exaggerated with fantastical *wuxia* elements. Kungfu is an accepted globalized term, and eventually as the global audience becomes more kungfu culturally literate the term *wuxia* will come to be equally recognizable and will lose the italics. Separating the terms is useful, as Stephen Teo notes:

> Simply put, "'*wuxia*'" and "'kung fu'" are genre-specific terms, while "'martial arts'" is a generic term to refer to any type of motion picture containing martial arts action, mostly including the martial arts of China, Korea and Japan but also Thailand and other countries in Asia. It is perhaps more useful to consider the martial arts cinema as a movement, as Jubin Hu has done. As a movement rather than a genre, we can then see more clearly how it engenders the genres of *wuxia* and kung fu and influences other genre (such as the comedy and gangster film).[4]

The title of the present study includes both "kungfu" and "martial arts fiction" and is situated relative to pop culture in not just Hong Kong,

Taiwan, Mainland and overseas Chinese popular culture, but also the globalization of pop culture in general. My analysis follows the growth of Hong Kong kungfu pop culture on a trajectory from the serialization of Jin Yong (and other) martial arts fiction in newspapers, to adaptation of the stories into television and film, and then expansion to the West (globalization). This paradigm importantly incorporates the development of the stars, directors, action choreographers and other structural elements such as stunt wires into Hollywood, and thus extends to the consciousness of global viewing audiences. Petrus Liu suggests a classification of four types of film adaptations of Jin Yong works:

> In schematic terms, I'd say that there are four major renditions of Jin Yong: kungfu movies that emphasize actions and spectacles and often showcase actors who are real trained martial artists; *wuxia* movies that are more about fantasy and rely on wires, trampolines, and CGI; art-house productions such as *Ashes of Time* (*Dong Xie Xi Du*) which care for neither action nor historical fantasy; and finally, Hong Kong style slap-stick comedy, which uses Jin Yong stories for their cultural familiarity but does not actually care about kungfu at all, and often features a distinctively Hong Kong *wulitou* (slapstick) sense of humor, which is indebted to Jin Yong's writing and also distinct from Sammo Hung and Jackie Chan's [comedy].[5]

In each rendition, the films are vehicles of Jin Yong's stories, the stars are the vehicles of objectified cultural capital who market the films, and a virtuous circle promotes the films, stars, and stories. To a lesser extent in the popular imagination, because of relatively less visibility in the film and television final product, is the role of the directors, secondary cast, and crew. Further down the ladder are the training schools/companies who prepared the actors for the opportunities to launch their careers. Jin Yong's novels build up his cultural authority chapter by chapter, accumulating and transmitting cultural capital in Bourdieu's conception. At the first level, Jin Yong's cultural capital was enabled by the newspapers Zha Liangyong (Jin Yong's actual name) sold, which at times relied on his fiction installments to sell the daily paper. Cultural capital economic capital and are intricately and cyclically related. The adaption of his novels to film and television further facilitated Jin Yong's cultural authority, and the success of these economic endeavors further accrued commensurate social and political capital, which feeds back into the construction of cultural capital.

Jin Yong interacted with and was inspired by other writers of New School Martial Arts Fiction, and he drew from the deep well of Chinese culture to inform his narratives. As a creative writer he had many influences. But when Jin Yong's works were adapted to television and film a much larger circle of artistic and technical talents was brought into the creative enterprise, and hyperbolically increased the pace of construction of the kungfu industrial complex. Television and film adaptations enhanced Jin Yong's cultural capital and established other foci of cultural and economic authority via the actors, directors, cast, and crew involved in translating the novels to the screen. Derivative products from the novels and films, such as comics and computer games, as well as online discussion venues and academic critiques, broadened Jin Yong's economic and cultural impact, and thus his cultural capital and influence. This chapter widens the analysis of Jin Yong's works, characters, and tropes, to encompass their adaptation for film and television in construction of the kungfu industrial complex by sketching how the characters and stories resonate in pop culture via actors, directors and crews involved in production.

Many successful actors in Hong Kong film industry from the 1970s–1990s followed a typical career development path that included training in an acting, acrobatic or martial arts school, establishing one's onscreen cred through television series, film, and music performance, and then transition from status as contracted actor to actor doing contracting. Film studios came and went, as "half the Hong Kong movie companies operating in the early 1970s were out of business 10 years later,"[6] and it was the stars who remained the common denominator in the industry. Studios even relied on star power to "presell a yet nonexistent film" and then to fill seats in theaters.[7] It is notable that actors like Bruce Lee, Jackie Chan, Stephan Chow, and later the Taiwan music and entertainment phenomenon Jay Chou, expanded their skillsets to include choreography, writing and directing. These stars became big enough to negotiate contracts and start their own production companies. The symbiosis in the Hong Kong film and television industries between stars, studios, and the music world, was crucial not only to commercial success, but also played a significant role in the construction of Chinese popular cultural consciousness. Synergy extends beyond specific film and television series, linking the careers of individual stars in music, videos, and other media, such as product endorsements. This kind of capitalization on star power is popular in Chinese media, for example the many endorsements and advertisements by the *Yazhou tianwang* (Asian heavenly king) Jay Chou:

> Unlike in the West, celebrity endorsements are not seen as "selling out" but are actually a positive testament to star status—an endorsement or many means you have "made it." This positive association with brands and celebrity endorsements results in a ton of money being thrown around to celebrities and multiple questions and studies on how to measure the ROI on these investments. In addition, mega celebrities are playing the game well and are becoming saturated with endorsements. Jay Chou alone has, at some point, endorsed the following global brands, let alone the local brands, Pepsi,

Panasonic, Motorola, China Mobile, Colgate, World of Warcraft 3, National Geographic, Metersbonwe, Sprite, and Levis.[8]

The transnational trajectory for Chinese stars from Bruce Lee to Jackie Chan to Jay Chou, who in fact reprised Bruce Lee's original role of Kato alongside Seth Rogen in the Hollywood blockbuster, *The Green Hornet* (2011) is situated in the matrix of the kungfu industrial complex. As an example of kungfu star power lineage, Jay Chou's version of Kato pays homage to Lee, playing on Lee's star power in a scene where Chou pages through illustrations that he has drawn showing Bruce Lee in kungfu poses. Image, cultural capital, and cultural authority, time and place intangibly combine to form and cyclically reinforce "star power."

BRUCE LEE ON STAR POWER

Bruce Lee was a hands-on kungfu practitioner and performer who saw through the hype of the concept of star or superstar. He was simultaneously a thinker and recorder of his insights into the application of kungfu and a translator of kungfu into film. His writing on kungfu shows that he had the philosophical and intellectual capacity to translate physical knowledge/practice to mental contemplation and back. This same ability is demonstrated by his performance-oriented view of "star":

> Well, let me say this. First of all, the word "superstar" really turns me off and I'll tell you why because the word "star" man, it's an illusion. It's something what the public calls you. You should look upon oneself as an actor, man. I mean you would be very pleased if somebody said, "hey man, you are a super actor!" It is much better than, you know, superstar.[9]

Bruce Lee abstracts the star analogy from kungfu to acting and demands of himself the same high standard in acting as in his martial art. Ironically, the humbler he is as this quote indicates, the greater his myth, which coincides with the humility/greatness dichotomy that the greater one's kungfu, the more modest one is about it.

Despite the popular myth of "greatest kungfu master of all time," Bruce Lee was not invincible, and his fallibility opened space and time for intellectual development of his own views on martial arts philosophy. To wit, Bruce Lee developed his book on practical martial practice and theory while recuperating from a back injury for six months.[10] Written primarily in English and published posthumously in 1975 with the title *Tao of Jeet Kune Do*, this work is a compilation of his writings and notes which presents itself as a kind of catalog of maxims on Jeet Kune Do (*jie quan dao*; literally meaning "the way of the intercepting fist"). *Tao of Jeet Kune Do* is comprised of style entries imbued with Chinese philosophy, particularly Daoism and Zen Buddhism, as well as martial strategy relating directly to practical combat techniques. The text includes illustrations of Lee's notes in Chinese on the Wing Chun (*yong chun*) style that he distilled from his master, the famous Yip Man (Ye Wen). Yip Man is often referenced in connection with Lee, his most famous student, and also in connection with Donnie Yen who starred in at least four movies and a television series (2013) about the master. *Tao of Jeet Kune Do* also includes Lee's drawings of kungfu moves as well as a variety of acupressure points (a martial arts fiction mainstay) with notes in Chinese.

An example of the mixture of Daoist philosophy and practice can be seen in Lee's quote that begins the chapter "Tools": "Before I studied the art, a punch to me was just a punch, a kick was just a kick. After I'd studied the art, a punch was no longer a punch, a kick no longer a kick. Now that I understand the art, a punch is just a punch, a kick is just a kick."[11] The Daoist basis for Lee's consciously figured "applied kungfu" indicated by the "action-inaction" expressed in this quote helps explain the paradox in the dichotomy of modesty and stardom—that a philosophical dimension is inherent to this cycle. Bruce Lee is the breakout global example of a kungfu practitioner intricately enmeshed in the entertainment industry. He costarred as Kato in the *Green Hornet* television series in the 1966–1967 season and then made a handful of Hong Kong and Hollywood kungfu films that turned him into an international idol and sparked a global craze for Chinese kungfu. Lee was working on an idea similar to what became the television series *Kung Fu* (run on ABC, October 1972 to April 1975) starring David Carradine. There is evidence that suggests the idea was developed independently by Ed Spielman in New York in the mid-1960s, years earlier than Lee's 1970s conception on the West Coast.[12] Some scholars assert outright that Lee "was supposed to star" in the series.[13] The controversy continued posthumously as Linda Lee indicated that Lee was the originator, but Carradine got the role he intended for himself.[14] A 2018 biography seems to lay this to rest, demonstrating these were parallel phenomena.[15] The issues in this controversy are prescient given contemporary discourse regarding the casting actors of different ethnicities for Asian roles.

Bruce Lee is seemingly pragmatic about the situation as indicated in his interview on the Pierre Burton Show in 1971, which addresses the issue of casting directly and diplomatically, demonstrating a nuanced understanding of cultural tension between racism and business at the time, and indicating an improved situation in Hollywood in his recent history: "business wise, it's a risk. And I don't blame them, I don't blame them. I mean, in the same way, it's like in Hong Kong, if a foreigner came and became a star, if I were the man, the man with the money, I probably would have my own worry of whether or not the acceptance would be there."[16] Lee also indicates in this interview that the issue of what is currently known as Hollywood "whitewashing" had vastly improved over forty years. Such interviews and his historical relativistic view may have enhanced the later Bruce Lee myth as a pivotal figure at a crucial point in the globalization of the kungfu. Lee was grounded in the reality of the time, highly composed and articulate as this interview shows, both a practitioner and teacher, as well as an actor, and was connected to Hollywood through his martial arts students. These students included the script writer Stirling Silliphant and actor James Coburn, who provided him an avenue to work on films, including his choreography of fight scenes in a few movies written by Silliphant. *The Green Hornet* wetted the American public's appetite for kungfu, which then followed with the 1972–1975 Carradine television series.

The contemporaneous Bruce Lee films symbiotically created a global recognition of the kungfu phenomenon through the vehicle of Bruce Lee. Though Lee is not directly connected to Jin Yong's work through film or television, he is connected in popular culture through academic and popular critique of his performativity: "[W]atching" a fighting scene in Cha's [Jin Yong's] novels is like watching Jet Li or Jackie Chan taking on Bruce Lee; the latter is superior to the former by virtue of the swiftness and agility of movement characteristic of Chinese *kungfu*."[17] Although Jet Li and Jackie Chan's kungfu are excellent, the level of Lee's performance most closely approaches the kungfu feats Jin Yong describes in his novels by virtue of his unparalleled, nearly mythical speed and agility (despite the fact that Lee also incorporated flashy techniques such as high kicks for film appeal). Other kungfu competent stars don't hit or kick so fast that they needed to be slowed down for the film to capture the action, but Lee did, and this is what makes him comparable to Jin Yong's fictional characters in kungfu ability.

Kungfu cultural literacy depicted in reference to Jin Yong's texts find real life parallels in Bruce Lee's training (sect), sacred text (his own book of secrets published posthumously), modesty (the more modest, the greater one's kungfu), as well as discursive interaction with other kungfu stars, studios and directors, and name recognition (symbolic of kungfu supremacy—being number one in the martial world). Importantly, Bruce Lee set a standard for kungfu star power after his first movie, *The Big Boss* (1971), broke box office records in Hong Kong and he contemplated "becoming a truly independent movie star, working with both major studios and with other independents."[18] This kind of desire for independence from the film factory was not unique, though few actors had the star power to realize it. Two stars who did were Jackie Chan and Andy Lau, both of whom eventually set up their own companies. Bruce Lee's success in his martial arts philosophy and film are situated within kungfu cultural literacy that embraces both *wushu* and *wuxia*, as well as a long history of Chinese military strategy. The most prominent example of this is Bruce Lee's well-known idea to "be formless, shapeless, like water," which quotes almost directly from the "Weak Points and Strong" (*Xu shi pian*) chapter of Sunzi's classic on martial strategy, *The Art of War* (*Sunzi bingfa*). This concept is also replicated by Jin Yong in works like *Companion* where Linghu Chong learns from Feng Qingyang that "formlessness defeats form" (*wu zhao sheng you zhao*).[19] Jin Yong frequently references *The Art of War* and even more frequently both quotes and narratively demonstrates the use of the popular *Thirty-Six Strategems* throughout his works.

This chapter examines the role of "star power" in the construction of the kungfu industrial complex by analyzing the career trajectory of selected stars crucial to the adaptation of Jin Yong's works to film and television in the 1970s and 1980s in Hong Kong. Analysis begins with discussion of the Shaw Brothers Studio, which produced the Jin Yong film adaptations and established Hong Kong's Television Broadcasting Limited Company (TVB). TVB operated a training course for actors who got roles in film and television programs TVB was producing. Here many of the top Hong Kong stars started to establish their reputations, launching their careers by performing in period martial arts dramas adapted from Jin Yong's novels. There are numerous star trajectories worthy of discussion because of the sheer quantity of actors, studios, producers, directors, and action choreographers who worked on Jin Yong related productions from the 1980s to the 2000s. The Five Tiger Generals of TVB most fully represent the star power phenomenon in the kungfu industrial complex. This chapter addresses the issues of the Shaw Brothers Studio versus Golden Harvest; directors King Hu, Chang Cheh, Chor Yuen (Chu Yuan), and Liu Jialiang; action choreographers (turned director) Ching Siu-Tung and Yuen Woo-ping; female martial stars (Carina Lau, Brigitte Lin, Barbara Yung), and other more direct and indirect associations that piece by piece combine to construct the production dimension of the kungfu industrial complex.

Jin Yong's works are representative of the trajectory of kungfu cultural literacy in the popular consciousness, but only one of the many dimensions of the kungfu industrial complex. For example, competition between *wuxia* and kungfu film genres likely increases audience demand for both, which in turn increases incentive for productions to meeting that demand. Audience tastes are not static, nor are the creative and business talents of directors and producers, who came up with triad "gunfu" films, which utilized (or capitalized on) the martial arts codes already embedded in the popular imagination. As Fredric Dannen puts it, "The triads in John Woo movies are modern gun-toting versions of honorable Chinese swordsman."[20]

SHAW BROTHERS STUDIO

Until the establishment of Golden Harvest in 1970, the dominant film studio in the Hong Kong entertainment industry during this period was Shaw Brothers (HK) Limited (Shaoshi xiongdi [Xianggang] youxian gongsi). TVB was the television branch of this company. The stars had grueling schedules:

> Stars at the Shaw Studios were normally contracted on a 3, 5- or 8-year basis and would work 6-day weeks to keep within the schedules. As the success of Shaw's brought more money into Hong Kong cinema, they actually became the victims of their own success as stars looked to more relaxed studios who also offered more competitive packages, such as ex-Shaw Raymond Chow's Golden Harvest. As a result of this and increasing issues surrounding piracy, the Shaw Studios in Hong Kong ceased operation in 1983 as a filmmaker to focus on TV production.[21]

Competition and piracy caused Shaw Brothers to shift its focus, whereupon it "sold its storied Movie Town backlot to its own subsidiary, TVB, which promptly renamed it TVB City and put it to work cranking out episodic soaps and swordsman dramas."[22] One measure of the popularity and impact of Jin Yong and other martial arts television series and movies that constitute the kungfu industrial complex is found in statistics of the overall number of productions, audiences/box office, proportion of the totals, the reissues, the numbers and frequency of new editions, as well as the spin-off products (vcds, DVDs, music, star interviews, product endorsements, etc.). Some general statistics are available, but most must be inferred and interpreted given conflicting data. The internet offers the tools to obtain an idea of the general trends because of the increasing availability of information, but the records are inevitably imperfect and should be used as qualitative indicators.

Hong Kong Shaw Brothers Studio and their subsidiaries, TVB and TVBI, were the focal points of martial arts television and movies from the 1960s thru the 1980s. The 1990s saw a gradual shift to mainland Chinese productions of martial arts features. Attendant with this shift is the production of new television adaptations of Jin Yong's works in the Mainland. The works of New School Martial Arts Fiction masters Gu Long and Liang Yusheng were also adapted to television series, but Jin Yong's works where more likely to be adapted repeatedly. While Gu Long's individual novels have many film adaptations, only five of his works have received multiple television adaptations.[23] The works of Liang Yusheng that have been adapted multiple times to television are also limited in comparison with Jin Yong's. One particularly prominent exception is the six television and three film adaptations of Liang Yusheng's *Bai fa mo nü zhuan* (The legend of the white-haired demoness).

Popular culture trends as mainland China opened to the West (and Hong Kong) during the 1980s openly embraced a triumvirate of imported popular culture from the Chinese diaspora. This specifically includes Jin Yong's martial arts novels, Qiong Yao's romance fiction, and Deng Lijun's songs.[24] Jin Yong's books had not been available in Maoist era mainland China, where politics tightly controlled cultural production, especially during the Cultural Revolution when Jin Yong was actively writing many of his masterpieces. Chinese audiences started reading Jin Yong's works in the 1980s in pirated editions. Jackie Chan's films were a fourth dimension of the massive importation of "Gang-Tai" (Hong Kong and Taiwanese) pop culture of this period. The Mainland "pop culture craze" during the final decades of the twentieth century stands in stark contrast to the earlier decades when Chinese politics was dominated by forces leading to the tragedies of the Great Leap Forward and the Cultural Revolution. It is notable that the Chinese pop culture juggernaut was being constructed in Hong Kong and Taiwan just when China was most sealed off.

Shaw Brothers Studio was one of the central industries crucial to this explosion of film and television pop culture. Shaw Brothers adapted many of Jin Yong's works to film and television, as well as those of Gu Long and Liang Yusheng. Statistics may be inferred from a variety of sources. For example, the Shaw Studio website states it produced 1,000 films from the 1950s to the 1980s,[25] which seems to be a generous rounding up, given other sources that cite 800 in the Shaw Brothers library.[26] TMDB movie database lists the number at 750 films.[27] Baidu lists 728 Shaw Brothers films.[28] Drilling down to kungfu, one list contains 341 Shaw Brothers produced martial arts films,[29] and another list contains 259 martial arts films.[30] These numbers indicate that martial arts films compose roughly 30–40 percent of Shaw Brothers total film production.

Of the four main directors of Shaw Brothers Studio, three are intimately related to the adaptation of martial arts novels. King Hu (Hu Jinquan) and Chang Cheh established the trend of the "New School Martial Arts Film."[31] Chor Yuen was the top director of Hong Kong and Taiwan film and worked on the most adaptations of Gu Long's martial arts novels.[32] Shaw Brothers Studio produced twenty-one films of Jin

Yong's works from 1967 to 1984, and then moved away from film and into television production. These films represent about three percent of a total of the approximately 750 films made by Shaw Brothers. It is more difficult to verify an accurate statistical measure of the percentage of martial arts films produced in this period because the titles do not always reflect the content, but if 30–40 percent of Shaw Brothers films were martial arts films, then these twenty-one films represent between seven and nine percent of Shaw Brothers martial arts films in total.

OVERVIEW OF KUNGFU FILM TRENDS

Shaw Brothers was the dominant force in Chinese film in the 1960s, 1970s, and 1980s, producing high production value Mandarin language films, with important competition from the Cathay Film Company (originally named "Motion Picture and General Investment Company) in the 1950s and 1960s.[33] Shaw Brothers stood alone when Cathay shut down in 1970, but around the same time Shaw Brothers' executives Raymond Chow (Zou Wenhuai) and Leonard Ho (He Guanchang) departed to found Orange Sky Golden Harvest Entertainment Co., Limited (*Cheng tian jiahe yule jituan youxian gongsi*; or simply Golden Harvest). Golden Harvest utilized the Cathay production studio and distribution system.[34] This departure created significant competition for Shaw Brothers in the Hong Kong film industry as Chow produced kungfu film hits by Bruce Lee and Jackie Chan, to name the most visible.

Golden Harvest's focus on kungfu film stood in contrast to Shaw Brothers continuation relative concentration on *wuxia* martial arts film productions, and it's timing favorably coincided with Bruce Lee's emergence. Golden Harvest even made the first coproduction between a Hollywood and Hong Kong studio, Bruce Lee's *Enter the Dragon* (*Long zheng hu dou*, 1973).[35] Golden Harvest quickly came to dominate the film industry, and in the early 1980s Shaw Brothers discontinued film production to focus on television. Kungfu film was strong into the mid-1970s, and even after Bruce Lee's death stars Jackie Chan and Sammo Hung continued kungfu film strength with the addition of comedy to the genre.[36] The 1980s and 1990s saw the rise of gangster/triad films replete with fists and guns that reenacted *wuxia* martial codes in this modernized form. The generalized kungfu "fist" versus *wuxia* "sword" subgenre bifurcation (always a mixture in *wuxia* film) still held qualitatively until 1990, when an apparent *wuxia* resurgence brought back swordplay in the Jin Yong derivative *Swordsman* trilogy filmed by Ching Siu-Tung (1990, 1992, 1993). *Wuxia*'s enduring appeal was then internationalized with the global phenomenon of *Crouching Tiger, Hidden Dragon* (2000).

The Hong Kong film industry was extremely dynamic. Martial arts ideological structures and values from *wuxia* fiction were continued in gangster/triad films which replicated the brotherhood aspects of the *jianghu* martial world in a modern setting. This is exemplified by John Woo's films such as *A Better Tomorrow* (*Yingxiong bense*, 1986), starring Chow Yun-fat, Leslie Cheung, and Ti Long, which "reinvented the gangster genre . . . by combining elements from Hollywood Westerns and Chinese swordplay movies."[37] Creation of the terms "gunfu"[38] and the related "wirefu"[39] testifies to both the linguistic and kungfu continuity between these subgenres in English film terminology. The *wuxia* swordplay films are a site where the kungfu "fist" and sword dimensions first merged, to be separated in the 1970s and 1980s as the pendulum swung toward Bruce Lee and Jackie Chan's more realistic kungfu, and then merged again in the 1990s and 2000s. Kungfu action movies maintained their appeal into the new millennium, and the *wuxia* megastars Andy Lau and Tony Leung, among others, easily translated their kungfu acting to the gangster and detective genres, scoring significant hits such as the movie *Infernal Affairs* (*Wu jian dao*, 2002) and its two sequels in 2003. Both Lau and Leung continue to shoot martial arts action films in the twenty-first century. Andy Lau's legacy of includes *Shaolin* (2011) and director Zhang Yimou's China-Hollywood coproduction, *The Great Wall* (2016) which also stars Matt Damon. Tony Leung's martial arts legacy includes *Red Cliff* (*Chi bi*, 2008 & 2009) and *The Grandmaster* (*Yi dai zongshi*, 2013), in which he played Ip Man opposite top female star Zhang Ziyi of *Crouching Tiger, Hidden Dragon*.

The primary elements that differentiate kungfu and *wuxia* in martial arts film discourse is relatively more realistic kungfu "fists and feet" versus fantastical "*wuxia* swords and *qi*." This is an important distinction in terms of style and substance, but the difference becomes increasingly relevant as movie trends develop from the period costume drama set in an unspecified dynastic (or early Republican) period to the more modern era of the mid-to-late twentieth century. The *wuxia* swordplay film was core to Shaw Brothers films in the 1960s and 1970s, and kungfu fist and feet began hold sway with the rise of Golden Harvest and Bruce Lee in the 1970s.

Advocates of kungfu film often oppose the fantastical nature of *wuxia* film because it lacks realism. The relative sense of realism with kungfu coincidentally translated better to the sensibilities of Hollywood action film and modern detective films of the late twentieth century. An implied time sensitivity to the aesthetics of reception informs tensions in the marketplace. At the turn of the twenty-first century, Hollywood action films seem to finally embrace *wuxia* film sword and *qi*, perhaps initially being conditioned by the *Star Wars* series introduction of "the force" throughout the 1980s and eventual innovations in digital technology that allowed fantastical elements to be seamlessly, if not always subtly, integrated into the realm that previously required an even greater suspension of disbelief.

Kungfu film choreography is not weapons free. Jackie Chan uses all manner of weapons, including the traditional broadsword and staff. It is nearly a trademark of his to use household items or whatever is at hand in his fight scenes. Conversely, many Jin Yong's *wuxia* characters also utilize fists and feet, and ordinary items as weapons, including the embroidery needle (*Wanderer*), the fishing pole (*Semi-Devils*), a coolie carrying rod (*Semi-Devils*), an official's writing brush (*Wanderer*), the zither (*Wanderer*), and the flute (*Book and Sword*) or just handy furniture (*Heroes*). In addition, Jin Yong's heroes employ throwing weapons (*anqi*) that vary from chopsticks to coins to stones, as well as more conventional items such as darts and knives. Jin Yong depicts sword-like *qi* emanating from fingers that never touch the enemy (*Semi-Devils*) or from the zither (*Wanderer*), or in connection with *neigong* internal energy (*Heroes*). When kungfu crosses to Hollywood, emphasis also focuses on the practice of *qi*, for example in *Kill Bill* where kungfu master Gordon Liu teaches Beatrix Kiddo to punch through wood and stone, or the light body kungfu *qinggong* of Neo and Trinity flying in *The Matrix*. It is an easy step to see that *qi* and *qinggong* are the basis of Jackie Chan's gymnastic parkour feats, which connect the imaginary and real realms of wirefu-enhanced *wuxia* movies and well-practiced stunts of his Jackie Chan Stunt Team.

TVB TELEVISION SERIES ADAPTATIONS OF JIN YONG NOVELS

TVB had a virtual television monopoly in Hong Kong except for the short-lived *Jiayi dianshi* (Commercial Television), which had a three-year lifespan from 1975 through 1978.[40] In 1976 TVB produced a sixty-episode adaptation of Jin Yong's first martial arts novel, *Book and Sword*, starring Zheng Shaoqiu (a.k.a. Adam Cheng). Zheng also starred in TVB's twenty-five-episode adaptation of Jin Yong's *Dragon Sabre* (1978), as well as TVB's sixty-five-episode adaptation of Gu Long's *Chu Liu Xiang* (1979), among other *wuxia* television adaptations.[41]

Television adaptations of Jin Yong works outnumber movie adaptations, employ even more stars, and are even more important to the kungfu industrial complex because of the time they occupied on the airways. These television dramas generally consist of between twenty and sixty episodes, are played and replayed over a long time period, and thus reached an immense viewing audience. Shaw Brothers television branches produced and programmed most adaptations of Jin Yong related works from its studios in Hong Kong through subsidiaries

TVB (established 1967) and TVBI Company Limited (established 1976)[42] as well as several other subsidiary entities. Mainland Chinese television productions of Jin Yong related works started in the 2000s and continue through the 2010s. The impact of TVB adaptations on the careers of actors who starred on them was great, like a catalyst that deepened the popular consciousness of kungfu with a multiplier-like affect.

THE FIVE TIGER GENERALS OF TVB

The sentient example of the symbiosis of Hong Kong television and movie worlds during the 1970s and 1980s is the "Five Tigers of TVB" (*wuxian wu hu*),[43] typically shortened to the "Five Tigers." Their appellations mirror the family-like hierarchy of martial arts sects: "big brother" (*laoda*) Michael Miu (Miao Qiaowei), "second brother" (*erdi*) Kent Tong (Tang Zhenye), "old third" (*laosan*) Felix Wong (Huang Rihua), "fourth brother" (*sige*) Andy Lau, and "little brother" (*xiaodi*) Tony Leung Chiu-Wai. Originating in Hong Kong, where both Cantonese and English are the local language, each of these stars has an English given name. Moreover, their Chinese names each have a different Mandarin pronunciation, thus a different Romanized spelling in English. The English given name is commonly paired with the Cantonese surname when writing in English.

The term "Five Tigers" was invented as a marketing tactic used to advertise a 1983 episode of a variety television program, called *All-star Challenge* (*Xingguang yiyi jingzheng hui*), in which they costarred.[44] These five actors represent what has been called the "golden era" of Hong Kong drama in the 1980s.[45] They all played important roles for TVB throughout the 1980s and all found significant success though their careers trajectories varied. The Five Tigers' success is initially tied to their Jin Yong connection, as a 2007 online entertainment news article indicates:

> In the short span of five years the Five Tigers replaced Adam Cheng and Chow Yun-fat's status in television circles. TVB produced and reproduced all of Jin Yong's long martial arts novels, the most important among them broadcast in these five years. *Heroes* (1983), *Companion* (1983), *Semi-Devils* (1982), and *Cauldron* (1984) were all done by the Five Tigers. Felix Wong and Tony Leung also played the leads in *Royal Sword*, *Dragon Sabre*, and *Ode to Gallantry*. The 1985 *Flying Fox* was originally set for Andy Lau as the lead, but because he refused a five-year contract, the lead was changed to Rui Lui (Lü Liangwei). That is to say, this was the era in which TVB was still the main production power in martial arts television series and it can be said that the Five Tigers had all the important roles.[46]

Felix Wong had roles in many movies, but his television and film credits demonstrate that he played in about twice as many television series as films and can be considered primarily a television star.[47] In contrast, the youngest two tigers, Andy Lau and Tony Leung, became megastars in Asia and familiar to the worldwide Chinese speaking diaspora over the last two decades of the twentieth century and into the twenty-first century. Lau and Leung also became familiar to international audiences at the start of the twenty-first century through the kungfu masterpieces *Hero* (2002) and *House of Flying Daggers* (2004).

The TVB actors training course (*Wuxian dianshi yiyuan peixun ban*) was established in 1971 and produced the Five Tigers in various cohorts (Kent Tong, 1979; Michael Miu & Felix Wong, 1980; Andy Lau, 1981; Tony Leung, 1982).[48] The Five Tigers may have been the most visible faces of martial arts adaptations in television and film, but they were not alone in the promotion and construction of kungfu culture. Other alumni of this training program include kungfu film and television stars Chow Yun-fat (1974), Ng Man Tat (Wu Mengda, 1974), Rui Lui (1977), Tony Leung Ka-fai (Liang Jiahui, 1981), Stephen Chow (1982), Carina Lau (Liu Jialing, 1983), Aaron Kwok (Guo Fucheng, 1984), Ekin Cheng (Zheng Yijian, 1987), and Donnie Yen (Zhen Zidan, 1989). All of these stars are linked to important kungfu films or to Jin Yong television series, or both.[49]

It was common in the TVB series to have one or more brother tigers in costarring or supporting martial arts roles. For example, the 1983 adaptation of Jin Yong's *Heroes* included eldest tiger brother, Michael Miu, costarring as antagonist Yang Kang opposite protagonist Felix Wong as Guo Jing. These same two tiger brothers starred in the 1985 TVB adaptation of Jin Yong's *Royal Blood*. Other brothers played opposite one another as well. Second tiger, Kent Tong, starred as Dali prince Duan Yu in the 1982 TVB adaptation of Jin Yong's *Semi-Devils* with Felix Wong's portrayal of the coprotagonist Xu Zhu, a young Shaolin monk, while Liang Jiaren[50] played the Beggar Gang leader Xiao Feng, and little tiger brother Tony Leung had a role as an extra.[51] Michael Miu also played the second male role in the TVB 1985 *Royal Blood* adaptation and had the title role in two of Gu Long's novels on the hero Chu Liuxiang. Miu played the role of Huang Yaoshi in the latest 2017 adaptation of *Heroes*, some thirty-four years after his original role as Yang Kang in 1983. It seems ironic that Miu played the father of the character (Huang Rong) in 2017 who was responsible for the death of the character (Yang Kang) he played in 1983. The works of Jin Yong are typically of such epic length and of such sustained popularity (generating remake after remake) that a star such as Michael Miu could reprise the role of one of the middle-aged characters later in life.

Third brother Felix Wong starred in more Jin Yong roles than his tiger brothers—five television adaptations from 1982 to 1999. He also starred in two Jin Yong movie adaptations and one spin-off prequel. Spin-offs are a common phenomenon, for example TVB's spin-off *Jian mo Dugu Qiubai* (Demon swordsman Dugu Qiubai, 1990) which creates the story of a swordsman whose technique is crucial to *Wanderer* and *Companion*.[52] Felix Wong's most significant role was as archetypical protagonist Guo Jing in the 1983 adaptation of *Heroes*, which costarred Barbara Yung as Huang Rong. While there have been at least nine adaptations of this *Heroes* to date, the Felix Wong/Barbara Yung version is still most memorable. This is perhaps due to its timing, coming out in 1983, not long after China opened to the outside world. A 2017 online article notes, "Frankly speaking, he still relies upon the classic character 'Guo Jing' to make a living in China because the Chinese audience has an extremely deep impression of this character."[53] Recall that mainland Chinese readers started having access to Jin Yong's works as early as the 1981[54] and a popular literature craze was in process by 1984–1985 even though the first authorized collected works of Jin Yong didn't appear until 1994.[55] It is reported that mainland Chinese readers had bought forty million volumes of Jin Yong's fiction in 1985 alone,[56] ample proof of the industrial-sized impact of Jin Yong works.

Note the neat coincidence of tiger brothers Kent Tong and Felix Wong playing roles in *Semi-Devils* in which they became sworn brothers. The relationship between students in the fictional martial arts schools/sects/temples in this important respect parallels the hierarchical working/acting "brotherhood" of the TVB training school.[57] Literary etymology of these brotherhood ideas is traces at least as far back as Ming fiction, specifically from the Peach Garden Oath in the Ming *Three Kingdoms*. In fact, the term "Five Tiger Generals" itself is found in the Ming novels *Three Kingdoms*[58] and *Water Margin*,[59] and it was also used as the name of a TVB series, *Wu hu jiang* (with the odd English title translation: "The Rise & Fall of a Stand-In")," which ran from 1986 to 1992 starring the two eldest of the Five Tigers, Michael Miu and Kent Tong.[60]

Kent Tong also had a minor part in the 1983 TVB adaptation of *Companion*, playing the Mongol Prince Huo Du next to fourth tiger Andy Lau's portrayal of protagonist Yang Guo.[61] The two most renowned of the Five Tigers are Andy Lau and Tony Leung. Fourth tiger Lau played the Qing Emperor Kang Xi in the 1984 TVB production of *Cauldron* opposite fifth tiger brother Tony Leung in the lead role of Wei Xiaobao. Lau and Leung's *Cauldron* is perhaps the most memorable and durable of early performances because of the exceptional on-screen chemistry between these two actors. They seem to actually like each other despite reports of conflict off screen regarding contract negotiations (which coincidentally mirrors the tension between their characters).

Figure 4.1. Tony Leung as Wei Xiaobao and Andy Lau as Emperor Kang Xi in television adaptation of *Cauldron* (1984), Episode 10

Their amity perhaps facilitates the ease of suspension of disbelief that creates room for the audience to accept the historically and socially unlikely prospect of friendship between an emperor and the son of a prostitute. Significantly, Jin Yong has endorsed this adaptation noting, "Of my novels that have been adapted into television series, I am most satisfied with Andy Lau and Tony Leung's *Cauldron*."[62] The Five Tigers have had varying degrees of success in their film and television careers, in particular Andy Lau who also became a singing superstar as well as movie superstar.

The Five Tigers of TVB are important nodes at the interstices of the matrix of the kungfu industrial complex. Their career trajectories corresponded with development of the Hong Kong entertainment business in the early 1980s and resonated for the next three decades. These five stars intersect directly with nearly all the other top and secondary stars, as well as directors, action directors, and crew in television, film, and music. Golden Harvest films which became dominant in the 1980s sometimes had common cast and crew as those in the TVB productions. In addition to Jin Yong television series, four of the Five Tigers also acted in fellow writer Gu Long's martial arts fiction television and/or adaptations.

The five-year contract period from 1980 to 1985 is important in the overall construction of the Five Tigers' celebrity images, setting the stage for their future success. However, "a high level TVB official's insider account revealed that the "Five Tiger Generals" toiled laboriously in the TVB system of high output factory style productions but didn't make much money."[63] This led to tensions among them as recognized that such multiyear contracts depressed their earnings.[64] Pirating of movies in the 1980s and contract tensions with their successful new stars, the Five Tigers, indicates a significant level of turmoil at TVB. For its part, TVB reportedly adopted the strategy of divide and conquer, resigning Leung, who appeared to be the weakest link in the union of brothers, to the chagrin of Lau and the others:

> Andy Lau, who always was simple and valued friendship, was pursued by many film companies at the time, but he basically set out with idea of "one for all" and knew that the other "tigers" also wanted to find a way out. So, he helped to contact other film companies. Higher levels at TVB of course knew about the secret revolt of the "Five Tigers," and were afraid of the effect of the five popular youngsters leaving the nest all at once, so quietly unfolded a battle to divide and conquer the Five Tigers. TVB attacked them one by one with contract talks in hopes of suppressing their revolt. According to a TVB producer, the poor young Tony Leung had a family to feed and was always careful and conservative, low key and not argumentative, with very few friends. So TVB focused on re-signing him, constantly urging him to be first to re-sign. Thus, the "revolution" of the Five Tigers collapsed. Lau

wouldn't submit and sign, so was immediately frozen out by TVB for a year. Moreover, even the promotion of albums they were originally going to do for him was suspended.[65]

The exact timing of these actions is not completely clear and such entertainment webpages may have dramatized events in retrospect trying to explain dynamics from earlier years. However, the break occurred about the time that Lau and Leung were in selection for *Cauldron*. There is indication that Leung was selected instead of Lau for the lead part of Wei Xiaobao because of the contract issue. Lau was made costar instead, playing Emperor Kang Xi: "In 1984, because of a conflict with TVB, TVB changed the male leading part for *Cauldron* from Lau to Leung, making Leung popular."[66]

This schism indicates a pivotal point in Andy Lau and Tony Leung's cultural capital. Leung's popularity increased with his role as Wei Xiaobao and with it came an increase in his cultural capital at the expense of Lau who played second lead. Here is an example of two agents in competition describing the dynamics of the field of cultural production in Bourdieu's terms. The actors have embodied cultural capital that informs their portrayal of the Jin Yong roles. In addition, their portrayal of those characters becomes iconic, in other words they themselves becomes the objectified cultural capital of the Jin Yong roles. The synergy of these two aspects of cultural capital contributes to the star power measured by "popularity" and viewership, increasing their social capital, which should lead to additional roles and remuneration (economic capital). TVB attempted to assert control over the careers of all Five Tigers by divide and conquer using economic leverage on Leung. Leung may have not earned as much for this role if he hadn't caved, but what he lost in remuneration was compensated by an increase in cultural capital for having played the main role. Lau would not budge, perhaps sensing his cultural and social capital (measuring his star power) was already sufficient to branch out into other areas of production like film and music. For his part, Lau says "I just wanted to get away . . . I want to make two movies a year, and they want me to keep on doing the TV series the rest of my life."[67] Lau's contract issues with TVB in this timeframe may have had an impact on his movement into the music world.

In 1985, Lau dropped his first album, which was well received, and he went on to make many more. During the early 1990s "tide of idolization" the media labeled him as one of the "Four Heavenly Kings" of Hong Kong music. While Leung also cut albums,[68] it was nowhere near the scale of Lau, who became a sensation in the music world. Martial arts roles were a reliable channel for Leung, who had played an extra in *Semi-Devils* (1982) and starred in *Cauldron* (1984). He played starring roles in two other Jin

Yong adaptations—the 1986 version of *Dragon Sabre* and the 1988 production of *Ode to Gallantry*. Besides Jin Yong novel adaptations, Leung also played in a 1988 TVB adaptation of Gu Long's renowned *wuxia* martial arts drama, *The Legendary Twins* (*Juedai shuang jiao*). Interestingly, Lau played in a film adaptation of the same novel in 1992 with Brigitte Lin and Sharla Cheung (Zhang Min) costarring.[69]

Tony Leung's portrayal of Wei Xiaobao in *Cauldron* opposite Lau's character Kang Xi in 1984 kicked off his "reign" period on screen.[70] And this was not the last time Leung played this same seminal Jin Yong character. To wit, in 1993 he also played Wei Xiaobao in a time displacement movie spin-off called *Hero from Beyond the Boundary of Time* (*Zheng pai Wei Xiaobao zhi fengzhi gounü*). This is a comedy where his character Wei Xiaobao time travels to 1990s Hong Kong.[71] The extrapolation of a Jin Yong character across decades (from novel to movie) and centuries (from the Qing dynasty to modern day Hong Kong) demonstrates the synergy of the novel, the character, and Tony Leung's cultural capital—all are linked through the ubiquitously recognizable character Wei Xiaobao and rely on the kungfu cultural literacy of the audience to interpret the new twists and turns in a modern setting on the way to the box office. In this case, the spin-off earned 54 million *renminbi* (approximately US$6.65 million) on a production cost of four million *renminbi*, a remarkable success.[72]

Kungfu cultural literacy here plays on the audience's identification of the character and characteristics of Wei Xiaobao in Leung's original reprisal, and moreover a curiosity of how the same character and star navigate time and space displacement. The official English translation of the movie's title, *Hero from Beyond the Boundary of Time* bears little relation to the Chinese title, which literally translates "the authentic Wei Xiaobao receives the imperial edict to seduce women." I argue that the kungfu culturally literate audience was sufficiently familiar with the character Wei Xiaobao to be curious about how his Qing dynasty love life, which included seven wives, would translate to a modern setting. Much comedy ensues as two of his wives from the novel come to modern Hong Kong to search for him. I suggest that Leung's embodied and objectified cultural capital through previous portrayal of Wei Xiaobao in 1984 factored heavily in the success of this movie ten years later, which would probably have had lower box office revenue without interest in how he would reprise the role.

Around this time, Leung also played the role of "Western Venom" Ouyang Feng in a spin-off film parody of *Heroes* titled *The Eagle-Shooting Heroes: Eastern and Western Accomplishments* (*She diao yingxiong zhuan zhi dong cheng xi jiu*, 1993). This movie has little relationship to the Jin Yong original besides the title and names of some characters. It was shot with the cast and crew of Wong Kar-wei's film, *Ashes of Time* (*Dong Xie Xi Du*, 1994), in which Leung played the Blind Martial Artist. *Ashes of Time* is a stylized art house prequel to *Heroes* borrowing its title and main characters from Jin Yong's novel. Those characters are virtually unrecognizable beyond name and place references. The details of *Ashes of Time* are discussed in a separate section of this chapter below. At this juncture it is sufficient to note that the movie ends with narration stating the fates of Jin Yong characters Hong Qigong, Huang Yaoshi and Ouyang Feng, putting them squarely into position to take up their roles in Jin Yong's novel, thus clearly validating a reading of the film as a "prequel" with many qualifications.

These selected television and film examples demonstrate the dynamics of star power in the kungfu industrial complex as novel is translated to television to film by vehicle of the actor, who draws upon familiarity with the character(s) and plots, or consciously studies the novel and previous adaptations to obtain such familiarity as the documentary on the production of the 1983 edition of *Cauldron* show. This familiarity facilitates the interpretation or (re)interpretation of the role and the construction of further "knowledge" about the character(s) and plot, perhaps even transferred to a non-Jin Yong written or related setting. New adaptations and even spin-offs capitalize on the actors' cultural capital and further build upon star power, which results in a virtuous cycle of construction of cultural capital, extending the "lives" of Jin Yong characters through the careers of stars who reifying them.

The kungfu cultural complex is a dynamic process of replication, reification, construction, and reconstruction. Star power (cultural and social capital that contribute to economic capital) hinges on the role and the actor. Cultural capital may have helped stars get their Jin Yong roles, but Jin Yong roles in turn sustained or even enhanced their cultural, social, and economic capital. Time displacement adds a creative twist transporting both the character and actor into different contexts, which then relies on the audience's cultural capital for successful interpretation. Time displacement can also work on the level of the film itself. Wong Kar-wai's 1994 *Ashes of Time* was given a redux in 2008, insinuating its previous fifteen years of popular and critical interpretive discourse to earn box office, while at the same time also reminding the audience of the original cast and their characters, thus informing and broadening the kungfu industrial complex.

ANDY LAU'S SYNERGY OF STAR POWER: THE KUNGFU INDUSTRIAL COMPLEX IN ACTION

Leung and Lau worked together in the *Infernal Affairs* film trilogy (2002–2003) in which Leung won the primary film awards.[73] Lau was codirector. Although Leung apparently achieved greater success in the movies and television series in which he played opposite Lau, over the two decades it was Lau who earned more box office revenue, outpacing both Stephen Chow and Jackie Chan from 1985 to 2005 in Hong Kong.[74]

The dual role of singer/actor is a defining feature of Hong Kong entertainment industry. Cultural capital earned in each dimension of their work contributes to their public persona (popularity and star power). The actor is first "educated" through a training school, gains roles and recognition in connection to those roles, and repeats the process as new roles provide additional "training," as it were. Playing Jin Yong roles adds a dimension to the cultural capital of the star because the roles are sufficiently well known among the audience that they have a cache of their own. Being type-cast is a double-edged sword for any actor, but the Hong Kong pop star has numerous outlets to maintain and enhance their career. It is common to find actors in Hong Kong, Taiwan, and increasingly mainland China with singing careers, some even singing the theme songs for their own television series or movies. Star power is enhanced in a virtuous cycle through trans-genre relationships in the kungfu industrial complex. Perhaps the most prominent example is Andy Lau's ranking as the single most recognizable Asian singing sensation of the 1980s and 1990s as one of the "Four Heavenly Kings" (*Si da tian wang*) of Cantopop/Mandopop, along with Jacky Cheung, Aaron Kwok, and Leon Lai. Having a nominal grouping such as the "Four Heavenly Kings" is part of a machinery of star marketing in which the media groups stars by associations and creates such appellations. Numeration parallels other of Jin Yong's grouping nomenclature, for example "The Four Great Evildoers" noted in chapter 3. Such linguistic groupings are common in Chinese. The "Four Heavenly Kings," for example, are originally protective deities in Buddhist temples, the opening up of China to import of the "four great populars" (which specifically included Jin Yong's works).[75] Groupings of four martial artists in Jin Yong works prominently include those connected to the cardinal directions, "Eastern Heritic, Western Venom, Northern Beggar, Southern Emperor" (*Dong Xie, Xi Du, Bei Gai, Nan Di*),[76] the "Four Ghosts of the Yellow River" (*Huanghe si gui*) in *Heroes*, and other secondary characters. Such numerology with respect to the kungfu industrial complex ties Jin Yong and his characters to pop culture phenomena past and present and reifies the deep roots of "star power" in contemporary cultural capital.

The synergy between Lau's television, movie and singing careers can be considered an archetypical example of star power in the construction and maintenance of the actor/idol pillar of the kungfu industrial complex. His television success noted above was directly related to the 1983 TVB adaptation of Jin Yong's *Companion* (a.k.a. *The Return of Condor Heroes*):

No matter how many variations of *The Return of Condor Heroes* Andy Lau has made in his acting career, or how many editions different Asian TV stations have produced, none can replace the 1983 TVB version in fans' mind. Andy Lau and Idy Chan have also been crowned as the most legendary Yeung Gor [Yang Guo] and Dragon Girl [Xiaolongnü] forever.[77]

In addition, the start of Lau's *music* career appears to be inextricably related to Jin Yong's novel by virtue of a test singing performance in costume at the Miss Hong Kong Pageant:

> There is indeed a story behind the selection of Andy Lau as Yeung Gor [Yang Guo]. When TVB decided to make *The Return of the Condor Heroes*, Idy Chan was already chosen to be Dragon Girl [Xiaolongnü]. However, producer Siu Sang had no clue whom to choose for the male lead. At that time, another TVB producer Lee Tim Shing, who worked with Andy Lau in the drama *Emissary* (1982) and saw his potential, recommended Andy Lau to Siu Sang. Siu Sang hesitated as Andy Lau had never tried any roles in ancient costume before, but he thought of a way to test audience acceptance. He arranged for Andy Lau to perform dressed in ancient costume at the Miss Hong Kong Pageant Contest in 1983. Positive feedback finally brought Andy Lau the chance to play this classic role, and his song performance at the show aroused the interest of Capital Artists Record Company, paving the way for Andy Lau to become a singer later.[78]

Lau had trained under the eminent singing instructor Dai Sicong since 1982, and his first album, *Zhi zhidao cike ai ni* (I Only Know that at this Moment I Love You), was cut in 1985.[79] Dai Sicong also trained Aaron Kwok and Leon Lai, as well as other well-known singers/actors such as Anita Mui (Mei Yanfeng). In addition, this instructor's trainees include all the Five Tigers and Barbara Yung, who played Huang Rong in the iconic 1983 TVB adaptation of Jin Yong's *Heroes*.

In addition to more than one hundred and sixty movies,[80] Andy Lau has recorded seventy-nine albums since 1985, not counting greatest hit compilations, concert compilations, and music video compilations.[81] He writes lyrics for many of his songs and also occasionally composes the music, currently having about one hundred and eighty credits for his lyrics,[82] including numerous movie and advertisement theme songs.[83] For example, Lau wrote the lyrics and sang the theme song "Zhen ai shi ku wei" (True love is bitter) for the 2003 animated version of Jin Yong's *Companion* although he turned down the request to dub the main character Yang Guo's voice (he had performed the role of Yang Guo in the 1983 TVB edition).[84] Moreover, Lau kept his connection to this animated version of *Companion* produced twenty years after the original:

> This animated edition is the tenth time *The Giant Eagle and Its Companion* has been adapted. The year TVB made Andy Lau and Idy Chan's *Companion*, it

was extraordinarily hot property in Hong Kong, and is the most popular of the adaptations because the male and female leads' appearance meshed well, and the script was faithful to the original. This time the cartoon edition is also faithful to the original work, and much of the script even maintains the original appearance of the novel. The producers even invited Andy Lau, the "Yang Guo" of old, to dub the cartoon Yang Guo. But because he didn't have the time in the end Andy Lau agreed to sing the theme song for the second and third parts. When *Companion* came to TVB for broadcast, Andy Lao also personally did the calligraphy for the two [title] characters, "*Shen Diao.*"[85]

Here the musical dimension of Lau's career meshes with his old television role and is supplemented with his own calligraphy for the title. Calligraphy is an elevation of the "popular" dimension to "high culture." Any number of calligraphers could have written these characters and any number of singers could have performed the theme songs for the cartoon edition, but Andy Lau, the original iconic Yang Guo, was chosen in this tenth adaptation of *Companion*. This demonstrates that Lau's cultural capital in connection with the Jin Yong role is incontestable. Lau's star power influenced his ability to get roles and draw an audience. His cultural capital built from experience in his early career, from training, to roles, and eventually informed his social capital thru a myriad of connections with other stars and the management of his image through other activities.

Andy Lau's musical productivity includes a multitude of concerts and awards, but he did not sing the theme songs for either of his earlier Jin Yong television series in the 1980s. Lau's prestige as an actor and singer has an even more admirable socially conscious dimension visible in his strong support of disabled athletes and his performance of two songs for the 2008 Paralympic Games in Beijing, one of which he wrote for a music video.[86] Lau continues to sing, make movies, and rack up awards. He was ranked 90th on the Forbes China Top 100 Celebrity List for 2020 (2020 *Fubusi Zhongguo mingren bang*), which also includes at least ten other kungfu film and television stars.[87]

Andy Lau did not leave Jin Yong's works behind in the 1980s but continued this connection through both investing and starring in two movies that drew their titles from *Companion*. These are retitled in English as *Savior of the Soul* (*Jiu yi Shen diao xia lü*, 1991)[88] and *Savior of the Soul II* (*Jiu er Shen diao xia lü zhi chixinqing chang jian*, 1992).[89] Directed by Corey Yuen (Yuan Kui), one of Jackie Chan's acting brothers, these two movies starred Lau, Anita Mui, Carina Lau, and Aaron Kwok. Although drawing on a Jin Yong title, the films were not based on Jin Yong's story, but some romantic and kungfu elements plot and characterization appear to resemble the story even though they are not period swordplay adventures. The choice of Chinese title for the films has been described as an "obsession" of Lau's: "Andy Lau's obsession with *The Return of the Condor*

Heroes is further reflected in the first movie in which he invested,[90] *Saviour of the Soul*" and "an obvious homage to the Chinese title of *The Return of the Condor Heroes*."[91] The sense of this "obsession" is also evident in the idea that "Andy Lau insisted that *Saviour of the Soul* feature the words "Godly Condor Hero Couple" as part of its Chinese title—he even sought Jin Yong's permission to do so."[92] Even if the content was not related to its Jin Yong title, the relationship between the characters in Andy Lau's film, and its sequel, was viewed in terms the protagonists of Jin Yong's novel: "The following year, Andy Lau made *Savior of the Soul 2*, with 'Godly Condor Hero Couple 1992' as its Chinese title. The film stars Andy Lau and Rosamund Kwan, and their relationship in the film, from the way he addresses her to his unfailing love for her, makes a clearer reference to Jin Yong's *The Return of the Condor Heroes*."[93]

There are many manifestations of Jin Yong adaptations in television and film, from straightforward adaptation, to bowdlerized comedy and satire. One wonders whether Lau's "obsessive" insistence on the Jin Yong titles for these two films was to give due credit to Jin Yong for parts of plot and characterization, or simply to draw box office. Lau could not have been unaware of the advantages of name identification with Jin Yong's work. This film was produced by Lau's fledgling film production company, *Tianmu zhizuo youxian gongsi* (Teamwork Production House, Limited). Andy both wrote the lyrics and performed the songs for the movie, which drew a Hong Kong box office more than HK$20,000,000.[94]

Note that the script writers for these two movies were Wong Kar-wai and Liu Zhenwei. Wong Kar-wai was in the lengthy, multiyear process of shooting the 1994 Jin Yong title-referenced film, *Ashes of Time* about the same time that *Savior of the Soul* was released. Recall that *Ashes of Time*, which also draw the title from characters in Jin Yong novels, was a virtual "prequel" to *Heroes*. It's difficult to determine if and how Wong's scripts for Andy Lau might have had an impact on his own writing of *Ashes of Time*. These are very complex films that only superficially attempt to capitalize on links to Jin Yong's works. The complexity comes with derivation and operates in a feedback loop within the matrix of the kungfu industrial complex. Actors, writers, producers, composers, singers, directors (and probably also crew) all participating, and also bringing previous direct Jin Yong adaptation experience with them to a new derivative dimension.

Jin Yong's *Companion* is a love story that includes a sixteen-year separation of lovers Yang Guo and Xiaolongnü as a plot device to drive the romantic ideology of an ideal love that will wait indefinitely for the one and only. After Yang Guo and Xiaolongnü are finally reunited, they eventually retire from the *jianghu* martial world, their denouement unclear. Lau's two *Savior of the Soul* movies portray the searching for love, and thus signify Jin

Yong's continuation of the ideal love drama in popular discourse. Lau's "obsession" with Jin Yong's *Companion* is paralleled by other producers who reference Jin Yong in derivative works. For example, Stephen Chow's two comic film adaptations of *Cauldron*, which carry the English titles *Royal Tramp* and *Royal Tramp II*, as well as his martial arts comedy *Kung Fu Hustle* (the subject of the next chapter) all recall Yang Guo and Xiaolongnü back to martial duty after "retirement" in the original novel. The volume of Jin Yong related derivative works demonstrates that producers recognized a Jin Yong connection to potential box office revenue. Jin Yong's characters, plots, and even titles may draw audiences eager to continue the narrative and curious about new twists in the original story. This is the power of the kungfu industrial complex at work: it assumes sufficient kungfu cultural literacy of the audience and thus extends Jin Yong's discourse through invention of possible futures (and pasts) of his characters. The 1991 *Saviour of the Soul* stars Andy Lau, Anita Mui, and Aaron Kwok, and the 1992 *Saviour of the Soul II* stars Andy Lau and Rosamund Kwan. These are top Hong Kong stars with martial arts swordplay adaptation resumes. Anita Mui's kungfu cred comes from starring in numerous Jackie Chan films, notably *Drunken Master II* (1993) as well as the female martial warrior classic, *Dongfang san xia* (Heroic Trio; alt. *The Eastern Three Heroes*, 1993). Aaron Kwok, another of the Four Heavenly Kings, is both a singing and film star who played roles in numerous *wuxia* film and television series, including the lead as Gu Long's Chu Liuxiang in the film *Xiao xia Chu Liuxiang* (1993) (*Legend of the Liquid Sword*, 1993). One element in which the 1991 *Savior of the Soul* resembles Jin Yong's original text is a segment called *"bi wu zhao qin"* (test one's martial ability to get a bride) in which Guo Fucheng and Andy Lau compete with a suitor dressed like a pirate for the woman's hand in marriage (she is leader of a secret all-female sect).[95] This reprises a similar trope in *Heroes* where Guo Jing initially meets Yang Kang. In the 1992 *Savior of the Soul II* Rosamund Kwan becomes old while Lau stays young—but their love survives, and they marry (or perhaps it is another of his dreams). Rosamund Kwan had also starred as Jin Yong character Ren Yingying in part two of the highly popular and widely acclaimed Jin Yong movie adaptation of *Wanderer*, titled *Xiao ao jianghu II: Dongfang Bubai* (*The Swordsman II:* Asia the Invincible, 1992).

In order to fill out the matrix of the kungfu industrial complex interactions of megastar Andy Lau, it is instructive to examine the extension of Lau's activities beyond his work as actor, singer, and lyricist into how he uses his star power. As noted above, Lau formed his own movie production company, Teamwork Production House, Limited in 1991. In 2005, through his other company, Yingyi yule youxian gongsi (Cinema arts entertainment company, Ltd.), Lau started "The Asian new star directors' program" (*Yazhou xin xing dao jihua*) to cultivate new directors by helping finance their projects.[96] Another dimension that plays on Lau's star power is his later career work as a philanthropist mentioned above. In addition to earning numerous awards for service, he established *Liu Dehua cishan jijinhui* (Andy Lau philanthropic foundation) in 1994 and took the post of member and Associate Chair of the executive council for the Chinese Disabled Persons Foundation in 2010.[97]

Success of these laudable activities is made possible in part by Lau's star power, which is a complex function of his cultural capital, social capital, and economic capital. Lau's star power has the tendency to loop back in various ways to Jin Yong's *Companion*. His starring role in the 1983 TVB Jin Yong television series *The Return of the Condor Heroes* (a.k.a. *Companion*) appears to have been a springboard for his career:

> Not only does the 1983 TVB version of *The Return of the Condor Heroes* remain in fans' hearts forever, it also means a lot to its male lead, Andy Lau. *The Return of the Condor Heroes* is a landmark in his acting career, earning him fame in TV, movie, and advertising fields, but also paving the way for his shining singing career. Andy Lau has admitted on many occasions that the time when he shot *The Return of the Condor Heroes* was his happiest time at TVB.[98]

Echoes of Jin Yong resonate through the kungfu industrial complex. Andy Lau's role in *Companion* is still relevant in the contemporary Hong Kong entertainment world, as demonstrated by a star-sighting report from March 17, 2016, which shows Lau photographed with Chen Shaoxia, the actor who played Yue Lingshan in the 1996 TVB adaptation of Jin Yong's *Wanderer*.[99] Again, here is the kungfu industrial complex in action: Lau and Chen Shaoxia are Jin Yong "products," objectified cultural capital. In the accompanying picture, the caption reads "Chen Shaoxia Nestled on Andy Lau's Chest." Then the description identifies Chen by the part she played in *Wanderer*, accompanied by internet speculation wondering when they are going to make a movie together again. The play of these two performers turns on Jin Yong kungfu cultural literacy beyond the level of his text. These two TVB stars of Jin Yong works from different generations are separated by fifteen years in age. Chen joined Lau's movie company and played husband and wife with him in the 1994 movie *Heaven and Earth*.[100] Then in this 2016 entertainment report they are associated through their generationally nuanced Jin Yong connection—although Lau played roles in both *Companion* and *Cauldron* and Chen Shaoxia had a role in *Wanderer*, they are connected through Jin Yong works with the appellations "Little Martial Sister" (*Xiao shimei*) and Elder Martial Brother (*Da shige*). This relationship mirrors the generational role they had as progeny of the TVB actors training course, which makes them as big brother–little sister in the entertainment *jianghu*.

Chen Shaoxia's TVB resume shows that in addition to her role in the 1996 *Wanderer*, she also had roles in the 1998 TVB adaptation of *Cauldron* (as Shuang'er), and the 2001 TVB adaptation of *Dragon Sabre* (as Zhu'er). Blog entries accompanying the photograph refer to Chen's roles as Shuang'er and also Zhu'er and chatter about her beauty in comparison to other Jin Yong characters.[101] The forty-eight photos accompanying the entertainment blog is composed a few recent poses of these Chen and Lau together, and a majority of screenshots of Chen in various Jin Yong roles.

Lau's image and star power are broadly influenced by his varied career activities outlined above, which far surpass his Jin Yong beginnings. Nevertheless, when his daughter was born in 2012, the news spread that many friends came to offer congratulations on the birth of his "Xiaolongnü," direct reference to the female leading role in the 1983 adaptation of *Companion* in which he starred nearly thirty years earlier. *Companion* received a 62 percent viewership rating at the time,[102] and generational resonance of this Jin Yong novel and its characters demonstrates star power in action via the kungfu industrial complex.

STAR POWER TAIWAN

Place is another dimension of the kungfu industrial complex. Jin Yong's works are known throughout Southeast Asia, as well as Japan and Korea. Hong Kong studios distributed films and television series targeted to the Chinese diaspora throughout the area since the 1950s. Many martial arts films, both *wuxia* and kungfu, are inextricably tied to issues involving nationalism and national identity. Jin Yong's works also touch directly on issues of ethnic nationalism and even identity through political allegory vis-à-vis the Mainland. The Chinese diaspora kept in touch with Chinese culture and history: "Entertainment in the form of theatre troupes and recordings of popular songs had always kept overseas Chinese in touch with home; the *wuxia* was just another form of a cultural link. Thus, filmmakers tailored the product to the tastes of their overseas audiences, focusing especially on stories lifted from swordplay *wuxia* novels."[103] Hong Kong was the center of Chinese cinema, with Shaw Brothers dominant in the 1960s and 1970s, but Golden Harvest rising in the 1970s to eventually become the dominant film company in the 1980s when Shaw Brothers turned to focus on television. Bordwell notes that Shaw Brothers "set up a Taiwanese production facility" in the 1960s,[104] and that Golden Harvest was "bankrolled by Thai and Taiwanese investors."[105] Taiwan was a market for Hong Kong films and also a production center that provided a pool of Chinese talent. After the United States recognized the Mainland diplomatically in 1979, Taiwan embassies were changed into economic and cultural offices. Thereupon, Bordwell points out, "Taiwan was forced to use culture as its primary means of maintaining international relations" with a strategy of making "its Golden Horse Awards—the Taiwanese version of the Oscars—into an internationally recognized film event."[106] Like Hong Kong, high level entertainers with complementary film and singing careers are readily found Taiwan. The seemingly wholescale appropriation of "Gang-Tai" popular culture in the Mainland during the 1980s and 1990s marks the great tide of "modernization of Chinese culture," a drastic break with the cultural trends of the first thirty years of the PRC. While Mainland stars and productions accelerated in the 2000s, many of the top martial arts movies produced through the 2000s utilized a bevy of established Hong Kong and Taiwanese stars, capitalizing on their music and film star power to draw audiences to the box office.

Taiwanese actors such as Brigitte Lin were highly successful in the Hong Kong movie industry. Entertainers like Emil Wakin Chau (Zhou Huajian), who was born in Hong Kong, moved to Taiwan for studies and developed their careers there. Emil Chau sang the theme songs for three Jin Yong television series, including Yang Peipei's 1994 production of *Dragon Sabre*.[107] Even Hong Konger Jackie Chan sang one of the closing credits songs for this 1994 adaptation of *Dragon Sabre*,[108] and was active in Taiwan during his early period when he was dating Taiwanese megastar singer Theresa Teng (Deng Lijun) at a time when she was more famous than him. Chan filmed part of *Boli zun* (Gorgeous, 1999) in Taiwan with Taiwan costars Shu Qi and Richie Jen, supported by Emil Chau and Tony Leung Chiu-wai in secondary roles.

Richie Jen (a.k.a. Richie Ren) represents a complementary Taiwan example to the phenomenon of Andy Lau's Hong Kong star trajectory, although he hasn't achieved the superstar level yet. His career highlights the impact of kungfu fiction and film on Hong Kong and Taiwanese popular culture. He started as a singer/musician writing some of his own lyrics and music. He released his first album in 1990 while still a senior at Taiwan's Chinese Cultural University and has compiled a total of thirty-eight albums to date.[109] Richie Jen acted in his first movie in 1991 and played in forty-five movies to date, some starring but mostly supporting roles.[110] In addition to endorsements and music awards, Richie also starred as Yang Guo, opposite Wu Qianlian playing Xiaolongnü, in the forty-seven-episode 1998 Taiwan Television (TTV) production of *Companion*. Following this series, Richie starred as Linghu Chong in the 2000 Taiwan Central Television (CTV) edition of Jin Yong's *Wanderer* (series title: *State of Divinity*) opposite Yuan Yongyi (Anita Yuen) as Ren Yingying. Richie recorded the theme song for these versions of

Companion and *Wanderer*.¹¹¹ In 2001 he also played the lead in the Gu Long television adaptation of *Xin Chu Liuxiang* (The new Chu Liuxiang) produced by China Television System (CTS).

Production is a dimension of the kungfu industrial complex matrix that must be addressed. The fifty-four-episode Richie Jen version of *Wanderer* was produced by Yang Peipei, a well-known Taiwanese producer of martial arts television series. In addition to this version of *Wanderer*, Yang produced the 1994 *Dragon Sabre* and 1998 *Companion* television adaptations. Jin Yong had mixed opinions of her work. In her own words Yang notes: "Jin Yong once said to me: 'Of my works put on screen, the best is made by you, and the one I like least is also made by you.' He liked my *Dragon Sabre* the most, and most disliked my *Companion*."¹¹² Richie sang both the theme song "Ren xiaoyao" (Being free) and the closing credits song "Shangxin Taipingyang" (Sorrowful Pacific Ocean), for Yang's 1998 adaptation of *Companion*. Although Jin Yong panned the production, both of Richie's renditions of these romantic songs were successful and are among his greatest hits. Richie's Weibo account from December 29, 2020, for example, posts a picture of him more than twenty years later in Taiwan's Hualian seaside looking out at the sea. One of his followers makes the joke, "This is where you lost love and were dumped!" Richie answers, "I did . . .? Why . . .?" To which the follower replies, "Because this is your 'Sorrowful Pacific Ocean.'" Whereupon Richie replies with a "relieved" smiley face emoji. Numerous other followers thereupon comment, with many females posting on how they love that song (and him).¹¹³ Twenty-two years after *Companion* Richie Jen is still something of a player in a drama between the most romantic of all Jin Yong's characters, Yang Guo and Xiaolongnü from *Companion*.

Crucial members of the production team are also the director and action director/choreographer. The action director for the year 2000 Richie Jen edition of *Wanderer* is Ching Siu-Tung (in Mandarin, Cheng Xiaodong). Ching Siu-Tung is known as one of the choreographers for the 2008 Olympic Ceremony in Beijing,¹¹⁴ for which renowned director Zhang Yimou was the General Director. Ching has a Jin Yong connection as action choreographer in the seminal 1983 TVB adaptation of *Heroes*.¹¹⁵ He was reportedly invited onto this production because his reputation and the high quality of his work, and then created numerous new martial moves for the production.¹¹⁶ Ching notes that *Heroes* was his first television series and he intentionally focused on lighting and photography to give the production a "movie like feeling."¹¹⁷ This series put Ching in intersection with the Five Tigers of TVB, as well as the actor Barbara Yung. Ching also codirected/directed the *Swordsman* trilogy based on Jin Yong's *Wanderer* in the 1990s. Ching worked on numerous other martial arts films and television series, including Stephen Chow's two 1992 films based on Jin Yong's *Cauldron, Royal Tramp* and *Royal Tramp II*, which also starred Brigitte Lin.[118] In addition, he worked as action director for Stephen Chow's *Shaolin Soccer* (2001).

FEMALE *WUXIA* SUPERSTAR

The role of the female *wuxia* martial artist in Jin Yong's novels is intriguing. There are a number of highly skilled female fighters, and although the majority of Jin Yong's protagonists are male, there seems to be egalitarianism in kungfu ability in most martial arts sects. Jin Yong created martial superstars, tough women with varying degrees of grace, guile and/or grudge among his female characters, including top rank fighters such as Huang Rong, Xiaolongnü and Ren Yingying who are protagonists with equal status and kungfu ability as their leading male counterparts and also play leadership roles in their kungfu sects. Jin Yong's stories also include other tough female antagonists and secondary characters. Antagonists Tianshan Tonglao and Li Mochou either surpass or are equal to male characters in martial arts skill while protagonist Wang Yuyan surpasses all other secondary characters in brains and kungfu textual knowledge. Here is space to consider the martial power of females on (nearly) equal ground with males.

While Guo Jing occupies the role of male protagonist in *Heroes*, the brains of the novel reside with female protagonist Huang Rong (Guo's eventual wife), who is considered by author Ni Kuang to be the "soul character" (*linghun renwu*) of the novel and termed a "tough-woman" (*nüqiangren*) by director Tsui Hark.[119] In addition to being a top martial artist, Huang Rong is perhaps Jin Yong's most intelligent and able character of *any* gender. She benefits from heredity, getting genes of intelligence from her mother and strategy from her father, the "Eastern Heretic" (*Dong Xie*) Huang Yaoshi. She learns kungfu specialties such as the Dog-Beating Staff Method (*da gou bangfa*) from her adoptive martial master Hong Qigong, the Northern Beggar (*Bei Gai*). Huang Rong eventually "inherits" his leadership of the Beggar Gang, the largest sect in the martial arts world. Identified by the cardinal coordinates in their nicknames, her father and master Hong are two of the four grandmasters, the elder generation of heroes in *Heroes*. The other two are "Western Venom" (*Xi Du*) Ouyang Feng and the "Southern Emperor" (*Nan Di*) Duan Zhixing.

Companion's Xiaolongnü and *Wanderer*'s Ren Yingying are equally capable martial artists, with a twist on their own individual character traits (Xiaolongnü: serenity; Ren Yingying: tolerance), in addition to specific martial abilities resulting from the narrative of their respective upbringing/development. Tales of romance in Chinese fiction from past dynasties provide a relational background of the love dimension in contemporary fiction, television, and film, appreciation for which has been finely honed over centuries of storytelling, reading, acting, and viewing. Dynastic historical documents also provide examples of martial women, such as Yang Miaozhen in the Song dynasty and Qin Liangyu in the Ming dynasty.[120] Legends of strong female martial figures, like general Hua Mulan, Hu Sanniang (*Water Margin*), and Lady Zhurong (*Three Kingdoms*) are handed down from classical fiction to contemporary film and television. Given this historical lineage, deployment of strong female characters in Jin Yong's *wuxia* fiction does not strain credulity or the suspension of disbelief. Although some feminist readings of his female characters may be negative, for example, criticism of the passivity of Xiaolongnü in *Companion*, the martial emotional range of Jin Yong's female characters equals or surpasses that of his male characters.

Early female stars of Jin Yong television series and films in the 1980s included Idy Chan (Chen Yulian), who was in the 1977 class of the TVB actors training course, and whose roles include Xiaolongnü, Huang Rong and Wang Yuyan.[121] Barbara Yung[122] made her fame as Huang Rong in the iconic 1983 TVB adaptation of *Heroes*. And Carina Lau both starred with Tony Leung Chiu-wai in numerous Jin Yong adaptations in the 1980s and 1990s and eventually married him. These female actors played opposite the seminal actors of the Hong Kong screen in crucial roles in Jin Yong works, particularly the Five Tigers of TVB. In addition to these early 1980s portrayals, other leading female stars who have taken up important Jin Yong roles include Anita Mui, Brigitte Lin, and Maggie Cheung.

The primary analysis of star power in the kungfu industrial complex up to this point focused on the Five Tigers of TVB, particularly Andy Lau and Tony Leung, which might make it seem that the *jianghu* is a man's world. While there is more than a grain of truth in this notion, a countercurrent of perceptible near egalitarianism exists in Jin Yong's martial arts novels. The novels are full of strong females who are martially equal to most, if not all, of the male heroes depicted. The ranks of female actors in the kungfu industrial complex are deep and interconnected. Tony Leung Chiu-wai's wife Carina Lau is an excellent example of a female star who played in many Jin Yong related roles. She was trained at TVB, played opposite Leung in *Cauldron* as one of his (Wei Xiaobao's) wives, and then actually did marry him in 2008. As expected for celebrities of their stature, their wedding was attended by numerous stars, including many with Jin Yong connections. Prominent among these stars are Faye Wong (Wang Fei), Wong Kar-wai, Brigitte Lin Ching-hsia, as well as Wong Kar-wai.[123] Faye Wong and top Mainland singer Liu Huan sang the closing credits song for the 2001 mainland Chinese version of *Wanderer*.[124] Wong Kar-wai directed *Ashes of Time* and wrote the script for Andy Lau's *Saviour of the Soul*, in which Carina Lau played a supporting role.

Carina Lau had numerous roles in movies with each of the Five Tigers, in addition to film roles alongside the Four Heavenly Kings of the Hong Kong music world, in Jackie Chan movies, and with other stars such as Chow Yun-fat, Leslie Cheung, and Brigitte Lin. Her Jin Yong bona fides include her role as Fang Yi, one Wei Xiaobao's wives in the 1984 *Cauldron*, and minor roles in the 1983 *Heroes* (starring Felix Wong) and the 1983 *Companion* (starring Andy Lau). In addition to playing in Andy Lau's 1991 *Saviour of the Soul*, Carina played Peach Blossom (the Blind Swordsman's wife) in the 1994 *Ashes of Time* (her husband Tony Leung played the Blind Swordsman). In the 1993 Jin Yong parody of *The Eagle-Shooting Heroes: Eastern and Western Accomplishments* she played Zhou Botong.[125]

Other female actors also played numerous such Jin Yong related roles. Idy Chan played Xiao Zhao (*Dragon Sabre*, 1978), Wang Yuyan (*Semi-Devils*, 1982), Xiaolongnü (*Companion*, 1983), Huang Rong (*Heroes*, 1988). Athena Chu (Zhu Yin) played Huang Rong (*Heroes*, 1993), Ah Ke (*Cauldron*, 2000), Yuan Ziyi (*Flying Fox*, 2006). Brigitte Lin, however, played the strongest and perhaps the most enigmatic roles in Jin Yong derivative works: Asia the Invincible in *Swordsman II* and the dual roles of Murong Yang—Murong Yin and Dugu Qiubai in *Ashes of Time* (1994).

Brigitte Lin is a fascinating example of the female star with deep and varied kungfu industrial complex connections. While her Jin Yong connections do not include television series, her major roles in a handful of movie adaptations of Jin Yong works are notable. For example, she played both Li Canghai and Li Qiushui in *Xin Tian long ba bu zhi Tianshan Tonglao* (The dragon chronicles—the maidens; alternately: The new demi-gods and semi-devils: Tianshan Tonglao, 1994). This film is a stylized excerpt of a plot line from Jin Yong's *Semi-Devils* directed by Qian Yongqiang and starring Mainland actor Gong Li in the title role of Tianshan Tonglao and Zhang Min as Ah Zi.[126] In the same timeframe, Brigitte Lin played Long'er in Stephen Chow's 1992 comedy, *Lu ding ji II: shenlong jiao* (Royal tramp II: mystical dragon cult) with Stephen Chow as protagonist Wei Xiaobao.

The ability to appear gender ambiguous was apparently a great asset. Prior to martial arts films, Brigitte Lin played in many adaptations of Taiwan writer Qiong Yao's love stories. But she had played male roles since as early as her 1977 depiction of Jia Baoyu, arguably China's most famous novel character, in the Shaw Brothers movie adaptation of the Ming dynasty novel *Dream of the Red Chamber*.[127] Her first significant role in a martial arts movie was the 1983 Tsui Hark film, *Zu Warriors from the Magic Mountain*. Tsui recalls frankly that he worked with her on this film because of her beauty.[128] It is a common trope to find a female martial artist dressed in men's clothing and being mistaken for male in martial arts fiction and film. This was the case for Zhang Ziyi's character in *Crouching*

Tiger. Authors and auteurs play with this ambiguity for irony, comedy, and narrative complexity, but readers and viewers are rarely deceived by such disguise, although some characters in the stories may be.

Brigitte Lin's seminal *wuxia* role is as Dongfang Bubai (Asia the Invincible)[129] in the hit 1992 film *Xiao ao jianghu zhi Dongfang Bubai* (*Swordsman II: Asia the Invincible*) and its follow-up, the 1993 *Dongfang Bubai zhi fengyun zaiqi* (*Swordsman III: The East Is Red*). Directed by Ching Siu-tung, these two films represent "the second peak of her film career."[130] *Swordsman II* starred Jet Li as protagonist Linghu Chong. Asia the Invincible is the implied antagonist of Jin Yong's *Wanderer*, the usurping leader of the "evil" Sun-Moon Cult (variably referred to in the text as the Demon Cult [*Mo jiao*]), and widely regarded as the top martial artist of the novel. Asia the Invincible is perhaps the top martial artist of all Jin Yong's works. Lin's casting as this character is intriguing because it relates to the issue of gender ambiguity in *wuxia* martial practice, which in itself is a significant plot line in the novel. To wit, in order to successfully practice the *Sunflower Classic*, a secret martial arts text written by a court eunuch, one must first castrate oneself. The desire to dominate the martial world is so strong among certain characters (for reasons including revenge, ambition, and pride) that castration does not deter many who seek access to the sacred text and realize the requirement for its practice. However, those who do so keep the requirement secret. Brigitte Lin's portrayal of this character fits the story's express narrative logic that castration has the effect of turning the male into female, as displayed by gender identification with stereotypical female traits of dress (colorful), pastime pursuits (embroidery), and sexual orientation (attraction to men). Jin Yong's novels often feature female characters who travel the *jianghu* in male garb to hide their gender without the complexification of actual gender ambiguity. In this case Lin deftly portrays Jin Yong's version of a man changed to woman. But more important is Jin Yong's suggestion in *Wanderer*, reflected in this film, that de-sexualization is required to practice the deepest secrets of kungfu and reach the pinnacle of the martial world. Unfortunately for those characters, the narrative logic of the novel suggests that castration (physical manifestation of breaking taboo of social norms) also leads to insanity, as does the quest for ultimate power in the *jianghu*. Asia the Invincible is one of the strongest martial artists in Jin Yong's novels and the name is fitting. The *Swordsman* film trilogy adaptations raises the role Asia the Invincible to a more prominent position than occupied in the novel. This represents a significant deviation from Jin Yong's original narrative wherein Asia the Invincible is an important secondary character.

Her reprisal of Asia the Invincible represented a second peak in Brigitte Lin's career and was problematic for her in because she was subsequently nearly type-cast, called on to reprise a similar type in many following

Figure 4.2. Brigitte Lin as Asia the Invincible, *Swordsman II* (1992)

movies. This touches on an aspect of the kungfu industrial complex yet unmentioned—the presence of triad gangsters in the Taiwan and Hong Kong film industry who coerced stars to work in films they produced because their names could draw box office revenue. Ming-Yeh T. Rawnsley notes the prevalence of triads and its grip on the biggest stars of the day:

> According to Curtin (2007, 72–75) almost one-third of new production houses that were established in Hong Kong in the early 1990s were triad owned. Several major Hong Kong movie stars, such as Andy Lau, Anita Mui, Stephen Chow, and Chow Yun-fat, were targeted by triad producers at the time. When Brigitte Lin's Asia the Invincible made her the center of attention, she found herself once again having to take on projects in which she was not particularly interested under pressure from triad producers (Lin 2011, 80–82). In total, Lin played various versions of the character Asia the Invincible in 13 different movies within one and a half years, until Lin and the audience were exhausted by it.[131]

Thirteen reprisals of Asia the Invincible is a remarkable record. Rawnsley suggests that this exhaustion eventually led to Lin's second retirement. The field of cultural production in Hong Kong and Taiwan at the time seemed particularly dangerous for successful actors. In Lin's case the cultural and economic capital she built via one Jin Yong movie adaptation multiplied into thirteen further roles, causing both her and the audience to burnout on those types of movies.

Brigitte Lin's other seminal *wuxia* role appears in the enigmatic Wong Kar-wai film, *Ashes of Time* (1994), which takes its title from the nicknames of two Jin Yong characters in *Heroes*, the "Eastern Heretic" and "Western Venom."[132] This film is a dark psychological work of post-textual cultural reprisal, a sort of prequel that creatively imagines the psychology of select characters in Jin Yong's *Heroes*. Lin plays three characters: the brother/sister twins Murong Yan and Murong Yan (different characters for the given name Yan), and Dugu Qiubai.[133] The two Murong characters are allusions to antagonist Murong Fu in Jin Yong's novel *Semi-Devils*, who is driven to restore his family's fourth-century state of Yan and eventually goes crazy. Murong's insanity in the novel is roughly paralleled by the split-personality characters that Lin plays in the film. The third character, Dugu Qiubai, is of importance in *Wanderer* since he is the greatest swordsman in the *jianghu*. Dugu Qiubai never actually appears in person in Jin Yong's novels, but he mentioned in three of them. He is the original source of sword skills secretly passed down to Linghu Chong by the Huashan Sect hermit elder, Feng Qingyang. Dugu Qiubai likewise plays a tangential but important role for Yang Guo in *Companion*. This greatest of all swordsmen is channeled through the giant eagle that was his companion and later became both Yang Guo's companion and trainer of Yang Guo in Dugu's swordsmanship (and source of his swords).

In the roles of Asia the Invincible and Murong Yan, Brigitte Lin plays a psychologically challenged, damaged, or deranged character by estimation of *jianghu* morality. She also participated in several other *wuxia* novel-based film productions. In the 1993 film adaptation novel of Liang Yusheng's *Bai fa monü zhuan* (Story of the white-haired demoness) she played the lead role of Lian Nichang whose hair turns white due to unrequited love. She also played the male character Hua Wuque opposite Andy Lau's lead in the 1992 film adaption of Gu Long's novel, *Juedai shuang jiao* (The legendary twins). Thus, within a three-year time frame Lin played characters from adaptations of novels the three great masters of New School Martial Arts Fiction: Jin Yong, Liang Yusheng, and Gu Long.

Through her Jin Yong referenced works, as well as films based on other *wuxia* novels, Brigitte Lin has 103 acting credits between 1973 and 2001.[134] She is in the company of many rising superstars of the time, some already discussed above, and also cast against the rising martial artist/actor, Jet Li. In her earlier films Lin also played in Jackie Chan's seminal detective movie, *Jingcha gushi* (Police story, 1985). She starred next to Maggie Cheung in the film *Xin longmen kezhan* (New dragon gate inn, a.k.a. Dragon inn, 1992), which also featured star kungfu film and television actors Tony Leung Ka-fai and Donnie Yen. Interconnections in the kungfu industrial complex run deep with *Dragon Inn*. This film was produced by Tsui Hark and had action directors Ching Siu-Tung and Yuan Biao. Recall that Lin's history with director/producer Tsui Hark goes back as far as the 1983 production of *Zu Warriors from the Magic Mountain*.

Brigitte Lin published a book of recollections in 2011 titled *Chuangli chuangwai* (Inside the window and outside the window), in which three essays reflect on her roles in the *Swordsman* movies and *Ashes of Time*. The essay titles are as follows: "Dongfang Bubai" (Asia the Invincible),[135] "Chong kan *Dong Xie Xi Du*" (Another look at *Ashes of Time*),[136] and "Da daoyan shouzhong de mangguo" (Mango in a great director's hands).[137] "Another look at *Ashes of Time*" recalls how she went into costume test shots for *Ashes of Time* with high self-confidence due to the surprising box office success of the 1992 *Swordsman II: Asia the Invincible*. Director Wong Kar-wai said that in all the test shots she looked like Asia the Invincible. She thought to herself, "Aren't I playing a man? Isn't this what a man looks like?"[138] In *Ashes of Time* she played a split male/female role, and says she was nearly driven crazy by Wong's obsessive number of retakes of scenes. Lin recalls in retrospect that this was how the director wanted her to look—crazy.

ASHES OF TIME: JIN YONG DERIVATIVE STAR POWER

Hong Kong superstar Leslie Cheung performed the theme song for Jin Yong's 1984 adaptation of *Cauldron* that starred Lau and Leung, and also played leading roles in numerous Jin Yong adaptations and spinoffs, including a 1983 Shaw Brothers film adaptation of *Companion* titled *Yang Guo yu Xiaolongnü* (Shaw English title: *Little Dragon Maiden*) and directed by Hua Shan. In 1994, Leslie Cheung also played the title character "Western Venom" (Xi Du) Ouyang Feng in Wong Kar-wai's *Ashes of Time* (Dong Xie, Xi Du). This Jin Yong derivative film gains its title from the martial appellations of two kungfu grandmasters in Jin Yong's *Heroes*. *Ashes of Time* is filmed with an all-star cast who had played numerous roles in other Jin Yong film and television adaptations, including Tony Leung Ka-fai, Brigette Lin, Tony Leung Chiu-wai, Maggie Cheung (Zhang Manyu), and Jacky Cheung (Zhang Xueyou).[139] Coincidentally, Leslie Cheung was playing "Western Venom" in one film at the same time he was playing "Eastern Heretic" in another. The difference is that his Eastern Heretic was for a parody of Jin Yong's martial arts films titled *The Eagle-Shooting Heroes: Eastern and Western Accomplishments* (1993). This parody was filmed using the cast of *Ashes of Time* to facilitate cash flow for director Wong Kar-wai because he was having difficulty wrapping that film.[140] Characters in these two films derived from Jin Yong's original novels, with Leslie Cheung playing both of cardinal direction title roles.

Ashes of Time is perhaps the most enigmatic product of the kungfu industrial complex. Wimal Dissanayake interviewed the director for his book on the film, *Wong Kar-wai's Ashes of Time* (Hong Kong University Press, 2003). While the film's narrative is difficult to understand given its flashbacks and character fluctuations, Wong Kar-wai's comments on its making shed light on the machinations of the kungfu industrial complex. First Dissanayake wonders if there are any elements from Jin Yong's original novel, and Wong replies:

> There is a relation. When we made this movie, we aimed to tell a story different from the book. At first, I was attracted by the names of two characters, Dong Xie and Xi Du, who, at the beginning of the design of the movie, we thought should be women. Later, we found out that there was not difference between buying the copyright of these two names and buying the entire book. Then, the idea of making this novel into a movie came to our minds. Another factor was that I enjoy reading this type of martial arts fiction, thus I was eager to turn it into a movie. The characters Dong Xie and Xi Du impressed me most because Dong Xie possesses natural grace but detests the world and its ways, something that we all thought was very cool. But I also had negative feelings about the selfish nature of Dong Xie. The character of Xi Du, on the other hand, appealed to me because he is a tragic figure.

At the beginning of the project, I wanted to contact Jin. I thought when he first designed these characters, he must have thought about their early histories but did not include it in his novel. In the end, it was good that I was unable to contact him because it allowed me to have more freedom in designing my characters. First, I imagined what these characters would be like when they were young. Then I developed my own story that leads up to and concludes where Jin Yong's story begins.[141]

These detailed remarks are instructive with respect to momentum and dynamism of the kungfu industrial complex. The idea that the director initially felt the title characters "should be women" is not explained. Although the title characters eventually remained male, the film itself ranged far from any semblance of Jin Yong's story. There is an implicit understanding that the cultural weight of Jin Yong's novel can provide a ready audience for the movie, a sense of market on which to capitalize.

Wong notes that the cost of acquiring the copyright for the names of the title characters and the whole novel was the same, and he thus considered making the book itself into a movie. This would have been a new adaptation, but instead Wong focused on two characters, Dong Xie (Eastern Heretic), who they "all thought was very cool" because he "detests the world and its ways," and Xi Du, who was appealing as a "tragic figure." Although explanation is limited to these two brief statements, the late twentieth-century socio-political situation of Hong Kong, which was to return to mainland China control only three years after *Ashes of Time* debuted (about six years after beginning the film project), may provide a clue to Wong's conception of "cool": detesting the world and its ways may be a coping strategy in the uncertain times. Jin Yong's character, Dong Xie, resided on Peach Blossom Island, somewhere indistinctly situated off the eastern coast of China, intentionally separated from the *jianghu* and the central plains by choice. Peach Blossom Island can be read as an allegory for Hong Kong, where it was possible to raise a family (as did the character Dong Xie) without outside interference of the mainland social and political demands. How "cool" is that? In terms of political allegory, Wong's reference to Xi Du (Western Venom) as a "tragic figure" is unclear but may refer to the inherent tension of colonialism in Hong Kong, the impact of which may not have been entirely negative despite the distinctly adverse power relationship from the point of view of ethnic nationalism.

The interviewer's questions probe for a connection to Jin Yong's texts. In answer, Wong says he likes the genre and expresses an initial desire to get background on the characters from the author. A margin of credibility for the film may come through connection with the author. Although unsuccessful in meeting with Jin Yong, he ultimately says he was satisfied because this allowed "more freedom in designing" the characters as a result. Wong understands there is a final line he must meet, noting that his story "concludes where Jin Yong's story begins." Thus, his work is perceived as a prequel, which inherently allows a degree of interpretive freedom up to a point.

Wong likes the *wuxia* genre and the audience, and moreover he knows the novels and characters. *Ashes of Time* was released in 1994, by which time the two novels in which the title characters appear had been published first serially and then as separate books in two editions over three decades at about 1,600 pages each. The novels were adapted for television series multiple times over the decades prior to *Ashes of Time*. *Heroes* saw eight adaptations and two derivatives up to 1994 (and three more adaptations since, including 2017). *Companion* was adapted three times by 1994 and six more times up to 2021. Furthermore, the third "new revised edition" of Jin Yong's collected works was finished in 2006.

The kungfu industrial complex assumes a basic kungfu cultural literacy on the part of the reading audience, which is carried over to the film and television viewing audiences through multiple repeated adaptations of each of Jin Yong's works. Director Wong Kar-wai enjoys "reading this type of martial arts fiction" and likes these characters, so is already predisposed to employ his kungfu cultural literacy during production. Furthermore, he can rely on the kungfu cultural literacy of his audience—they already know the story and the characters too. The question of how well the story and characters are depicted/interpreted by the scriptwriters, directors, film and televisions stars of the day, within or outside the expectations of the audience, becomes a focal point in the later critique of *Ashes of Time*. Many of the cast are luminaries from the Hong Kong film world who had previous experience acting in Jin Yong adaptations to film and television. Thus, director Wong did not start from such a blank slate since much of the audience was certainly familiar with those Jin Yong roles depicted by the actors. Wong suggests that the audience will recognize references to the novel, an assumption of the kungfu cultural literacy of the audience. But this is film is difficult to understand. Initial audience reaction indicates that the director's interpretation pushed the audience's imagination beyond expectations, resulting in negative evaluation of the film and ticket sales falling far short of recouping production costs. Since the critics and audience didn't like the film, some alternative interpretation is necessary. The interviewer Dissanayake argues: "It is our conviction that *Ashes of Time* carries a certain structure of feeling that relates to the sense of confusion and anguish that characterized Hong Kong in the 1990s in the face of the impending handover. Hence, this is one way of seeing the relevance of *Ashes of Time* to the dynamics of contemporary Hong Kong."[142] In this reading, Wong's prequel to Jin Yong's story captures the enigma of the separation/reunification anxiety. With the advantage of historical hindsight, Dissanayake's analysis and conclusion astutely elaborate eight facets of the contemporary socio-political situation in Hong Kong (time, fate/destiny, loss, consumer capitalism, disappearance of heroism, evil, failure to connect, and hope).[143] These facets derive from analysis of *Ashes of Time* vis-à-vis Wong Kar-wai's other works, critical film theory, and historical contingencies of the time. Dissanayake sheds light on Wong's astute cultural reading of star power (read cultural capital) in terms of an actor's public persona and a character's personality:

> The way Wong Kar-wai makes use of stars like Leslie Cheung, Maggie Cheung, Tony Leung Chiu-wai and Brigitte Lin in his films is most interesting, and it is an arena in which he has influenced subsequent film directors. He is fully aware of the implications of stardom in modern commercial film culture and how stardom is located at a complex crossroads of art, popular entertainment, commerce, industry, popular psychology, cultural icons, and other factors. Stars can be popular cultural icons, bearers of cultural meaning, performers with distinct public images, commercial attractions and an important element of cinematic meaning. Wong makes use of them as performers who bring their own public persona in to the characters that they are playing in his films and precipitate a tension between their public personas and the nature of the characters that are being played.[144]

Dissanayake's critical intent is to "examine *Ashes of Time* in relation to the creativity of Wong Kar-wai,"[145] and thus has "sought to locate it in the larger social, cultural, historical and conceptual contexts which it both reflects and inflects."[146] Wong Kar-wai worked on all aspects of the film, from the writing, acting, directing, to the artistic elements. *Ashes of Time* was produced by a collection of film companies, led by the Taiwan based Scholar Films Company, Limited. As Dissanayake outlines, it was presold in Taiwan, Singapore, Malaysia, and Korea, then also France and Japan, as the money was used up at a fast pace.[147] Wong kept on working on the film even as it was entered in the Venice Film Festival in 1994. Dissanayake notes that this was illustrative of the director's temperament and work style, and that throughout the course of the film many changes were made, even in casting. The general audience reaction was "one of bewilderment and disappointment," as "people walked out of the theatres in droves in the middle of the film." This was further expressed in "a furious battle in the pages of newspapers and journals, between those who liked it and those who did not, with an intensity that had hardly been witnessed before."[148] Even Maggie Cheung who played in the picture had to see it three times before she thought she understood it.[149]

There was discussion that Wong's "business head" could be seen in this "peak of the golden era of Hong Kong film," meeting the investors' three basic requirements for cast, film genre, and story: "The cast was eight megastars, the genre was the first most popular *wuxia*, and the story was one of Jin Yong's gold-plated novels. Because of this, Wong Kar-wai casually and 'carefreely' got a huge investment of a few tens of millions."[150] Despite the star power and Jin Yong's "gold plated novel," reception of the film was negative, and the box office was in the red. Although the critical evaluation of the film has improved markedly since its original release, the investment of an estimated HK$40 million didn't pay off, even when one adds the original Hong Kong box office of about HK$9 million in 1994 to the box office for the *Ashes of Time Redux* (*Dong Xie Xi Du: zhongji ban*) in 2008, which amounted to about US$2 million (HK$15.5 million). In terms of the kungfu industrial complex, this indicates that a work must meet expectations of audience kungfu cultural literacy in the short term. Although it was reasonable that "Wong Kar-wai was seeking to unsettle and challenge the images of the leading characters that had been etched into the imaginations of Hong Kong audiences,"[151] he recognizes that Hong Kong audiences were disappointed with the film. On this level, perhaps he didn't appreciate the nature of kungfu cultural literacy that drives audience interpretation/reception. The film's reception may change over time, but that change will probably come with rereading of the film back against elements of the kungfu industrial complex, itself a function of historical socio-cultural-political distance. Wong was aiming for both a work of art and a commercial success, betting that the all-star cast and Jin Yong's character name recognition would cover the costs. The final measure of the film and director may be delayed to a future date, but from the perspective of the kungfu industrial complex it can be predicted that *Ashes of Time* will eventually conquer the rotten tomatoes as the cultural capital of Wong Kar-wai and his superstar cast further develop. The initial interpretive indeterminacy of *Ashes of time* will actually open space for further film interpretations beyond the expectation of profit, and perhaps ironically survive longer in martial arts film consciousness as a result of the "art."

THE LEGENDARY MARTIAL ARTS HERO

The intersection of kungfu action stars and legendary martial arts heroes forms another interstice of the kungfu film and pop culture matrix that resonates with "authenticity." Typically, this meshes with a narrative of nationalism placing the work in sync with the audience expectations for the film or television series. Nationalism is furthered through fictional narratives of real-life martial arts heroes such as Huo Yuanjia, Huang Feihong, Fang Shiyu, and Ip Man, all of whom are mythologized through innumerable repetitions on screen and television. Historical martial artists have been long portrayed by celebrities of Hong Kong and Chinese film and television. In Bruce Lee's *Jingwu men* (*Fist of Fury*, 1972), fictional character Chen Zhen is the disciple of famous real-life martial artist, Huo Yuanjia. The role of Chen Zhen has pop-cultural depth with a timeline. Chen Zhen was also played by Jet Li in the film *Fist of Legend* (*Jingwu yingxiong*, 1994). Donnie Yen played Chen Zhen in a thirty-episode television series *Fist of Fury* (1995) and also played Chen Zhen in the sequel to Jet Li's film *Legend of the Fist: The Return of Chen Zhen* (*Jingwu fengyun*, 2010). In fitting symmetry, Yen starred in the title role of the movie *Ip Man* (*Ye Wen*, 2008), whose title reference is Bruce Lee's real-life Wing Chun master. Bruce Lee's Hong Kong box office revenue in 1972 was HK$4,430,000.[152] This record was broken by Donnie Yen's Chen Zhen in 2008, which grossed HK$1,764,105 in Hong Kong and approximately $27 million USD worldwide."[153] Bruce Lee, Jet Li and Donnie Yen are trained martial artists and actors who project a certain authenticity that comes with that training. In addition, Jet Li and Donnie Yen are both "at home with special effects" in the twentieth-first century.[154] Beyond entertainment value, this level of star power brought to bear on these film characters reifies both the history of Ip Man, Huo Yuanjia, and Huo's fictional student Chen Zhen, as well as the nationalist discourse of the narratives. Bruce Lee, as Bowman notes, "is the constitutive element uniting both these figures,"[155] the historical Ip Man and Huo Yuanjia. Going one step further, the real Bruce Lee and fictional Chen Zhen are vehicles in the construction of the kungfu industrial complex.

Chen Zhen is a fictional character, but his kungfu master was the real-life martial artist Huo Yuanjia (1868–1920) whose legend as a patriot includes the actual defeat of foreign fighters in Shanghai and his presumed poisoning by Japanese henchmen. Huo Yuanjia established the Jingwu Athletic Association (*Jingwu tiyuhui*) shortly before his death. To date there have been six television series about his legend filmed in Taiwan, Hong Kong, and mainland China. The most recent versions are those starring Vincent Zhao (Zhao Wenzhuo) in 2001, singer/actor Ekin Cheng in 2007, and Vincent Zhao's 2020 sequel to his 2001 series. Vincent Zhao also starred in the 2003 television series adaptation of Jin Yong's *Book and Sword*. Ekin Cheng played parts in numerous *wuxia* television series, also including *Book and Sword* (1987). There are eight films which use Huo's name in their title from 1944 to 2020, as well as the total of seven related television series.[156] To cap off Huo's legend, his village birthplace in what is part of today's Tianjin was renamed *Jingwu zhen* (martial essence town). Retranslating in line with the inexact English translation of the Bruce Lee's movie title, this town would now be called "Fist of Fury Town."

Figure 4.3. Bruce Lee as Huo Yuanjia's disciple Chen Zhen, *Fist of Fury* (1972)

Taiwan singing sensation Jay Chou produced and sang the theme song for the 2006 television series *Huo Yuanjia* starring Jet Li.

The 1940s, 1950s, and 1960s Hong Kong film world was populated by Cantonese martial arts films of both the "swordplay" *wuxia* and kungfu variety. The most popular kungfu film series featured the martial artist and actor Kwan Tak-hing (Guan Dexing, 1905–1996), who played the martial artist Wong Fei-hung (Huang Feihong) in a series of black and white Cantonese movies. Thirty-nine of these movies were directed by Hu Peng between 1949 to 1957. In 1956 alone, twenty-five Huang Feihong films debuted, twenty-two of which were directed by Hu Peng.[157] Supporting actors included Shi Jian (in Cantonese, Shih Kien) as villain, as well as the actor Liu Zhan playing one of Huang Feihong's disciple. Liu is the father of action choreographer Liu Jialiang.[158]

The real-life Huang Feihong (Wong Fei-hung, 1847–1924) is one of the most mythologized martial artists in Chinese popular culture. Huang is a nationalist hero even more visible in film and television than Huo Yuanjia or Ip Man. Jeff Wang notes that after the near demise of Cantonese cinema in Japanese occupied Hong Kong during World War II, "Canto-cinema" was saved in 1949 by introduction of the story of Huang Feihong, "a Cantonese physician and martial artist renowned for his patriotism and virtue."[159] Kwan Tak-hing who played him "already had the nickname of 'The Patriotic Entertainer' due to his avid fundraising activities during the war."[160] Of his 130 movies over his sixty year career, Kwan Tak-hing starred as Huang Feihong in eighty-six of them.[161] He also played Huang Feihong in a thirteen part TVB television series in 1976,[162] one of at least five television series related to Huang.[163] The role of Huang Feihong has been played by numerous well known stars of Hong Kong and Chinese cinema: Gordon Liu (1976, 1981), Jackie Chan (1978, 1994), Kwan Tak-hing (1979), Jet Li (1991, 1992, 1993, 1997), Vincent Zhao (1994, 1995), and Sammo Hung (2004).[164] There are many seminal performances in this illustrious group. Jackie Chan's two films, *Drunken Master* and *Drunken Master II*, are particularly significant to the legend of Huang Feihong as well as kungfu film in general. Jet Li's series of Huang Feihong movies, directed by Tsui Hark, were also well received at the box office and by critics. In addition, Jackie Chan also sang the Mandarin version of the theme song for the second Huang Feihong movie in Tsui Hark's series in 1992.[165]

The kungfu industrial complex is exemplified by the impact of the success of the first movie, *The Story of Wong Fei Hung* (1949):

> The film was an enormous success, spawning an incredible chain of sequels; dozens of directors and stars learned their craft working on the series, including celebrated director Lau Kar Leung (ironically, the student of a student of a student of the *real* Wong Fei Hung). Lau went on to try his own

hand at the Wong Fei Hung legend with *Challenge of the Masters* (1976). Lau's novel concept was to show Wong as an awkward young man rather than a mature elder statesman; the film proved to be a key influence for one of the greatest kung fu movies of all time, *Drunken Master* (1978), directed by Yuen Woo Ping and starring Jackie Chan at the dawn of his stardom.[166]

Prior to Bruce Lee putting kungfu on the global map, Kwan Tak-hing played the nationalist hero Huang Feihong and Chan took over the role in 1978 in his seminal kungfu masterpiece, *Zui quan* (Drunken master), which was followed by the even more excellent sequel, *Zui quan* II (Drunken master II; 1994). Actors from *Drunken Master II* play in numerous Jin Yong movie and television adaptations (e.g., Andy Lau, Felix Wong, Di Long, Anita Mui, etc.). In Chan's portrayal, the mischievous young Huang Feihong causes a lot of trouble, often embarrassing his upright father, who consequently threatens to beat him. Critic Kin-Yan Szeto has characterized Chan's portrayal of Huang Feihong as follows:

> Whereas Jet Li's empowering Chinese martial arts in the *Once Upon a Time in China* series (1991–1997) merely affirmed "Chinese-ness as a 'national style' in the face of imperialist oppression (Teo 2001: 153), Chan used the drunken style to undermine such assertion of patriarchal masculinity and its strong association with Chinese nationalism. This use of animal gestures, drunken postures, and comic personae, which symbolically and comically contests fatherhood, hegemonic masculinity, and Chinese nationalism, would have been unlikely in the earlier film or in a more "serious" film of the time.[167]

Such symbolic contestation of fatherhood implies a common understanding of the hierarchical roles of father and son in Chinese cultural consciousness. In *Drunken Master* Chan plays both sides for comic relief. After Feihong (Jackie Chan) defeats the fighters of an enemy school, the enemy finally finds a champion named Yan Tiexing to challenge him. Yan handily kicks Feihong around, and the following dialogue ensues:

> Yan: With only these limited abilities you still think you'll make it in the Jianghu? Who taught you?
>
> Huang Feihong: My dad taught me.
>
> Yan: It appears your dad's kungfu isn't any good either. Have him join my school.
>
> Yan: Hurry up and become my obedient son.
>
> Huang Feihong: Screw your mother.
>
> Yan: Sit down, stand up, sit down. Obedient son surprisingly listens well.[168]

Framing this dialogue Yan has already used the pejorative *xiaozi* (punk) and *ni zhege xiaozi* (you this punk) to bully and insult Jackie/Feihong as he kicks him around. Such humiliation is a wakeup call to Feihong, who vows to train seriously in order to recoup his honor. Feihong thereupon returns with humility to his adopted beggar master and earnestly dedicates himself to learning the Drunken Fist style.

Drunken Master II continues the comedy of the original but takes the tension between strict disciplinarian father and mischievous, but generally obedient son, to an extreme. Speaking as a doctor, his father lectures against the evils of alcohol and has forbidden Feihong to drink or fight using the Drunken Fist style. Conflict between father and son reaches a peak after Feihong uses the Drunken Fist style while defending his stepmother, thereby defeating an evil Japanese plant manager and his henchmen, the fight finally broken up by his father, who scolds him for drinking.

After returning home a customer comes to their family compound and complains about receiving fake ginseng from Dr. Huang. It was Feihong who switched the real ginseng, and he thereupon is beaten by his father for tarnishing the reputation of the family business. Feihong's stepmother (played by the brilliant Anita Mui) tries to defend him at first, saying Feihong was defending her after being insulted by the foreigner, and also stressing that she was the one who supplied the wine he used for Drunken Fist style. While he is being beaten, the still drunk Feihong inadvertently defends himself by first smashing a wine flask and then hitting his father using Drunken Fist kungfu. The dialogue follows:

> "Huang Qiying [father]: You dare fight back? I truly have wasted my time raising you. Get out of here. I, Huang Qiying, don't have such a son as you. Get out, get out, get out. . . .
>
> Huang Taitai [stepmother]: Are you crazy? He is your father!"[169]

Even as his father is beating him, she had continued to defend him. But when she sees him hit his father her attitude immediately reverses. Feihong has obviously crossed a line of propriety and she concludes he is "crazy" because he hit his father. This extreme example insinuates that hierarchical kungfu is to be used against outsiders and must not be translated into actual kungfu action against one's own real family.

The humbled and remorseful Feihong later sings songs of respect about his father and even refuses to fight back using Drunken Fist style when the Japanese manager and his henchmen challenge him to a rematch. Consequently, Feihong is hung naked from the town gates with a sign (ironically) proclaiming his skill at Drunken Fist style kungfu. The extreme transgression of hitting one's father results in his exile and being termed "crazy." It does not matter that Feihong was drunk when

Figure 4.4. Jackie Chan using Drunken Fist kungfu and scolded by his father, *Drunken Master II* (1994)

he hit his father or that he was originally protecting his stepmother from the foreigner's insults and slap. In the film's denouement, the ultimately filial Feihong makes up for his transgression by using the Drunken Fist style to unmask the foreigners and their henchmen who are plundering precious art treasures and thereby save the face of the entire Chinese nation. At this point it becomes clear that facing up to challenges to the nation (*guojia*) is prioritized over obedience to one's own family (*jia*).

Discussion of kungfu and *wuxia* film is always complicated by the fact of China's gradual opening to the outside world in the 1980s, well after Jin Yong's works were initially serialized and in the process of being revised, reserialized, and adapted over and over. The kungfu industrial complex was already operating when the mainland Chinese market was added to the mix, broadening the audiences, and associated cultural industry. There were many advantages after the Mainland opened up. Television and film adaptations could be filmed on site in the Mainland instead of in a mocked-up studio elsewhere. Mainland actors also began to revise Jin Yong's seminal roles as well as other famous roles. Jet Li was the first mainland Chinese martial artist to take kungfu and *wuxia* roles. He played the nationalist hero Huang Feihong at the same time Jackie Chan was playing the hero in the 1990s. Supporting actors in Jet Li's first 1991 Huang Feihong film included Jacky Cheung, Yuan Biao (Jackie Chan's martial brother), and Rosamund Kwan. Jet Li starred in four Huang Feihong films directed by Tsui Hark, played the title role in the nationalist film narratives on the life of *Huo Yuanjia* (2006), portrayed the title character in two *Fang Shiyu* films (1993), and played the fictional protagonist Chen Zhen in *Fist of Legend* (1994). In the same period, Jet Li also starred in *Shaolin Temple* (1982) and in *Taiji Zhang Sanfeng* (Yuen Woo-ping, dir., 1993), and as Jin Yong's character Linghu Chong in the last two of the *Swordsman* films costarring Brigitte Lin. In addition, Jet Li played the Jin Yong character Zhang Wuji in the 1993 film *Yi tian tu long ji zhi mo jiao jiaozhu* (Kungfu cult master; a.k.a. Demon cult master of The Demi-gods and Semi-devils). Jet Li's roles took him to the Shaolin Temple, Wudang Mountain, and included the range of real life kungfu heroes and fictional characters from *wuxia* novels. After building this impressive kungfu and *wuxia* film pedigree in Asia, he went to Hollywood and continued his kungfu film success.

The acting, directing, stunt choreography, cast and crew of Hong Kong film are an extended family affair, and sometimes also an actual family affair. Sons follow fathers in the business, and martial brothers, such as the "Seven Little Fortunes" stars Sammo Hong, Jackie Chan, Yuan Biao, and the others work together in movies, split off on their own, and rejoin forces later. The value structure of the film world mirrored the *yiqi* of *wuxia* novels, and emphasized taking care of your family, and especially your *xiongdi* (brothers):

> When former *One-Armed Boxer* Jimmy Wang Yu decided to make a comeback as actor/producer, he made sure that the film, *Island of Fire*, featured an all-star cast. He used his influence to get Jackie, Sammo Hung, singer Andy Lau and *The Lover* (1992) star Tony Leung to make this "charity" film for a fraction of their usual fees. . . . "I had no choice," says Jackie when asked why he made the film. "it's 'heng dai,' the older brother/younger brother relationship."[170]

The brotherhood, "'heng dai,' the older brother/younger brother relationship" feeds the "human capital" element of the kungfu industrial complex, crossing subgenre lines from *wuxia* to kungfu to comedy kungfu and onward. In addition to the stars, directors, and crew, human capital in the film industry includes the less visible actors and supporting actors who play parts without whom the stories could not be told.

VILLAIN SHI JIAN (SHIH KIEN)

Protagonists are the actors who get the lion's share of the glory, the recognition, the visibility, and probably the remuneration in the film industry. These heroes may be male or female, but they can't exist in literature or film without supporting casts that make them the center. The supporting cast includes minor characters, but also the antagonists, the villains against whom protagonists struggle in the narrative process that defines their characters. To have a hero requires a villain. To have strong heroes, authors create strong villains, and to have superheroes there must be supervillains. Jin Yong created a variety of types of antagonists, male and female of all different levels who help define his protagonists large and small. *Heroes'* Guo Jing and Huang Rong fight Western Venom Ouyang Feng and his surrogates. *Wanderer's* Linghu Chong meanders on a developmental journey through which he discovers a host of villains from *both* good and evil sects, including Asia the Invincible and also his own master Yue Buqun. *Book and Sword's* protagonist Chen Jialuo is portrayed against turncoat Zhang Zhaozhong of the Wudang sect who sold out to the Qing government. Scheming and treacherous antagonists are found vying for power in secret, sometimes hidden (if temporarily) from the reader as well as the protagonists.

Meta-narratively speaking, in Jin Yong's works historically based nationalist sects and societies such as the anti-Manchu Qing Red Flower Society and the Heaven and Earth Society are set against officialdom of the Qing empire. In another twist, *Cauldron's* Wei Xiaobao defines herodom in terms of the *jianghu* ideology of *yiqi* (righteous loyalty/friendship), which guides the opportunistic line he walks in his status as anti-Qing leader and friend of Emperor Kang Xi, while also fighting the Ming traitor Wu Sangui's political ambitions to overthrow the Qing rulers whom he has helped install in power. The complexity of Jin Yong's heroes and villains throughout his oeuvre imbues his narratives with power and longevity. Although extensive television adaptations can provide a sense of this depth because there are many hours in which to develop characters, the mediums of film and television unfortunately often simplify the good/evil dichotomy between protagonists and antagonists. Informed readers can either easily supply the details of such character twists when viewing adaptations if they possess the requisite kungfu literacy or have the opportunity to expand their kungfu literacy if they so desire.

Among all the stars who played villains in the kungfu industrial complex, there is one outstanding example, the villain among villains, Shi Jian. Shi Jian played numerous Jin Yong villain roles, but his status was already well established through his roles in hundreds of movies over a long career. Those frequent villain roles resulted in a pun on his name, *jianren Jian* (villain Jian), a moniker that was so well-known that for "many years thereafter Hong Kongers used the term *jian guo Shi Jian* (more traitorous than Shi Jian)" to refer to villains who surpassed Shi's treachery.[171] Although he didn't always play the antagonist, his casting as a villain stuck and it took a lifetime to change this image, as indicated in a 2007 headline from *Pingguo ribao* (Apple daily) which notes that he is cleansed from his villainous air at age ninety-four.[172]

Shi Jian played in 554 movies over his sixty-four-year career running from 1940–2004. In addition, he played in thirty-one TVB television series. Jin Yong adaptations constitute seven of Shi Jian's thirty-one roles in those television productions. These series include *Book and Sword* (1976), *Dragon Sabre* (1978), *Semi-Devils* (1982), *Heroes* (1983), *Companion* (1983), *Wanderer* (1984), *Royal Blood* (1985), and *Flying Fox* (1985).[173] In general, the role that Shi Jian plays for Jin Yong based television series (or films) is antagonist. Examples include his role as Xiao Yuanshan in the 1982 TVB adaptation of *Semi-Devils*, Qiu Qianren and his twin Qiu Qianzhang in the 1983 TVB adaptation of *Heroes*, Jinlun Fawang (Golden wheel Sakyamuni) in the 1960 two-part film adaptation of *Companion*, the treacherous Zhang Zhaozhong in the 1960 film and the 1976 TVB series adaptations of *Book and Sword*. Some of his roles like Xiao Yuanshan in *Semi-Devils* and Xie Xun in *Dragon Sabre* are complicated because they are not explicitly evil but fall on the negative side of neutral.

While Shi Jian is more famous for his multitude of roles in non-Jin Yong movies based on the historical martial arts characters Huang Feihong and Fang Shiyu, he also acted in at least seventeen movie adaptations of Jin

Yong's works from 1958 thru 1964.[174] Positive roles include the part of the Daoist fighter Qiu Chuji in the first part of the film adaptation of *Heroes* (1958) and the partially positive role of Eastern Heretic Huang Yaoshi in the second part of the film adaptation of *Heroes* (1959). These Cantonese language movie adaptations of Jin Yong's *Heroes* were started in 1958 even before he had finished writing the work that ran serially from 1957–1959.[175]

Shi Jian's most famous villain role is arguably as Mr. Han in Bruce Lee's quintessential kungfu film, *Enter the Dragon* (*Long zheng hu dou*, 1973). The final fight scene between Lee and Mr. Han is a classic, with Shi Jian using a bladed hand prosthetic to make cuts across Bruce's body and face. Audiences will not forget Lee's iconic action of licking his own blood from those cuts prior to killing Shi Jian in the finale of the movie. Shi Jian's 2009 obituary associates him with a list of kungfu stars: "Shi Jian, who acted in excess of 300 movies over more than 50 years, had cooperated with stars including Wu Chufan, Guan Dexing, Chow Yun-fat, Brigitte Lin, Jackie Chan, Bruce Lee, etc."[176] The short obituary also mentions five television series, two of which are adaptations of Jin Yong's works. Shi Jian's breadth of film and television kungfu experience extends from early Jin Yong movies through roles in Jin Yong television series. Shi Jian links other important stars in the kungfu industrial complex not directly related to Jin Yong, particularly Bruce Lee and peripherally Jackie Chan.

BRUCE LEE HOMAGE

It is impossible to consider the concept of a kungfu industrial complex without talking about Bruce Lee, even if Jin Yong and his works are the kernel of the present study. And even Jin Yong wasn't immune to Lee's cultural impact. Hamm notes that in Jin Yong's *wuxia* magazine, *Martial Arts and History*, "for a period in the early 1970s featured movie stills or photos of luminaries from the Bruce Lee-inspired craze for kungfu movies."[177] Lee was learning his craft and making his movies in the heyday of Hong Kong production of *wuxia* and kungfu film. He created immense cultural capital, and his image continues to produce social and economic capital long after his death. I have not located any source confirming that Bruce Lee actually read Jin Yong's novels, but it is a good guess that he was exposed to the movies and/or the early television series at some point in Hong Kong even though he spent his 20s in Washington and California. Kungfu training, movies, and novels all construct the discourse of cultural capital necessary to translate kungfu ideology successfully on the screen. Lee is known, as previously mentioned, as having invented his own school of kungfu thought represented in his book, *Tao of Jeet Kune Do*. Not only did he utilize kungfu cultural capital to inform his acting and practice, but he also constructed it, literally writing a book on the "way" (*Tao*; pinyin spelling is *dao*; complicated by Cantonese "*do*" making a double usage in the title) that posthumously became part of kungfu cultural literacy. Moreover, at least one commentator notes that the base of Lee's philosophy boils down to be the same as that of Dugu Qiubai represented in Jin Yong's *Companion*: "formless move defeats form move" (*wu zhao sheng you zhao*).[178] In his book Lee's most similar concept is the notion "To float in totality, to have no technique, is to have all technique."[179] This idea is akin to Lee's well known remarks on strategy to "be formless, shapeless, like water," both of which can be traced back to *Sunzi The Art of War*:

> Military tactics are like unto water; for water in its natural course runs away from high places and hastens downwards. So, in war, the way is to avoid what is strong and to strike at what is weak. Water shapes its course according to the nature of the ground over which it flows; the soldier works out his victory in relation to the foe whom he is facing. Therefore, just as water retains no constant shape, so in warfare there are no constant conditions. He who can modify his tactics in relation to his opponent and thereby succeed in winning, may be called a heaven-born captain.[180]

This classic text of Chinese martial strategy was compiled over centuries. Jin Yong quotes directly from it and also refers to the strategy therein indirectly. Bruce Lee deserves credit for the application of these ideas and putting them in his own words for the twentieth-century audience that he was also introducing to Chinese kungfu. He was not thinking (or acting) in a vacuum, but rather steeped in deep study of kungfu and associated cultural knowledge. It is the area of kungfu cultural literacy that connects Bruce Lee and Jin Yong in the kungfu industrial complex.

Bruce Lee's kungfu cultural capital was the first step in the globalization of Hong Kong kungfu film. Although he was only making films for about five years, his five films represent the first wave of Hong Kong kungfu films successfully introduced to the world. Bruce Lee was a catalyst: "On May 16, 1973, *Fists of Fury*, *Deep Thrust—the Hand of Death*, and *Five Fingers of Death* were ranked 1, 2 and 3 respectively, on *Variety's* list of the week's top box-office draws."[181] Desser also notes that the industry was primed and ready to deliver more in this kungfu craze: "Bruce Lee's stardom accounts for the spectacular ascension of kung fu, and, luckily for U.S. distributors, there was a huge backlog of films that could be brought into overseas distribution immediately, along with an industry able to produce, no less hurriedly, films to cater to this sudden fad."[182] His films provided the introduction of terms and philosophy behind kungfu that three decades later led to the embrace of martial arts films like *Crouching*

Tiger, Hidden Dragon in 2000. And Bruce Lee's images, his kungfu moves and thoughts, became both the iconic metaphors to be imitated and symbols to be wielded in the construction of global kungfu cultural capital.

Kungfu cultural literacy was being assimilated in Hollywood action films often through "Bruce Lee embedding," visual references which pay him homage. These come in the form of both archetypical Bruce Lee hand signals and fight scenes which pit a lone martial arts hero against a gang. The honed and handsome Lee died young, so he is thus forever young, and audiences are reminded of him and his iconic kungfu imagery channeled by stars in movie after movie. The repeated embedding of his fighting gestures into movies cements his image and legacy ever deeper in kungfu cultural consciousness. Examples of such homage are found in numerous films and television series, variously performed by Jackie Chan in *City Hunter* (1993), Louis Koo (Gu Tianle) in the television series *A Step Back to the Past* (2001), Stephen Chow in *Shaolin Soccer* (2001) and *Kung Fu Hustle* (2004), and Jet Li in *Kiss of the Dragon* (2001). Hollywood pays Bruce Lee homage through Keanu Reeves in *The Matrix* (1999), Uma Thurman in *Kill Bill: Vol. 1* (2003), and Jay Chou in *The Green Hornet* (2011). Scholar Kenneth Chan refers to such borrowed embedding as "citationality," or "visual quotation," or "filmic allusions," which can have the effect of " enabling" films to "enter the popular cultural mainstream."[183]

Bruce Lee homage is an exploitation of his star power for cultural and economic capital. For example, his image is used as the logo for the popular "True Kungfu" (*zhen gongfu*) restaurant chain established in 1990 with shops in 57 cities throughout China.[184] Jackie Chan himself is a walking "Bruce homage" advertisement by virtue of his name. Lee is "Li Xiaolong" (little dragon Lee), and Jackie Chan took the name "Cheng Long" (becoming a dragon) "in honor of Bruce Lee" when he was cast in the Golden Harvest sequel to Lee's original, *New Fist of Fury* (1976).[185] The idea was that Bruce Lee is already a dragon and Jackie Chan would succeed him in becoming a dragon. In his 1993 film *City Hunter*, Chan performs the most extensive reenactment of the Bruce Lee legend during a fighting scene with tall black opponents that literally mirrors Lee's fight in his posthumous film *The Game of Death* (1978). The scene in *City Hunter* takes place in a movie theatre. Jackie Chan watches Bruce Lee's fight with Kareem Abdul-Jabbar on screen while he himself fights tall black martial artists.

When he encounters difficulties fighting opponents so much taller than himself, he looks to the screen and observes the techniques Lee uses against Kareem, then implements them on the spot. There are differences between the Bruce Lee and Jackie Chan in spirit. Lee's fight scene was designed as a serious encounter where he must defeat increasingly difficult

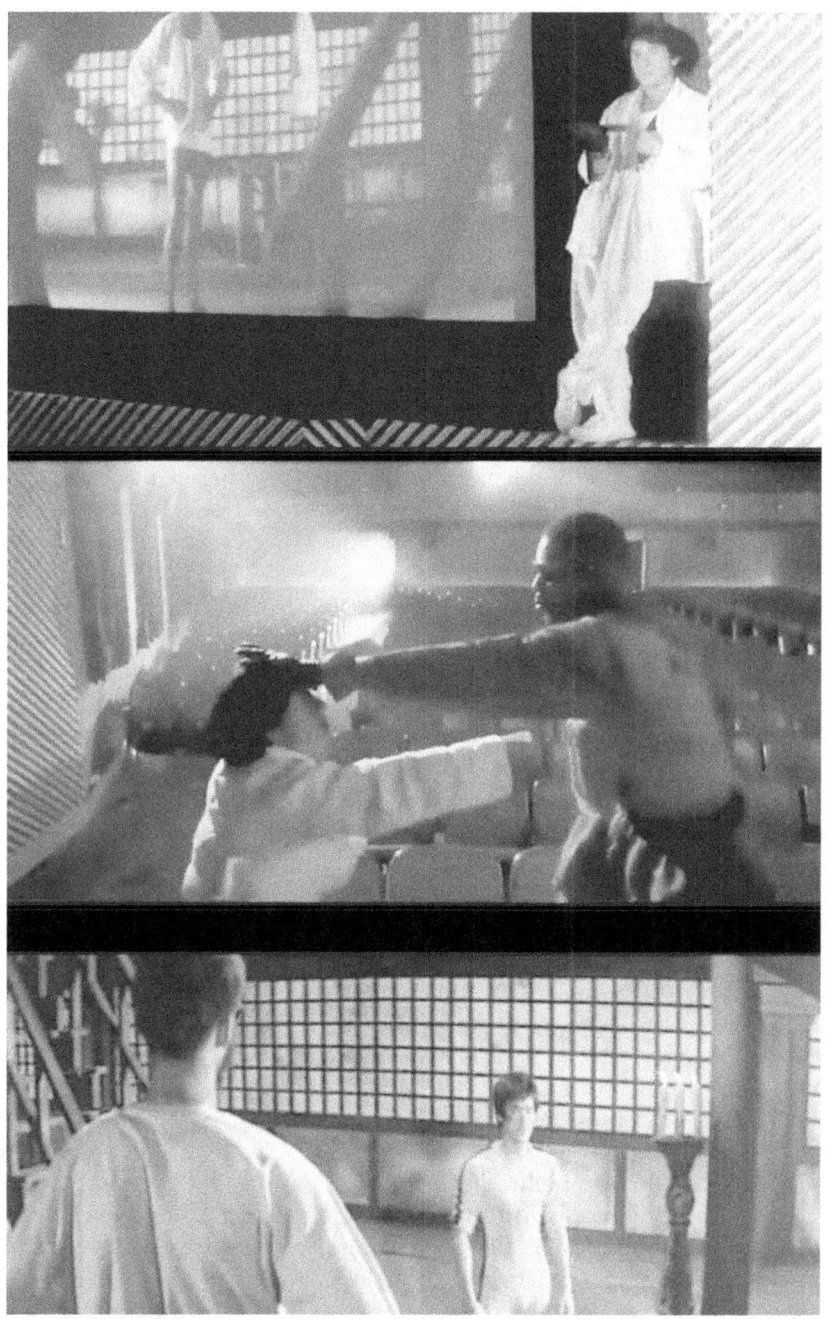

Figure 4.5. Jackie Chan, *City Hunter* (1993), movie theater scene in which he learns from Bruce Lee how to fight tall opponents, direct homage to Lee's iconic fight in *Game of Death* (1978)

opponents representing various schools of martial arts as he moves from floor to floor up a pagoda. Chan fights with slapstick humor enhanced through mirroring Lee's moves. Learning at the feet of the "master" is a realization of his name "becoming a dragon," thus a true genuflection to the iconic Bruce Lee. This was not the first time Chan "learned" from Lee. He had minor roles in *Fist of Fury* (1972) and *Enter the Dragon* (1973). In *Fist of Fury* "Lee kicked [him] through a wall" and in *Enter the Dragon* "he snapped Chan's neck."[186]

Having dispatched those opponents in *City Hunter*, Chan looks over to the movie screen and says thanks for Lee's martial instruction. Much to Chan's surprise, Lee replies from the screen saying, "You're welcome." This is the most extensive homage paid to Lee in Jackie Chan's movies, but it is not the only instance. *Rush Hour 2* (2001) plays on the stereotype of black virility, copying scenes from Lee's *Enter the Dragon*. Chan and Chris Tucker go to a Hong Kong massage parlor where Chris selects numerous girls to service him. A similar scene from Lee's *Enter the Dragon* has black actor Jim Kelly choosing four or five girls to accompany him for the night.

The play on kungfu cultural capital based in Bruce Lee knowledge is broad and deep. The yellow jump suit that he wears fighting Kareem in *The Game of Death* is another iconic emblem of his image that numerous stars have directly borrowed. Uma Thurman's Beatrice Kiddo in *Kill Bill: Vol. 1* (2003) dons the yellow jump suit and rides a motorcycle (another replicated element) to the bar in which she takes on O-Ren Ishii's (actor Lucy Liu) team of yakuza, the Crazy 88. It is no surprise that director Quentin Tarantino is an avid fan of Hong Kong film, "and his active promotion of Hong Kong cinema has helped filmmakers like John Woo and Yuen Woo-ping make their mark in Hollywood.[187] The film in fact begins with homage to Shaw Brothers film company, directly using its opening scene Shaw logo.

The yellow jump suit is also a favorite and Uma Thurman fills it out in style. In Stephen Chow's *Shaolin Soccer* (2001), the goalie wears a nearly identical exercise suit and also replays Bruce Lee's fighting style and iconic hand signals (bring it on) and arrogant expression (you're going to get it). Not surprisingly, Stephen Chow is "an avowed admirer of Bruce Lee,"[188] and in the same movie his own character uses these Bruce Lee signals to taunt an opponent. The bring it on hand signals, its accompanying arrogant facial expression, and occasionally Bruce's footwork, are also copied by other actors. For example, Louis Koo (Gu Tianle), plays Xiang Xiaolong (little dragon Xiang) in the television series called *A Step Back to the Past* where as a Hong Kong detective he travels in time back 2,000 years. Fighting against Qin dynasty opponents, Koo uses Bruce Lee's footwork, and taunting hand signals—pointing, calling with the finger, thumbs down—to rile his opponent.[189]

These selected examples are only a handful of the multitude of visual references that illustrate the cross-fertilization of Bruce Lee himself as a metaphor/symbol of kungfu in Hong Kong and Hollywood over half a century. Taiwanese pop music icon Jay Chou co-starred as Kato in the

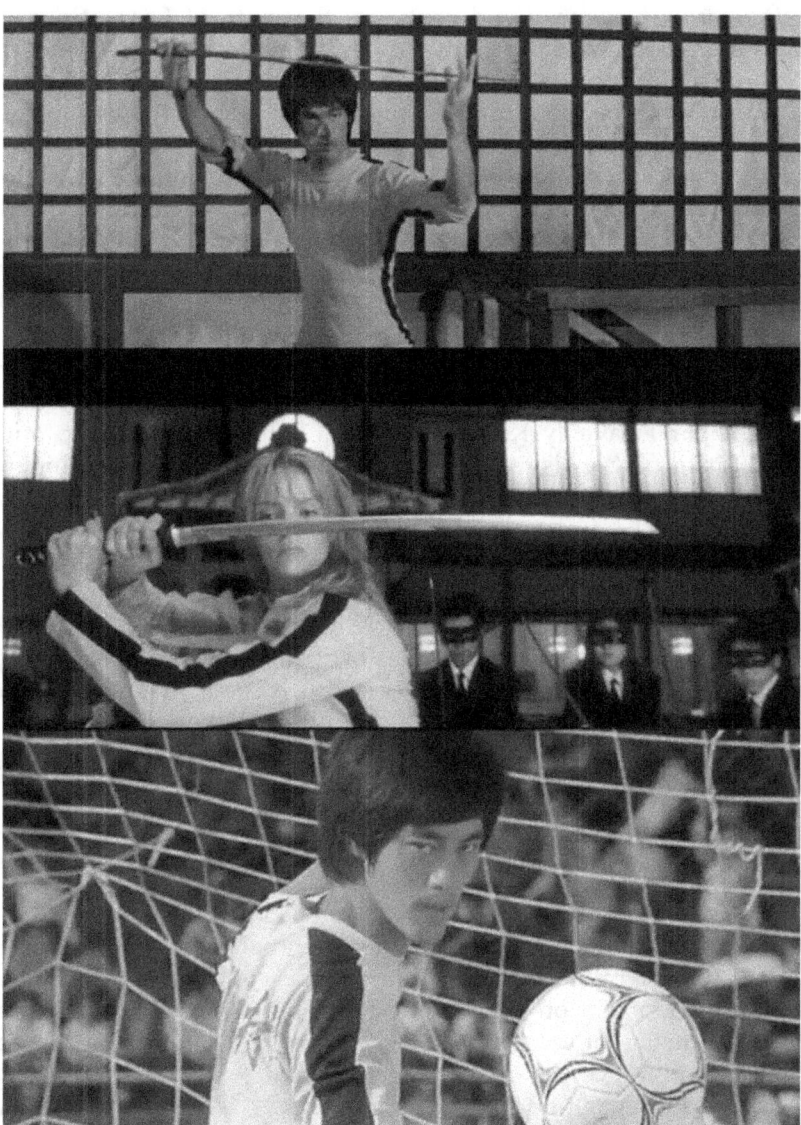

Figure 4.6. Visual References to Bruce Lee's iconic costume in *The Game of Death* (1978), *Kill Bill* (2003), *Shaolin Soccer* (2001)

Hollywood version of *The Green Hornet* (2011). This role is a reprisal of Bruce Lee's breakout television role in the original 1966 television series. Chou is shown paging through sketches he made of Bruce Lee in various fighting poses. As a film reprisal of the original television show, it should be expected that the kungfu abilities of the twenty-first-century Kato would be equal in quality of the original. Referencing Bruce Lee and his kungfu in the sketchbook is an act of validation of Chou's own kungfu training through homage and continues the myth of Lee's star power while staking a claim to the myth for Jay Chou himself.

While Jay Chou has not been involved directly in Jin Yong adaptations, he is linked to the kungfu industrial complex through Bruce Lee and his reprisal of Kato. However, Chou is an Asian megastar in his own right. He doesn't need to use Bruce Lee homage to validate his cultural capital in Asia where he is readily recognized. The visual reference does, however, help the Western audience situate the extraordinary kungfu he executes in his rendition of Kato. In fact, Jay Chou is a virtual pop culture industry in himself, a highly talented singer/musician who earned fame writing, singing, and producing music in Taiwan and China. His music career led him into film, production, advertising, and all other manner of cultural production. He has collaborated with many other stars, including the "Four Heavenly Kings" of 1990s Cantopop/Mandopop music. Kungfu film is part of his repertoire with credits that include leading roles in Zhang Yimou's *Curse of the Golden Flowers* (2006) alongside superstars Chow Yun-fat and Gong Li, as well as *Kung Fu Dunk* (*Gongfu guanlan*, a.k.a. *Da guanlan*; 2008), a film in which he combines his longtime interest in basketball with kungfu. Jay Chou not only stars in this movie, but also composed the theme song called "Zhou daxia" (Great knight Zhou [Chou]), which is a combination of his own surname and the *wuxia* concept of the ultimate hero (*xia*). His act of Bruce Lee homage in *The Green Hornet* should be viewed as laying a claim to Lee's kungfu legacy, a utilization of cultural capital in an attempt to help Chou *globalize* his image.

MEGASTAR POWER: JACKIE CHAN AND JIN YONG

Jay Chou does not have the cultural capital of a global superstar yet, but the kungfu industrial complex may eventually help him reach that level of cultural capital. Jackie Chan, on the contrary, is immediately recognizable globally on Bruce Lee's level, but in contrast to Lee's abbreviated timeline of less than ten years, it took Chan decades to reach such recognition. The vehicles of global recognition are the same, kungfu and film. Jackie Chan performed a tour de force costarring as Mr. Han in the Hollywood remake of *The Karate Kid* (2010) with actor Jaden Smith. Hollywood's myopic marketing apparently figured the cultural capital of the original film was greater than Jackie Chan's own given Hollywood's conflation of the Japanese term karate with the Chinese term kungfu. Indeed, the *Christian Science Monitor* review of the movie points out a more accurate title would be "The Kung Fu Kid."[190] You don't have to be a linguist to understand the cultural origins of "karate" versus "kungfu." Going to the Chinese market the film was renamed "Kungfu Dream" (*Gongfu meng*), perhaps a reference to popularization of the concept of "the Chinese Dream" (*Zhongguo meng* or *Zhongguo mengxiang*) which articulates aspirations for a great Chinese national revival/future expressed in similar linguistic currency of "the American Dream." The movie is set in Beijing where Jackie Chan explicates the idea of kungfu as a way of life, as a greater morality. In terms of the kungfu industrial complex, Chan describes his own trajectory in which kungfu was his path from poverty to national and international fame. Using kungfu as a vehicle, he completes the circle of globalization by bringing the international audience back home to China. The idea of kungfu as an ultimate morality (cultural, not politicized) coincides with the narratives of Stephen Chow's *Shaolin Soccer* (2001), as well as *Kungfu Panda* (2008), for which Chan did the voice of Monkey. *Kungfu Panda* is notable in terms of transnationalism because it caused angst among some Chinese critics who engaged in introspection, asking: "Why didn't Chinese make this movie?" Set in Beijing, *The Karate Kid* complicates this issue, having Chinese stars and tracing the martial lineage of Jackie Chan's character, Mr. Han, to the Wudang Mountain kungfu sect. The founder of the Wudang Sect also invented Chinese Taiji. The moral and physical power of Chinese kungfu is demonstrated by Jaden Smith who capably overcomes bigger and stronger adversaries that practice a cruel application of the martial arts. Jackie Chan thus becomes a "trans-transnational star" by reprising the original Hollywood Japanese role with Chinese cultural sensibilities and martial/moral philosophy.

No single person has the bandwidth to represent the kungfu industrial complex as a whole (Michelle Yeoh may stand as an exception in *Everything Everywhere All at Once* [2022]). While Jackie Chan's direct connection to Jin Yong's works is limited, he has lengthy and deep connections with many directors and stars of Jin Yong related works. In *Kungfu Yoga* (2017), Chan demonstrates variety of kungfu styles while fighting off attackers, including Chinese and Indian kungfu, but the first kungfu he declares is *xiang long shiba zhang* (eighteen palms subduing the dragon). This kungfu is practiced by Jin Yong's renowned characters Xiao Feng, Guo Jing, and Hong Qigong. Chan's single direct connection to a Jin Yong work is recording a theme song to the 1994 Taiwan television adaptation of *Dragon*

Sabre. On closer examination, this surface level simplicity of a "single" connection has deeper structural dimensions that include connections to directors, actors, as well martial arts archetypes and *wuxia* film in general. Kungfu connections run deep through the industry.

YUEN WOO-PING: TECHNICAL KUNGFU MASTER DIRECTOR

The kungfu industrial complex is a multidimensional matrix of connections that interweave, intersect, and feed off each other in a myriad of ways. While the creation of cultural capital first prioritizes the authors (who are already working within a discourse of cultural capital), the next level of credit for production of cultural capital should go to the auteurs who work with scriptwriters to adapt the novels to screen, and then the actors who interpret the characters (along with the production crews that facilitate the technical aspects of those interpretations). The relationship between Jackie Chan and Yuen Woo-ping (Yuan Heping) is illustrative of this. Yuen is an important director and action director/choreographer who directed Chan's two breakthrough films in 1978, *Snake in the Eagle"s Shadow* and *Drunken Master*. Not surprisingly, Yuen has worked with virtually all the important kungfu stars in Hong Kong and is credited as action director for the hugely popular forty-three-episode, mainland Chinese adaptation of the Ming Dynasty literary masterpiece, *Water Margin* (1998). Among his other credits, Yuen was also action director for *Bruce Lee and I* (*Lee Xiaolong yu wo*, 1976), a "biographical action film" which also stars Betty Ting and purports to tell the story of Lee and Ting in whose apartment Bruce Lee died.[191] He also directed Donnie Yen in *Su Qi Er* (a.k.a. *Hero Among Heroes*, 1993), as well as Michelle Yeoh in *Wing Chun* (*Yong chun*, 1994), and was action director for Yeoh's *Crouching Tiger, Hidden Dragon* (2000). He was action director for Stephen Chow's *Kung Fu Hustle* (2004) and numerous Jet Li movies, such as *Huo Yuanjia* (*Fearless*, 2006). Yuen was action director for *Gongfu zhi wang* (*The Forbidden Kingdom* [King of Kungfu], 2008), which starred Jackie Chan and Jet Li together. Yuen also connects to Tony Leung and Zhang Ziyi in *Yi dai zongshi* (*The Grandmaster*, 2013) as action choreographer. Yuen Woo-ping's father, Yuen Siu-tian, played kungfu master, the beggar Su Qi Er, in *Drunken Master* (1978), where he taught Jackie Chan's character Huang Feihong the "Drunken Fist" style of kungfu. The title *Su Qi Er* itself is used again for a 2010 film (the English title this time is *True Legend*) and was directed by Yuen Woo-ping with a starring cast of kungfu cinema notables including Vincent Zhao, Michelle Yeoh, David Carradine (in his last movie), and Gordon Liu, as well as pop singers Zhou Xun and Jay Chou. While this movie bombed at the box office, its multigenerational kungfu pop culture pedigree of director and actors is unsurpassed.

Yuen Woo-ping is directly connected to Jin Yong's martial arts novels as action director for the 1984 Chow Yun-fat adaptation of Jin Yong's *Wanderer*. He is also connected indirectly through his work with Chinese film stars Stephen Chow and Gordon Liu, both of whom starred in adaptations of Jin Yong novels to television series and films. Yuen is the quintessential director and action choreographer who ties globalization of the kungfu industrial complex together literally in a matrix of action adventure. In addition to credit as action choreographer for *Crouching Tiger* (2000), his transnational action choreography creds also include *The Matrix* (1998) and its sequels, as well as then Quentin Tarantino's *Kill Bill: Vol. 1* (2003) and *Kill Bill: Vol. 2* (2004).

The *Kill Bill* movies reconnect Yuen Woo-ping to the early days of globalization of the kungfu industrial complex through the David Carradine, who starred Kwai Chang Caine in the sixty-three-episode ABC television series, *Kung Fu* (1972–1975). Carradine appears as Bill, the title character of *Kill Bill*. Moreover, *Kill Bill* completes a full homage circle through the Hong Kong actor, Gordon Liu, who stars as the Shaolin master Pai Mei (Bai Mei). Liu trains Bill and later Bill's disciple Kiddo and the other members of the Deadly Viper Assassination Squad. He indirectly connects the kungfu circle to television adaptation of Jin Yong's novels. Gordon Liu portrayed Emperor Kang Xi in the 1983 film adaptation of *Cauldron* about the time that Andy Lau played that part in the TVB series.[192] Liu also had parts in Jin Yong television adaptations including the TVB derivative *Jianmo Dugu Qiubai* (Sword demon Dugu Qiubai, 1990), the adaptations *She diao yingxiong zhuan zhi jiu yin zhenjing* (*The Eagle-Shooting Heroes* nine yin classic, 1993), *Companion* (1995), *Flying Fox* (1999), and *Dragon Sabre* (2001).[193] Gordon Liu's 1983 portrayal of Emperor Kang Xi and his 1995 portrayal of Jinlun Fawang are major roles, but most of the other parts are secondary level characters in Jin Yong novels.

Perhaps the quintessential example of star power in the kungfu industrial complex may be come in production the 2017 movie short *Gong shou dao* (literally: "kungfu protecting the way") written and produced by Jet Li, directed by Wen Zhang, with action directors Sammo Hong, Yuen Woo-ping, and Ching Siu-Tung, and starring Alibaba billionaire Jack Ma along with a list of A-list kungfu film and superstars including Donnie Yen, Wu Jing, and Jet Li. The plot of this short film centers on Jack Ma as a "nondescript middle-aged man who passes by 'Huashan Sect' gate and uses his brain to defeat six martial artists and obtain a book of martial secrets."[194] The extended metaphor is Jack Ma taking on the world with his business acumen. Jack Ma's Jin Yong connection was previously noted

Figure 4.7. Gordon Liu as Kangxi in the Shaw Brothers film adaptation of *Caldron* (1983) and as the dual role of Johnny Mo and Pai Mei in the *Kill Bill* films

through reference to his Alibaba nickname, Feng Qingyang, which derives from the name of the Huashan Sword Sect elder who taught Linghu Chong the unrivaled sword style, the Nine Swords of Dugu. For this film, however, it is Jack Ma's unparalleled economic status that brought all these actors and directors together (without remuneration) for a 22-minute film to promote a "common dream" and "by means of the film pay respect to the contributions of all the progenitors of Chinese kungfu, pay respect to Chinese culture, and at the same time share Chinese culture with the whole world."[195]

Action choreographers like Yuen Woo-ping and Ching Siu-Tung became directors in their own right. They are lynchpins in the kungfu industrial complex, and they eventually worked in Hollywood like many of the stars with whom they worked. While others in the West may claim the invention of parkour (free running) for themselves, the briefest look at an early Jackie Chan movie is enough to demonstrate that he was engaged in the marvelous acrobatics of parkour long before its codification with a name. Similarly, Yuen Woo-ping and Ching Siu-Tung brought wirefu and gunfu techniques to global action film, which stand as *wuxia* and kungfu contributions to Hollywood even as the stars come and go. Jackie Chan explains this phenomenon in his biography, *I Am Jackie Chan* (New York: Ballantine Books, 1998), where he comments on the mutual borrowings between Hong Kong cinema and Hollywood, with the directionality being from Hong Kong to Hollywood in the latter part of the twentieth century:

> We didn't have the money, or the technical expertise, or the marking and distribution clout of the American studios, but we had things that Hollywood didn't have—including the kind of raw, yet beautifully choreographed action that required intense training and "unacceptable" risks to create....
> But that [is] what makes our movies unique.
> Ten years later, take a look at Hollywood today. Every major Hong Kong action film director has been recruited to shoot American pictures—from John Woo to Tsui Hark to Ringo Lam, and more. Chow Yun-fat, Michelle Yeoh, and I, we've all recently done Hollywood films. And even the pictures that aren't shot by Hong Kong directors and that don't feature a Hong Kong star—every frame, every sequence, every choreographed turn, twist, and leap—you couldn't copy a Hong Kong film more closely if you used a Xerox machine.
> Things sure do change, don't they?[196]

Chan may be exaggerating here with the use of "every" with respect to Hollywood action films adopting Chinese kungfu and the Hong Kong technical expertise to depict it in film, but his comment indicates the enormity of the impact of both kungfu actors, directors, and the depiction of kungfu techniques on the action film worldwide. Expertise imported from the Hong Kong film industry is a highly significant achievement and a crucial step in the globalization of the kungfu industrial complex.

This chapter has broadened the analysis of Jin Yong and his works in the kungfu industrial complex to include film and television adaptations, focusing on the cast and crews that facilitated the dissemination of kungfu cultural capital. Hong Kong (and Taiwan) television and film studios played a pivotal role in production of Jin Yong's *wuxia* television series and films. Shaw Brothers Studio was particularly important in this process and its transition from producing primarily films to mainly television series through its subsidiary Television Broadcasts Limited (TVB) was facilitated by its actor training course, which was instrumental in the career trajectories of numerous Jin Yong related stars, the Five Tigers of TVB being representative of the role of star power in the kungfu industrial complex. The careers of the two most prominent of the Five Tigers, Tony Leung and Andy Lau, transcended their early Jin Yong *wuxia* roles, but those roles initially facilitated their long careers in action film and dramas. Lau and Leung are thus outstanding examples of the increasingly global phenomenon of the kungfu industrial complex, measured by their status as Asian superstars with increasingly global visibility.

Tony Leung and Andy Lau are examples of the trajectory of cultural capital, as a virtuous star power cycle: initiation in their TVB acting training courses, application through their Jin Yong roles, promotion through their rise in popularity, enhancement of their careers through further roles, all of which feeds back into their image and star power. The cultural field represented by the Five Tigers of TVB was both competitive and complicated by TVB's desire to keep its stars under contract, not allowing them out of house to make more money or pursue other opportunities. This initially pitted Lau and Leung against each other, causing the lead role of Wei Xiaobao in the 1984 adaptation of *Cauldron* to be switched from Lau to Leung (who had re-signed with TVB out of economic necessity against Lau's drive for solidarity). Leung's rise in the entertainment field is punctuated by this course of events, which apparently stalled Lau's career for a year or two, although both eventually became megastars. This example demonstrates that the construction of star power is relatively complicated, more than just a measure of the star's ability to get roles and draw box office. To wit, construction of an actor's image and star power is vastly more intangible than success in a breakout film implies, but rather relies on cultural capital elements from the actor's early education (and specific roles), training in theater and foundational kungfu craft, and synergy within the industry as a whole. While it may appear that considerable luck and coincidence is involved construction of star power, approaching the star phenomenon from the perspective of cultural capital provides tools to demystify the process and also demonstrates the myriad of connections that form the kungfu industrial complex beyond the waxing and waning of a single star's image and career. The lengthy identification of Lau and Leung with Jin Yong works and roles over a period of decades is implicit testimony to the recognition that the stars themselves are conscious of how Jin Yong figures in their own cultural capital, which in turn has an impact on a star's social and economic capital.

This chapter demonstrates that the kungfu industrial complex is dynamic and growing. The influence of the Hong Kong literary and film industry cannot be underestimated in the globalization of kungfu and *wuxia* film. Furthermore, Jin Yong's works intersect with geography and politics as Mainland and Taiwan stars became important elements in the matrix. Star power both grapples with and transcends gender as analysis of Brigitte Lin's complex *wuxia* roles reveal, particularly in Wong Kar-wai's enigmatic film *Ashes of Time*. The kungfu cultural capital of Jin Yong works and characters is open-ended, indeterminant, as demonstrated by a phenomenon I call "Jin Yong derivative star power." Such an oblique film as *Ashes of Time* can be made at least partially intelligible through the analysis of kungfu cultural literacy. Finally, the kungfu industrial complex approach shows that legendary martial arts heroes are indirectly connected to Jin Yong works through the actors who portray them or through derivative works based on loose connections to Jin Yong's stories or characters. Thus, the villain Shih Kien who played roles in Jin Yong *wuxia* film adaptations links to Bruce Lee's iconic kungfu films. Furthermore, Bruce Lee homage in other martial arts films inform the greater globalization of kungfu cultural capital. Increasingly indirect and derivative examples demonstrate the breadth of the kungfu industrial complex and offer an interpretation of how and why Jackie Chan's assertion that "every frame, every sequence, every choreographed turn, twist, and leap" were copied from Hong Kong film is valid. Though only indirectly linked to Jin Yong and his works, essential kungfu stars such as Bruce Lee and Jackie Chan have important linkages within the kungfu industrial complex via studios, directors, and other cast and crew, all of whom populate an entertainment *jianghu* through their roles in the globalization of Chinese kungfu and culture.

NOTES

1. John Minford, "Translator's Introduction," in *The Deer and the Cauldron: The First Book, A Martial Arts Novel by Louis Cha* (New York: Oxford University Press, 1997): xi.
2. David Bordwell, *Planet Hong Kong: Popular Cinema and the Art of Entertainment* (Boston: Harvard University Press, 2000): 67.
3. Stephen Teo, *Chinese Martial Arts Cinema*, 2.
4. Ibid.
5. Petrus Liu, private communication, December 2016.
6. Lisa Odham Stokes, *Historical Dictionary of Hong Kong Cinema* (Lanham, MD: Scarecrow Press, 2007): xxxvi.
7. Ibid.
8. "Jay Chou—An Insight from enoVate China," accessed December 30, 2020, https://www.mgientertainment.com/2010/01/jay-chou/.
9. "Bruce Lee: The Lost Interview (filmed in 1971 --> first aired 1994)," 18:09–18:35, *The Pierre Burton Show*, total 24 minutes, 36 seconds, accessed May 24, 2016, https://archive.org/details/BruceLeeTheLostInterview.
10. "Introduction," Linda Lee, *Tao of Jeet Kune Do* (Burbank, CA: Ohara Publications, 1975): 4.
11. Bruce Lee, *Tao of Jeet Kune Do* (Burbank, CA: Ohara Publications, 1975): 70.
12. Herbie J. Pilato, *The Kung Fu Book of Caine: The Complete Guide to TV"s First Mystical Eastern Western* (Boston: Charles E. Tuttle, 1993), 13–17. See also "Kung Fu (TV series): Bruce Lee's Involvement."
13. Kenneth Chan, *Remade in Hollywood: The Global Chinese Presence in Transnational Cinemas* (Hong Kong: Hong Kong University Press, 2009), 153.
14. Linda Lee, *Bruce Lee: The Man Only I Knew* (New York: Warner Books, 1976): 130–131.
15. Matthew Polly, *Bruce Lee: A Life* (New York: Simon & Schuster, 2018). Cited in Richard Bejtlich, "The Truth about the Creation of the Kung Fu TV Series," May 20, 2019, https://web.archive.org/web/20210130134124/https://www.martialjournal.com/the-truth-about-the-creation-of-the-kung-fu-tv-series/.
16. "Bruce Lee: The Lost Interview," 20:50–21:17.
17. Laurence K. P. Wong, "Is Martial Arts Fiction in English Possible? With Reference to John Minford's English Version of the First Two Chapters of Louis Cha's *Luding Ji*," In *The Question of Reception: Martial Arts Fiction in English Translation* (Hong Kong: Lingnan College, 1997): 112.
18. Stephen Teo, *Chinese Martial Arts Cinema*, 76.
19. Jin Yong, *Companion*, 520.
20. Fredric Dannen and Barry Long, *Hong Kong Babylon: An Insider's Guide to the Hollywood of the East* (New York: Miramax Books, 1997): 38.

21. "Shaw Brothers History," accessed February 20, 2016, http://www.hkcinema.co.uk/Articles/shawbronews.html.

22. Jeff Yang, *Once Upon a Time in China: A Guide to Hong Kong, Taiwanese, and Mainland Chinese Cinema* (New York: Atria Books, 2003): 78.

23. Certain characters become titles for novels, or series of novels, that are then adapted into television series, and occasionally readapted. These title characters/titles are *Xiao Li Feidao* [Young Li's flying daggers], *Chu Liuxiang*, *Xiao Shiyilang*, and *Lu Xiaofeng*. See "Gu Long xiaoshuo gaibian dianying shoucang da quanji" [Complete collected adaptations of Gu Long's films], accessed January 6, 2021, https://www.douban.com/doulist/111533282/.

24. Sheldon H. Lu, *China, Transnational Visuality, Global Postmodernity* (Stanford: Stanford University Press, 2001): 197.

25. "Shaw Studios," accessed May 26, 2016, http://www.shawstudios.hk/who_we_are.htm.

26. "Shaw Brothers History."

27. TMDB, "Shaw Brothers," accessed March 28, 2022, https://www.themoviedb.org/company/5798/movie.

28. "Shao shi dianying gongsi" [Shaw Brothers film company], accessed May 26, 2016, http://baike.baidu.com/view/124639.htm#4.

29. "Shaw Brothers Martial Arts Films," accessed May 26, 2016, http://www.silveremulsion.com/review-series/ongoing-review-series/shaw-brothers-martial-arts-films/.

30. "Complete List of SHAW BROTHERS Martial Arts Movies," accessed May 26, 2016, http://rateyourmusic.com/list/gigiriva/complete_list_of_shaw_brothers_martial_arts_movies/.

31. "Shaoshi dianying gongsi: zuopin" [Shaw Brothers film company works], accessed March 18, 2016, http://baike.baidu.com/view/124639.htm?fromtitle=邵氏兄弟（香港）有限公司&fromid=859804&type=syn#4.

32. Ibid.

33. Bordwell, *Planet Hong Kong*, 64.

34. Ibid., 68.

35. Stokes, *Historical Dictionary*, xxxiv.

36. Bordwell, *Planet Hong Kong*, 68.

37. Stokes, *Historical Dictionary*, xxxv.

38. Kevin Lincoln, "From John Woo to John Wick, Here's Your Guide to Gun Fu," Vulture, October 12, 2016, https://www.vulture.com/2016/10/john-wick-gun-fu.html.

39. Mark Rahner, "'Wire-fu' Flicks: Pouncing Public, Hidden Treasures," *Seattle Times*, December 24, 2004, https://web.archive.org/web/20150102125529/http://seattletimes.com/html/movies/2002129305_martialarts24.html.

40. "tvb," accessed May 18, 2009, http://baike.baidu.com/view/926.htm.

41. "Adam Cheng," accessed July 31, 2018, https://www.imdb.com/name/nm0155532/.

42. "Established in 1976, TVBI Company Limited (TVBI) is the worldwide operating arm of Television Broadcasts Limited (TVB), which enjoys exclusive rights to distribute TVB programs to more than 40 countries and 100 cities, accessible

to over 300 million households." "TVBI," accessed March 18, 2016, http://b.tvb.com/tvbi/.

43. Another formulation of this is the "Five Tiger Generals" (wu hu jiang).

44. "Duo nian enyuan jiuchan bu qing dangnian 'wuhujiang' jinchao 'si que yi'" [Many years of grievances and irresolvable entanglements; the "five tiger generals" of those years are the "Four missing one" of today], May 31, 2007, http://ent.news.cn/2007-05/31/content_6177413.htm.

45. "Wuxian wu hu" [TVB five tigers], accessed May 28, 2016, http://baike.baidu.com/view/45291.html.

46. "Duo nian enyuan," accessed May 27, 2016.

47. "Huang Rihua," accessed January 6, 2021, https://baike.baidu.com/item/黃日華#3_2.

48. Run as a yearlong course until 1984, it was contracted to three months thereafter. See tvb," accessed June 29, 2009, http://baike.baidu.com/view/115923.html.

49. "Wuxian dianshi yiyuan xunlianban" [TVB actors training course], accessed March 28, 2022, https://baike.baidu.com/item无线电视艺员训练班#2.

50. Liang Jiaren played roles in three Jin Yong series in 1980: *Semi-Devils* (1982), *Companion* (1983), and *Wanderer* (Taiwan Television, 1985). He also played Hong Qigong in the 1998 Taiwan Television production of Jin Yong's *Companion* and the same role in the 2008 production, which starred Hu Ge. Liang also played Feng Qingyang in the 2012 production of Jin Yong's *Wanderer*, as well as Xiao Yuanshan in the 2013 production of *Semi-Devils*. In addition, he also played other non-Jin Yong roles, such as the historical martial arts hero Huang Feihong for TVB in several movies in the 1990s. "Liang Jiaren," accessed January 6, 2021, https://search.douban.com/movie/subject_search?search_text=梁家仁電視劇&cat=1002.

51. "Liang Chaowei, Zhou Xingchi, dou lai paolongtao de 82 ban *Tian long ba bu*" [Tony Liang (Leung) and Stephen Chow both play bit roles in the 1982 version of *The Semi-Gods and Semi-Devils*], Lu ju ba [Mainland theater], July 8, 2021, https://lujuba.cc/zh-hans/580802.html.

52. "Dugu Qiubai," accessed May 27, 2009, http://baike.baidu.com/view/893659.htm.

53. "56 sui Huang Rihua xueguan sai.buxiang tai pinming gouyong jiu hao," September 27, 2017, http://www.sinchew.com.my/node/1685885.

54. Hamm, *Paper Swordsman*, 240.

55. Ibid., 244.

56. Ibid., 241.

57. Jackie Chan's school also had such a structure, but even more entrenched since TVB's training lasted a mere three to twelve months, very short by comparison to the ten years Chan spent during his "Seven Little Fortunes" period at Master Yu Zhanyuan's Chinese Drama Institute.

58. "San Guo wu hu jiang" [Three kingdoms five tiger generals]," accessed January 6, 2021, https://baike.baidu.com/item/五虎上將/22566?fromtitle=三國五虎將&fromid=3620090.

59. "Liangshan wu hu jiang [Five tiger generals of Liangshan]," accessed January 6, 2021, https://baike.baidu.com/item/梁山五虎將/2786362?fromtitle=馬軍五虎將&fromid=638088.

60. "Wu hu jiang (1984)" [Five tiger generals (1984)], accessed January 6, 2021, https://movie.douban.com/subject/5401549/.

61. In addition, Tong played the Kang Xi emperor in Zhou Xingchi's comedy movie *Zheng pai Wei Xiaobao zhi fengzhi gounü* [Hero from Beyond the Boundary of Time, 1993], which takes Jin Yong's character Wei Xiaobao as its title character. See *"Zheng pai Wei Xiaobao zhi fengzhi gounü,"* accessed June 5, 2016, http://baike.baidu.com/view/1460127.htm.

62. "Wu ban *Lu ding ji* sishiwu wei zhujue chuanyue shikong da bipin" [Five editions of *The Deer and the Cauldron*: Forty-five main characters transcend time to compete], November 3, 2008, http://yule.sohu.com/20081103/n260321411.shtml.

63. "Duo nian enyuan," accessed May 27, 2016.

64. These "long-term 'management' contracts' that guaranteed TVB a piece of future showbiz earnings" of the stars translated to "pay that amounted to a few dollars an hour." Jeff Yang, *Once Upon a Time in China*, 78.

65. "Duo nian enyuan," accessed May 27, 2016.

66. "Wuxian wuhu/Liu Dehua/chudao jingli" [Five tigers of TVB/Liu Dehua /steps in his career start], accessed March 19, 2016, http://baike.baidu.com/item /无线五虎#5_2.

67. Dannen and Long, *Hong Kong Babylon*, 105.

68. Tony Leung is listed with nineteen albums from 1988 to 2016. "Liang Chaowei yinyue zhuanji [Tony Leung Chiu-wai albums]," accessed January 6, 2021, https://baike.baidu.com/item/梁朝偉#3_3.

69. Gu Long's *Jue dai shuang jiao* is rendered in English by a few translations: *The Twins*, *Handsome Siblings*, *Legendary Siblings*, *The Twin Heroes*, or *Amazing Twins*. Mention of Gu Long's novel adaptation here provides an example of the general phenomenon that the Five Tigers also worked on many non-Jin Yong kungfu works produced by TVB.

70. *Zhongshi xinwen tai* 中視新聞台 [CTV News Channel], Haixia yehang "Jin Yong de jianghu rensheng" [Night navigation on the Straits: "Jin Yong's life in the martial world"]. No date. YouTube, "Wuxia dash—Jin Yong chuanqi" [Martial arts grandmaster—the legend of Jin Yong], 39:28, posted April 23, 2014, accessed May 18, 2016, https://www.youtube.com/watch?v=opIdAMYowqI.

71. *"Zheng pai Wei Xiaobao,"* accessed January 6, 2016.

72. *"Zheng pai Wei Xiaobao,"* accessed August 1, 2017.

73. "Duo nian enyuan," accessed May 27, 2016.

74. "In 2005, Lau was awarded 'No.1 Box office Actor 1985–2005' of Hong Kong, yielding a total box office of HKD 1,733,275,816 for shooting 108 films in the past 20 years." "Andy Lau Biography," IMDb, accessed March 28, 2022, https://www.imdb.com/name/nm0490489/bio.

75. See *"Tian long ba bu ruxuan gaozhong yuwen duben."*

76. Note that connected with these important four characters is also "Middle Mystic Wang Chongyang" who has already died and only plays a reference point in Jin Yong's *Heroes*. That said, a 20-episode TVB spin-off television series based on this character was made in 1992 starring Ekin Cheng and Fiona Leung.

77. Monjeh, "The Return of the Condor Heroes," *Yumcha*, February 6, 2006, http://www.yesasia.com/us/yumcha/the-return-of-the-condor-heroes/0-0-0-arid.59-en/featured-article.html.

78. Ibid.
79. "Liu Dehua," accessed January 6, 2021, https://baike.baidu.com/item/刘德华/114923.
80. "Andy Lau Biography," IMDb, accessed March 28, 2022, https://www.imdb.com/name/nm0490489/bio.
81. "Liu Dehua," https://baike.baidu.com/item/刘德华/114923>, accessed January 6, 2021.
82. "Liu Dehua ziji zuoci, zuoqu de geming shi shenme? You naxie? Qing fenlei!" [What are the names of songs for which Andy Lau has written lyrics and music? Which ones? Please classify!"], May 5, 2009, http://zhidao.baidu.com/question/95922231.html.
83. "Liu Dehua," accessed March 17, 2009, http://baike.baidu.com/view/1758.htm.
84. "Jin Yong baiwan gangyuan maichu *Shen diao xia lü* katong banquan" [Jin Yong sells the animation copyright for *The Giant Eagle and Its Companion* for one million HKD], July 4, 2003, http://yule.sohu.com/23/62/article210726223.shtml.
85. Ibid.
86. "Beijing Paralympic theme song shows love for life," September 6, 2008. https://www.chinadaily.com.cn/paralympics/2008-09/06/content_7005411.htm.
87. "2020 Fubusi Zhongguo mingren bang 2020" 福布斯中國名人榜 [Forbes China Top 100 Celebrity List for 2020], accessed December 31, 2020, https://www.forbeschina.com/lists/1744.
88. "*Savior of the Soul*," accessed May 30, 2016, http://www.imdb.com/title/tt0104322/.
89. "*Savior of the Soul II*," accessed July 10, 2009, http://www.imdb.com/title/tt0104560/.
90. Andy Lau's film company is Focus Films Limited, established in 2002 based on Heavenly Screen Film Company Limited, which produced *Savior of the Soul*. Focus Films also invested in Feng Xiaogang's direction of *A World Without Thieves*, which starred Andy Lau. "Yingyi yule youxian gongsi" [Yingyi entertainment, ltd.], accessed June 26, 2010, http://baike.baidu.com/view/203889.html?tp=8_01.
91. Monjeh, accessed July 21, 2009.
92. Ibid.
93. Ibid.
94. "*Jiu yi Shen diao xia lü*" [1991 Savior of the Soul], accessed March 28, 2022, https://baike.baidu.com/item/九一神雕俠侶/10721519.
95. "*Jiu yi Shen diao xia lü*" [1991 Savior of the Soul], minute 40:00, accessed July 1, 2010, http://www.tudou.com/programs/view/ODxP4QMbdCE/.
96. "Yazhou xin xing dao" [Asian new star directors], accessed May 31, 2016, http://baike.baidu.com/view/1866371.htm.
97. "Liu Dehua," accessed May 31, 2016, http://baike.baidu.com/subview/1758/18233157.htm.
98. Monjeh, "Condor Heroes."

99. "'Xiao shimei' yu Liu Dehua heying qinmi xiangyong" ["Little martial sister" and Andy Lau pictured together in intimate embrace], March 18, 2016, http://m.chinadaily.com.cn/cn/2016-03/18/content_23938297.htm.

100. "Chen Shaoxia," accessed March 19, 2016, http://baike.baidu.com/view/386338.htm.

101. "'Xiao shimei' yu Liu Dehua heying qinmi xiangyong: remen gentie" ["Little martial sister" and Andy Lau pictured together in intimate embrace: popular posts], March 18, 2016, http://ent.163.com/photoview/00AJ0003/591416.html#p=BIE4T04K00AJ0003?baike.

102. "Liu Dehua," accessed May 31, 2016, http://baike.baidu.com/subview/1758/18233157.htm.

103. Allan Cho, *The Hong Kong Wuxia Movie: Identity and Politics, 1966–1976* (Saarbrücken, Germany: Lambart Academic Publishing, 2010): 25.

104. Bordwell, *Planet Hong Kong*, 66.

105. Ibid., 68.

106. Jeff Yang, *Once Upon a Time in China*, 79.

107. Chau sang "Dao jian ru meng" [Sabre and sword like a dream' for the 1994 Ma Jingtao Taiwan Television (TTV) series adaptation of *Dragon Sabre* (*Yi tian tu long ji* [The heaven sword and the dragon sabre], accessed March 30, 2022, https://baike.baidu.com/item/倚天屠龙记/6893552); he sang "Shenhua qinghua" [God-speak and love-speak] for the 1995 Gu Tianle TVB television series adaptation of *Companion* (*Shen diao xia lü* [The Giant eagle and its companion], accessed March 30, 2022, https://baike.baidu.com/item/神雕侠侣/7906915); and he sang "Nan nian de jing" [Difficult scriptures to chant] for the 1997 Felix Wong TVB television series adaptation of *Semi-Devils* (*Tian long ba bu* [The demi-gods and semi-devils], accessed March 30, 2022, https://baike.baidu.com/item/天龙八部/5480147).

108. "Ni gei wo yi pian tian" [You give me a new world], accessed June 9, 2016, http://baike.baidu.com/view/9096551.htm.

109. "Ren Xianqi" (Richie Ren), accessed March 28, 2022, https://baike.baidu.com/item/任贤齐/145904.

110. "Richie Ren Xian-Qi," Xianggang yingku [Hong Kong Movie Database], accessed March 28, 2022, https://hkmdb.com/db/people/view.mhtml?id=12636&display_set=big5.

111. The theme song for *Wanderer* is "Canghai yi sheng xiao" [A laugh in the vast sea]. Ren Xianqi also sang the closing credits song for this adaptation, "Si bu liao" [Will not die].

112. "Yang Peipei: renwu pinglun" [Yang Peipei: character commentary], accessed June 2, 2016, http://baike.baidu.com/view/1724293.htm#4.

113. Ren Xianqi, Weibo, December 29, 2020, https://weibo.com/1288803057/JAJpQ46Ke?filter=hot&root_comment_id=0&ssl_rnd=1609435931.0128&type=comment#_rnd1609435935657.

114. "Cehua: Huangjin zhenrong dazaode diyi bu dianshi shi chaoji daju" [Plan: golden battle lines making up the first super-series in television history], February 5, 2009, http://news.sina.com/v/2009-02-06/14232365418_2.shtml.

115. "Ta shi xing erdai, ta shi 83 ban *She diao yingxiong zhuan* de dongzuo daoyan, ta shi dongzuo sheji dashi Cheng Xiaodong" [He is a star of the second

generation, he is the action director for the 1983 adaptation of *The Eagle Shooting Heroes*, he is the master action designer Cheng Xiaodong], accessed January 6, 2021, https://zhuanlan.zhihu.com/p/147224952.

116. "*She diao yingxiong zhuan* zhizuo teji fanyi gao—zhuan tie zi zhongyang qingbao 5-3" [The production of a special translation draft of *The Eagle-Shooting Heroes*—forward post from the CIA 5-3], accessed April 11, 2016, http://www.barbarayung.net/club/post006b.htm.

117. Ibid.

118. "Ta shi xing erdai."

119. "*She diao yingxiong zhuan* zhizuo teji fanyi gao—zhuan tie zi zhongyang qingbao 5-1" [The production of a special translation draft of *The Eagle-Shooting Heroes*—forward post from the CIA 5-1], accessed March 30, 2016, http://www.barbarayung.net/club/post006.htm.

120. In his book, *The Sword or the Needle: The Female Knight-Errant (Xia) in Traditional Chinese Narrative* (Bern: Peter Lang, 2009), Roland Altenburger notes: "While a biographical entry in for a woman general in a dynastic history was exceptional, accounts about martial women in historical documents nevertheless were not particularly rare" (47).

121. She also played in TVB Gu Long adaptations. "Idy Chan," accessed January 6, 2021, https://www.douban.com/search?q=陳玉蓮.

122. "2011 Documentary—Barbara Yung (Weng Meiling)," accessed April 6, 2016, https://www.youtube.com/watch?v=RopW27MekzE.

123. Vivienne Chow, "After 20 years, stars wed in royal style," *South China Morning Post*, July 22, 2008, https://www.scmp.com/article/646096/after-20-years-stars-wed-royal-style.

124. "*Xiao ao jianghu* (Liu Huan yanchang gequ)" [*Xiao ao jianghu* (song performed by Liu Huan)], accessed June 29, 2016, http://baike.baidu.com/subview/10786/13369510.htm.

125. "She diao yingxiong zhuan zhi dong cheng xi jiu 1993" [The eagle-shooting heroes: eastern and western accomplishments (1993)], accessed January 6, 2021, https://movie.douban.com/subject/1316510/.

126. "*Xin Tian long ba bu* (1994) [*The New Demi-gods and the semi-devils* (1994)], accessed January 6, 2021, https://movie.douban.com/subject/1297517/.

127. *Jin yu liangyuan Hong lou meng* (Gold Jade good karma dream of the red chamber), Shaw Brothers Studios, 1977.

128. "Lin Qingxia mingan: Jin Yong fandui ta yan Dongfang Bubai" [Lin Qingxia is sensitive, Jin Yong objected to her playing Asia the Invincible], July 21, 2008, http://www.yn.xinhuanet.com/ent/2008-07/21/content_13882940.htm.

129. English subtitles for the film translate this as "Invincible Asia," but there are numerous translation possibilities confounded by the fact that this is a character's name. The surname Dongfang literally means "the East" or "the Orient," the second of which is problematic given negative association with the discourse of Orientalism. I follow Ming-Yeh T. Rawnsley, who translates this name as "Asia the Invincible" in "Stars as Production and Consumption: A Case Study of Brigitte Lin," in *East Asian Film Stars*, eds. Leung Wing-Fai and Andy Willis (New York: Palgrave Macmillan, 2014): 199.

130. Ibid.

131. Ibid., 200.

132. Wimal Dissanayake, *Wong Kar-Wai's* Ashes of Time (Hong Kong: Hong Kong University Press, 2003), uses "Malevolent East" and "Malicious West" which skews the meaning of Huang Yaoshi's moniker.

133. The film's narrator describes Murong Yan's split personality and explains at about 12:50 that "A few years later a strange swordsman appeared in the *jianghu*, and nobody knew her [*ta*] background. He [*ta*] liked to practice in front of his own reflection. He has a peculiar name, Dugu Qiubai." Note that the subtitles continue the gender bifurcation play of words, and the scene of Dugu Qiubai is played by Lin, with ambiguity regarding gender.

134. "Brigitte Lin," IMDb, accessed March 29, 2022, https://www.imdb.com/name/nm0510857/.

135. Lin Qingxia, "*Dongfang Bubai* ganku tan (1)" [Talking of good times and hardships in *Swordsman II*], July 3, 2008, http://lz.book.sohu.com/chapter-1226510.html.

136. Lin Qingxia, "Chong kan *Dong Xie Xi Du*" [Another look at *Ashes of Time*], September 26, 2008, http://lz.book.sohu.com/chapter-1226509.html.

137. Lin Qingxia, "Da daoyan shouzhong de mangguo" (Mango in a great director's hands), August 1, 2006, http://reading.caixin.com/111078/111111.html.

138. Lin Qingxia, "Chong kan *Dong Xie Xi Du*."

139. Wimal Dissanayake, *Ashes of Time*," 170.

140. "*She diao yingxiong zhuan zhi dong cheng xijiu*: muhou huaxu" [Interesting facts behind the scenes of *The Eagle Shooting Heroes eastern and western accomplishments*], accessed May 31, 2016, http://baike.baidu.com/subview/15834/7184865.htm?fromtitle=射雕英雄传之东成西就&fromid=2899193&type=syn#5.

141. Dissanayake, *Ashes of Time*, 149–150.

142. Ibid., 141.

143. Ibid., 143–145.

144. Ibid., 70.

145. Ibid., 3.

146. Ibid.

147. Ibid., 18.

148. Ibid., 20.

149. Ibid., 21.

150. "Cehua: Wang Jiawei 'Dugu Qiubai' geming jiujian weizhen jianghu (2)" [Plan: Wang Jiawei's "Dugu Qiubai" revolutionary nine swords storm the martial world (2)], March 24, 2009, http://news.sina.com/m/2009-03-25/14312437898_2.shtml.

151. Dissanayake, *Ashes of Time*, 27.

152. "Liu bu Li Xiaolong dianying Xianggang piaofang paihang: sanbu dapo jilu, *Jing wu men* pai di'er" [Six of Bruce Lee's movies on the Hong Kong box office charts: Three break records, *Fist of fury* is ranked number two], accessed March 29, 2022, https://new.qq.com/omn/20211003/20211003A05MAA00.html.

153. "Legend of the Fist: The Return of Chen Zhen (2010)," Box Office Mojo by IMDb, accessed March 29, 2022, https://www.boxofficemojo.com/title/tt1456661/?ref_=bo_se_r_1.

154. Leon Hunt, "Too Late the Hero? The Delayed Stardom of Donnie Yen," in *East Asian Film Stars*, eds. Leung Wing-Fai and Andy Willis (New York: Palgrave Macmillan, 2014): 154.

155. Paul Bowman, "Return of the Dragon: Handover, Hong Kong Cinema, and Chinese Ethno-nationalism," in *A Companion to Hong Kong Cinema*, eds. Esther M. K. Cheung et al. (West Sussex, UK: John Wiley & Sons, 2015): 317.

156. "Huo Yuanjia," accessed January 6, 2021, https://www.douban.com/search?source=suggest&q=霍元甲.

157. Wei Junzi, *Xianggang dianying shiji* [A history of Hong Kong films] (Beijing: Zhongguo renmin daxue chubanshe, 2013): 128.

158. "Huang Feihong zhuan (shangji)" [Huang Feihong biography (part 1)], accessed April 16, 2016, http://baike.baidu.com/item/黄飞鸿传（上集）?fr=aladdin.

159. Wang, *Once Upon a Time in China*, 39.

160. Ibid.

161. Wei Junzi, *Xianggang dianying shiji*, 129.

162. "Guan Dexing," accessed January 6, 2021, https://baike.sogou.com/v5744920.htm.

163. "Huang Feihong dianshiju" [Huang Feihong television series], accessed January 6, 2021, https://search.douban.com/movie/subject_search?search_text=SimSun&cat=1002.

164. "Huang Fehong xilie yingshi" 黃飛鴻系列影視 [Huang Feihong film and television series]," accessed March 30, 2022, https://hongkong.fandom.com/zh-hk/wiki/黃飛鴻系列影視.

165. "Huang Feihong zhi er nan er dang ziqiang" 黃飛鴻之二男兒當自強 [Once upon a time in China 2; a.k.a. Huang Feihong part 2, real men do self-strengthening], accessed March 31, 2022, https://hkmdb.com/db/movies/view.mhtml?id=7576&display_set=big5.

166. Linn Haynes, "Wong Fei Hung," in Jeff Yang, *Once Upon a Time in China*, 41.

167. Kin-Yan Szeto, "Jackie Chan's Cosmopolitical Consciousness and Comic Displacement," *Modern Chinese Literature and Culture*, vol. 20, no. 2 (Fall 2009): 229–261.

168. *Zui quan* [Drunken Master], dir. Yuan Heping, prod. Wu Siyuan, starring Jackie Chan, (1978, Guangdong: Guangdong Yinxiang chubangongsi, 1990): disc A, 46:46–48:20.

169. *Zui quan II* [Drunken Master II], dir. Lau Kar-Leung (Liu Jialiang). starring Jackie Chan (Golden Harvest, Paragon Films, 1994): disc 1, 50:41–52:23.

170. Bey Logan, *Hong Kong Action Cinema* (Woodstock, NY: Overlook Press, 1996): 77.

171. Wei Junzi, *Xianggang dianying shiji*, 130.

172. "Bao [Da] Zhang Jin ting [Li] Keqin guorichen 94 sui Shi Jian xijin jianqi" [Watching television drama (*Dae*) *Jang Geum* and listening to songs of (Li) Kejin to pass the morning, the 94-year-old Shi Jian is cleansed of his villainy], January 20, 2007, http://hk.apple.nextmedia.com/template/apple/art_main.php?iss_id=20070120&sec_id=462&subsec_id=830&art_id=6734345.

173. "Shi Jian," accessed March 29, 2022, https://www.maochangfood.com/mingxing/shijian/dianshiju.html.

174. "Shi Jian" (Sek Kin), Xianggang yingku HKMDB, accessed March 29, 2022, https://hkmdb.com/db/people/view.mhtml?id=1167&complete_credits=1&display_set=big5.

175. *She diao yingxiong zhuan (1958)*" [Story of the vulture conqueror (1958)], accessed January 6, 2021, https://movie.douban.com/subject/3369388/.

176. "'Jianren Jian' Shi Jian cishi, zeng hezuo Zhou Runfa Cheng Long Li Xiaolong" ["Villain Jian" passes away, had cooperated with Zhou Runfa, Jackie Chan, and Bruce Lee], June 4, 2009, http://news.sina.com/sin acn/502-104-103-107/2009-06-04/1915763140.html.

177. Hamm, *Paper Swordsman*, 131.

178. "Li Xiaolong he Jin Yong d guanxi, yange lai shuo, Li Xiaolong shi Jin Yong de tudi" [The relationship between Bruce Lee and Jin Yong, strictly speaking, Li Xiaolong is Jin Yong's disciple], *Kuai Zi Xun*, December 12, 2019, https://www.360kuai.com/pc/9cdf52c893d600cce?cota=3&kuai_so=1&sign=360_7bc3b157.

179. Bruce Lee, *Tao of Jeet Kune Do* (Burbank, CA: Ohara Publications): 201.

180. Translation Lionel Giles, "Xu shi pian" [Weak points and strong], *Sunzi bingfa* [*Sunzi Art of War*], Chinese Text Project, accessed January 4, 2021, https://ctext.org/art-of-war/weak-points-and-strong.

181. David Desser, "The Kung Fu Craze: Hong Kong Cinema's First American Reception," in *The Cinema of Hong Kong: History, Arts, Identity*, eds. Poshek Fu and David Desser (Cambridge: Cambridge University Press, 2000): 20.

182. Ibid.

183. Kenneth Chan, *Remade in China*, 146.

184. "Zhen gongfu canyin guanli youxian gongsi" [True kungfu restaurant management company, ltd.], accessed March 29, 2022, https://www.qcc.com/firm/373dc2faf053f5424042fd24750d5d10.html.

185. Stokes, *Historical Dictionary*, 35.

186. Ibid.

187. Kenneth Chan, *Remade in China*, 146.

188. Siu Leung Li, "The Myth Continues," 53.

189. *Xun Qin ji: Ershiqi die Xianggang dianshi lianxuju* [*A Step Back to the Past*: Twenty-seven-disc Hong Kong television series], Disc 10, 4:45–4:54. TVBI Zhongkai wenhua, Jiuzhou yinxiang chubangongsi, 2001.

190. Peter Rainer, "Jackie Chan stars in 'The Karate Kid' (except it should be called 'The Kung Fu Kid')," June 11, 2010, http://www.csmonitor.com/The-Culture/Movies/2010/0611/Jackie-Chan-stars-in-The-Karate-Kid-except-it-should-be-called-The-Kung-Fu-Kid.

191. "Bruce Lee: His Last Days," accessed January 6, 2021, https://www.grindhousedatabase.com/index.php/Bruce_Lee:_His_Last_Days.

192. "Lu ding ji (1983 nian Hua Shan zhidao Xianggang Shaoshi dianying)" [The deer and the cauldron (1983 Hua Shan directed Shaw Brothers movie)], accessed January 6, 2021, https://baike.baidu.com/item/鹿鼎記/9411195.

193. "Liu Jiahui," accessed March 30, 2022. https://baike.baidu.com/item/刘家辉/5482824.

194. "Movie *Kungfu Protects the Way* a film popularizes Taiji with Jet Li, Donnie Yen, Wu Jing" Dianying *Gong shou dao* tuiguang Taiji yipian jijie Li Lianjie Zhen Zidan Wu Jing, Renmin wang, October 31, 2017. http://tj.people.com.cn/n2/2017/1031/c375366-30872104.html.

195. Ibid.

196. Jackie Chan and Jeff Yang, *I Am Jackie Chan: My Life in Action* (New York: Ballantine Books, 1998): 296.

Five

The *Kung Fu Hustle* Hustle

Jin Yong's fellow New School Martial Arts Fiction writer Gu Long encapsulated the dictum that conformity to the rules of the martial world is fundamental to *wuxia* morality, as expressed in his iconic Chinese martial saying, *"ren zai jianghu, shen bu you ji"* (in the *jianghu* [martial world] there is no individual choice).[1] This expression appears in several of Gu Long's novels and has been interpolated into television adaptations of both his and Jin Yong's novels.[2] It appears simple on the surface but has an ideological depth that belies simplicity. The *wuxia* martial artist may struggle with the constraints implied therein, but in the end must accept it as a dictate, as a moral compass with which to navigate the myriad of conflicts that drive the narrative. Readers and viewers are reminded of this dictum in order to guide their interpretation of the actions (and interactions) of the vast array of characters populating the stories. Audiences may sympathize with even the worst of the characters by recognizing this dictum despite any personal moral qualms. Interesting narratives are propelled through the choices characters make when they have to apply this dictum in compromising, no-win situations. The dictum is an element of kungfu cultural literacy that informs the basic interpretive mode upon which a whole range of non-kungfu human relations intersect in plot and subplot, from romance to political intrigue.

Jin Yong's authorial role in construction of the kungfu industrial complex is richly informed by Chinese literature and culture, as well as his own literary and commercial interests. He went from a founder of the New School of Martial Arts Fiction to become the grandmaster. Jin Yong's novels, characters, and the world he constructed were immediately and repeatedly adapted to film, television, and other media, growing the audience demand for such works and subsequently impacting the careers of actors and directors while furthering the globalization of kungfu's cultural contribution to film and television. This process is mirrored in the other authors of his generation on a similar scale. The opening of China led to Jin Yong's fiction being widely read in the Mainland and caused much deliberation in literary circles regarding the value of his works during the process of his canonization in Chinese literary discourse.

Jin Yong's works and characters are well known in Chinese cultural discourse. A translation project of all of Jin Yong's works into English is currently underway and its successful completion may remedy the general lack of penetration of his stories and characters in the West.[3] Martial arts films, on the contrary, have been increasingly well received by audiences since the 1970s and kungfu action now permeates Hollywood. The groundwork for enhanced appreciation of Chinese language and culture has been laid. A limited amount of *wuxia* film is now available in the West in a variety of streaming platforms. Can Chinese *wuxia* television series replicate the success that Korean dramas have found in the West? *Crouching Tiger*'s director Ang Lee notes: "[W]hen it comes to martial arts, we are an inspiring force in filmmaking. Those are films we excel at, and there is something special about them. I cannot think of another genre that we do better than America."[4] This international excellence in martial arts film complements Jackie Chan's assertion, referenced in chapter 4, that Hollywood action movies are deeply imprinted with Chinese kungfu at every level. Martial arts films are part and parcel of the process of globalization. Chang Cheh, director of Shaw Brothers films in 1960s and 1970s, offers insight into how and why kungfu film could be so effective at transnational assimilation: "Action is a world language, thus Hong Kong's action films were accepted by Cantonese speakers and Mandarin speakers, by Southeast Asian countries which didn't understand Chinese, and gradually, by Europe and America."[5]

Directors astutely see "action" as a common language available to different linguistic communities in Asia and the rest of the world and capitalize on it. The cultural capital necessary to appreciate a *Chinese language* martial arts novel takes years for to accumulate. Film however is a ready vehicle for distribution of kungfu action globally because action is visible, even if the deeper underlying cultural machinations may be indistinct to some viewers. Outstanding heroes and villains battling with their hands, feet, wits, and emotion are essential to action. Jin Yong has created numerous such unforgettable characters in his novels. Many of the actors who portrayed those characters in film and television assimilated a degree of the cultural capital associated with those heroic roles, as the example of Andy Lau's depiction of Yang Guo previously demonstrated. The idea of an "industrial complex" suggests a multitude of dimensions and connections between many factors involved at all levels of cultural and commercial processes, including the authors, stories, characters, actors, directors, and innumerable technical staff at every level. The industrial complex also suggests that capitalizing (making money) on the core product at every level motivates the players to further construction characters, narratives, and stories in derivative iterations, thus perpetuating the cycle of industry.

The kungfu industrial complex could be termed the "kungfu cultural complex" wherein the martial arts narratives challenge both overt and covert subversion of cultural norms outlined by the tenants of Confucianism, Daoism, and Buddhism and other schools of Chinese thought. This myriad of threads throughout Jin Yong's narratives draws on culture in all its manifestations—from literature to philosophy to religion to history—and informs culture through self and social analysis in both virtuous and vicious cycles. The kungfu industrial complex is moreover an economic construction where the interested parties (including readers and viewers) function to reify the cultural, social, and political capital—symbolic and political power are continually tested and even expanded through the globalization of kungfu film.

In the first three decades of the PRC, Chinese film production was tightly controlled for didactic propaganda purposes. Hong Kong was the epicenter of film production in the Chinese-speaking world, lying outside the PRC sphere of censorship. Starting with opening to the outside world in the 1980s, China gradually loosened proscriptions on the film industry. These changes over two decades seem to be synchronically capped by the success of *Crouching Tiger* in 2000, which was an international coproduction filmed on location in China directed by Taiwanese Ang Lee. Foreign audience enthusiasm for *Crouching Tiger* and its economic success abroad, despite a tepid reception by domestic Chinese audiences, demonstrated the significant symbolic power of the genre, even a form of cultural soft power. Following that lead, many of China's most talented directors pursued similar formulas hoping for blockbuster commercial success. The moneymaking potential of *wuxia* kungfu films was proven. Great films mixing kungfu and *wuxia* elements were developed by Zhang Yimou, Stephen Chow, Tsui Hark, and many others in the twenty-first century, thus carrying water for globalization of the kungfu industrial complex. Specific elements of *Crouching Tiger*'s production have action authenticity in the "Jackie Chan sense" where action stunts are "real" and create a synergy that overcomes the twentieth-century divide between supposed "real" kungfu and fantastical *wuxia*. One key is the myth that many *wuxia* stunts are actually performed by the lead actors themselves:

> Everything we see is real, Lee told me. Computers were used only to remove the safety wires that held the actors. "So those were stunt people up there?" I asked, trying to hold onto some reserve of skepticism. "Not for the most part," he said. "Maybe a little stunt work, but most of the time you can see their faces. That's really them in the trees." And on the rooftops, too, he told me.[6]

Figure 5.1. The qinggong (light-body kungfu) of Zhang Ziyi and Chow Yun-fat in *Crouching Tiger* (2000)

There is value in such a myth of kungfu stunt authenticity that goes back to the films of Bruce Lee and Jackie Chan. It is a qualified myth that Chan did "all" his own stunts, which may be in large part true, but must be significantly clarified with respect to the debt he owes to stunt doubles who blocked out and rehearsed many of his stunts before he did them on film.[7] Mythology is good for the bottom line and is a valued aspect connecting cultural capital to commercial success in the kungfu industrial complex. Myth and legend both work within a structure of cultural capital and vice versa.

If action is a global language, it is connected to authenticity, which is arguably earned to an extent in *Crouching Tiger* as the previous quote asserts, by having actors do their own stunts. While Chan's films did not use many wires at first, more complex and dangerous later stunts were enhanced by wirefu by necessity, which some critics may see as a dilution of the "real." I would rather frame this "real" as the use of production techniques (and technology) to elaborate the fantastical *wugong* martial ability that permeates Jin Yong's *wuxia* narratives and are translated into *wuxia* film, such as the *qinggong* light-body kungfu flying stunts or *neigong* internal *qi* mastery. It is of artistic and commercial interest in the kungfu industrial complex to keep Chan alive producing ever more and ever greater movies. Although the *wushu* martial arts of Bruce Lee and Jackie Chan competed in the 1970s and 1980s with the wire-enhanced special martial arts effects of *wuxia* films, the *wuxia* films have always been imbued with *wushu* that helps audiences suspend disbelief and appreciate Jin Yong's imaginative martial arts (*wugong*) inventions. The wires reified some fantastical *wugong* elements described in the novels that could not otherwise be well depicted. However, by the end of the twentieth-century martial arts film from China had become a synergy of these subgenres, replete with the complexities of *wuxia* fiction, its rhetorical kungfu tropes and plots, but now enhanced (for better or worse) by CGI—wirefu makes room for the appreciation of acrobatic and production techniques whereas CGI precludes that important synergy by being too obviously fake and easy.

THE KUNGFU INDUSTRIAL COMPLEX AS *JIANGHU*

In order to explicate Jin Yong's role in the kungfu industrial complex and broaden the view of his cultural impact, this concluding chapter examines the *wuxia* ideological matrix and identifies points of intersection with crucial extratextual discourse in Chinese society. Jin Yong's novels are informed by the tension between self and society that can be represented by two iconic expressions found in new martial arts fiction of the mid-to-late twentieth century. The first expression is Gu Long's contrasting neologism quoted at the start of this chapter, *"ren zai jianghu, shen bu you ji"* ("in the *jianghu* [martial world] there is no individual choice"—in other words one has no choice but to conform to *jianghu* rules/morality. The second is *"xiao ao jianghu,"* a concept taken from Jin Yong's novel by that same name—*Wanderer*—a trope which literally translates as "laughing proudly, rivers and lakes" but contextually means "laughing haughtily at *jianghu* [rules/morality]."

Read as a pseudo-allegory of Chairman Mao's Great Proletarian Cultural Revolution (ca. 1965–1975), which was contemporaneous with its serialization, *Wanderer* attacks the incoherence of the *wuxia* Good/Evil ideological dichotomy through the narrative construction of protagonist Linghu Chong's acquisition of martial abilities in parallel with his gradual awakening of political consciousness. Wandering the *jianghu*, Linghu Chong struggles against increasing alienation from his martial master and Good sect brethren as he gradually realizes the "evil" hypocrisy of the Good leadership, as well as the flipside—relativization of "good" in characters of ostensibly Evil sects. His reticence to take power himself brings into relief his leadership's lust for it, and his wandering thus becomes a critique of their manipulation of martial mores and the extremes to which they are willing to go in order to realize ambitions of ultimate power.

The well-meaning, happy-go-lucky Linghu Chong continually fails to meet his master's demands to toe the line of collective Good sect *jianghu* expectations. Linghu Chong encounters situations where he hesitates, straddling the deterministic divide between Good and Evil, thus challenging the dogma of his master and other Good sect leaders. He typically chooses *yiqi* (righteous friendship) over *zhongxiao* (obedient filial loyalty) to his master/father figure, who in one example orders him to kill a particularly vile opponent, the rapist Tian Boguang for whom Linghu Chong had developed a qualified mutual respect through a series of events as he fought to save the virtue of the nun Yilin. Tian repeatedly spared Linghu Chong's life and Linghu Chong only "defeated" him by employing a clever stratagem that turned on the martial ethic of standing by one's word (*shuohua suanshu*). Although tricked by Linghu Chong, Tian keeps his word and thus furthers the weak bond of *yiqi* between them. This incurs the wrath of both his master and other representatives of the "Good" martial sects who insist that Linghu Chong now kill his "friend." This sets in motion Linghu Chong's subsequent punishment for refusing his master's order (disguised as a self-inflicted injury). The conflict between *yiqi* friend-loyalty and obedience/loyalty to his master highlights the dogmatic position of absolute Good versus Evil in *jianghu* mentality. Linghu Chong's punishment, banishment to "face the wall" for a year high on Huashan, leads unexpectedly to his crucial martial training opportunity and the parallel awakening of his political consciousness. Collective (unfair) perception of disloyalty to his master causes Linghu Chong to experience internal conflict, resulting in psychological depression that he treats with copious quantities of wine and by physically distancing himself from his Good brethren. He thus wanders in the direction of so-called Evil. His depression is compounded by the fact that his romantic interest, his master's daughter, shifts her love allegiance to his younger martial brother.

The *jianghu* within which this "smiling, proud wanderer" of Jin Yong's novel operates has an implied and recognizable moral structure. Members who bend or break the rules of morality are either corralled back into line or ostracized (mercilessly slaughtered), thus reifying Gu Long's expression, *ren zai jianghu, shen bu you ji*. The expression encapsulates the complex codes of martial culture that govern the fighter's actions within that world, an inescapable predicament that articulates what everyone knows and which functions to remind the individual of prioritization of collective over individual desire. A brief dialogue between two of Gu Long's characters explains it succinctly. The youngster in the following quote is perhaps a descendant of Gu Long's famous character Chu Liuxiang. He is conversing with an old man, who elaborates on the commonly accepted idea of one's role in the *jianghu* is unalterable regardless of fame, glory, reputation, or even the "immortality" or "un-defeat-ability" of certain fighters:

> The youngster said: "Sometimes fame seems like baggage. The greater your fame, the heavier the baggage." He said: "Most awful is that everything is in this baggage." . . . There is reputation, wealth, status, friends, sensual pleasures, good wine, but there are also burdens, outrageous treatment, injury, inciting disharmony, treachery, and slaughter.
>
> So, this kind of person is always most able to understand the saying: *ren zai jianghu, shen bu you ji* (in the *jianghu* there is no individual choice [one has no choice but to conform to *jianghu* rules/morality]).
>
> Of course, the old man also understood this point. In his life he had done who knows how many things he himself certainly didn't want to do, but he didn't complain at all. Because he knows . . . a person must force themself to do a few things in their life that they don't want to do, and only then will their life have meaning. This is also the meaning of "there are things you mustn't do and things you must do."[8]

Thus, the saying *ren zai jianghu, shen bu you ji* is an inescapable predicament that pithily articulates what everyone in the *jianghu* knows and functions to remind the martial artist why collective desire is prioritized over individual desire, summed up here: "only then will their life have meaning."

Figure 5.2. Characters Liu Zhengfeng and Qu Yuan perform title song, "Xiao ao jianghu," *Wanderer* (2001), Episode 5

Jin Yong's title trope from *Wanderer*, "laughing haughtily at the *jianghu* [rules/morality]," stands in stark contrast to Gu Long's moral vector. Both expressions recognize the contemporary ethico-moral truth, but Linghu Chong yearns for another option to the prescribed martial norms. *Xiao ao jianghu* "Laughing haughtily at the *jianghu* [rules/morality]" is impacted at multiple levels, standing as both the title of the novel and the name of a musical piece/score performed at critical junctures in the novel. The crucial scene where Liu Zhengfeng and Qu Yuan perform their musical composition, for which they have sacrificed position and ultimately their lives, brings these ideas together, challenging ideological conformity that Linghu Chong will explore throughout the novel.

Linghu Chong's consciousness of *xiao ao jianghu* metaphorically implies departure from the contemporaneous norms of the martial world, the desire to separate oneself from that martial world, but he simultaneously recognizes the inextricability of the situation. Removing himself from the martial world that produced him is impossible, no matter how much he longs to do so.

Although Jin Yong doesn't use Gu Long's exact terminology *"ren zai jianghu, shen bu you ji"* in his novels proper, he exactly cites Gu Long's expression in the 1980 "Afterword" to *Wanderer*, demonstrating his intimate familiarity with his fellow writer's trope and connecting it directly to the thoughts and actions of his characters in *Wanderer*:

> In the traditional arts of China, whether in poetry, essay, drama, or painting, the most prominent main theme is the pursuit of liberation of the personality. The more chaotic an era and the more bitter the people's lives, the more prominent this main theme.
>
> *"Ren zai jianghu, shen bu you ji"* (in the *jianghu* there is no individual choice [one has no choice but to conform to the *jianghu* (rules/morality)]), [means] it is no easy thing to retire. Liu Zhengfeng pursued artistic freedom and emphasized friendship that didn't go against his heart, and thus wanted to wash his hands [of the martial world]. The Four Friends of Plum Villa hoped to secretly ensconce themselves in the solitary mountains and enjoy the pleasures of zither, chess, calligraphy, and painting. None of them could do it and they lost their lives because the power struggle (politics *zhengzhi*) wouldn't permit it.
>
> ... Linghu Chong is not a great martial hero, but rather a hermit like Tao Qian who pursued a kind of personality liberation. Feng Qingyang [who taught Linghu Chong unparalleled swordsmanship] was discouraged and retired in shame and dejection. But by his nature, Linghu Chong can't stand to be fettered.... The carefreeness of *"xiao ao jianghu"* is the object of pursuit of the type of character like Linghu Chong.[9]

So Linghu Chong has an explicit antecedent in the form of a famous hermit Tao Yuan of China's Six Dynasties period who became the archetype for leaving society (eschewing politics) in order to pursue individual liberation. When faced with the moral dogma of *ren zai jianghu, shen bu you ji* he comes very close to transcending it. Linghu Chong doesn't explicitly express that dogma in the exact terms of the saying in the novel itself. However, at least one television adaptation of *Wanderer* does directly incorporate Gu Long's phraseology. In a scene in the 2000 television series adaptation Linghu Chong's future lover, Ren Yingying, fights Xiang Wentian, a ranking member in her own Sun Moon Cult's hierarchy. Telling him to flee without her, she says, "I am also a member of the *jianghu*, and have no choice but to conform [to *jianghu* rules/morality]" (*wo ye shi jianghuren, shen bu you ji*).[10]

Further conflation of Gu Long's expression in this television adaptation of Jin Yong's novel is also found in the novel's title scene where the meaning of *"xiao ao jianghu"* is explicated. The orthodox Hengshan Sword Sect elder Liu Zhengfeng's entire clan is massacred by "Good" Songshan Sword Sect brethren ostensibly because Liu had befriended the Sun Moon Cult elder Qu Yang over mutual infatuation with music. Liu had decided to retire from the *jianghu* to protect their musical friendship, but Songshan Sword Sect leadership insists they must be killed in order to redress the serious breach of *jianghu* morality represented by his attempted retirement. In this television adaptation Liu quotes Gu Long's dictum directly, *ren zai jianghu, shen bu you ji*.[11] Both these cases prioritize individual, private *yiqi* over collective sectarian identification in direct contradiction to the rigid *jianghu* hierarchy of value. The cost for Liu Zhengfeng is extreme—annihilation of his entire clan right before his eyes and death for him and his allegedly "evil" friend as they fight to survive. The Cultural Revolution allegory is clear.

The tension between attempting to retire from the *jianghu* and not being allowed to do so generates the trope that names *Wanderer*. Plot contextualization may perhaps explain the implicit sense of Jin Yong's own translation for the title in English—*The Smiling, Proud Wanderer*. A wanderer is unmoored from sect and society, and thus may be "laughing haughtily at the *jianghu* [rules/morality]"—a closer translation. Liu and Qu had formed a friendship over their mutual interest in music, which overcame their own inherent biases represented by their sects, also indicated in their names, *zheng* (upright, orthodox, Good) and Qu (crooked) related through *xie* (heterodox, Evil) prior to forming their musical friendship. The perfect manifestation of music uniting these ostensible *jianghu* opposites is their musical composition for zither and flute titled "Xiao ao jianghu," the novel's exact title. Realizing the breach of *jianghu* morality, Liu wishes to retire, to metaphorically "wash his hands" (*jin pan xi shou*) from *jianghu* obligations but is not permitted to do so. The maxim *ren zai jianghu, shen bu you ji* explicates that personal existence in the *jianghu* is also subordinated to the *jianghu* norms, and that there are mortal consequences of prioritizing righteous friendship over the loyalty owed to one's master and sect. Herein lies central the tension for this analysis, the dilemma of private desire to withdraw from the world out of alienation arising from personal experience that challenges the Good/Evil dichotomy, in tension with public demands that preclude the possibility of questioning that dichotomy. Retirement is not permitted, period, and death is punishment if you try.

Despite its martial trappings—beatings, stabbings, dismemberment, poisonings, creative and multifaceted killing mechanisms—Jin Yong's *jianghu* resembles the Confucian moral model of the world, with familial social hierarchy, dictum of unquestioning filial loyalty and obedience to one's superiors, prioritization of the pursuit of learning, etc. As a pseudo-political allegory, *Wanderer* reads as a critique of Mao's Cultural Revolution in theme and character, and consciously situates author Jin Yong in the privileged place of both literary creator and social critic. Recall that Jin Yong wrote *Wanderer* from 1967 to 1969 in Hong Kong as an active outside observer of the Cultural Revolution. The power struggle between Maoist factions is skillfully portrayed in the pages of *Wanderer* as a death struggle between Good and Evil. In his 1980 "Afterword" to the novel Jin Yong clarifies the sense of daily crisis and its general applicability to historical Chinese political life:

> Each day I wrote social critique for the newspaper, *Ming Pao*, with an intense revulsion to the despicable political situation. Naturally this is reflected in the martial arts installment I wrote each day. . . . The all-out struggle for power is a fundamental situation of political life in China and abroad. . . . In my conception, these characters Ren Woxing, Asia the Invincible, Yue Buqun, and Zuo Lengchan are not experts of the martial world, but rather political characters.[12]

Jin Yong critiques contemporary China from the outside looking in through the eyes of his critical avatar in the novel, the character Linghu Chong. This is not a perfect allegory to historical events, but rather the "portrayal of human nature" which Jin Yong sees as firmly situated within Chinese cultural history. Cultural capital is thus situated in a grasp on "human nature" and the dynamics of the "all-out struggle for power." Jin Yong as intellectual and author situated in British Hong Kong is alienated from the mainland Chinese masses and uses his newspaper to critique the ideological power struggle, and "unintentionally" reflects this in his novel. Jin Yong, however, is not against Chinese culture, but rather explicates a broad view that the Cultural Revolution is characteristic of power struggles throughout history. Jin Yong's depiction of a greater value within Chinese tradition, represented by the ultimate Shaolin and

Wudang sect martial/moral superiority in *Wanderer*, demonstrates his faith in and support of Chinese culture. Shaolin and Wudang martial sects are temporarily unable to assert their martial/moral superiority, but find an ally in the character Linghu Chong, with whom they readily identify despite his conflicted morality.[13] The greater truth is that Shaolin and Wudang sects represent a norm of behavior and path of martial morality that transcends the sectarian struggles within the Five Mountain Sword Sect (read Cultural Revolution leadership) and between Good/Evil. Jin Yong's lesson is that Chinese culture and the framing processes that reify culture ultimately transcend Cultural Revolution ideology and that there is no escape from one's culture and its constructions.

Ironically, despite their superficial oppositional stances, the Good and Evil sects operate by the similar hierarchical *jianghu* rules and motivations, among which are the demand of obedience to authority, pursuit of sacred martial tomes (books of secrets) to enhance one's kungfu, and a "black and white" view of right and wrong based on political/sectarian identity. The Good and Evil sects contend for ultimate control of the *jianghu* and the leaders of each sect scheme and struggle among themselves for supremacy (they would even attempt to subsume/conquer Shaolin and Wudang—metaphors for all of Chinese culture). Linghu Chong's trajectory of martial development from minor to major player is the main discursive thread of the novel. His development casts the political struggles into relief by introducing indeterminacy as he questions the *jianghu* morality. These leaders have access to, or strive to acquire, sacred texts that teach techniques for martial mastery that would ostensibly make them *tianxia diyi* (supreme power in the world). They consciously scheme to advance their positions on the path to domination while secretly hiding their motivations.

Jin Yong's narrative of these *jianghu* power struggles reads like Lu Xun's critique of the cannibalistic world in "Diary of a Madman." Lu Xun's "clearheaded" madman realizes the horror of his cannibalistic society, and likewise Jin Yong's Linghu Chong realizes the insanity and metaphorically cannibalistic nature of the practitioners of those "sacred" martial texts. Those who have thus castrated themselves in pursuit of ultimate power subsequently meet ignominious ends. Lu Xun's madman was "cured" and returned to cannibalistic society. The madman's final plea to "save the children" resonates with Linghu Chong's quest to break from *jianghu* norms of morality. Rank and file fighters who resemble the masses and like Lu Xun's Ah Q are manipulated by their *jianghu* leaders. The madmen (and latent madman, Linghu Chong) are awake under the bright moon to the political reality of a *jianghu* that controls, dominates, protects and/or enlarges its leaders' sphere of influence. The sacred kungfu text that the players strive to acquire, the *Sword Manuel to Ward of Evil,* alludes to Mao's "little red book," the knowledge and interpretation of which yield ultimate power in the *jianghu*. Jin Yong's story demonstrates that the Good and Evil leaders of are ethically the same, both immensely cruel and increasingly insane. They may start out normal, but lust for power corrupts them, and they willingly go to any extreme to learn the techniques that bestow martial prowess (read political power) to consolidate and expand their privileged positions.

In reading Jin Yong's novel as a critique of the Cultural Revolution, I align his authorial omniscience with that of the protagonist Linghu Chong. In other words, Linghu Chong is an avatar for Jin Yong's critical consciousness throughout much of the novel. He has a privileged, albeit not always reliable, view of developing *jianghu* struggles, and he himself suffers the strict bifurcation of Good and Evil. Like Lu Xun's madman seeing the bright moon clearly for the first time in thirty years, *jianghu* society is observed from Linghu Chong's increasingly clear/reliable but increasingly depressed point of view as his master and martial brethren unfairly ostracize him. Jin Yong constructs his own "elite subject position" critiquing mainland power struggle, literally writing social critique by day and martial arts fiction by night. The *jianghu* is corrupt. Would-be champions of *jianghu* Good morality, such as Linghu Chong's master Yue Buqun (style name, the "gentleman sword"), are exposed as *wei junzi* ("hypocrites" or "false gentleman"), a play on Yue Buqun's moniker. They scheme for their own interests, subverting the very moral code they tout in their struggle for power. Martial hermit Feng Qingyang early in the novel teaches Linghu Chong a lesson that carries through the next 1600-plus pages: "The most fearsome [kungfu] moves in the world lie not in martial ability, but in conspiracy, treachery and traps."[14] Linghu Chong's increasing ambivalence separates him from his brethren, though he desperately wants his master's approval and his martial sister's love. A reluctant and manipulated pawn in the power struggle, Linghu Chong was unwilling to recognize his master's scheming hypocrisy until the very end of the novel. He subsequently distanced himself from his sect, which ironically brought him recognition for moral character from the Shaolin and Wudang sects. He unwillingly becomes leader of the Hengshan Sect of nuns, and by the final pages of the novel, he and the Sun Moon Cult's Ren Yingying establish harmony and peace in the *jianghu*, bringing together "Good" and "Evil" in their marriage, where they performed the composition "Xiao ao jianghu" demonstrating that "the intent of bridging the divide between sects and dispelling years of [the cycle of] revenge as envisioned by the elders Liu and Qu [who wrote it] was finally achieved."[15] Performing the title musical score for the novel with his now wife Ren Yingying at their wedding is the symbolic bookend of Linghu Chong's critique, and he thereupon "retires" with Yingying, having put the *jianghu* back in balance. *Wanderer*'s musical score itself ironically becomes a sacred text more powerful than the contested tomes of swordsmanship because it symbolically unites Good and Evil and opens space for "retirement." Thus, the problem is "solved," and like the madman at the end of Lu Xun's story they "return" to sanity (peace). The moral order is restored and the dictum "in the *jianghu* one has no choice but to conform to *jianghu* rules/morality" is upheld. Those who should die have died, and those who should survive have survived.

On the metanarrative level Linghu Chong and *Wanderer*'s trajectory, like that of Jin Yong's other novels (and the characters therein), does not stop when the novel finishes serialization, but rather continues to inform the contemporary pop culture narrative, being repeatedly reprised in movies, television series, and other contemporary cultural products. The characters and concepts have been active the decades of cultural discourse, performing as cultural touchstones long after the characters' [and Jin Yong's] ostensible "retirement" at the end of the novel. Such revision, recreation, and reenactment of the dynamic cultural discourse, the relatively intangible manifestations of the kungfu industrial complex, becomes inseparable from the *jianghu,* acquiescent to the *jianghu* dictum that "in the *jianghu* one has no choice but to conform to *jianghu* rules/morality."

Among the derivative adaptations of *Wanderer* include a three-part adaptation released from 1990–1993: the movies *Swordsman* (1990), *Swordsman II: Asia the Invincible* (1992), and *Swordsman III: The East Is Red* (1993). *Swordsman* directly adapts the retirement theme, beginning the movie with Linghu Chong and his whole sect of martial brothers attempt to retire from the *jianghu*, but are intercepted on the way. Similarly, retirement is not an option as reprised in Tsui Hark and Ching Siu-Tung's *Swordsman II: Asia the Invincible* (1992), which continues in twists and turns to amplify the tension between the idea of *Wanderer* and the Gu Long articulated theme. To wit, the evil Sun Moon Cult leader Ren Woxing laughingly explains to Linghu Chong: "Retire from the *jianghu*? . . . *jianghu,* as long as there are people there will be feelings of gratitude and resentment, and as long as there are feelings of gratitude and resentment there will be *jianghu*. People are *jianghu*, how are you going to retire from it?"[16] Ren Woxing thereupon encourages Linghu Chong to join his Sun Moon Cult and offers him second in command, complete with his daughter Yingying's hand in marriage. Despite his love for Yingying, Linghu Chong sees her father's insanity and declines his terms. The film directly echoes Gu Long's theme with a twist, addition of the term *enyuan* (feelings of gratitude/obligation and resentment), thus forcing the focus away from individual desire onto the social interplay of gratitude and resentment, with final assertion of the inevitable inescapability from the "revenge" cycle. It is simply impossible to retire from *jianghu* because you can't retire from human relations, humanity is *jianghu*, and therefore *shen bu you ji* (one has no choice [but to conform to the *jianghu* rules/morality]).

Pop culture discourse has a multitude of manifestations of the idea of *jianghu*. Pivoting to the cultural penetration of the *jianghu* and the role of the individual fighter in Jin Yong's works, it is instructive to examine *Swordsman II*'s oblique angle on the "retirement theme" in a different movie, Wong Kar-wai's epic reenvisioning of two characters of Jin Yong's *Heroes* in the movie *Ashes of Time* (1994). *Ashes of Time* centers on the two characters indicated in the Chinese title, Jin Yong's "Eastern Heretic" Huang Yaoshi, and "Western Venom" Ouyang Feng. This reinterpretation of Jin Yong heroes transcends Jin Yong's depiction, positing a post-textual definition of *jianghu* focusing on a cycle of obligation and revenge, participation in which is not voluntary. In this reading, *Ashes of Time* reifies and twist the concept that "in the *jianghu* one has no choice but to conform to *jianghu* rules/morality," leaving no space for wandering/retiring from the *jianghu* as expressed by the trope "*xiao ao jianghu*" (laughing haughtily at the *jianghu* [rules/morality]). *Ashes of Time* completely swings the interpretive space away from "laughing haughtily at the *jianghu* [rules/morality]" to "in the *jianghu* one has no choice but to conform to *jianghu* rules/morality." Here in a bleak and forbidding desert nobody can retire, especially not the killers who owe obligation in the revenge cycle. The *jianghu* in *Ashes of Time* appears as an infinite desert, a cultural dystopia in which only obligation and revenge have meaning, though entwined with love and eating. Retirement, withdrawing from this *jianghu*, happens only with death, and even death itself is not closure, but rather continues like the cycle of sandstorms depicted in the film. In one scene Ouyang Feng gets to bare basics of the *jianghu* while trying to recruit Hong Qi as an assassin:

Ouyang Feng: "Do you know why I invited you to eat?"

Hong Qi: "No."

Ouyang Feng: "Because I know you are hungry. Actually, I've noticed you for a long time, seeing you squatting at the base of that wall, not moving all day long. I've seen a lot of young people like you who know a little kungfu and think they can run riot throughout the world. In fact, *zou jianghu* [wandering the *jianghu*] is a very painful thing. Knowing kungfu, there are a lot of things you aren't able to do. You're not gonna farm, right? And it's shameful to rob, and even less do you want to show your face street performing, so how are you going to live? Somebody with really strong kungfu still has to eat. There is one profession suited to you, which can both help you earn a little money and also let you fight for justice and righteousness. Are you interested? You just think about it for a while but make it quick. You know you'll be hungry soon."[17]

The lesson from this scene in *Ashes of Time* is that being a hired killer is the only *jianghu* profession suitable for the kungfu hero who must *xing xia zhang yi* (do the upholding of justice of the moral system). The twist is that selling out can be rationalized as "righteous" in terms of *jianghu* morality, since you've got to survive/eat, but this can be done with "honor." Riven by the existential angst of *jianghu* society, Hong Qi can acquiesce to *jianghu* morality by becoming an assassin. If he acquiesces like Lu Xun's madman, he may then return to "sanity," and if doesn't acquiesce, he is going to starve. This, however, is a false choice because having only one choice is the absence of choice. You can't fight *jianghu* nature just like you

Figure 5.3. Hong Qi and Ouyang Feng discussing the *jianghu* in *Ashes of Time* (1994)

can't sanely starve yourself, so the madman/martial hero clears up his/her insanity and returns to the "normality" of killing.

What amount of cultural capital would be required to survive departure from the *jianghu*, such a seeming impossibility? Even the cache of Jack Ma with his billions seems to be metaphorically bound by this dictum. Consider once again his Alibaba nickname, Feng Qingyang, taken from the hermit Huashan elder who taught Linghu Chong the unparalleled swordsmanship of Dugu Qiubai. The *jianghu* is a cultural field and enormous cultural capital is necessary to even attempt to reject it. Being the number one martial artist in the *jianghu* (like Jack Ma) is still too fleeting as the denouement of Asia the Invincible—insanity—implies. The tragedy of Feng Qingyang's enforced hermetism (*Wanderer*) and Xiao Feng's loss of soulmate (*Semi-Devils*), both demonstrate the transience of human volition, not to mention Dugu Qiubai's unrequited yearning for a worthy opponent whom he hoped could defeat him (*Companion*).

The holistic approach of viewing the kungfu industrial complex as the *jianghu* is revealed and validated when considering the fact, noted in chapter 4, that Brigitte Lin had to do thirteen film variations of Asia the Invincible role in a year and a half and was only "allowed" by the triads to "retire" from acting after she and the audience were "exhausted" with the role. What will be the conditions under which audiences finally stop patronizing Jin Yong and kungfu movies in general? This probably won't happen for a long time since, as Jackie Chan notes, action is a world language and kungfu has permeated world cinema. Rather than lose their ability to understand and appreciate the language of action, the kungfu industrial complex is increasingly globalized, and audiences find kungfu action informing ever more subgenres. In this sense the game is "rigged," as it were, a culturally conditioned and socially sustained hustle.

THE *KUNG FU HUSTLE* HUSTLE

Director and actor Stephen Chow has deep experience playing off Jin Yong's characters in a variety of movies, and also draws from the novels of fellow kungfu fiction master Gu Long. For example, Chow's movie *Da ne mitan linglingfa* (*Forbidden City Cop*, 1996) begins with Gu Long's characters Ximen Chuixue, Lu Xiaofeng, Ye Gucheng, and Hua Manlou meeting on a rooftop for a seminal battle. They are old, and as imperial "protector" Chow laughs at them as they introduce themselves with their full martial appellations. Ye Gucheng gives Chow a martial book of secrets called *Tianwai fei xian* (Flying immortal from space) and asks him to let them off the hook. Mimicking the prologue to a James Bond movie, this scene is played out in the first four minutes where Chow also satirizes Bond (*ling ling qi*—007) by introducing himself as *"ling ling fa"* (homophone for 008), a gynecologist inventor. Chow's inventions infuriate the emperor, who is only interested in pursuing actual kungfu.

The *ultimate* Jin Yong derivative work is Stephen Chow's *Kung Fu Hustle* (2004). *Kung Fu Hustle* is a work of homage to not only Hong Kong martial arts film, but also to the kungfu and *wuxia* mythology that form the literary-filmic background upon which the movie is constructed. *Kung Fu Hustle* is the prime example of the manipulation of cultural capital in the martial *jianghu*, the zenith of the kungfu industrial complex in operation.

First note that Jin Yong wrote one other key protagonist whose ambivalence toward *jianghu* morality resembles Linghu Chong's. Yang Guo is the protagonist in *Companion*, which was the first novel serialized in Jin Yong's own newly established newspaper[18] and perhaps Jin Yong's ultimate love story. The primary *jianghu* tension in *Companion* is the conflict between love and duty. Yang Guo observes the moral order in the *jianghu* from a distance, skeptical from youth because he was first bullied by martial brothers/sisters and later ostracized for disobedience to his Qing Zhen Sect master. He runs away and eventually falls in love with his new master, Xiaolongnü (Little Dragon Girl), a maiden not much older than him who is highly accomplished in martial arts. Both abandoning his martial sect and falling in love with one's own master (read as martial incest) constitute mortal breaches of *jianghu* morality. Yang Guo and Xiaolongnü require nearly 1600 pages of heroic action to overcome the stigma that their relationship causes to their reputations in the martial world. In the end, after a myriad of heroic acts and being separated for over a decade, they are finally reunited. The novel ends with these two heroes departing to places unknown, taking their leave from the *jianghu*. However, like *Wanderer*'s Linghu Chong, Yang Guo and Xiaolongnü appear and reappear in post-textual cultural discourse over the decades as their characters are reprised in television series adaptations in 1976, 1983, 1984, 1995, 1998 (twice), 2006, 2014, and 2019, as well as movie and game adaptations.

The epitome of post-textual derivation of Yang Guo and Xiaolongnü is found in Stephen Chow's *Kung Fu Hustle* (2004).[19] *Kung Fu Hustle* is a brilliant caricature of kungfu/*wuxia* film which draws directly on Jin Yong's rich literary and film legacy.[20] The movie won at least twenty-one awards and nominations in Hong Kong and Taiwan and took in $17 million domestically and $83 million internationally.[21] *Kung Fu Hustle* portrays a future for Yang Guo and Xiaolongnü. As writer, director, and actor, Stephen Chow taps into mythic archetypical action styled by Bruce Lee, himself a writer and director and actor, as well as the cultural currency of these two seminal Jin Yong characters.

A high level of kungfu cultural literacy is necessary to earnestly appreciate the rapid-fire inside jokes and allusions that permeate virtually every scene of *Kung Fu Hustle*. The movie has high production value and commensurately high degree of visual surface appeal, as well as a variety of action that easily appeals to the Western viewer without recourse to a background in Chinese studies. However, the cultural capital acquired through reading Jin Yong's novels (and consumption of other *wuxia* fiction and film) is crucial to enhanced appreciation of the "hustle" of *Kung Fu Hustle* (the film's Chinese name is simply "Kungfu").

Kung Fu Hustle's narrative is framed at beginning and end by a satirical sketch involving a beggar who hawks sacred kungfu texts (titles found in Jin Yong works) to a child on some nameless street. In the opening scene the beggar, played by action director Yuen Woo-ping's real father Yuen Siu-tien (Yuan Xiaotian), sells the *Rulai shen zhang* (Buddha's Mystical Palm) text to the adolescent Chow.[22] The movie ends with the same beggar peddling a set of five books, four of which are also Jin Yong secret kungfu manuals. Like the Buddhist *samsara* (wheel of life), the kungfu educational cycle continues its unending course.

Next the film jumps a couple of decades to a small suburb called "Pigsty Alley" where Yang Guo and Xiaolongnü live an ostensibly quiet "retirement" as landlords. Here they "temporarily have peace and tranquility" earned by many years of anonymity. They are soon forced by events, however, to reveal their kungfu skills when the peace of Pigsty Alley is disrupted by the now grown-up would-be hoodlum played by Stephen Chow. Yang Guo and Xiaolongnü unwillingly come out of retirement to successfully fight the Axe Gang. After suffering a humiliating defeat,

Figure 5.4. The old beggar peddling Jin Yong martial tomes at conclusion of *Kung Fu Hustle* (2004)

the Axe Gang hires powerful assassins who shoot *qi* from their zither's to even the score, but they are also defeated. The Axe Gang thereupon seeks out "The Beast" (Huoyun xieshen), a kungfu master with unparalleled ability who is self-confined to an insane asylum because there are no worthy opponents in the outside world (read this as a Dugu Qiubai analogy). The Beast is enticed out of retirement by the possibility of a real match with such worthy adversaries as Yang Guo and Xiaolongnü. In an epic battle he pits his *hama gong* (toad kungfu), the signature kungfu of *Heroes* antagonist Western Venom Ouyang Feng, against the two now middle-aged lovers. The Beast is victorious.

The poorly skilled Stephen Chow inexplicably comes to the unlikely rescue through the process of being beaten to a pulp (reduced to his most elemental form) by the Beast. This thorough thrashing awakens in Chow some "natural born ability" to channel his *qi*, clearing a path through his meridians and allowing him to attain the highest consolidation of martial abilities realized in the *Buddha's Mystical Palm* kungfu text. Chow thereupon uses the *Buddha's Mystical Palm* to finally defeat the Beast.

Kung Fu Hustle demonstrates that retirement is transitory or impossible. Yang Guo and Xiaolongnü discover that no matter how well they cover up their kungfu powers to facilitate their "peaceful" retirement, in the end they must return to the *jianghu*. They first surreptitiously battle the Axe Gang minions, then its hired killers, and finally The Beast, whom the Axe Gang literally recruits straight from the insane asylum to kill them. Do they have any choice but to fight? Yangguo and Xiaolongnü retired into the obscurity of this small hamlet, just like Linghu Chong and Ren Yingying who relinquished leadership in their respective sects. Their kungfu skills are well hidden from the occupants of the village, even from three other highly skill martial artists who are also living there in common obscurity. Yangguo and Xiaolongnü are depicted comically interacting with the inhabitants, who fail to recognize the considerable foreshadowing of their kungfu skills. This pattern of lovers removing themselves from the *jianghu* at the height of their martial prowess superficially allows them to realize the *"xiao ao jianghu"* ideal. However, like Lu Xun's madman, who returns to "sanity" and retakes his place in the cannibalistic social structure, Yangguo and Xiaolongnü are forced back to the *jianghu* to restore the peace and tranquility of their retirement at the cost of further mayhem and insanity.

Chow's *Kung Fu Hustle* demonstrates that the scope of the kungfu industrial complex is far wider than Jin Yong and his works. It is not only the epitome of synthesis of *wuxia* and kungfu films and fiction, but also demonstrates Jin Yong's rich legacy of martial arts fiction. *Kung Fu Hustle* shows Jin Yong readers a vision of his archetypical characters over the decades, still alive in pop cultural consciousness through repeated production in television series. That they can't ever really "retire" is the price of immortality as eternal archetypes. *Kung Fu Hustle* does a hustle, a con, resolving one of the greatest mysteries from Jin Yong's *Companion*—the denouement of Yang Guo and Xiaolongnü. Moreover, *Kung Fu Hustle* uses

Figure 5.5. Companions martial lovers, Yang Guo and Xiaolongnü, come out of retirement to battle the Beast in *Kung Fu Hustle* (2004)

a plethora of kungfu characters, terms, and techniques with legacy from Chinese classics through Jin Yong and Hong Kong film throughout the decades. The usages may not be "pure" or "standard," but the etymology of the *Buddha's Mystical Palm* and "The Beast," as is the case with many of the kungfu allusions in *Kung Fu Hustle*, have a long provenance.[23] The legacy of Chow's use of such kungfu terms is broad, deep, and rich. *Kung Fu Hustle* demonstrates a deep vision of continuity to martial arts fictional tradition. The use of slapstick comedy hustles the audience by taking the emotional edge off the extreme violence and virtually nonstop mass murder occurring throughout the film.

Continuing the hustle, in 2007 Stephen Chow had plans to develop all Jin Yong's characters into a single movie, and met with Jin Yong to discuss his cooperation:

> According to a Hong Kong media report, on the evening of February 5, Stephen Chow met Jin Yong for dinner, together along with Ni Kuang, Cai Lan, Xu Xiaofeng, and other celebrities. During dinner both sides discussed Stephen Chow's future outline of a new drama that would put together all the famous characters of Jin Yong's works as a subject, and thus his hope for Mr. Jin Yong's future collaboration in making this new movie. Last night, the reporter addressed this with [Chow's] Xinghui Film Company's Tian Qiwen, who acknowledged "We have maintained this concept."[24]

The kungfu "hustle" draws on the long and deep cultural discourse of martial arts fiction and film. Stephen Chow went from playing minor roles in early TVB television adaptations of *Semi-Devils* (1982) and *Companion* (1983)[25] to dining with Jin Yong and other celebrities and proposing additional Jin Yong based film adaptations. There is a practical creative function of the kungfu industrial complex developing along the lines of humorous self-satire in *Kung Fu Hustle*. While Wong Kar-wai's *Ashes of Time* provided a vision of prequel for Jin Yong characters, *Kung Fu Hustle* provides a vision of sequel, and derivation. Ambitions of cooperation with Jin Yong indicated in the quote above points to a potentially more complex future for the kungfu industrial complex, seeming to assure that further prequels and sequels are forthcoming. Where will Stephen Chow's hustle take the narrative of Jin Yong characters in his future production of *Kung Fu Hustle II*? The *Kung Fu Hustle* hustle is to be continued, because after all, people cannot retire from the *jianghu*, since "the *jianghu* is people," though they may periodically laugh haughtily at the *jianghu*, its rules and morality.

Gu Long's eight-character dictum, *ren zai jianghu, shen bu you ji* proves true. In *Kung Fu Hustle* neither Yangguo and Xiaolongnü nor The Beast could successfully escape into anonymous obscurity. Gu Long continued his observations noted in the block quote at the beginning of this chapter, following his dictum with commentary on violence in the *jianghu*, saying that by daylight some people seem "cultured," but "At midnight of the full moon, many of them will go crazy, some will rape, some will commit violence, and some will kill people."[26] This dichotomy leads to the tentative conclusion that *ren zai jianghu, shen bu you ji* can only be temporarily challenged by the idea of *xiao ao jianghu* at the cost of innumerable martial artists going insane—committing horrific acts and/or dying horrible deaths.

Post-textual interpretive performance of Jin Yong's plots/subplots seems to amplify the tension between the two crucial *wuxia* themes: "*ren zai jianghu, shen bu you ji*," and "*xiao ao jianghu*." Derivative works also prioritize the *jianghu* social order over the individual *wuxia* self-desire for separation or disassociation from the *jianghu*. Prioritization is a mirror of the return of Lu Xun's madman to society no longer "insane" (while the entire text of Lu Xun's story clearly explicates the irony that returning to sanity is proof of "insanity"). This conundrum indicates that a slight modification of Gu Long's dictum is warranted, in the Lu Xun sense, as it were. Here I add the character *"kuang"* (crazy) to the dictum: *kuangren zai jianghu, shen bu you ji* (in the *jianghu* the madman has no choice but to conform to *jianghu* rules/morality). Thus updated, the dictum indicates that *jianghu* madmen have either death as an option, or like Linghu Chong and Ren Yingying, or Yang Guo and Xiaolongnü, they may temporarily "retire," but will necessarily continue along the trajectory of Lu Xun's madman and eventually be forced to return to "sanity" of the insane *jianghu* moral order. Such a return to "sanity" finally explicates the denouement of such characters in post-textual reinterpretations and derivations of Jin Yong's works. Insanity is the "stable state" of the "sane" *jianghu*. This ironic reality helps elucidate the narrative twist in *Swordsman II* in which Linghu Chong eventually sees his lover Ren Yingying morph into their mortal enemy, Asia the Invincible. If pushed to even farther extratextual boundaries, the contradiction of insanity/sanity may ironically explain the improbability of Linghu Chong and Ren Yingying's retirement song, "Xiao ao jianghu," morphing into a contemporary pop television comedy variety show, such is the malleability of cultural capital.

Construction of the kungfu industrial complex is multifaceted, ever broadening and deepening. The variety of characters, plots, and tropes in Jin Yong's novels trace their cultural currency back through the history of Chinese literature, and into the future or "afterlives" up to the present. Kungfu cultural literacy is a phenomenon impacted by more than the author Jin Yong and his works alone and encompasses other authors and their creative use of the language of kungfu, as well as imaginative production of characters and stories that draw upon millennia of myths and legends, which then take on a life of their own and continue to resonate throughout pop culture. The rhetorical kungfu discussed in chapter 2 demonstrated how Jin Yong's humorously subversive language might resonate with readers and audiences. Jin Yong and his works resonate in the academy as well, as shown in chapter 3, where debates among academicians and literary figures in the process of determining the literary value of Jin Yong's martial arts fiction set in the context of his entry into the canon of Chinese literature. Analysis of the discourse of canonization and cultural authority from the perspective of the national character critique demonstrated that Jin Yong's holistic portrayal of national character both complements and surpasses the one-sided negative critique supplied by the modern literary master Lu Xun. Chapter 4 described the significant dimension of star power in the construction of the kungfu industrial complex. Here are multitudes of actors, directors, casts, and crews who give life to the martial arts moves and mores in Jin Yong screen adaptations. While action is a language that transcends national boundaries and explains the success of kungfu film from Bruce Lee to Ang Lee, kungfu also presents an opening, or a window, through which to explore and interpret Chinese language, literature, and culture on a whole.

This concluding chapter 5 examined the ideological predicament of the characters from two of Jin Yong's seminal novels, *Wanderer* and *Companion*, and presented the tension between society and the individual through their struggles as a dichotomy of the *jianghu*, expressed through the framing concepts, *"ren zai jianghu, shen bu you ji"* and *"xiao ao jianghu."* While Linghu Chong may laugh haughtily at the *jianghu* norms and rules, the *jianghu* is social, it is political, it is in the end people, and one can't retire from it. Yang Guo and Xiaolongnü resemble Linghu Chong and Ren Yingying. The *Kung Fu Hustle* hustle demonstrates that Jin Yong's characters and themes return again and again, retirement impossible as material from kungfu novels is adapted to movies. The "comedy" of *Kung Fu Hustle* is entertainment, but moreover used as social and cultural critique which transcends politics while implying universal themes of good versus evil made intelligible by the interpretive lens of kungfu cultural literacy. This kungfu cultural literacy plays on the process described in chapter 4, whereupon stars, actors, directors, reify the kungfu novels' characters, stories, and ethico-moral universe in an unceasing discourse constructing and reconstructing the kungfu industrial complex.

The legacy of Jin Yong, Bruce Lee, Jackie Chan, Stephen Chow, and multitudes of others is visible through the kungfu techniques and their choreographic representations which have been adopted wholesale in the transnational ascendance of actual and metaphorical kungfu from Asia to

Hollywood. The kungfu culturally literate audience can now more ably read the subtexts of action films that carry on the themes, sayings, characters, conflicts, sacred texts and kungfu sects, while reveling in China's language, history, geography, and culture as stars participate in power struggles of romance and revenge in pursuit of a semblance of world peace and harmony. The heroes can't retire from the *jianghu* because the *jianghu* is people, a people whose *jianghu* is perpetually imagined, reified, reimagined and rereified in the construction of the kungfu industrial complex. This is the cultural field composed of writers, critics, actors, directors, producers, and cast and crew, as well as audiences who make up the kungfu industrial complex, thus demonstrating the immeasurable extent to which cultural capital informs and reproduces at all the nodes in the matrix of kungfu culturalism.

The *Kung Fu Hustle* hustle demonstrates the individual elements of the kungfu industrial complex come together in a dynamic equilibrium and suggests that China may likewise eventually find such equilibrium and transcend the narrow issues of nationalism and national identity through full embrace its own cultural forms. The globalization of the kungfu industrial complex suggests that in the twenty-first century, China no longer needs to make nationalist pronouncements about cultural subjugation in modern global society. China has become an international producer of artistic and aesthetic culture, not just consumer products, and continues to move up the manufacturing chain to create higher value-added cultural artifacts. As such, kungfu film internationalism supplies both Chinese and foreign audiences with a nuanced mythologized view of Chinese cultural prowess.

NOTES

1. This appears in two places in Gu Long's works, the first in volume 6 of the *Xiao Li fei dao* (Young Li's flying dagger) series, *Feng ling zhong de dao sheng* (Sound of a sword in the wind), *Gu Long zuopin ji* (The collected works of Gu Long), vol. 34, (Zhuhaishi: Zhuhai chubanshe, 1995): 258. The second is in *Chu Liuxiang chuanqi* (The tales of Chu Liuxiang), vol. 48 of *Gu Long zuopin ji* (The collected works of Gu Long), 2085.

2. Television adaptations include episode 18 of the Taiwan edition of Jin Yong's *Wanderer* (2000), as well as episodes 10, 12, and 17 of the mainland edition of Gu Long's *San Shaoye de jian* (2000).

3. "Jin Yong's Heroes now in English," February 13, 2018, https://www.straitstimes.com/lifestyle/arts/jin-yongs-heroes-now-in-english.

4. Ang Lee, quoted in Kin-Yan Szeto, *The Martial Arts Cinema of the Chinese Diaspora: Ang Lee, John Woo, and Jackie Chan in Hollywood* (Carbondale: Southern Illinois University Press, 2011): 1.

5. Zhang Che, quoted in Kin-Yan Szeto, *The Martial Arts Cinema of the Chinese Diaspora*, 1.

6. Roger Ebert, "Crouching Tiger Hidden Dragon," *Chicago Sun Times*, December 20, 2000, https://www.rogerebert.com/reviews/crouching-tiger-hidden-dragon-2000.

7. Wang Lu. "Zhumin tishen yanyuan Luo Lixian xiemi: Cheng Long yizhi yong tishen" [Famous stunt double Luo Lixian reveals secret: Jackie Chan used stunt double all along], April 3, 2007, http://ent.sina.com.cn/m/c/2007-04-03/10181502981.html.

8. Gu Long, *Chu Liuxiang*, 2085.

9. Jin Yong, *Wanderer*, 1683–1684.

10. Note that the dubbed words cited here do not exactly match the subtitles. The subtitles follow Gu Long's expression directly with the addition of the initial "I am also," "*Wo ye shi ren zai jianghu, shen bu you ji*" [I am also (in the situation of) in the *jianghu* there is no individual choice (i.e., one has no choice but to conform to *jianghu* rules/morality)]. "*Xiao ao jianghu*" (2000), episode 18.

11. "*Xiao ao jianghu*" (2000), episode 6, 49:51.

12. Jin Yong, *Wanderer*, 1682.

13. Reading *Wanderer* as a loose allegory to Chairman Mao's Cultural Revolution, Jin Yong narratively makes the case here that ultimate knowledge, truth, and wisdom of Chinese culture is located in institutions, in this case represented by the Shaolin and Wudang Sects, which hold moral authority established through long history and tradition.

14. Jin Yong, *Wanderer*, 396.

15. Ibid., 1674–1675.

16. "Xiao ao jianghu: Dongfang Bubai (Guo Yue) [*Swordsman II: Asia the Invincible* (Mandarin, Cantonese)], 1:32:03, accessed December 13, 2016, https://www.youtube.com/watch?v=WIz2M0bBWYY.

17. "Dong Xie Xi Du taici (quanben)" [Ashes of Time script (complete)], accessed June 20, 2016, http://www.douban.com/group/topic/1316973/.

18. Jin Yong, *Companion*, 1661.

19. Chow has ample experience with Jin Yong character parts, having played Wei Xiaobao in his comedy depiction of Jin Yong's *The Deer and the Cauldron* through his films *The Royal Tramp* (1992) and *The Royal Tramp II* (1992). Moreover, Chow ostensibly promoted kungfu as the answer to improving Chinese health and spiritual being in his movie *Shaolin Soccer* (2001). And "industrial complex" does imply money in an important dimension.

20. Siu Leung Li interprets this movie in terms of commodification, "crossing kung fu over to other genres to produce an often hybrid from in order to make money." Siu Leung Li, "The Myth Continues," 54.

21. "*Kung Fu Hustle*," accessed January 6, 2021, https://www.boxofficemojo.com/title/tt0373074/?ref_=bo_se_r_1.

22. The beggar character is interpreted in the later *Kung Fu Hustle* video games as "The Nine Fingered Mystical Beggar," a direct allusion to Jin Yong's character Hong Qigong who goes by that appellation. See He Ye, "Xiang Xingye yiyang xue shengong gongfu Jiu zhi shengai wanfa puguang" [Just like Zhou Xingchi learn-

ing mystical kungfu the Nine Fingered Mystical Beggar's method of playing is exposed," March 16, 2012, http://news.07073.com/zixun/577098.html.

23. The Buddha's Mystical Palm appears to be an ironic reference to a 1965 Hong Kong film series, the 1968 Hong Kong film, *Rulai shenzhang zai xian shenwei* (The Buddha's mystical palm again demonstrates its mystical power), in which the main character is also named Huoyun xieshen (a.k.a. the Beast in *Kung Fu Hustle*), and his primary kungfu is *Jiu shi rulai shenzhang* (Nine styles of the Buddha's mystical palm). "Rulai shenzhang" (The Buddha's mystical palm), accessed March 30, 2022, https://baike.baidu.com/item/如来神掌/19730380.

24. "Zhou Xingchi she yan yao Jin Yong hepai dianying juben dawang yi nihao" [Stephen Chow gives a banquet and invites Jin Yong to collaborate on a movie, the script outline is already finished], February 8, 2007, www.ifensi.com.

25. "Zhou Xingchi (Stephen Chow)," accessed January 6, 2021, https://baike.baidu.com/item/周星驰.

26. Gu Long, *Chu Liuxiang*, 2086.

GLOSSARY

A Q jingshen	阿Q精神
A Q shi	阿Q式
A Q sixiang	阿Q思想
A Q zhuyi	阿Q主義
anqi	暗器
baba	爸爸
Bai fa monü zhuan	白髮魔女傳
bangzhu	幫主
Bei Gai	北丐
bei Qiao Feng nan Murong	北喬峰南慕容
beifen gongfu	輩分功夫
beifen	輩分
bi wu zhao qin	比武招親
Bixie jianpu	辟邪劍譜
Boli zun	玻璃樽
bu qiu tongnian tongyue tongri sheng, dan yuan tongnian tongyue tongri si	不求同年同月同日生，但願同年同月同日死
Chan, Idy (Chen Yulian)	陳玉蓮
Chan, Jackie (Cheng Long)	成龍
Chang Cheh (Zhang Che)	張徹
Chau, Emil Wakin (Zhou Huajian)	周華健
Chen Shaoxia	陳少霞
Chenbao	晨報
Cheng, Adam (Zheng Shaoqiu)	鄭少秋
Cheng, Ekin (Zheng Yijian)	鄭伊健
Cheng tian jiahe yule jituan youxian gongsi	橙天嘉禾娛樂集團有限公司
Cheung, Jacky (Zhang Xueyou)	張學友
Cheung, Julien (Zhang Zhilin)	张智霖

Cheung, Leslie (Zhang Guorong)	張國榮
Cheung, Sharla (Zhang Min)	張敏
Chi bi	赤壁
Ching Siu-Tung (Cheng Xiaodong)	程小東
chongzhi	蟲豸
Chor Yuen (Chu Yuan)	楚原
Chou, Jay (Zhou Jielun)	周杰倫
Chow, Raymond (Zou Wenhuai)	鄒文懷
Chow, Stephen (Zhou Xingchi)	周星馳
Chow Yun-fat (Zhou Runfa)	周潤發
Chu, Athena (Zhu Yin)	朱茵
Chu Liuxiang	楚留香
Chu Liuxiang xilie	楚留香系列
Chuangli chuangwai	窗里窗外
chusheng	畜牲
da fei zhu	大肥豬
da gou bangfa	打狗棒法
Da ne mitan linglingfa	大内密探零零发
Dai Sicong	戴思聰
dajiuzi	大舅子
Diao Yu	刁羽
die	爹
Ding Chunqiu	丁春秋
Do (*dao*)	道
Dong Xie Xi Du	東邪西毒
Dong Xie Xi Du: zhongji ban	東邪西毒：終極版
Dong Xie	東邪
Dongfang Bubai	東方不敗
Dongfang Bubai zhi fengyun zaiqi	東方不敗之風雲再起
Dongfang san xia	東方三俠
Du bi dao	獨臂刀
Duan Yu	段譽
Dugu jiu jian	獨孤九劍
Dugu Qiubai	恩怨
enyuan	恩怨
erzi da laozi	兒子打老子
erzi hao da ye de	兒子好打爺的
erzi ti laozi	兒子提老子
faluo gong	法螺功
Fang Shiyu	方世玉

fengci gongfu	諷刺功夫
Gang-Tai	港台
Gong shou dao	功守道
Gongfu guanlan	功夫灌籃
	(a.k.a., *Da guanlan* 大灌籃)
Gongfu meng	功夫夢
gongfu pian	功夫片
Gongfu zhi wang	功夫之王
gongfu	功夫
gou ming	狗命
Gu Long	古龍
guai haizi	乖孩子
Guan Dexing	關德興
Guo Jing	郭靖
guo ma	國罵
guominxing	國民性
Gushi xinbian	故事新編
guzhuang	古裝
hama gong	蛤蟆功
Hengshan	恆山
Hengshan	衡山
Ho, Leonard (He Guanchang)	何冠昌
hou yan gong	厚顏功
Hu, King (Hu Jinquan)	胡金銓
Hu Peng	胡鵬
Hua Mulan	花木蘭
Hua Wuque	花無缺
Huanghe si gui	黃河四鬼
Huashan pai diyi daodangui	華山派第一搗蛋鬼
hunao bang	胡鬧幫
Huo Yuanjia	霍元甲
Huoyun xieshen	火雲邪神
hutu xiaozi	糊塗小子
Jeet Kune Do (jie quan dao)	截拳道
Jen, Richie (Ren Xianqi)	任賢齊
ji di zhi ji	激敵之計
ji jiang ji	激將計
Jia Baoyu	賈寶玉 (假寶玉)
jian guo Shi Jian	奸過石堅
jianghu	江湖

Jianmo Dugu Qiubai	劍魔獨孤求敗
jianren Jian	奸人堅
Jiayi dianshi	佳藝電視
jie wei xiongdi	結為兄弟
jiebai cheng le jinlan xiongdi	結拜成了金蘭兄弟
jin pan xi shou	金盤洗手
Jin shi baihua	金式白話
Jin Yong *xueqi*	金庸學期
Jingcha gushi	警察故事
jingshen shengli de daiyong pin	精神勝利的代用品
jingshen shengli fa	精神勝利法
Jingwu fengyun	精武風雲
Jingwu men	精武門
Jingwu tiyuhui	精武體育會
Jingwu yingxiong	精武英雄
Jingwu zhen	精武鎮
Jinlun Fawang	金輪法王
jiu ban	舊版
Jiu er Shen diao xia lü zhi chixinqing chang jian	九二神鵰俠侶之痴心情長劍
Jiu ni zhe liangxiazi hai xiang chulai chuang jianghu? Shei jiao ni de?	就你這兩下子還想出來闖江湖？誰教你的？
Jiu shi rulai shenzhang	九式如來神掌
Jiu yi Shen diao xia lü	九一神鵰俠侶
jue zi jue sun	絕子絕孫
Juedai shuang jiao	絕代雙驕
junzi ke ru, bu ke qu	君子可辱，不可屈
kaifang	開放
kuangren zai jianghu, shen bu you ji	狂人在江湖，身不由己
Kwan Tak-hing (Guan Dexing)	關德興
Kwok, Aaron (Guo Fucheng)	郭富城
lao biaozi	老婊子
lao qianbei	老前輩
Lao Sun	老孫
lao wantong	老頑童
lao wugui	老烏龜
laoda	老大
loaning	老娘
laosan	老三
laoyezi	老爺子
laozi	老子

Lau, Andy (Liu Dehua)	劉德華
Lau, Carina (Liu Jialing)	劉嘉玲
Lee, Bruce (Li Xiaolong)	李小龍
Lee Xiaolong yu wo	李小龍與我
Leung, Tony Chiu-Wai (Liang Chaowei)	梁朝偉
Leung, Tony Ka-fai (Liang Jiahui)	梁家輝
Li, Jet (Li Lianjie)	李連杰
lian chusheng ye bu ru	連畜牲也不如
Liang Jiaren	梁家仁
Liang Yusheng	梁羽生
Linghu yeye	令狐爺爺
linghun renwu	靈魂人物
lishi ta ri you fu gongxiang, you nan tongdang	立誓他日有福共享, 有難同當
Liu Dehua cishan jijinhui	劉德華慈善基金會
Liu, Gordon (Liu Jiahui)	劉家輝
Liu Huan	劉歡
Liu Jialiang	劉家良
Liu Zhan	劉湛
Liu Zhengfeng	劉正風
Liu Zhenwei	劉鎮偉
liuxing ban	流行版
Long zheng hu dou	龍爭虎鬥
Lu ding ji II: shenlong jiao	鹿鼎記 II 神龍教
Lu ding ji	鹿鼎记
Lu Xiaofeng	陸小鳳
ma pi gong	馬屁功
Ma, Jack (Ma Yun)	馬雲
Mao Weitao	茅威濤
mapi gong	馬屁功
maren gongfu	罵人功夫
Miao Renfeng	苗人鳳
ming zheng yan shun	名正言順
minzu hun	民族魂
Miu, Michael (Miao Qiaowei)	苗僑偉
Mo jiao	魔教
Mui, Anita (Mei Yanfang)	梅艷芳
Murong Fu	慕容復
Murong Yan	慕容嫣
Murong Yan	慕容燕

muzhu	母豬
Nahan	吶喊
Nan Di	南帝
neigong	內功
Ng Man Tat (Wu Mengda)	吳孟達
ni erzi	你兒子
ni hui sunzi	你灰孫子
ni laogong	你老公
ni nainaide lao zazhong, wo cao ni Mao jia shiqiba dai lao zusong, wugui wangbadan	你奶奶的老雜種，我操你茅家十七八代老祖宗，烏龜王八蛋
ni nainaide	你奶奶的
ni zhe chou wangba, sibutou de lao jiayu	你這臭王八，死不透的老甲魚
ni zhe zei wangba, chou wugui lucao shi, gei ren zhanshang yiqian dao de zhuluo	你這賊王八，臭烏龜，路倒屍，給人斬上一千刀的豬玀
ning si bu qu	寧死不屈
numu er shi	怒目而視
numu zhuyi	怒目主義
nüqiangren	女強人
ouxiang pai	偶像派
Pai Mei (Bai Mei)	白眉
Panghuang	彷徨
pingbei pengyou	平輩朋友
qi	氣
Qian Yongqiang	錢永強
Qiao Feng	喬峯 (a.k.a., Xiao Feng 蕭峯)
qingshen gongfu	輕身功夫
rao wanzi ma ren	繞彎子罵人
Ren xiaoyao	任逍遙
Ren zai jianghu, shen bu you ji	人在江湖，身不由己
renqing	人情
Rui Lui (Lü Liangwei)	呂良偉
Rulai shen zhang	如來神掌
Rulai shenzhang zai xian shenwei	如來神掌再顯神威
San jian xia	三劍俠
Shangxin Taipingyang	傷心太平洋
Shaoshi xiongdi (Xianggang) youxian gongsi	邵氏兄弟（香港）有限公司

She diao san bu qu	射鵰三部曲
She diao yingxiong zhuan zhi dong cheng xi jiu	射鵰英雄傳之東成西就
She diao yingxiong zhuan zhi jiu yin zhenjing	射雕英雄传之九阴真经
She diao yingxiong zhuan zhi nandi beigai	射鵰英雄傳之南帝北丐
She diao yingxiong zhuan	射鵰英雄傳
Shen long jiao	神龍教
shi bu sha yi ren, qian li bu liu xing	十步殺一人，千里不留行
Shi ji	史記
Shi Jian (Shih Kien)	石堅
shi ke sha bu ke ru	士可殺不可辱
shifu	師父
shili pai	實力派
shishu	師叔
shishuzu	師叔祖
Shu Qi	舒淇
shuangzi xing	雙子星
shuohua suanshu	說話算數
Si bu liao	死不了
Si da e'ren	四大惡人
Si da ming zhu	四大名著
Si da su	四大俗
Si da tian wang	四大天王
Sichuan Qingcheng pai	四川青城派
sige	四哥
Su Qi Er	蘇乞兒
Sun Wukong	孫悟空
Sunzi bingfa	孫子兵法
sunzi ti yeye	孫子提爺爺
ta mada	他媽的
tai shishuzu	太師叔祖
Teng, Theresa (Deng Lijun)	鄧麗君
Tian di hui	天地會
Tianmu zhizuo youxian gongsi	天幕製作有限公司
Tianwai fei xian	天外飛仙
tianxia diyi	天下第一
To, Johnnie (Du Qifeng)	杜琪峯
Tong, Kent (Tang Zhenye)	湯鎮業

Tsui Hark	徐克
Wang, Jimmy (Wang Yu)	王羽
wei junzi	偽君子
Wei Xiaobao	韋小寶 (偽小寶)
Wei, wei, wugui erzi wangbadan, nimen tuo laozi ganshenme?	喂，喂，烏龜兒子王八蛋你們拖老子幹甚麼？
wen wu quan cai	文武全才
wenhua xiaoshuo	文化小說
wenhuaren	文化人
Wing Chun (yong chun)	詠春
wo huisunzi	我灰孫子
wo ye shi jianghuren, shen bu you ji	我也是江湖人，身不由己
Wo zong suan bei erzi dale	我總算被兒子打了
Wong Kar-wai (Wang Jiawei)	王家衛
Wong, Faye (Wang Fei)	王菲
Wong, Felix (Huang Rihua)	黃日華
wu hu jiang	五虎將
Wu jian dao	無間道
Wu Jing	吳京
Wu Qianlian	吳倩蓮
wu zhao sheng you zhao	無招勝有招
wu	武
wuda pian	武打片
wugong	武功
wulitou	無釐頭
wushu	武術
wuxia	武俠
wuxia pian	武俠片
wuxia xiaoshuo	武俠小說
Wuxian dianshi yiyuan peixun ban	無線電視藝員培訓班
wuxian wu hu	無綫五虎
wuyi	武藝
Xi Du	西毒
xia	俠
Xia ke xing	俠客行
xiang long shiba zhang	降龙十八掌
Xianlang, ni que meili, nali erzi hao da ye de?	賢郎，你卻沒理，那裏兒子好打爺的
Xianzai de shijie tai bu chenghua, erzi da laozi	現在的世界太不成話，兒子打老子
xiao	孝

xiao ao jianghu	笑傲江湖
Xiao ao jianghu II: Dongfang Bubai	笑傲江湖II：東方不敗
Xiao ao jianghu zhi Dongfang Bubai	笑傲江湖之東方不敗
Xiao Feng	蕭峯 (a.k.a., Qiao Feng 喬峯)
Xiao Li Feidao	小李飛刀
Xiao Shiyilang	蕭十一郎
Xiao xia Chu Liuxiang	笑俠楚留香
xiao zazhong, ni nainaide	小雜種，你奶奶的
xiaodi	小弟
Xiaoyaozi	逍遙子
xiaozi	小子
xiayi	俠義
xie	邪
xie pai	邪派
Xie Xun	谢逊
xin ban	新版
Xin Chu Liuxiang	新楚留香
Xin longmen kezhan	新龍門客棧
Xin pai wuxia xiaoshuo	新派武俠小說
Xin shushan jianxia	新蜀山劍俠
Xin Tian long ba bu zhi Tianshan Tonglao	新天龍八部之天山童姥
xin xiu ban	新修版
xing xia zhang yi	行俠仗義
Xingguang yiyi jingzheng hui	星光熠熠勁爭輝
xiongdi	兄弟
xixing dafa	吸星大法
Xu Zhu	虛竹
Yan	燕
Yang Guo *yu* Xiaolongnü	楊過與小龍女
Yang Peipei	杨佩佩
Yazhou tianwang	亞洲天王
Yazhou xin xing dao jihua	亞洲新星導計劃
Yecao	野草
Yen, Donnie (Zhen Zidan)	甄子丹
yeye	爺爺
yi dai zongshi	一代宗師
Yi jian nigu, feng du bi shu	一見尼姑，封賭必輸
Yi tian tu long ji zhi mo jiao jiaozhu	倚天屠龍記之魔教教主
Yi yang zhi	一陽指

Yingxiong bense	英雄本色
yingxiong dahui	英雄大会
yingxiong haohan	英雄好漢
Yip Man (Ye Wen)	葉問
yiqi	義氣
you fu gong xiang, you nan tong dang	有福共享、有難同當
youxia	遊俠
Youxia liezhuan	遊俠列傳
Yu Zhanyuan	于占元
Yuan Biao	元彬
yuanyang hudie pai	鴛鴦蝴蝶派
Yuen, Anita (Yuan Yongyi)	袁詠儀
Yuen, Corey (Yuan Kui)	元奎
Yuen Siu-tian (Yuan Xiaotian)	袁小田
Yuen Woo-ping (Yuan Heping)	袁和平
Yung, Barbara (Weng Meiling)	翁美玲
zawen	雜文
Zhao hua xi shi	朝花夕拾
Zhao, Vincent (Zhao Wenzhuo)	趙文卓
zhen gongfu	真功夫
zheng	正
zheng pai	正派
zhengren junzi	正人君子
zhi bi zhi ji, bai zhan bu dai	知彼知己，百戰不殆
zhi ji zhi bi, bai zhan bai sheng	知己知彼，百戰百勝
zhi zhidao cike ai ni	只知道此刻愛你
zhi'er	侄兒
Zhongguo gongfu zhizun dajiang	中國功夫至尊大獎
Zhongguo meng	中國夢
Zhongguo mengxiang	中國夢想
Zhongguoren de dianxing	中國人的典型
zhongxiao	忠孝
zhongxin	忠心
zhongyuan	中原
Zhou *daxia*	周大俠
Zhu Lingfeng	朱凌锋
Zhuang Zi	莊子
zou jianghu	走江湖
zou wei shang ji	走為上計
zuo nide pianyi dajiuzi	做你的便宜大舅子

BIBLIOGRAPHY

"56 sui Huang Rihua xueguan sai.buxiang tai pinming gouyong jiu hao." September 27, 2017. http://www.sinchew.com.my/node/1685885.

"2011 Documentary—Barbara Yung (翁美玲)." Accessed April 6, 2016. https://www.youtube.com/watch?v=RopW27MekzE.

"2020 *Fubusi Zhongguo mingren bang*" 2020 福布斯中國名人榜 [Forbes China Top 100 Celebrity List for 2020]. Accessed December 31, 2020. https://www.forbeschina.com/lists/1744.

"Adam Cheng." Accessed July 31, 2018. https://www.imdb.com/name/nm0155532/.

"Ali gaoguan huaming jun qu zi Jin Yong xiaoshuo" 阿里高管花名均取自金庸小說，馬雲叫"風清揚"，其他人叫什麼？ [Alibaba upper management all take nicknames from Jin Yong's novels, Jack Ma is called "Feng Qingyang," what are others called?]. Accessed January 20, 2020. https://new.qq.com/rain/a/20181105A14EKN.

Altenburger, Roland. *The Sword or the Needle: The Female Knight-Errant (Xia) in Traditional Chinese Narrative*. Bern; New York: Peter Lang, 2009.

Anderson, Benedict. *Imagined Communities*. 1983. Rev. ed. London: Verso, 1991.

"Andy Lau Biography." IMDb. Accessed March 28, 2022. https://www.imdb.com/name/nm0490489/bio.

"Bai Biao" 白彪. Accessed March 31, 2022. https://baike.baidu.com/item/彪/3179.

"Bao [*Da*] *Zhang Jin* ting [*Li*] *Keqin guorichen 94 sui Shi Jian xijin jianqi*" 煲[大]長今聽[李]克勤過日辰 94歲石堅洗盡奸氣 [Watching television drama (*Dae*) *Jang Geum* and listening to songs of (Li) Kejin to pass the morning, the 94-year-old Shi Jian is cleansed of his villainy]. January 20, 2007. http://hk.apple.nextmedia.com/template/apple/art_main.php?iss_id=20070120&sec_id=462&subsec_id=830&art_id=6734345.

Bao Jing 鮑晶, ed. *Lu Xun "guominxing sixiang" taolun ji* 魯迅 "國民性思想" 討論集 [Collection of discussions on Lu Xun's "national character ideas"]. Tianjin: Tianjin renmin chubanshe, 1982.

Barmé, Geremie R. "TRINKET, a Common Property." In *The Question of Reception: Martial Arts Fiction in English Translation*. Hong Kong: Lingnan College, 1997. 41–63.

Beasley-Murray, Jon. "Pierre Bourdieu." *The Johns Hopkins Guide to Literary Theory and Criticism*, 2nd ed. Eds. Michael Groden, Martin Kreiswirth, and

Imre Szeman. Baltimore: Johns Hopkins University Press, 2005. Accessed July 26, 2017. http://litguide.press.jhu.edu.proxy.library.emory.edu/cgi-bin/view.cgi?eid=37.

"Beijing Paralympic Theme Song Shows Love for Life." September 6, 2008. https://www.chinadaily.com.cn/paralympics/2008-09/06/content_7005411.htm.

Bejtlich, Richard. "The Truth about the Creation of the Kung Fu TV Series." May 20, 2019. https://web.archive.org/web/20210130134124/https://www.martialjournal.com/the-truth-about-the-creation-of-the-kung-fu-tv-series/.

Bordwell, David. *Planet Hong Kong: Popular Cinema and the Art of Entertainment*. Boston: Harvard University Press, 2000.

Bourdieu, Pierre. *Distinction: A Social Critique of the Judgement of Taste*. London: Routledge, 1984.

———. *The Fields of Cultural Production*. Cambridge: Polity Press, 1993.

———. "The Forms of Capital." Trans. Richard Nice. *Handbook of Theory and Research for the Sociology of Education*. Ed. J. E. Richardson. New York: Greenword Press, 1986. 241–258.

Bourdieu, Pierre, and Jean Claude Passeron. *The Inheritors: French Students and Their Relation to Culture*. Chicago: University of Chicago Press, 1979.

Bowman, Paul. "Return of the Dragon: Handover, Hong Kong Cinema, and Chinese Ethno-nationalism." *A Companion to Hong Kong Cinema*, eds. Esther M. K. Cheung et al. West Sussex, UK: John Wiley & Sons, 2015. 307–321.

"The Brave Archer (1977)." Accessed April 29, 2016. http://hkmdb.com/db/movies/view.mhtml?id=5811&display_set=eng.

"Brigette Lin." IBDb. Accessed March 29, 2022. https://www.imdb.com/name/nm0510857/.

"Bruce Lee: His Last Days." Accessed January 6, 2021. https://www.grindhouse-database.com/index.php/Bruce_Lee:_His_Last_Days.

"Cehua: Huangjin zhenrong dazaode diyi bu dianshi shi chaoji daju" 策劃：黃金陣容打造的第一部電視史超級大劇 [Plan: golden battle lines making up the first super-series in television history]. February 5, 2009. http://news.sina.com/v/2009-02-06/14232365418_2.shtml.

"Cehua: Wang Jiawei 'Dugu Qiubai' geming jiujian weizhen jianghu (2)" 策劃：王家衛 '獨孤求敗' 革命九劍威震江湖 (2) [Plan: Wang Jiawei's "Dugu Qiubai" revolutionary nine swords storms the martial world (2)]. March 24, 2009. http://news.sina.com/m/2009-03-25/14312437898_2.shtml.

Chan, Jackie, and Jeff Yang. *I Am Jackie Chan: My Life in Action*. New York: Ballantine Books, 1998.

Chan, Kenneth. *Remade in Hollywood: The Global Chinese Presence in Transnational Cinemas*. Hong Kong: Hong Kong University Press, 2009.

Chen Mo 陳墨. *Gudu zhi xia: Jin Yong xiaoshuo lun* 孤獨之俠：金庸小說論 [The solitary knight: a treatise on Jin Yong's novels]. 3rd ed. Shanghai: Sanlian shudian, 1999.

———. "Jin Yong banben" 金庸版本 [Jin Yong editions]. *Chen Mo ping Jin Yong xilie* 陳墨評金庸系列 [Chen Mo critiques Jin Yong series]. Vol. 13. Beijing: Haitun chubanshe, 2014.

———. *Jin Yong wenhua* 金庸文化 [Jin Yong culture]. In *Chen Mo ping Jin Yong xilie* 陳墨金庸系列 [Chen Mo critiques Jin Yong series]. Vol. 7. Beijing: Haitun chubanshe, 2014.

———. *Langman zhi lü: Jin Yong xiaoshuo shenyou* 浪漫之旅：金庸小说神游 [A romantic journey: a mental journey through Jin Yong's novels]. Shanghai: Sanlian shudian, 2000.

Chen Pingyuan 陳平原. "Qiangu wenren xiake meng—wuxia xiaoshuo leixing yanjiu" 千古文人俠客夢：武俠小說類型研究 [Knight errant dream of the literati through the ages—research on types in martial arts fiction]. In *Chen Pingyuan xiaoshuo shi lun ji* 陳平原小说史论集 [Collection of Chen Pingyuan's essays on the history of fiction]. Vol. 2. Shijiazhuang: Hebei renmin chubanshe, 1997. 919–1165.

———. "Literature High and Low: 'Popular Fiction' in Twentieth-century China." In *The Literary Field of Twentieth Century China*. Trans. and ed. Michel Hockx. Honolulu: University of Hawaii Press, 1999. 113–133.

———. "Transcending 'High' and 'Low' Distinctions in Literature: The Success of Jin Yong and the Future of Martial Arts Novels." Trans. Jianmei Liu and Ann Huss. Eds. Ann Huss and Jianmei Liu, *The Jin Yong Phenomenon: Chinese Martial Arts Fiction and Modern Chinese Literary History*. Youngstown, NY: Cambria Press. 55–72.

"Chen Shaoxia" 陈少霞. Accessed March 19, 2016. http://baike.baidu.com/view/386338.htm.

Cheng Long 成龍 and Zhu Mo 朱墨. *Cheng Long: hai mei zhangda jiu laole* 成龍：還沒長大就老了 [Jackie Chan: Still haven't grown up and already old]. Hong Kong: Fenghuang chuban, 2015.

Chengshi Langzi 城市浪子. "Qinggong zhende cunzai ma? Gudairen hui, xiandairen que buhui? Kanwan zhongyu mingbaile!" 輕功真的存在嗎？古代人會，現代人卻不會？看完終於明白了！ (Does light-body kungfu really exist? The ancients could do it, why can't modern people? After finishing reading, I finally understand!). January 20, 2021. https://www.163.com/dy/article/G0PMFO4M0543NQXQ.html.

Cho, Allan. *The Hong Kong Wuxia Movie: Identity and Politics, 1966–1976*. Saarbrücken, Germany: Lambart Academic Publishing, 2010.

Chow, Vivienne. "After 20 Years, Stars Wed in Royal Style." *South China Morning Post*, July 22, 2008. Accessed January 6, 2021. https://www.scmp.com/article/646096/after-20-years-stars-wed-royal-style.

"Complete List of SHAW BROTHERS Martial Arts Movies." Accessed May 26, 2016. http://rateyourmusic.com/list/gigiriva/complete_list_of_shaw_brothers_martial_arts_movies/.

Dai, Jinhua. "Order/Anti-Order: Representation of Identity in Hong Kong Action Movies." In *Hong Kong Connections: Transnational Imagination in Action Cinema*. Eds. Meaghan Morris et al. Hong Kong: Hong Kong University Press, 2005. 81–94.

Dannen, Fredric, and Barry Long. *Hong Kong Babylon: An Insider's Guide to the Hollywood of the East*. New York: Miramax Books, 1997.

Denton, Kirk A., ed. *Modern Chinese Literary Thought: Writings on Literature, 1893–1945*. Stanford: Stanford University Press, 1996.

Desser, David. "The Kung Fu Craze: Hong Kong Cinema's First American Reception." In *The Cinema of Hong Kong: History, Arts, Identity*. Eds. Poshek Fu and David Desser. Cambridge: Cambridge University Press, 2000. 19–43.

Dissanayake, Wimal. *Wong Kar-Wai's Ashes of Time*. Hong Kong: Hong Kong University Press, 2003.

"Dong Xie Xi Du taici (quanben)" 《東邪西毒》台詞 （全本）[Ashes of Time script (complete)]. Accessed June 20, 2016. http://www.douban.com/group/topic/1316973/.

Douban dianying 豆瓣電影 [Douban movies]. "Shediao yingxiong zhuan zhi xiang long shiba zhang" 射雕英雄傳之降龍十八掌 (2021) [The eagle-shooting heroes eighteen palms subduing the dragon]. Accessed March 26, 2022. https://movie.douban.com/subject/35043784/.

"Dugu Qiubai." Accessed May 27, 2009. http://baike.baidu.com/view/893659.htm.

"Duo nian enyuan jiuchan bu qing dangnian 'wuhujiang' jinchao 'si que yi,'" 多年恩怨糾纏不清 当年"五虎將"今朝"四缺一" [Many years of grievances and irresolvable entanglements; the "five tiger generals" of those years are the "Four missing one" of today]. May 31, 2007. http://ent.news.cn/2007-05/31/content_6177413.htm.

Ebert, Roger. "Crouching Tiger Hidden Dragon," *Chicago Sun Times*, December 20, 2000. https://www.rogerebert.com/reviews/crouching-tiger-hidden-dragon-2000.

Elegant, Simon. "The Storyteller: What Makes Louis Cha's Martial Arts Novels so Wildly Popular in Asia?" *Far East Economic Review* (September 5, 1996): 38–44.

Feng Jicai 馮驥才. *Shouxia liuqing: xiandai dushi wenhua de youhuan* 手下留情：現代都市文化的憂患 [Show leniency: The suffering of modern city culture]. Shanghai: Xuelin chubanshe, 2000.

Foster, Paul B. *Ah Q Archaeology: Lu Xun, Ah Q, Ah Q Progeny and the National Character Discourse in Twentieth Century China*. Lanham, MD: Lexington Books, 2006.

———. "The Geopolitics of Kung Fu Film." *Foreign Policy in Focus*, February 8, 2007. http://www.fpif.org/fpiftxt/3980.

———. "Jin Yong and the Kungfu Industrial Complex." *Chinese Literature Today* 今日中國文學, Vol. 8, No. 2. (2019): 68–76.

———. "Jin Yong's Linghu Chong Faces Off against Lu Xun's Ah Q: Complements to the Construction of National Character." *Twentieth-Century China*, Vol. 30, No. 1 (November 2004): 82-117.

Giles, Lionel. Trans. "Xu shi pian" 虛實篇 [Weak points and strong], *Sunzi bingfa* 孫子兵法 [*Sunzi Art of War*]. Chinese Text Project. Accessed January 4, 2021. https://ctext.org/art-of-war/weak-points-and-strong.

"Gossip Most: Wanted Men." Accessed May 26, 2008. http://www.cityweekend.com.cn/en/beijing/features/2002_11/Gossip_MostWantedMen.

Gu Long 古龍. *Chu Liuxiang chuanqi* 楚留香傳奇 (The tales of Chu Liuxiang). *Gu Long zuopin ji* 古龍作品集 (The collected works of Gu Long). Vol. 48. Zhuhaishi: Zhuhai chubanshe, 1995.

———. *Xiao Li fei dao* 小李飛刀 (Young Li's flying dagger). Vol. 34 of *Feng ling zhong de dao sheng* 風鈴中的刀聲 (Sound of a sword in the wind). *Gu Long zuopin ji* 古龍作品集 (The collected works of Gu Long). Zhuhaishi: Zhuhai chubanshe, 1995.

"Gu Long xiaoshuo gaibian dianying shoucang da quanji" 古龍小說改編電影收藏大全集 [Complete collected adaptations of Gu Long's films]. Accessed January 6, 2021. https://www.douban.com/doulist/111533282/.

"Guan Dexing 關德興." Accessed January 6, 2021. https://baike.sogou.com/v5744920.htm.

Hamm, John Christopher. *Paper Swordsmen: Jin Yong and the Modern Chinese Martial Arts Novel*. Honolulu: University of Hawai'i Press, 2005.

———. *The Unworthy Scholar from Pingjiang: Republican Era Martial Arts Fiction*. New York: Columbia University Press, 2019.

Haynes, Linn. "Wong Fei Hung." In Jeff Yang, *Once Upon a Time in China: A Guide to Hong Kong, Taiwan, and Mainland Chinese Cinema*. New York: Atria Books, 2003. 40–41.

He Ye 何葉. "Xiang Xingye yiyang xue shengong gongfu Jiu zhi shengai wanfa puguang" 像星爺一樣學神功功夫九指神丐玩法曝光 [Just like Zhou Xingchi learning mystical kungfu the Nine Fingered Mystical Beggar's method of playing is exposed." March 16, 2012. http://news.07073.com/zixun/577098.html.

"Heilongjiang wenhua yinxiang chubanshe" 黑龍江文化音像出版社 [Heilongjiang culture film publishing]. Accessed April 29, 2016. http://baike.baidu.com/view/4772362.htm.

"Huang Feihong dianshiju" 黃飛鴻電視劇 [Huang Feihong television series]. Accessed January 6, 2021. https://search.douban.com/movie/subject_search?search_text=黃飛鴻电视剧&cat=1002.

"Huang Fehong xilie yingshi" 黃飛鴻系列影視 [Huang Feihong film and television series]. Accessed March 30, 2022. https://hongkong.fandom.com/zh-hk/wiki/黃飛鴻系列影視.

"Huang Feihong zhi er nan er dang ziqiang" 黃飛鴻之二男兒當自強 [Once upon a time in China 2; a.k.a. Huang Feihong part 2, real men do self-strengthening]. Accessed March 31, 2022. https://hkmdb.com/db/movies/view.mhtml?id=7576&display_set=big5.

"Huang Feihong zhuan (shangji)" 黃飛鴻傳（上集）[Huang Feihong biography (part 1)]. Accessed April 16, 2016. http://baike.baidu.com/item/黄飞鸿传（上集）?fr=aladdin.

"Huang Rihua 黃日華." Accessed January 6, 2021. https://baike.baidu.com/item/黃日華#3_2.

Hunt, Leon. "Too Late the Hero? The Delayed Stardom of Donnie Yen." In *East Asian Film Stars*. Eds. Leung Wing-Fai and Andy Willis. New York: Palgrave Macmillan, 2014. 143–155.

"Huo Yuanjia" 霍元甲. Accessed January 6, 2021. https://www.douban.com/search?source=suggest&q=霍元甲.

Huss, Ann, and Jianmei Liu, eds. *The Jin Yong Phenomenon: Chinese Martial Arts Fiction and Modern Chinese Literary History*. Youngstown, NY: Cambria Press, 2007.

"Idy Chan 陳玉蓮." accessed January 6, 2021. https://www.douban.com/search?q=陳玉蓮.

"Jay Chou—An insight from enoVate China." Accessed December 30, 2020. https://www.mgientertainment.com/2010/01/jay-chou/.

"'Jianren Jian' Shi Jian cishi, zeng hezuo Zhou Runfa Cheng Long Li Xiaolong" "奸人堅"石堅辭世 曾合作周潤發成龍李小龍 ["Villain Jian" passes away, had cooperated with Zhou Runfa, Jackie Chan and Bruce Lee). June 4, 2009. http://news.sina.com/sinacn/502-104-103-107/2009-06-04/1915763140.html.

Jin Yong. "Against the Authors of 'Foreign Books in Chinese Language': An Interview with China's Most Popular Writer of Adventure Novels." *Modern Chinese Writers Self Portrayals*. Trans. Marty Backstrom. Ed. Helmut Martin. Armonk, NY: M.E. Sharpe, 1992. 172–78.

Jin Yong 金庸. "Houji" 後記 [Afterword]. *Lu ding ji* 鹿鼎記 [The duke of the Mount Deer]. Vol. 36 of *Jin Yong zuopin ji* 金庸作品集 [The collected works of Jin Yong]. 2nd ed. Taibei: Yuanliu chuban gongsi, 1992. 2119–21. Originally written 22 January 1981.

———. "Houji" 後記 [Afterword]. *Shen diao xia lü* 神鵰俠侶 [The giant eagle and its companion]. Vol. 12 of *Jin Yong zuopin ji* 金庸作品集 [The collected works of Jin Yong]. 2nd ed. Taibei: Yuanliu chubanshe, 1993.

———. "Houji" 後記 [Afterword]. *Xiao ao jianghu* 笑傲江湖 [The smiling, proud wanderer]. Vol. 31 of *Jin Yong zuopin ji* 金庸作品集 [The collected works of Jin Yong]. 2nd ed. Taibei: Yuanliu chubanshe, 1992. 1681–1684.

———. *Jin Yong zuopin ji* 金庸作品集 [The collected works of Jin Yong]. 2nd ed. 36 vols. Taibei: Yuanliu chuban gongsi, 1986–1987.

———. *Lu ding ji* 鹿鼎記 [The duke of the Mount Deer]. 5 vols. 2nd ed. *Jin Yong zuopin ji* 金庸作品集 [The collected works of Jin Yong]. Vols. 32–36. Taibei: Yuanliu chuban gongsi, 1986.

———. *She diao yingxiong zhuan* 射鵰英雄傳 [*The Eagle-shooting Heroes*]. 4 vols. 3rd printing. Vols. 5–8. Taibei: Yuanliu, 1998.

———. *Shendiao xialü* 神鵰俠侶 [*The Giant Eagle and Its Companion*]. 4 vols. 2nd ed. *Jin Yong zuopin ji* 金庸作品集 [The collected works of Jin Yong]. Vols. 9–12. Taibei: Yuanliu, 1992.

——— & Ikeda Daisaku 池田大作 (Chitian Dazuo). *Tanqiu yige canlan de shiji* 探求一個燦爛的世紀 [Seeking a splendid century]. Hong Kong: Minghe she, 1998.

———. *Tian long ba bu* 天龍八部 [The Semi-Gods and Semi-Devils; or The Demi-Gods and Semi-Devils]. 5 vols. *Jin Yong zuopin ji* 金庸作品集 [The collected works of Jin Yong]. 2nd ed. Vols. 21–25. Taibei: Yuanliu chuban gongsi, 1987.

———. "Wei Xiaobao zhege xiao jiahuo!" 韋小寶這個小傢伙 [This little punk Wei Xiaobao!]. In Liu Tiansi 劉天賜, *Wei Xiaobao shengong* 韋小寶神功 [Wei Xiaobao's mystical power]. *Jin xue yanjiu congshu* 金學研究叢書 [A collection of Jinology research]. Vol. 12. Taibei: Yuanjing chubanshe, 1985. 153–175. Originally published in *Mingbao yuekan* (October 1981).

———. *Xiao ao jianghu* 笑傲江湖 [*The Smiling, Proud Wanderer*]. 4 vols. *Jin Yong zuopin ji* 金庸作品集 [The collected works of Jin Yong]. 2nd ed. Vols. 28–31. Taibei: Yuanliu chuban gongsi, 1992.

———. "Xiaoshuo chuangzuo de jidian sikao—Jin Yong zai bimu shi shang de jianghua" 小說創作的幾點思考—金庸在閉幕式上的講話 [A few points to contemplate on the creation of fiction—Jin Yong's remarks at the closing ceremony]. In *Jin Yong xiaoshuo yu ershi shiji Zhongguo wenxue: guoji xueshu yantaohui lunwen ji* 金庸小說與二十世紀中國文學：國際學術研討會論文集 [Jin Yong's fiction and twentieth-century Chinese literature: collection of essays from an international academic conference]. Ed. Liu Zaifu et al. Hong Kong: Minghe she, 2000. 23–28.

———. *Yi tian tu long ji* 倚天屠龍記 [*The Heaven Sword and Dragon Sabre*]. 4 vols. *Jin Yong zuopin ji* 金庸作品集 [The collected works of Jin Yong]. 2nd ed. Vols. 16–19. Taibei: Yuanliu chuban gongsi, 1992.

"Jin Yong baiwan gangyuan maichu *Shen diao xia lü* katong banquan" 金庸百萬港元賣出《神鵰俠侶》卡通版權 [Jin Yong sells the animation copyright for *The Giant Eagle and Its Companion* for one million HKD]. July 4, 2003. http://yule.sohu.com/23/62/article210726223.shtml.

"Jin Yong ruxuan Lu Xun chu: Beijing yuwen keben gaige zheng yi ru chao 金庸入選魯迅出：北京語文課本改革爭議如潮 [In with Jin Yong and out with Lu Xun: the tide of discussion of Beijing language textbook reform]. August 18, 2007. http://www.chinareviewnews.com/doc/1004/3/2/1/100432100.html?coluid=0&kindid=0&docid=100432100.

"Jin Yong Zuopin ji (Sanlian ban) xu" 金庸作品集（三联版）序 [Preface to the Joint Publishing edition of *The Collected Works of Jin Yong*]. Accessed June 3, 2016. http://cnnovels.com/wx/jingyong/014.htm.

"Jin Yong's Heroes now in English." February 13, 2018. https://www.straitstimes.com/lifestyle/arts/jin-yongs-heroes-now-in-english.

"Jiu yi Shen diao xia lü" 九一神鵰俠侶 [1991 Savior of the Soul]. Accessed March 28, 2022. https://baike.baidu.com/item/九一神雕俠侶/10721519.

"*Jiu yi Shen diao xia lü*" 九一神鵰俠侶 [1991 Savior of the Soul]. Minute 40:00. Accessed July 1, 2010. http://www.tudou.com/programs/view/ODxP4QMbdCE/.

Jin yu liangyuan Hong lou meng 金玉良缘红楼梦 [Gold Jade good karma dream of the red chamber]. Shaw Brothers Studios, 1977.

"Kong Qingdong jiaoshou zuoke da yuwang tan wuxia wenzi fangtan shilu" 孔慶東教授做客大渝網談武俠文字訪談實錄 [The accurate record of Professor Kong Qingdong's visit to cq.qq.com discussing martial arts fiction language]. August 28, 2007. http://cq.qq.com/a/20070828/000510.htm.

Kowallis, Jon. *The Lyrical Lu Xun*. Honolulu: University of Hawai'i Press, 1996.

"Kung Fu Hustle." Accessed January 6, 2021. https://www.boxofficemojo.com/title/tt0373074/?ref_=bo_se_r_1.

Lee, Bruce. "Bruce Lee: The Lost Interview (filmed in 1971 --> first aired 1994)." *The Pierre Burton Show*, total 24 minutes, 36 seconds. Accessed May 24, 2016. https://archive.org/details/BruceLeeTheLostInterview.

———. *Tao of Jeet Kune Do*. Burbank, CA: Ohara Publications, 1975.

Lee, Haiyan. "Mo Yan, Inaugural Newman Laureate, Honored in Oklahoma." *The China Beat*, March 10, 2009. http://thechinabeat.blogspot.com/2009/03/mo-yan-inaugural-newman-laureate.html.

Lee, Leo Ou-fan. *Voices from the Iron House: A Study of Lu Xun*. Bloomington: Indiana University Press, 1987.

Lee, Linda. *Bruce Lee: The Man Only I Knew*. New York: Warner Books, 1976.

———. "Introduction." In *Tao of Jeet Kune Do*. Burbank, CA: Ohara Publications, 1975. 4.

"Legend of the Fist: The Return of Chen Zhen (2010)." Box Office Mojo by IMDb. Accessed March 29, 2022. https://www.boxofficemojo.com/title/tt1456661/?ref_=bo_se_r_1.

Leng Xia 冷夏. *Jin Yong zhuan* 金庸傳 [Biography of Jin Yong]. Taibei: Yuanjing chuban shiye gongsi, 1995.

Li Baojia 李寶嘉. *Guanchang xianxing ji* 官場現形記 [Record of the current state of officialdom]. Accessed May 25, 2016. http://chengyu.game2.tw/archives/25427#.V0Y4_-RH7fc.

Li Li 李莉. "*She diao yingxiong zhuan* ruxuan Beijing Zhaoyang qu xiaoxue tushuguan jiben shumu" 《射雕英雄傳》入選北京朝陽區小學圖書館基本書目 [*The Eagle-Shooting Heroes* selected for the basic library reading list at Beijing Zhaoyang district elementary school]. April 2, 2013. http://news.ifeng.com/society/2/detail_2013_04/02/23800442_0.shtml.

Li, Siu Leung. "The Myth Continues: Cinematic Kung Fu in Modernity." In *Hong Kong Connections: Transnational Imagination in Action Cinema*. Eds. Meaghan Morris et al. Hong Kong: Hong Kong University Press, 2005. 49–61.

Li Tuo. "The Language of Jin Yong's Writing: A New Direction in the Development of Modern Chinese." Trans. John Christopher Hamm. Eds. Ann Huss and Jianmei Liu, *The Jin Yong Phenomenon: Chinese Martial Arts Fiction and Modern Chinese Literary History*. Youngstown, NY: Cambria Press. 39–53.

"Li Xiaolong he Jin Yong de guanxi, yange lai shuo, Li Xiaolong shi Jin Yong de tudi" 李小龍和金庸的關係，嚴格來說，李小龍是金庸的徒弟 [The relationship between Bruce Lee and Jin Yong, strictly speaking, Li Xiaolong is Jin Yong's disciple]. *Kuai Zi Xun* 快資訊. December 12, 2019. https://www.360kuai.com/pc/9cdf52c893d600cce?cota=3&kuai_so=1&sign=360_7bc3b157.

"Liang Chaowei yinyue zhuanji 梁朝偉音樂專輯 [Tony Leung Chiu-wai albums]." Accessed January 6, 2021. https://baike.baidu.com/item/梁朝偉#3_3.

"Liang Chaowei, Zhou Xingchi, dou lai paolongtao de 82 ban *Tian long ba bu*" 梁朝偉、周星馳都來跑龍套的82版《天龍八部》，這才是童年的江湖 [Tony Liang (Leung) and Stephen Chow both play bit roles in the 1982 version of *The Semi-Gods and Semi-Devils*]. Lu ju ba [Mainland theater] 陸劇吧. July 8, 2021. https://lujuba.cc/zh-hans/580802.html.

"Liang Jiaren 梁家仁." Accessed January 6, 2021. https://search.douban.com/movie/subject_search?search_text=梁家仁電視劇&cat=1002.

Liang Qichao 梁啟超. "Lun xiaoshuo yu qunzhi zhi guanxi" 論小說與群治之關係 [On the relationship between fiction and the government of the people]. *Xin xiaoshuo* 新小說 (1902). In trans. Gek Nai Cheng. *Modern Chinese Literary Thought: Writings on Literature, 1893–1945*. Ed. Kirk A. Denton. Stanford: Stanford University Press, 1996. 74–81.

"Liangshan wu hu jiang 梁山五虎將 [Five tiger generals of Liangshan]." Accessed January 6, 2021. https://baike.baidu.com/item/梁山五虎將/2786362?fromtitle=馬軍五虎將&fromid=638088.

Lin Qingxia. "Chong kan *Dong Xie Xi Du*" 重看東邪西毒 [Another look at *Ashes of Time*]. September 26, 2008. http://lz.book.sohu.com/chapter-1226509.html.

———. "Da daoyan shouzhong de mangguo" 大導演手中的芒果 [Mango in a great director's hands]. August 1, 2006. http://reading.caixin.com/111078/111111.html.

———. "*Dongfang Bubai* ganku tan (1) 《東方不敗》 甘苦談（1）[Talking of good times and hardships in *Swordsman II*]. July 3, 2008. http://lz.book.sohu.com/chapter-1226510.html.
"Lin Qingxia mingan: Jin Yong fandui ta yan Dongfang Bubai" 林青霞敏感：金庸反對她演東方不敗" [Lin Qingxia is sensitive, Jin Yong objected to her playing Asia the Invincible]. July 21, 2008. http://www.yn.xinhuanet.com/ent/2008-07/21/content_13882940.htm.
Lincoln, Kevin. "From John Woo to John Wick, Here's Your Guide to Gun Fu." Vulture. Oct. 12, 2016. https://www.vulture.com/2016/10/john-wick-gun-fu.html.
Link, Perry. *Mandarin Ducks and Butterflies: Popular Fiction in Early Twentieth-Century Chinese Cities*. Berkeley: University of California Press, 1981.
"Liu bu Li Xiaolong dianying Xianggang piaofang paihang: sanbu dapo jilu, *Jing wu men* pai di'er" 六部李小龙电影香港票房排行：三部打破纪录，《精武門》排第二 [Six of Bruce Lee's movies on the Hong Kong box office charts: Three break records, *Fist of fury* is ranked number two]. Accessed March 29, 2022. https://new.qq.com/omn/20211003/20211003A05MAA00.html.
"Liu Dehua" 劉德華. Accessed March 17, 2009. http://baike.baidu.com/view/1758.htm.
"Liu Dehua" 劉德華. Accessed May 31, 2016. http://baike.baidu.com/subview/1758/18233157.htm.
"Liu Dehua" 劉德華. Accessed January 6, 2021. https://baike.baidu.com/item/刘德华/114923.
"Liu Dehua ziji zuoci, zuoqu de geming shi shenme? You naxie? Qing fenlei!" 劉德華自己作詞，作曲的歌名是甚麼？有哪些？請分類！[What are the names of songs for which Andy Lau has written lyrics and music? Which ones? Please classify!"]. May 5, 2009. http://zhidao.baidu.com/question/95922231.html.
"Liu Jiahui" 劉家輝. Accessed March 30, 2022. https://baike.baidu.com/item/刘家辉/5482824.
Liu, James J. Y. *The Chinese Knight-Errant*. London: Routledge and Kegan Paul, 1967.
Liu, Petrus. *Stateless Subjects: Chinese Martial Arts Literature & Postcolonial History*. Ithaca: Cornell University Press, 2011.
Liu Zaifu 劉再復. "Huiyi daoyan: Jin Yong xiaoshuo zai ershi shiji Zhongguo wenxue shi de diwei" 會議導言：金庸小說在二十世紀中國文學史的地位 [Conference keynote speech: The status of Jin Yong's novels in twentieth century Chinese literary history]. In *Jin Yong xiaoshuo yu ershi shiji Zhongguo wenxue: guoji xueshu yantaohui lunwen ji* 金庸小說與二十世紀中國文學：國際學術研討會論文集 [Jin Yong's fiction and twentieth century Chinese literature: collection of essays from an international academic conference]. Ed. Liu Zaifu 劉再復, et al. Hong Kong: Minghe she, 2000. 13–22.
Liu Zaifu 劉再復, Howard Goldblatt & Zhang Dongming, eds. *Jin Yong xiaoshuo yu ershi shiji Zhongguo wenxue: guoji xueshu yantaohui lunwen ji* 金庸小說與二十世紀中國文學：國際學術研討會論文集 [Jin Yong's fiction and twentieth-century Chinese literature: collection of essays from an international academic conference]. Hong Kong: Minghe she, 2000.
Logan, Bey. *Hong Kong Action Cinema*. Woodstock, NY: Overlook Press, 1996.
Lovell Julia. *The Politics of Cultural Capital: China's Quest for a Nobel Prize in Literature*. Honolulu: University of Hawaii Press, 2006.

"Lu ding ji (1983 nian Hua Shan zhidao Xianggang Shaoshi dianying) 鹿鼎記（1983年華山執導香港邵氏電影）[The deer and the cauldron (1983 Hua Shan directed Shaw Brothers movie)]. Accessed January 6, 2021. https://baike.baidu.com/item/鹿鼎記/9411195.

"*Lu ding ji*: zhizuo teji" 鹿鼎記：製作特輯 [The Making of *The Duke of Mount Deer*]. In *Lu ding ji* [*The Duke of Mount Deer*]. 40 episodes, 24 discs. Hong Kong. Dianshi guangbo youxian gongsi 電視廣播有限公司 (TVBI). 1984, 2001.

Lu Li 陸離. "Jin Yong fangwen ji" 金庸訪問記 [Record of calling on Jin Yong]. In Weng Lingwen 翁靈文, et al., *Zhuzi baijia kan Jin Yong (3)* 諸子百家看金庸 (3) [Philosophers and writers of all schools read Jin Yong (3)]. *Jin xue yanjiu congshu* 金學研究叢書 [A collection of Jin-ology research]. Vol. 16. Taibei: Yuanjing chubanshe, 1985. 33–54.

Lu, Sheldon H. *China, Transnational Visuality, Global Postmodernity* Stanford: Stanford University Press, 2001.

Lu Xun 魯迅. "A Q zhengzhuan" 阿 Q 正傳 [The true story of Ah Q]. *Lu Xun quanji* 魯迅全集 [The complete works of Lu Xun]. Vol. 1. Taipei: Gufeng 谷風, 1989. 485–529.

———. "A Q zhengzhuan" 阿 Q 正傳 ["The true story of Ah Q"]. Trans. Yang Xianyi and Gladys Yang. *Lu Xun: Selected Works*. Vol. 1. 2nd ed. Beijing: Foreign Languages Press, 1980. 102–154.

———. "Da *Xi zhoukan* bianzhe yan" (Reply to the editor of *Theater Weekly*). In *Lu Xun: Selected Works*. Trans. Yang Xianyi and Gladys Yang. Vol. 4. 2nd ed. Beijing: Foreign Languages Press. 139–144.

Lun Xun yanjiu xueshu lunzhu ziliao huibian (1913–1980) 鲁迅研究学术论著资料汇编 (1913–1980) [A corpus of data of academic theses and works on Lu Xun (1913–1983)]. 1985. Gen. ed. Zhang Mengyang. 5 vols. Beijing: Zhongguo wenlian.

Luo Guanzhong 儸貫中. *Sanguo yanyi* 三國演義 [Romance of the three kingdoms]. 1970. 2 vols. Hong Kong: Zhonghua shuju, 1987.

Lyell, William A., trans. *Lu Xun: Diary of a Madman and Other Stories*. Honolulu: University of Hawaii Press, 1990.

Mao Dun 茅盾. "Da Guotang xiansheng" 答國堂先生 [Reply to Mr. Guotang]. *Xiaoshuo yuebao*, Vol. 13, No. 2 (February 10, 1922): 5.

Meyers, Richard. *Great Martial Arts Movies from Bruce Lee to Jackie Chan and More*. 1985. New York: Citadel Press, 2001.

"Mi Xue 米雪 (Michelle Yim)." Accessed January 6, 2021. https://search.douban.com/movie/subject_search?search_text=米雪&cat=1002&start=45.

Minford, John. "Kungfu in Translation, Translation as Kungfu." In *The Question of Reception: Martial Arts Fiction in English Translation*. Hong Kong: Lingnan College, 1997. 1–40.

———. "Translator's Introduction." *The Deer and the Cauldron: The First Book, A Martial Arts Novel by Louis Cha*. Ed. John Minford. New York: Oxford University Press, 1997.

Monjeh, "The Return of the Condor Heroes." *Yumcha*, February 6, 2006. http://www.yesasia.com/us/yumcha/the-return-of-the-condor-heroes/0-0-0-arid.59-en/featured-article.html.

"Movie *Kungfu Protects the Way* a film popularizes Taiji with Jet Li, Donnie Yen, Wu Jing" 电影《功守道》推广太极 一片集结李连杰甄子丹吴京 Dianying *Gong shou dao* tuiguang Taiji yipian jijie Li Lianjie Zhen Zidan Wu Jing, Renmin wang 人民网. October 31, 2017. http://tj.people.com.cn/n2/2017/1031/c375366 -30872104.html.

"Ni gei wo yi pian tian" 你給我一片天 [You give me a new world]. Accessed June 9, 2016. http://baike.baidu.com/view/9096551.htm.

Pilato, Herbie J. *The Kung Fu Book of Caine: The Complete Guide to TV's First Mystical Eastern Western*. Boston: Charles E. Tuttle, 1993.

Polly, Matthew. *Bruce Lee: a life*. New York: Simon & Schuster, 2018.

Rahner, Mark. "'Wire-fu' Flicks: Pouncing Public, Hidden Treasures." *The Seattle Times*, December 24, 2004. https://web.archive.org/web/20150102125529 /http://seattletimes.com/html/movies/2002129305_martialarts24.html.

Rainer, Peter. "Jackie Chan stars in 'The Karate Kid' (except it should be called 'The Kung Fu Kid')." June 11, 2010. http://www.csmonitor.com/The-Culture /Movies/2010/0611/Jackie-Chan-stars-in-The-Karate-Kid-except-it-should -be-called-The-Kung-Fu-Kid.

Rawnsley, Ming-Yeh T. "Stars as Production and Consumption: A Case Study of Brigitte Lin." In *East Asian Film Stars*. Eds. Leung Wing-Fai and Andy Willis. New York: Palgrave Macmillan, 2014. 190–204.

"Ren Xianqi" 任賢齊 (Richie Ren). Accessed March 28, 2022, https://baike.baidu. com/item/任贤齐/145904.

Ren Xianqi 任賢齊. Weibo, December 29, 2020. https://weibo.com/1288803057 /JAJpQ46Ke?filter=hot&root_comment_id=0&ssl_rnd=1609435931.0128&type =comment#_rnd1609435935657.

Richie Ren Xian-Qi 任賢齊." Xianggang yingku 香港影庫 [Hong Kong Movie Database]. Accessed March 28, 2022. https://hkmdb.com/db/people/view. mhtml?id=12636&display_set=big5.

"Rulai shenzhang" 如來神掌 [The Buddha's mystical palm]. Accessed March 30, 2022. https://baike.baidu.com/item/如来神掌/19730380.

"San Guo wu hu jiang" 三國五虎將 [Three kingdoms five tiger generals." Accessed January 6, 2021. https://baike.baidu.com/item/五虎上將/22566?fromtitle=三 國五虎將&fromid=3620090.

"*Savior of the Soul*." Accessed May 30, 2016. http://www.imdb.com/title /tt0104322/.

"*Savior of the Soul II*." Accessed July 10, 2009. http://www.imdb.com/title /tt0104560/.

Szeto, Kin-Yan. "Jackie Chan's Cosmopolitical Consciousness and Comic Displacement." *Modern Chinese Literature and Culture*, Vol. 20, No. 2 (Fall 2009): 229–261.

"Shaolin monk runs atop water for 125 meters, sets new record." August 29, 2015. Posted September 2, 2015. https://www.youtube.com/watch?v=YrncG8NvZJI.

"Shao shi dianying gongsi" 邵氏電影公司 [Shaw Brothers film company]. Accessed May 26, 2016. http://baike.baidu.com/view/124639.htm#4.

"Shaoshi dianying gongsi: zuopin" 邵氏電影公司 [Shaw Brothers film company: works]. Accessed March 18, 2016. <http://baike.baidu.com/view/124639. htm?fromtitle=邵氏兄弟（香港）有限公司&fromid=859804&type=syn#4.

"Shaw Brothers History." Accessed February 20, 2016. http://www.hkcinema .co.uk/Articles/shawbronews.html.

"Shaw Brothers Martial Arts Films." Accessed May 26, 2016. http://www.silver-emulsion.com/review-series/ongoing-review-series/shaw-brothers-martial-arts-films/.

"Shaw Studios." Accessed May 26, 2016. http://www.shawstudios.hk/who_we_are.htm.

"*She diao yingxiong zhuan*" 射雕英雄傳 [*The Eagle-Shooting Heroes*]. Accessed April 28, 2016. http://www.ijq.tv/yingshi/14615726502298.html.

"*She diao yingxiong zhuan* (1958)" 射雕英雄傳 (1958) [Story of the vulture conqueror (1958)]. Accessed January 6, 2021. https://movie.douban.com/subject/3369388/.

"*She diao yingxiong zhuan* ruxuan Beijing Zhaoyang qu xiaoxue jiben shumu, Huaren online" 射雕英雄传入选北京朝阳区小学基本书目 _华人online [*The Eagle-Shooting Heroes* is selected for Beijing Zhaoyang elementary school basic reading list, Huaren online]. Accessed May 11, 2016. https://www.youtube.com/watch?v=yIEN87BHE94.

"*She diao yingxiong zhuan zhi dong cheng xijiu*: muhou huaxu" 射雕英雄傳之東成西就：幕后花絮 [Interesting facts behind the scenes of *The Eagle Shooting Heroes eastern and western accomplishments*]. Accessed May 31, 2016. http://baike.baidu.com/subview/15834/7184865.htm?fromtitle=射雕英雄传之东成西就&fromid=2899193&type=syn#5.

"*She diao yingxiong zhuan zhi Jiu yin zhenjing*" 射雕英雄傳之九陰真經 [*The Eagle-Shooting Heroes* nine yin true classic]. Accessed April 29, 2016. http://baike.baidu.com/view/3943843.htm.

"*She diao yingxiong zhuan* zhizuo teji fanyi gao—zhuan tie zi zhongyang qingbao 5-1" 「射鵰英雄傳」製作特輯翻譯稿—轉貼自中央情報局 5-1 [The production of a special translation draft of *The Eagle-Shooting Heroes*—forward post from the CIA 5-1]. Accessed March 30, 2016. http://www.barbarayung.net/club/post006.htm.

"*She diao yingxiong zhuan* zhizuo teji fanyi gao—zhuan tie zi zhongyang qingbao 5-3" 「射鵰英雄傳」製作特輯翻譯稿—轉貼自中央情報局 5-3 [The production of a special translation draft of *The Eagle-Shooting Heroes*—forward post from the CIA 5-3]. Accessed April 11, 2016. http://www.barbarayung.net/club/post006b.htm.

"*She diao yingxiong zhuan zhi dong cheng xi jiu* 1993" 射雕英雄傳之東成西就 (1993) [The eagle-shooting heroes: eastern and western accomplishments (1993)]. Accessed January 6, 2021. https://movie.douban.com/subject/1316510/.

Shen diao xia lü 神鵰俠侶 [The giant eagle and its companion]. Accessed March 30, 2022, https://baike.baidu.com/item/神雕俠侶/7906915.

Shendiao xialü: sishiqi ji 神鵰俠侶：四十七集 [The giant eagle and its companion: forty-seven-episode television series). Prod. dir. Jiang Xiaorong 蔣曉榮. Starring Ren Xianqi 任賢齊. 47 vcds. Joint prod. Yang Peipei Workshop 楊佩佩工作室，Beijing guangbo xueyuan dianshi zhiquo zhongxin 北京廣播學院電視製作中心，Beijing Hailong dianshi yishu youxian gongsi 北京海龍電視藝術有限公司. Guangzhou junqu: Haichao yinxiang chubanshe (South Wave), 1999.

"Shi Jian" 石堅. Accessed March 29, 2022. https://www.maochangfood.com/mingxing/shijian/dianshiju.html.

"Shi Jian" 石堅 (Sek Kin), Xianggang yingku 香港影庫 HKMDB, accessed March 29, 2021, https://hkmdb.com/db/people/view.mhtml?id=1167&complete_credits=1&display_set=big5.

Shi Nai'an 施耐庵. *Shuihu zhuan* 水滸傳 [Water margin]. 2 vols. Taibei: Lianjing chuban shiye gongsi, 1987.

Shih, Shu-mei. *The Lure of the Modern: Writing Modernism in Semicolonial China, 1917–1937*. Berkeley: University of California Press, 2001.

Stokes, Lisa Odham. *Historical Dictionary of Hong Kong Cinema*. Lanham, MD: Scarecrow Press, 2007.

"Story of the Vulture Conqueror (1958)." Accessed April 29, 2016. http://hkmdb.com/db/movies/view.mhtml?id=2741&display_set=eng.

"Story of the Vulture-Conqueror (Part 2) (1959)." Accessed April 29, 2016. http://hkmdb.com/db/movies/view.mhtml?id=2894&display_set=eng.

Szeto, Kin-Yan. *The Martial Arts Cinema of the Chinese Diaspora: Ang Lee, John Woo, and Jackie Chan in Hollywood*. Carbondale: Southern Illinois University Press, 2011.

"Ta shi xing erdai, ta shi 83 ban *She diao yingxiong zhuan* de dongzuo daoyan, ta shi dongzuo sheji dashi Cheng Xiaodong" 他是星二代、他是83版射雕的動作導演、他是動作設計大師程小東 [He is a star of the second generation, he is the action director for the 1983 adaptation of *The Eagle Shooting Heroes*, he is the master action designer Cheng Xiaodong]. Accessed January 6, 2021. https://zhuanlan.zhihu.com/p/147224952.

Teo, Stephen. *Chinese Martial Arts Cinema: The Wuxia Tradition*. 2nd ed. Edinburgh: Edinburgh University Press, 2016.

Tian long ba bu 天龍八部 [The demi-gods and semi-devils]. Accessed March 30, 2022. https://baike.baidu.com/item/天龙八部/5480147.

"*Tian long ba bu* ruxuan gaozhong yuwen duben" 《天龍八部》入選高中語文讀本 [*The Demi-Gods and Semi-Devils* selected for high school language reader]. *Jiaoyu, Renmin wang* 教育-人民網 [edu.people.cn]. March 2, 2005. Accessed May 11, 2016. http://edu.people.com.cn/GB/44071/3212362.html.

Tian long ba bu: sishi ji mingzhu wuxia dianshiju 天龍八部：四十集名著武俠電視劇 [Eight parts of the heavenly dragons: forty-episode classic martial arts television series]. Joint production by Jiangsu sheng guangbo dianshi zongtai & Jiuzhou yinxiang chuban gongsi. 2 vols. Guangdong: Weijia yinxiang chuban gongsi, 2003.

TMDB. "Shaw Brothers." Accessed March 28, 2022. https://www.themoviedb.org/company/5798/movie.

"tvb." Accessed May 18, 2009. http://baike.baidu.com/view/926.htm.

"tvb." Accessed June 29, 2009. http://baike.baidu.com/view/115923.html.

"TVBI." Accessed March 18, 2016. http://b.tvb.com/tvbi/.

Wang Jingwen 王靜雯. "Jin Yong qudai Lu Xun yuwen keben de beihou" 金庸取代魯迅語文課本的背後 [Behind the scenes of Jin Yong replacing Lu Xun in language texts]. September 10, 2007. Accessed June 13, 2022. https://www.epochtimes.com/b5/7/9/10/n1828703.htm.

Wang Lu 王璐. "Zhumin tishen yanyuan Luo Lixian xiemi: Cheng Long yizhi yong tishen" 著名替身演員罗礼贤揭秘：成龙一直用替身 (Famous stunt double Luo Lixian reveals secret: Jackie Chan used stunt double all along). April 3, 2007. http://ent.sina.com.cn/m/c/2007-04-03/10181502981.html.

Wei Junzi 魏君子. *Xianggang dianying shiji* 香港电影史记 [A history of Hong Kong films] (Beijing: Zhongguo renmin daxue chubanshe, 2013).
"Wibmer's Law—Fabio Wibmer." Accessed July 18, 2021. https://www.youtube.com/watch?v=ZDbNe3mS0aw.
Wong, Laurence K. P. "Is Martial Arts Fiction in English Possible? With Reference to John Minford's English Version of the First Two Chapters of Louis Cha's *Lu ding Ji*." In *The Question of Reception: Martial Arts Fiction in English Translation*. Hong Kong: Lingnan College, 1997. 105–124.
"Wu ban *Lu ding ji* sishiwu wei zhujue chuanyue shikong da bipin" 五版《鹿鼎記》四十五位主角穿越時空大比拼 [Five editions of *The Deer and the Cauldron*: forty-five main characters transcend time to compete]. November 3, 2008. http://yule.sohu.com/20081103/n260321411.shtml.
Wu Cheng'en 王承恩. *Xi you ji* 西遊記 [Journey to the west]. 3 vols. Beijing: Renmin wenxue chubanshe, 1996.
"Wu hu jiang (1984) 五虎將 (1984) [Five tiger generals (1984)]. Accessed January 6, 2021. https://movie.douban.com/subject/5401549/.
"*Wuxia dashi—Jin Yong chuanqi*" 武俠大師-金庸傳奇 [Martial arts grandmaster—the legend of Jin Yong]. 39:28, posted April 23, 2014. Accessed May 18, 2016. https://www.youtube.com/watch?v=opIdAMYowqI.
"Wuxian wu hu" 無線五虎 [TVB five tigers]. Accessed May 28, 2016. http://baike.baidu.com/view/45291.html.
"Wuxian wuhu/Liu Dehua/chudao jingli" [Five tigers of TVB/Liu Dehua/steps in his career start]. Accessed March 19, 2016. http://baike.baidu.com/item/无线五虎#5_2.
"Wuxian wuhu: chudao jingli" 無線五虎：出道經歷 [Five Tigers of TVB: History of Their Career Start]. Accessed March 19, 2016. http://baike.baidu.com/view/45291.htm.
"Wuxian dianshi yiyuan xunlianban" 無綫電視藝員訓練班 [TVB actors training course]. Accessed March 28, 2022. https://baike.baidu.com/item无线电视艺员训练班#2.
Xi you ji: ershiwu ji dianshi lianxu ju 西遊記：二十五集電視連續劇 [The journey to the west: twenty-five-episode television series]. Dir. Yang Jie 楊潔. Starring Liu Xiaolingtong 流小齡童. N.p.: Heilongjiang yinxiang chubanshe, n.d.
"Xiao ao jianghu: Dongfang Bubai (Guo Yue)" 笑傲江湖：東方不敗（國粵）[Swordsman II: Asia the Invincible (Mandarin, Cantonese)]. 1:32:03. Accessed December 13, 2016. https://www.youtube.com/watch?v=WIz2M0bBWYY.
"*Xiao ao jianghu* (Liu Huan yanchang gequ)" 笑傲江湖（劉歡演唱歌曲）[*Xiao ao jianghu* (song performed by Liu Huan)]. Accessed June 29, 2016. http://baike.baidu.com/subview/10786/13369510.htm.
Xiao ao jianghu: sanshi ji dianshi lianxuju 笑傲江湖：三十集電視連續劇 [The Smiling, Proud Wanderer: thirty-episode television series]. Gen. dir. Huo Yaoliang 霍燿良. Prod. Li Dinglun 李鼎倫. Action dir. Ching Siu-Tung 程小東. Starring Zhou Runfa 周潤發. 20 vcds. Guangdong Feishi yinxiang youxian gongsi [FACE]. Guangdong yinxiang chuban gongsi, 1984. TVBI, 2001.
Xiao ao jianghu: sishi ji dianshi lianxuju 笑傲江湖：四十集電視連續劇 [The Legendary Swordsman: forty-episode television series]. Dir. Huo Zhikai 霍志楷. Star-

ring Ma Jingtao 馬景濤. 27 vcds. Produced by *Xinjiapo dianshi jigou* 新加坡電視機搆 [Singapore TV]. Shenzhen: Dongfang Liren, 2003.

Xiao ao jianghu: wushisi ji dianshi lianxuju 笑傲江湖：五十四集電視連續劇 [State of divinity: fifty-four-episode television series]. Dir. Lai Shuiqing 賴水清 & Li Huimin 李惠民. Prod. Yang Peipei 楊佩佩. Action dir. Ching Siu-Tung 程小東. Starring Ren Xianqi 任賢齊. 27 vcds. Xi'an meiya yingshi wenhua chuanbo youxian gongsi. Shaanxi wenhua yinxiang, 2000.

"Xiao Sheng" 蕭笙. Accessed January 6, 2021. https://search.douban.com/movie/subject_search?search_text=蕭笙&cat=1002&start=15.

"'Xiao shimei' yu Liu Dehua heying qinmi xiangyong" "小師妹"與劉德華合影親密相擁 ["Little martial sister" and Andy Lau pictured together in intimate embrace]. March 18, 2016. http://m.chinadaily.com.cn/cn/2016-03/18/content_23938297.htm.

"'Xiao shimei'" yu Liu Dehua heying qinmi xiangyong: remen gentie," "小師妹"與劉德華合影親密相擁：熱門跟貼" ["Little martial sister" and Andy Lau pictured together in intimate embrace: popular posts]. March 18, 2016. http://ent.163.com/photoview/00AJ0003/591416.html#p=BIE4T04K00AJ0003?baike.

"*Xin Tian long ba bu* (1994) 新天龍八部之天山童姥 (1994) [*The New Demi-gods and the semi-devils* (1994)]. Accessed January 6, 2021. https://movie.douban.com/subject/1297517.

Xun Qin ji: Ershiqi die Xianggang dianshi lianxuju 尋秦記：二十七碟香港電視連續劇 [*A Step Back to the Past:* Twenty-seven-disc Hong Kong television series]. Disc 10, 4:45–4:54. TVBI Zhongkai wenhua 中凱文化, Jiuzhou yinxiang chubangongsi 九州音像出版公司, 2001.

Yang, Jeff. *Once Upon a Time in China: A Guide to Hong Kong, Taiwanese, and Mainland Chinese Cinema*. New York: Atria Books, 2003.

"Yang Peipei: renwu pinglun" 楊佩佩：人物評論 [Yang Peipei: character commentary]. Accessed June 2, 2016. http://baike.baidu.com/view/1724293.htm#4.

"Yazhou xin xing dao" 亞洲新星導 [Asian new star directors]. Accessed May 31, 2016. http://baike.baidu.com/view/1866371.htm.

Ye Hongsheng 葉洪生. *Lun jian: wuxia xiaoshuo tan yi lu* 論劍：武俠小說談藝錄 [Discussing swords—a record of artistic discussion on martial arts fiction]. Shanghai: Xuelin chubanshe, 1997.

Yi tian tu long ji 倚天屠龍記 [The heaven sword and the dragon sabre]. Accessed March 30, 2022. https://baike.baidu.com/item/倚天屠龙记/6893552.

"Yingyi yule youxian gongsi" 映藝娛樂有限公司 [Yingyi entertainment, ltd.]. Accessed June 26, 2010. http://baike.baidu.com/view/203889.html?tp=8_01.

Yu Huiming 余慧明. "*Wuxia xiaoshuo ershi nian huimou*" 武俠小說二十年回眸 [A look back at twenty years of martial arts fiction]. January 21, 2002, http://www.people.com.cn/GB/paper39/5269/551667.html.

Zhang Dachun 張大春. "Jin Yong tan yi lu" 金庸談藝錄 [Jin Yong talks about art]. In Shen Deng'en 沈登恩, ed., *Zhuzi baijia kan Jin Yong (di si ji)* 諸子百家看金庸（第四輯）[Philosophers and writers of all schools read Jin Yong (vol. 4)]. Vol. 17 of *Jin xue yanjiu congshu* 金學研究叢書 [A collection of Jin-ology research]. Taibei: Yuanjing chubanshe, 1985. 35-47. Originally published in *Zhongguo shibao* 中國時報 [China times], October 30, 1970.

"Zhen gongfu canyin guanli youxian gongsi" 真功夫餐饮管理有限公司 [True kungfu restaurant management company, Ltd.]. Accessed March 29, 2022, https://www.qcc.com/firm/373dc2faf053f5424042fd24750d5d10.html.

"*Zheng pai Wei Xiaobao zhi fengzhi gounü*" 正牌韋小寶之奉旨溝女 [Hero from Beyond the Boundary of Time, 1993]. Accessed June 5, 2016. http://baike.baidu.com/view/1460127.htm.

"Zhong shentong Wang Chongyang" 中神通王重陽 [Middle mystic Wang Chongyang]. Accessed January 6, 2021. https://search.douban.com/movie/subject_search?search_text=中神通王重陽&cat=1002.

"Zhongguo gongfu quanqiu shengdian (6)" 中国功夫全球盛典（6）[Chinese kungfu global festival (part 6)]. October 12, 2007. 10:20–11:00. http://www.tudou.com/programs/view/XG_GS__1ODY/.

"Zhongguo gongfu quanqiu shengdian" 中國功夫全球盛典 [Chinese kungfu global festival]. October 12, 2007. http://baike.baidu.com/view/1197603.htm.

Zhongshi xinwen tai 中视新闻台 [CTV News Channel], *Haixia yehang "Jin Yong de jianghu rensheng* 海峽夜航 "金庸的江湖人生" [Night navigation on the Straits: "Jin Yong's life in the martial world]. No date. YouTube, *Wuxia dashi—Jin Yong chuanqi* 武俠大師-金庸傳奇 [Martial arts grandmaster—the legend of Jin Yong], 39:28. Posted April 23, 2014, accessed May 18, 2016. https://www.youtube.com/watch?v=opIdAMYowqI.

"Zhou Xingchi 周星馳 (Stephen Chow)." Accessed January 6, 2021. https://baike.baidu.com/item/周星馳.

"Zhou Xingchi she yan yao Jin Yong hepai dianying juben dawang yi nihao" 周星馳設宴邀金庸合拍電影 劇本大綱已擬好 [Stephen Chow gives a banquet and invites Jin Yong to collaborate on a movie, the script outline is already finished]. February 8, 2007, www.ifensi.com.

Zhou Zuoren 周作人 (Zhong Mi 仲蜜). "A Q zhengzhuan" 阿 Q 正傳 ["(On) The true story of Ah Q"]. Reprinted in *Lun Xun yanjiu xueshu lunzhu ziliao huibian (1913–1980)* 魯迅研究學術論著資料彙編 (1913–1980) [A corpus of data of academic theses and works on Lu Xun (1913–1980)]. Gen. ed. Zhang Mengyang. Vol. 1. Beijing: Zhongguo wenlian, 1985. 27–29. Originally published in *Chenbao fukan* (March 19, 1922).

Zui quan 醉拳 [Drunken Master)]. Dir. Yuan Heping 袁和平. Prod. Wu Siyuan 吳恩遠. Starring Jackie Chan 成龍. 1978. Guangdong: Guangdong Yinxiang chubangongsi, 1990.

Zui quan II 醉拳 II [Drunken Master II]. Dir. Lau Kar-Leung (Liu Jialiang) 劉家良. Starring Jackie Chan 成龍. Golden Harvest. Paragon Films, 1994.

INDEX

Ah Q, 47–48, 58, 61–62, 79, 80; and the "method of spiritual victory," 58, 61, 75, 76, 79, 86; and "The True Story of Ah Q," 68, 98
Anderson, Benedict, 69–70, 90, 94
antihero, 34–35, 39, 56, 58, 80–81
Ashes of Time (*Dong Xie Xi Du*), 39, 109, 131, 144–148, 197–199

Barmé, Geremie R., 90–91
Bixie jianpu (Sword manual to ward off evil), 84
Bordwell, David, 134–135
Bourdieu, Pierre, 2, 17, 45, 69, 93; cultural capital and literary field, 8–10
Bowman, Paul, 149

canonization, 92–99
Carradine, David, 112–13
Cathay Film Company, 117
Chan, Idy (Chen Yulian), 29, 39, 129, 138, 139
Chan, Jackie, 1, 6, 15, 21, 97, 107, 109, 110, 111, 113, 114, 116–119, 128, 130, 132, 135, 139, 143, 156, 158, 167, 169, 171, 184, 185, 187, 199, 206; Bruce Lee homage in *City Hunter*, 160–162; and megastar power with Jin Yong, 164–166; playing Huang Feihong, 151–155
Chang Cheh (Zhang Che), 16, 27, 36, 114, 116, 184
Chen Mo, 43n16, 48, 76, 79, 81, 94–95

Chen Pingyuan, 49, 68, 92, 93, 95
Chen Shaoxia, 133–134
Chen Zhen, 42n4, 149–150, 155
Cheung, Leslie (Zhang Guorong), 27, 40, 118, 139, 144, 147
Ching Siu-Tung (Cheng Xiaodong), 36, 114, 117, 136–137, 140, 143, 167, 169, 196
Chor Yuen, 114, 116
Chou, Jay, 109–111, 151, 160, 163–164, 166
Chow, Raymond (Zou Wenhuai), 115, 117
Chow, Stephen, 13, 40, 110, 121, 128, 132, 136, 137, 139, 142, 174n51, 185; and *Kungfu Hustle*, 166, 199–207; and *Shaolin Soccer*, 160, 162, 165, 167
Chow Yun-fat (Zhou Runfa), 36, 39, 118, 120, 121, 139, 142, 158, 164, 167, 181, 186
City Hunter, 160–162
Confucian and Confucianism, 12, 19, 24, 32, 46, 48, 52, 58, 63, 76, 78, 81, 83, 86, 89, 90, 185, 193
Crouching Tiger, Hidden Dragon, 1, 5–6, 96, 117, 185–187; and cultural capital, 17–18
cultural capital, 2–3, 5–6, 7–11, 12–14, 16, 17–19, 21, 25–27, 31, 34–35, 41, 67, 73, 75, 78, 81, 92–95, 97–98, 107, 109–111; actors and, 125–127, 128, 130, 133, 147, 148, 170–171; Bruce Lee homage and, 158–160, 162, 164; director Yuen Woo-ping and,

166; Jack Ma and, 199; Jackie Chan and, 164; Jin Yong's writing and, 193; Jin Yong and Lu Xun and the construction of, 92–93; Jin Yong's Rhetorical Kungfu and Cultural Capital of Humor, 45–49, 58–65; *Kungfu Hustle* and, 200; matrix of the kungfu industrial complex and, 207; national identity and, 69; readers and, 201; social function of literature and, 99–100
Cultural Revolution, 14, 50, 100, 102, 107, 116, 188, 192–195
cursing kungfu (*maren gongfu*), 49–53

Dai Sicong, 129
Dannen, Fredric, 115
Dissanayake, Wimal, 144–147
Dream of the Red Chamber, 49
Dugu jiu jian (The nine swords of Dugu), 22, 38, 84

Enter the Dragon (*Long zheng hu dou*), 117, 158, 162

female *wuxia* superstar, 137–144
Feng Jicai, 74, 77, 78
Fist of Fury (*Jingwu men*), 149, 150, 159, 162
Five Tiger of TVB, 114, 120–127; contract issues, 124–125
flattery kungfu (*ma pi gong*), 49, 53–56
formlessness defeats form (*wu zhao sheng you zhao*), 114, 159
four great populars (*si da su*), 97
Four Heavenly Kings (*Si da tian wang*), 97, 125, 128, 132, 139, 164

Golden Harvest, 114, 115, 117, 134; Bruce Lee and, 117–118, 160
Green Hornet, The, 111, 112, 113, 160, 163–164
Gu Long, 7, 11, 15–16, 115–116, 119,121, 124, 126, 132, 136, 143, 199; and concept of *ren zai jianghu, shen bu you ji*, 183–192, 196, 204, 205

Hamm, John Christopher, 26, 158
hero concept *yingxiong haohan*, 32, 53, 90
hierarchical kungfu (*beifen gongfu*), 48, 58–63
Hockx, Michel, 8, 103n80
Hong Kong Commercial Daily (*Xianggang shangbao*), 26
Hu Ge, 29, 30, 39, 174n50
Huang Feihong (Wong Fei-hung), 16, 36, 148, 151–155, 157, 166, 174n50
Huo Yuanjia, 42n4, 148–151, 155, 166

Jen, Richie (Ren Xianqi), 36, 40, 135–136
jianghu (martial world), 18, 24, 25, 35, 36, 50, 51, 53, 54–56, 58, 61–62, 75, 82, 83, 90, 94, 118, 131, 138, 140, 142, 143, 145, 152, 157, 183, 200, 202, 204, 205; kungfu industrial complex as, 187–199
Jin Yong, 1, 97; biography, 25–26; cultural capital and, 8–11; construction of cultural capital, 25–31; cultural penetration of, 35–41; *Dagong bao* and, 25; derivative star power and, 171; form and spirit in literature, 77; geography and scale of works, 23–24, 36–38, 83; Jackie Chan and, 15, 164–166; kungfu cultural literacy and, 7–9; Jack Ma and, 21–22; Jin Yong Semester, 21; linguistic cultural capital, 31–35; Lu Xun and, 69, 77–78; method of spiritual victory and, 61; Ming Ho Publication Corporation Limited, 22; national character complements and, 75–76; national character critique, 80; plot devices, 25; table of 12 major novels, 23; table of abbreviations of works, 23; table of film adaptations and derivatives of *The Eagle-Shooting Heroes*, 27; table of television adaptations of *The Eagle-Shooting Heroes* and its derivatives by year, 29; television and film adaptations, 26–31; wealth, 26; *Xin wanbao* and, 25; villains, 156–158

Jin Yong, fictional characters: Bao Butong, 56–58; Constellation Sect, 56–58; Dongfang Bubai (Asia the Invincible), 37–38, 132, 139, 140–143, 156, 193, 196, 199, 205; Duan Yu, 34, 53–56; Dugu Qiubai, 22, 122, 142, 159; Feng Qingyang, 21–22, 42n10, 84, 114, 142, 169, 174n50, 191, 195, 199; Four Great Evildoers (*Si da e'ren*), 54–56; Guo Jing, 22, 28, 30, 32, 34, 35, 39, 40, 121–122, 132, 137, 156, 165; Huang Rong, 28, 39, 121, 122, 129, 137, 138, 139, 156; Huang Yaoshi, 39, 40, 121, 127, 137, 158, 178n132, 197; Kang Xi, 12, 39–40, 50–51, 61–62, 76, 122–123, 125, 126, 157, 167; Linghu Chong, 22, 24, 25, 38–40, 75–76, 78, 82–92, 114, 135, 140, 142, 155, 156, 169, 188–189, 191–196, 199, 200, 202, 205–206; Mao Shiba, 51–53, 59; Ouyang Feng, 39, 40, 126, 127, 137, 144, 156, 197–198, 202; Ren Yingying, 40, 86, 132, 135, 137, 149, 192, 195, 202, 205; Wei Xiaobao, 12, 34–35, 39–40, 46–48, 49, 50–53, 56, 58–63, 75–76, 79–81, 83, 91, 97, 122–123, 125–126, 139, 156, 170, ; Xiao Feng (Qiao Feng), 24, 34, 39–40, 43n22, 53–54, 81–82, 121, 165, 199; Xiaolongnü, 24, 39–40, 129, 131–132, 134, 135, 136, 137–139, 200–205, 206; Yang Guo, 24, 39–40, 122, 129–130, 131, 132, 135, 136, 142, 184, 200–205, 206; Yilin, 86–87, 88–89; Zhou Botong, 32, 35, 139

Jin Yong, works of: *Book and Sword, Gratitude and Revenge*, 24, 26, 29, 34, 119, 149, 156, 157; *Collected Works of Jin Yong*, 23; *The Deer and the Cauldron*, 11–12, 20, 31, 34, 35, 46, 48, 49–53, 58, 60–62, 68, 71, 75–76, 78–80, 83, 91, 107, 120, 122–127, 133, 134, 137, 138–139, 144, 156, 167, 170; *The Demi-Gods and Semi-Devils*, 12, 23, 24, 34, 49, 53–56, 56–58, 96, 120, 142, 81, 82, 96, 98, 119, 120, 121, 122, 125, 139, 142, 155, 157, 199, 204; *The Eagle-Shooting Heroes*, 12, 23–24, 26–30, 32, 34, 35, 38–39, 98, 119, 120, 121, 122, 127, 129, 121, 132, 136, 137, 138, 139, 142, 144, 146, 156, 157, 158, 167, 197, 202; *The Giant Eagle and Its Companion*, 24, 26, 29, 53, 114, 120, 122, 127–133, 134, 135, 136, 137, 138, 139, 142, 144, 146, 157, 159, 167, 199–204, 206; *The Heaven Sword and the Dragon Sabre*, 24, 29, 31, 119, 120, 126, 134–136, 139, 157, 167; *Flying Fox on Snowy Mountain*, 29, 31, 98, 120, 139, 157, 167; Ode to Gallantry, 31, 33, 120, 126; *The Smiling, Proud Wanderer*, 21–22, 24, 25, 31, 35–38, 75–76, 82–92, 100, 107, 119, 122, 132–134, 135–136, 137, 138, 140, 142, 156, 157, 167, 187–189, 190–197, 199, 200, 206; *The Sword Stained with Royal Blood*, 26, 29, 120; *The Young Flying Fox*, 31

Journey to the West, 33, 46–47, 80

Kill Bill, 119, 160, 162–163, 167–168
King Hu (Hu Jinquan), 114, 116
Kong Qingdong, 97–98
Kowallis, Jon, 68
kungfu cultural literacy, 12, 15–41, 201, 205–206; cultural capital and, 17–22
kungfu film: gunfu and 115, 118, 169; overview, 117–119; wirefu and, 118, 119, 169, 187
Kung Fu Hustle, 13–14, 132, 160, 166, 183, 199–207
kungfu industrial complex, 3–6, 7; canonization and the construction of, 92–99; construction of, 19; hierarchical kungfu and, 48; kungfu cultural literacy and, 15–41; rhetorical kungfu and, 47–65; as *jianghu*, 187–199
Kwan Tak-hing (Guan Dexing), 151, 152

laozi (I, me, your father), 46–48, 55, 58–63, 83, 86, 87
Lau, Andy (Liu Dehua), 20, 38–39, 114, 118, 120–123, 135, 138, 139, 142,

143, 144, 152, 156, 167, 170–171, 184; Godly Condor Hero Couple, 131; singing career, 125, 129; star power and, 127–134; Tony Leung and, 124–127
Lau, Carina Kar-ling (Liu Jialing), 114, 121, 130, 138–139
Lee, Ang, 1, 185–187
Lee, Bruce, 1, 6, 7, 21, 107, 109; Chen Zhen role and, 149–150; *Enter the Dragon* and, 117; film homage and, 158–164; *Fist of Fury* and, 149–150, 159; *The Game of Death* homage and, 160–162; homage by Jackie Chan and, 160; homage by Jay Chou in *Green Hornet*, 163–164; homage in *Kill Bill*, 162–163; homage in *Shaolin Soccer*, 162–163; Pierre Burton Show interview and, 112–113; star power and, 111–114; *Tao of Jeet Kune Do*, 111–112, 158–159
Lee, Leo Ou-Fan, 70–71
Leung Chiu-Wai, Tony (Liang Chaowei), 20, 27, 39, 120, 121, 123, 124–127, 138, 170–171
Li, Jet (Li Lianjie), 36, 113, 140, 143, 149, 151, 152, 160, 166, 167; as legendary martial arts figures, 155
Li, Siu Leung, 2, 208n20
Li Bai, 33
Li Yapeng, 36–38
Liang Jiaren, 36, 40, 121
Liang Qichao, 94, 99
Liang Yusheng, 7, 11, 15–16, 25, 116, 126, 135, 137, 143
light body kungfu (*qinggong*), 2, 40–41, 119
Lin, Brigitte (Lin Qingxia), 27, 36, 39, 114, 135, 138, 139, 147, 155, 158, 171, 199; as Asia the Invincible, 140–143
Liu, Gordon (Liu Jiahui), 119, 151, 166–168
Liu, Petrus, xi, 33, 49, 109
Liu Zaifu, 92–93
Lu Xun, 47, 68, 69, 77, 96–99, 206; cultural industry and, 70–72; "Diary of a Madman" and, 194–196, 198, 202, 205; Jin Yong and, 70, 93, 95; Jin Yong's criticism of, 73, 77–78; on negative national character and Ah Q, 58–61, 74–76, 78–80, 83, 86, 91–92, 98

Ma, Jack (Ma Yun), 21, 199
Ma Jingtao, 36, 40
Mao Weitao, 37–38
Matrix, The 5, 119, 160
May Fourth, 7, 11, 26, 76–77, 92, 98, 99–100
method of spiritual victory (*jingshen shengli fa*), 58, 61, 75, 76, 79, 86
Meyers, Richard, 6
Minford, John, 1, 107
Miu, Michael (Miao Qiaowei), 40, 120, 121, 122

national character, 67–92, 80; Linghu Chong and Wei Xiaobao and, 78–92; Lu Xun's critique of, 58–61, 74–76, 78–80, 83, 86, 91–92, 98
national character complements, 75–76, 78–93, 95
national identity, 69–70, 73–74
New School Martial Arts Fiction, 1, 7, 108, 109, 115, 143, 183; in Hong Kong, 11
New School Martial Arts Film, 116
Newman Prize for Chinese Literature, 67–68
Ni Kuang, 16, 137, 204
Nobel Prize in Literature, 67–68, 72, 94, 107

qi (internal energy force), 2, 7, 17, 19, 41
Qiong Yao, 97, 116, 139

Rawnsley, Ming-Yeh T., 142
ren zai jianghu, shen bu you ji (in the *jianghu* [martial world] there is no individual choice), 183; contrast with *xiao ao jianghu* (laughing haughtily at *jianghu* [rules/morality]), 187–199

renqing (human sentiment), 61–62, 80
rhetorical kungfu, 7; 47–65, applied cultural capital and, 63–65; cursing kungfu and, 49–53; flattery kungfu and, 49, 53–56; hierarchical kungfu and, 48, 58–63; sarcasm kungfu and, 49, 56–58
Rush Hour 2, 161

sarcasm kungfu (*fengci gongfu*), 49, 56–58
Seven Little Fortunes, 155–156
Shaolin Temple, 15, 24, 62, 155
Shaw Brothers Studios, 16, 27, 36, 114–117, 118, 119, 134, 139, 144, 162, 168, 170, 184; contract period, 115
Shi ji (Records of the grand historian), 32
Shi Jian (Shih Kien), 146–158; moniker "villain Jian," 157
Shih, Shu-mei, 76
Si da ming zhu (The four great classical Chinese novels), 33
star power, 9, 39, 107–171; *Ashes of Time* and, 144–148; Bruce Lee on, 111–114; female *wuxia* superstar, 137–144; legendary martial arts hero and, 148–156; Jackie Chan and Jin Yong and, 164–166; Taiwan and, 134–137
storytelling, 5, 46
Sun Wukong, 46–47, 58, 61, 80
Sunzi Art of War, 64, 114, 159
suspension of disbelief, 2, 7, 40

"*Taohua haojie san jie yi*" (Three heroes swear brotherhood in the peach garden), 33–34; *Book and Sword* and, 34; *Heroes* and, 34; *Cauldron* and, 33–34
Tarantino, Quentin, 162
Television Broadcasting Limited Company (TVB), 114; contract issues, 124–125; Five Tiger of, 114, 120–127; adaptation of Jin Yong novels, 119–120
Teng, Theresa (Deng Lijun), 116, 135

Teo, Stephen, 108
Three Kingdoms, 33–34, 107–108; and "*Taohua haojie san jie yi*" (Three heroes swear brotherhood in the peach garden), 33–34
Tong, Kent (Tang Zhenye), 120–122
Tsui Hark (Xu Ke), 36, 143

Wang Dulu, 1, 96
Wang Shuo, 69, 96–98
Water Margin, 25, 33, 46, 107–108
Wibmer, Fabio, 41
Wolf Warrior, 6
Wong, Felix, (Huang Rihua), 28, 29, 39, 120–122, 152
Wong Kar-wai, 27, 131, 138; *Ashes of Time* and 127, 142, 143, 144–148, 197, 204; *Ashes of Time Redux* and, 148
Wu Jing, 6
Wudang mountain/sect, 18, 36, 155, 156, 165, 194, 195
Wulin (Martial forest), 23
wushu (martial arts/technique), 1, 2, 4, 6, 19, 21, 25, 114, 187
wuxia (martial arts, knight-errant, martial chivalry), 1, 2, 3, 4, 16–19, 21, 25, 26, 34, 41, 119, 126, 132, 149, 164, 166, 170, 183, 184, 187–188, 200–205; kungfu/*gongfu* as film genres and, 6–7, 108, 109, 114, 117–18, 134, 146, 148, 151, 155–156, 169, 171, 185, 202; female superstars and, 137–144

xiao ao jianghu (laughing haughtily at *jianghu* [rules/morality]), contrast with *ren zai jianghu, shen bu you ji* (in the *jianghu* [martial world] there is no individual choice), 187–199, 205

Yan Shunkai, 71
Yen, Donnie (Zhen Zidan), 18, 112, 121, 143, 149, 166, 167
yiqi (righteous loyalty to one's friends), 61–62, 80, 81, 88, 90, 91, 94, 155, 157, 188, 192

Yuen Siu-tien (Yuan Xiaotian), 201
Yuen Woo-ping (Yuan Heping), 5, 114, 155, 162, 166–167, 169, 201; and *Kill Bill*, 167
Yung, Barbara (Weng Meiling), 28, 29, 39, 114, 122, 129, 136, 138

Zhang Ziyi, 18, 118, 139, 166, 186
Zhao, Vincent (Zhao Wenzhuo), 40, 149, 151
Zhuang Zi, 33

About the Author

Paul B. Foster is Associate Professor of Chinese at the Georgia Institute of Technology in Atlanta, Georgia. He is author of *Ah Q Archeology: Lu Xun, Ah Q, Ah Q Progeny and the National Character Discourse in Twentieth-Century China* (2006). He has published in the journals *Modern Chinese Literature and Culture, Asian Studies Review, Twentieth-Century China, Frontiers, China Information, Foreign Policy in Focus,* and *China Currents.* In addition to his course on martial arts fiction, he teaches classes on kungfu film and pop culture, strategy and *The Art of War*, Lu Xun and modern Chinese literature, and Chinese science fiction. An avid rock climber, he has climbed throughout the United States, Europe, Japan, and Taiwan. He also enjoys juggling, wire walking, ultra-endurance mountain biking, and growing and producing his own tea.

www.ingramcontent.com/pod-product-compliance
Lightning Source LLC
Chambersburg PA
CBHW061440300426
44114CB00014B/1761